D1483171

E
184
P 85
C 68

Cordasco, Francesco.
The Puerto Rican
experience.

DEC 16 '77

THE PUERTO RICAN EXPERIENCE

A Sociological Sourcebook

THE PUERTO RICAN EXPERIENCE

A Sociological Sourcebook

BY

FRANCESCO CORDASCO
Montclair State College

FORMER CONSULTANT, MIGRATION DIVISION
COMMONWEALTH OF PUERTO RICO

EUGENE BUCCHIONI
City University of New York

ROWMAN AND LITTLEFIELD
TOTOWA, NEW JERSEY

Published 1973 by Littlefield, Adams & Co.

Copyright 1973 by Francesco Cordasco and Eugene Bucchioni

All rights reserved. No part of this book may be reproduced in any form without permission in writing from
the publisher except by a reviewer who wishes to
quote brief passages in connection with a review
written for inclusion in a magazine, newspaper or
broadcast.

Library of Congress Cataloging in Publication Data

Cordasco, Francesco, 1920-   comp.
The Puerto Rican Experience.

CONTENTS: The island background: Bourne, D. D.
and Bourne, J. R. Thirty years of change in Puerto
Rico: a case study of ten selected rural areas. Mintz,
S. W.   Puerto Rico: an essay in the definition of
national culture. Wagenheim, K. Puerto Rico: a profile.
Myerson, M. Puerto Rico, our backyard colony. [etc.]
1. Puerto Ricans in the United States.
I. Bucchioni, Eugene, joint comp. II. Title.
E184.P85C67   301.45'16'87295073   72-90922
ISBN 0-87471-162-2

Printed in the United States of America

For

JUAN

MIGUEL

MILAGROS

OLGA

MANUEL

Quiénes somos? Somos un Pueblo compasivo, porque hemos sufrido mucho; somos un Pueblo pacífico, en cuyo escudo de armas el Pueblo de San Juan Bautista tiene un Cordero que a mí se me antoja que no es otro que Aquel que quita los pecados del mundo . . . Somos un Pueblo humilde; somos un Pueblo pobre, donde la vergüenza todavía vale más que la plata, donde la honradez todavía vale más que cualquier otra medalla de honor. Somos un Pueblo que tiene tres patrias, y sin embargo no tenemos dominio sobre ninguna de ellas hasta la fecha.

—PABLO RIVERA ALVAREZ

PREFACE

In the proliferating literature on ethnic communities in the United States, there has been no neglect of Puerto Ricans. How vast (and expanding) this literature has become is amply recorded in the bibliography on the Puerto Rican mainland experience recently published;[1] and beyond the literature addressed to the mainland communities, there is a vast (as yet, essentially uncharted) literature on Puerto Rico both before and after its affiliation with the United States. If anything, a serious problem has presented itself to students who sought a convenient sourcebook which afforded an overview of the Puerto Rican mainland experience (with some notice of the island backgrounds), essentially compact, but dimensionally comprehensive.[2] This documentary sourcebook is addressed to that need. It is intended as a classroom text (in a wide range of classes, *e.g.* urban sociology; ethnic relations; minority groups in the United States, *etc.*), and it should equally prove valuable to a broad readership which wishes to place the Puerto Rican experience in meaningful perspectives.

We have adopted a flexible framework for the text. Part I (*The Island Background*) provides a politico-economic-cultural kaleidoscope of island life (at best, a miniscule social portrait deriving from the huge literature noted above) and is intended as a background against which the mainland experience is to be understood. Part II (*The Migration*) brings together the data for a correct appraisal of the phenomenon, including return migration. Part III (*Life on the Mainland: Conflict and Acculturation*) furnishes multi-dimensional perspectives on the mainland experience, with particular notice

[1] Francesco Cordasco, Eugene Bucchioni, and Diego Castellanos. *Puerto Ricans on the United States Mainland: A Bibliography of Reports, Texts, Critical Studies and Related Materials* (Totowa, N.J.: Rowman & Littlefield, 1972).

[2] Limitedly, this has been provided for one facet of the mainland experience: Francesco Cordasco and Eugene Bucchioni, *Puerto Rican Children in Mainland Schools: A Sourcebook for Teachers* (Metuchen, N.J.: Scarecrow Press, 1968; 2nd ed., 1972).

of the restiveness and new awareness of needs translated into the postures of defiance, *e.g.* the Young Lords Party and the politicization of the mainland experience; and Part IV (Education on the Mainland) explores the experience in schools, the most sensitive of the social institutions.

We are keenly aware that no clear consensus can be achieved (both within and outside a community) on what should be included in a collection of documents; and it is hardly necessary to add that we do not subscribe to all of the statements recorded. However, the documents have been carefully chosen and the authenticity of the composite delineation of the Puerto Rican experience which emerges in the text is an attestation of the sound scholarship found in the materials which have been brought together.

Inevitably, we have incurred a multiplicity of obligations in the preparation of the text. Our first indebtedness is to those individuals who have provided the materials in the text; and, both within and outside the academic community, our perspectives have been sharpened by our privileged association with a wide range of individuals whose identity with the mainland Puerto Rican community (in a variety of roles) has allowed the assessment of both materials and experience from their vantage points; only a handful are mentioned here: Dr. Maria Teresa Babin; Gloria del Toro; Dr. Trina Rivera de Rios; Maximiliano Soriano; Diego Castellanos; and Pablo Rivera Alvarez. Special thanks are due to Angela B. Jack for handling the difficult manuscript.

F.C.
E.B.

TABLE OF CONTENTS

INTRODUCTION

In February 1971, the U.S. Census Bureau published its November 1969, sample-survey estimate that the fifty states and the District of Columbia had 1,454,000 Puerto Rican residents—811,000 born on the island, 636,000 born in the states and district, 1,000 in Cuba, and 6,000 elsewhere. In March 1972, the Census Bureau released preliminary and a few final state population totals from the 1970 census for three categories—persons of Spanish language, persons of Spanish family name, and Puerto Ricans. Puerto Rican counts were for three states only—New York (872,471; 5% of the state population); New Jersey (135,676; 2% of the state population; and Pennsylvania (44,535).

Puerto Ricans have been on the mainland for many years; in the 19th century, a small colony of Puerto Ricans, gathered largely in New York City, worked for the independence of the island. After the annexation of the island in 1898 by the United States, a continuing migration to the mainland began. In 1910 some 1,500 Puerto Ricans were living in the United States; by 1930, they numbered close to 53,000. The migration was reversed during the depression of the 1930s; and again was substantially impeded by World War II in the early 1940s. After the end of World War II (and concurrent with the advent of cheap air transport) it increased steadily until it reached its peak in the early 1950s (in 1953, 304,910 persons left the island and 203,307 returned, leaving a net balance of 74,603). The state of the economy on the mainland has always been an indicator of the migration. The decline in Puerto Rican migration to the mainland in 1970 and continuing into 1971 was precisely due to economic hardship in the states.[1]

[1] For Puerto Rican passenger traffic for fiscal years 1940-1969, see the reports of the Puerto Rico Planning Board. The major source of information on Puerto Rican migration is the Department of Labor, Migration Division, Commonwealth of Puerto Rico. See further, H. C. Barton, Jr., "The Employment Situation in Puerto Rico and Migratory Movements between Puerto Rico and the United States," *Summary of Proceedings: Workshop on Employment Problems of Puerto Ricans* (Graduate School of Social Work, New York University, 1968). See

In a prescient book on Puerto Rican Américans, the Jesuit sociologist, Rev. Joseph P. Fitzpatrick, observes that Puerto Ricans have found it difficult to achieve "community solidarity" and suggests that they may work out adjustment "in very new ways" differing from those of past immigrants (technically, as American citizens, Puerto Ricans are migrants to the mainland United States); and Father Fitzpatrick cogently observes:

> A book about the Puerto Ricans in mainland United States, with a special focus on those in New York City, is very risky but also is very necessary. It is risky because the Puerto Rican community is in a state of turbulent change in a city and a nation which are also in a state of turbulent change. So many different currents of change affect Puerto Ricans at the present time that it is foolhardy to attempt to describe this group adequately or put them into focus. Nor is it possible to point out clearly any one direction in which the Puerto Rican community is moving in its adjustment to life on the mainland. Its directions are often in conflict, and no single leader or movement has given sharp definition to one direction as dominant over others. . . . What is most needed at this moment of the Puerto Rican experience, both for Puerto Ricans and other mainland Americans, is *perspective*: a sense of the meaning of the migration for everyone involved in that migration, for the new-comers as well as the residents of the cities and neighborhoods to which the Puerto Ricans come.[2]

also, *The New York Puerto Rican: Patterns of Work Experience.* U.S. Department of Labor, Bureau of Labor Statistics [Middle Atlantic Regional Office], New York, 1971.

[2] Joseph P. Fitzpatrick, *Puerto Rican Americans: The Meaning of Migration to the Mainland* (Englewood Cliffs, N.J.: Prentice Hall, 1971), p. xi. The Puerto Rican migration is, in many ways, a unique phenomenon for the United States. "The Puerto Ricans have come for the most part in the first great airborne migration of people from abroad; they are decidedly newcomers of the aviation age. A Puerto Rican can travel from San Juan to New York in less time than a New Yorker could travel from Coney Island to Times Square a century ago. They are the first group to come in large numbers from a different cultural background but who are, nevertheless, citizens of the United States. They are the first group of newcomers who bring a cultural practice of widespread intermingling and intermarriage of people of many different colors. They are the first group of predominantly Catholic migrants not accompanied by a native clergy. Numerous characteristics of the Puerto Ricans make their migration unique." (Fitzpatrick, p. 2)

How varied the Puerto Rican experience on the mainland has been can be best indicated by the sharp contrasts provided in four juxtaposed excerpts from Puerto Rican reactions registered over a period of time.

In 1948, J. J. Osuna, the distinguished Puerto Rican educator, on a visit to New York City schools, observed:

> As far as possible something should be done in Puerto Rico to discourage migration of people who do not have occupations to go into upon their arrival in this country, or of children whose parents live in Puerto Rico and who have no home in New York. Too many people are coming, hoping that they may find work and thereby better themselves economically, and in the case of the children, educationally. It is laudable that they take the chance, but the experience of the past teaches us that as far as possible, people should not come to the continent until they have secured employment here.[3]

In 1961, Joseph Monserrat, at the time Director of the Migration Division, Commonwealth of Puerto Rico, in speaking on "Community Planning for Puerto Rican Integration in the United States," cautioned that:

> If all Puerto Ricans were to suddenly disappear from New York City, neither the housing problem nor other basic issues confronting the city would be solved. In fact, without the Puerto Ricans, New York would be faced with one of two alternatives: either "import" people to do the work done by Puerto Ricans (and whoever was imported from wherever they might come would have to live in the very same buildings Puerto Ricans now live in for the simple reason that there is nothing else); or industries would have to move to other areas where there are workers, causing a severe economic upheaval in the city. Obviously, neither one is a viable solution. Nor will the stagnation of the past resolve our dilemma. . . . The Puerto Rican, although he comes from a close knit neighborhood in the Commonwealth, has found the best possi-

[3] J. J. Osuna, *Report on Visits to New York City Schools* [Government of Puerto Rico]. Reprinted in F. Cordasco and E. Bucchioni, *Puerto Rican Children in Mainland Schools: A Sourcebook for Teachers* (Metuchen, N.J.: Scarecrow Press, 1968), pp. 227–239.

bility for social action and self-improvement on the city-
wide level. The community of Puerto Ricans is not the
East Side or the South Side. It is New York City, Lorain,
Chicago, Los Angeles, Middletown. City living is learned
living. The migrants must be helped to learn the facts of
city life and how to function effectively as a pressure
group in a pressure group society.[4]

Both of these statements are in stark contrast to the ideology
of revolution and separatism evident in the animadversions
which follow. First, from a spokesman for "La Generación
Encojonada:"

Violence is the essence of a colonial society. It is established as a system in the interests of the ruling classes.
Colonial society "is the meeting of two forces, opposed to
each other by their very nature, which in fact owe their
originality to that sort of substantification which results
from and is nourished by the situation in the colonies.
Their first encounter was marked by violence and their
existence together . . . was carried on by dint of a great
array of bayonets and cannon." Puerto Rican history has
been witness to this violent confrontation between people
and oppressor. We see it in daily events: in schools,
churches, factories, the countryside, in strikes, demonstrations, and insurrections. As soon as an individual confronts
the system, he feels its violence in the way of life colonialism imposes on him: the feudal-type exploitation in the
countryside, the capitalist exploitation in the cities.

The lifeblood of every colonial society is the profit it
offers to its exploiters. Its basis is the authority of an
exploiting system—not the authority that comes from a
majority consensus, but the paternal authority with which
a minority tries to justify a system beneficial to it. Around
that system is built a morality, an ethic, rooted in the
economic co-existence of colonizers and colonized. Thus
the system envelops itself in forms that create the illusion

[4] Joseph Monserrat, "Community Planning for Puerto Rican Integra-
tion in the United States," [An Address at the National Conference on
Social Welfare, Minneapolis, Minnesota, May 1961]. Published in F.
Cordasco and E. Bucchioni, *op. cit.*, pp. 221–226.

of sharing, of a brotherhood and equality that don't exist. The Puerto Rican elections held every four years exemplify this. We must not confuse the ox with the fighting bull, the causes with the problem, the root with the branches.[5]

And from a theoretician for the Young Lords Party, spawned in the socio-pathology of the urban *barrio*:

To support its economic exploitation of Puerto Rico, the United States instituted a new educational system whose purpose was to Americanize us. Specifically, that means that the school's principal job is to exalt the cultural values of the United States. As soon as we begin using books that are printed in English, that are printed in the United States, that means that the American way of life is being pushed . . . with all its bad points, with its commercialism, its dehumanization of human beings.

At the same time that the cultural values of America are exalted, the cultural values of Puerto Rico are downgraded. People begin to feel ashamed of speaking Spanish. Language becomes a reward and punishment system. If you speak English and adapt to the cultural values of America, you're rewarded; if you speak Spanish and stick to the old traditional ways, you're punished. In the school system here, if you don't quickly begin to speak English and shed your Puerto Rican values, you're put back a grade—so you may be in the sixth grade in Puerto Rico but when you come here, you go back to the fourth or fifth. You're treated as if you're retarded, as if you're backward—and your own cultural values therefore are shown to be of less value than the cultural values of this country and the language of this country.[6]

[5] Juan A. Silén, *We, The Puerto Rican People: A Story of Oppression and Resistance* (New York: Monthly Review Press, 1971), pp. 118–119. Originally, *Hacia una Visión Positiva del Puertorriqueño* (Rio Piedras: Editorial Edil, 1970).

[6] David Perez, "The Chains that have been Taken off Slaves' Bodies are put Back on their Minds." *Palante: Young Lords Party.* [Photographs by Michael Abramson; Text by Young Lords Party and Michael Abramson] (New York: McGraw Hill, 1971), pp. 65–66. Palante is the Spanish equivalent of "Right On" or "Forward." The Young Lords Party is a revolutionary political organization formed in New York City in 1969. The concerns of the Young Lords Party range from prisons and health

It is no accident that this strident voice registers anger particularly with the schools; for, it is in the schools that Puerto Rican identity is subjected to the greatest pressures, and it is the educational experience on the mainland which, for Puerto Ricans, is generally bad and from which despair and alienation emerge. It is in mainland schools that the dynamics of conflict and acculturation for Puerto Ricans are best seen in clear perspective; and it is a grim irony that, generally, educational programs for Puerto Ricans have failed despite the multitudinous educational experiments encapsulated in those new attentions born in Johnsonian America to the culture of the poor and the massive programmatic onslaughts on poverty. In the Puerto Rican mainland communities, there has been a subtle shift (following Black models) from civil rights and integration to an emphasis on Puerto Rican power and community solidarity.

And the Puerto Rican poor in their urban barrios have encountered as their chief adversaries the Black poor in the grim struggle for anti-poverty monies and for the participative indentities on Community Action Programs (funded by the Office of Economic Opportunity) which are often the vehicles and leverages of political power in the decaying American cities; additionally, a Puerto Rican professional presence in schools and a myriad of other institutional settings has been thwarted by exiled middle-class Cuban professionals. "Most of the Cubans are an exiled professional middle-class that came to the United States for political reasons. They are lauded and rewarded by the United States government for their rejection of Communism and Fidel Castro. The Cubans lean toward the political right, are fearful of the involvement of masses of poor people. Being middle-class they are familiar with 'the system' and operated successfully in this structure. They are competitive and upwardly mobile. They have little sympathy for the uneducated poor." (Hilda Hidalgo, *The Puerto Ricans of Newark, New Jersey*. Newark: Aspira, 1971, p. 14)

It is hardly strange that the Puerto Rican community has

care to sexism; they have cleaned up the streets of *El Barrio*, organized free breakfast programs for school children, and conducted door-to-door testing for lead poisoning and tuberculosis. See Frank Browning, "From Rumble to Revolution: The Young Lords," *Ramparts* (October 1970); and, Richard C. Schroeder, *Spanish-Americans: The New Militants*. Washington: Editorial Research Reports, 1971.

looked to the schools, traditionally the road out of poverty, as affording its best hope for successfully negotiating the challenges of an hostile mainland American milieu.

There is a continuing poignancy in the observations made by Lawrence R. Chenault as long ago as 1938 as he studied the plight of the Puerto Rican migrant in New York City: "The social adjustment necessitated by the migration results from the abrupt change of people but slightly removed from the peasant class from a simple rural environment to the slum section of an enormous city. The migration causes disintegrating forces to affect the family. In addition to this painful adjustment, the worker and his family are exposed to conditions which have long been recognized as harmful to the happiness and well-being of all people regardless of background. Often mixed with other families under extremely crowded conditions, without funds or employment, and in many cases suffering from malnutrition or some chronic disease, it is not strange that the worker and his family feel the influence of the antisocial behavior which is prevalent in these neighborhoods. Having come from an island where he has already acquired a feeling of mistreatment at the hands of the American people and their government, he is often resentful as a result of the clash in culture, racial antagonisms, and the failure to realize many expectations because of what he feels are discrimination and indifference."[7]

It is hazardous to predict what the continuing Puerto Rican experience on the mainland will be. The novelist Piri Thomas (whose *Down These Mean Streets* is a bitter portrait of life in the East Harlem *barrio*) comments sardonically on the evolving new postures of young Puerto Ricans: "During the past few years, I have had many opportunities to speak with young American-born Puerto Ricans in our communities, schools, and universities. They have developed an awareness of, and identity with, the land of their heritage and a strong desire to preserve its language and culture. They have told me that they are tired of the stereotyped picture of Puerto Ricans as a meek, submissive, or sexually immoral people. They are tired of reading books in English about Puerto Ricans written from a

[7] Lawrence Chenault, *The Puerto Rican Migrant in New York City* (New York: Columbia University Press, 1938; reissued with a New Foreword by F. Cordasco, New York: Russell & Russell, 1970), pp. 157–158.

politically or sociologically up-tight viewpoint that they consider to be a put-down."[8] And much of this sentiment (stripped of its ideological underpinning) is clearly evident in the haunting pathos of the following Young Lords verses (as though sung by hierophants) which are an apostrophic lament for dead Puerto Ricans and the end (for them) of the mainland hegira:

Juan
Miguel
Milagros
Olga
Manuel
Will right now be doing their own thing
Where beautiful people sing
And dance and work together
Where the wind is a stranger
To miserable weather conditions
Where you do not need a dictionary
To communicate with your hermanos y hermanas
Aquí se habla español all the time
Aquí you salute your flag first
Aquí there are no dial soap commercials
Aquí everybody smells good
Aquí TV dinners do not have a future
Aquí wigs are not necessary
Aquí we admire desire
And never get tired of each other
Aquí que passa Power is what's happening
Aquí to be called negrito y negrita
Means to be called Love.[9]

In the final analysis, the Puerto Rican mainland experience is still evolving and no past experiences of other groups furnish models adequate to its comprehension; in many ways it remains unique. Father Fitzpatrick (in speaking of the Puerto Rican experience in New York City), perhaps, best captures the *ethos* of the mainland communities at this point in time: "It is not yet clear what will become the basis of community strength which will enable the Puerto Ricans to move securely and confidently into full participation in the city's life. In the process,

---

[8] In Kal Wagenheim, *Puerto Rico: A Profile* (New York: Prager, 1970), p. xi.

[9] *Palante: Young Lords Party*, pp. 21–22.

both New York City and Puerto Ricans will have changed. As New York becomes more Puerto Rican, and as Puerto Ricans become more intimately a part of New York, both can become enriched in the process."[10]

[10] Fitzpatrick, *op. cit.*, p. 184.

PART I

THE ISLAND

BACKGROUND

Dorothy D. Bourne and James R. Bourne

THIRTY YEARS OF CHANGE
IN PUERTO RICO: A CASE STUDY
OF TEN SELECTED RURAL AREAS[*][1]

Planning is defined and described by Rafael Pico, first president of the Puerto Rican Planning Board: "It is a rational way of projecting the future from the experience of the past and the present."[2] As Pico points out, planning is of ancient origin, and among the Spaniards, was copied from the Romans. A drawing exists of the plan for San Juan, dated September 12, 1519. In 1932, James R. Beverley, Governor of Puerto Rico, brought to the island the architect Harland Bartholomew, who pointed out the need for zoning in San Juan and for a regional plan for the island. The work done by the Puerto Rico Relief Administration (PRERA), 1933–36, which carried out thousands of projects in the island, was limited in its planning by the emergency character of its program but attempted to relate its work to basic as well as temporary needs. ,

In May, 1942, the first law establishing planning was passed. The act established a planning board to work toward these goals. Its powers and duties were laid out in a master plan approved May 12, 1942.

The board shall prepare and adopt a Master Plan, which shall show, with any accompanying maps, charts and explanatory matter, its recommendations for the develop-

[*] From Dorothy D. Bourne and James R. Bourne, *Thirty Years of Change in Puerto Rico: A Case Study of Ten Selected Rural Areas*. New York: Prager, 1966, pp. 27–46. Reprinted with permission.

[1] A great part of the material for this section has been taken from Rafael Pico's book *Puerto Rico: Planificación y Acción* (Baltimore: Waverly Press, 1961). The other main source is the *Economic Report to the Governor*, 1963.

[2] Rafael Pico, *Puerto Rico: Planificación y Acción* (Pamphlet), (San Juan: Banco Gobernamental de Fomento para Puerto Rico, 1962).

ment of Puerto Rico and may include the general location, character and extent of the land, minerals, water, vegetation and animal life and their present and possible future utilization for mining, power, irrigation, flood control, navigation, draining, domestic and industrial uses of water, fishing, recreation and the general welfare; and of residential, commercial, recreational, manufacturing, transportation, institutional, governmental and public utility facilities and operations by whatever desirable categories, and the possible future utilization and development for these or other purposes and for the general welfare.

The Board shall include in the Master Plan the urban, suburban and rural parts of the island, but the Master Plan of Puerto Rico need not include minor resources, uses or facilities which are of a strictly local character. The Board may adopt the Master Plan as a whole or in parts, and may amend, add to, or itemize it or any part thereof. The Board may in its discretion prepare a separate master plan for the possible and advisable development of any municipality or its urban area, which may include resources, uses or facilities not included in the Master Plan of the island.[3]

These statements make clear the scope and purpose of planning in Puerto Rico. The act of 1942 was made possible by the vision and wisdom of a group of men of unusual devotion and ability. The leadership of Governor Muñoz Marín, then president of the Senate, was essential to the changes that had taken place. This legislation had many roots in the past and reflected the influence of many personalities, but without this expressed ideal and its practical organization, Puerto Rico would have been largely at the mercy of haphazard socioeconomic forces.

This project is designed to show that the changes which have taken place are good, that they represent measurable progress toward the goals set up in the General Purpose and that the organization of the Planning Board, with its coordinating functions, is competent to continue this progress in the future.

Although the approach of the Planning Board and its predecessors was concerned primarily with the economic situation of the island they were, sometimes unconsciously, also dealing

[3] Puerto Rico Planning Board, *Planning Act* (rev. ed.; Santurce: Planning Board, 1962), Section 3, pp. 2, 3–4. (Act No. 213 of May 12, 1942.)

with the cultural and human problems of developing societies: the changes from traditional to modern ways of life and the difficulties of the transition involved.

The first work of the Planning Board included: a division of engineering, a division of finances for the preparation of the Economic Program, a division of insular industries and services, and a division of urbanization.

Much work was necessary to overcome public opposition and to make clear what the real meaning of planning is and how it protects the individual in the exercise of his rights; it was also necessary to meet objections from some of the government departments which saw in the Planning Board a threat to the development of their respective programs.

In 1950, the Planning Board was assigned to the Governor's office. The Governor would coordinate its work with that of the Office of the Budget and Personnel. The Board would also be advisory to the Legislature and would maintain relations with the municipalities on local matters—revising and approving permanent projects in their relationship to over-all plans.

The work of the Board includes, of necessity, planning for cooperative action between the public and private sectors of the Commonwealth. This has become one of the keys to planned change in Puerto Rico. Both the incentives to private capital and the control of its development characterize the industrial and commercial planning. The establishment of government corporations, financed by the sale of bonds on the open market, demonstrates the possibility of combining patterns of capitalistic and government financing. This has made it possible to finance the initial costs of electrification, water, and other programs, each operating as an entity within the over-all plan and making available to communities and individuals improvement in living standards, sanitation, etc. through the sale of these commodities combined with the resources of the Puerto Rican Government.

The Government Development Bank is the agency responsible for long-term intermediate and short-term financing through a central system of marketing bonds. The bank serves public corporations, such as the Water Resources Authority and the Industrial Development Company, the municipalities and the Free Associated State of Puerto Rico, represented by the Treasury Department. The largest proportion of this financing goes to the public corporations.

Recognition must also be given to the part played by the

Federal Government and private investment from the United States in the economy of Puerto Rico. Heilbroner has said in his book *The Great Ascent* that in developing countries "the necessary germinal core of industrial capital must be obtained from abroad."[4] This can come through "trade, investment or aid." In the case of Puerto Rico, all three are involved, with the replacement of aid by federal programs applied to Puerto Rico in the form of matching appropriations and federal financial programs.

Although Puerto Rico receives far more financial advantage from its political status as part of the United States than any Latin American country through a U.S. aid program, nevertheless there is some basis for theoretical comparison. Planning in Puerto Rico has been based from its beginning on the analysis and use of *all* available resources. It recognized the necessity first to put its own house in order. This meant consideration of such obvious requirements as modifying the tax structure and tax collection and other revolutionary changes in land tenure and industrial development.

Economic and social planning rest fundamentally on the natural and human resources of the island. The understanding of these resources comes first, and then their use for development. The budget must represent in fiscal terms the decisions on proportions, priorities, and specific allocations. This is done by the preparation of a yearly model budget and its relation to a six-year plan. (In the Department of Health, planning is done through 1975.) It becomes the blueprint for present and future organization and growth.

The original budget of the Planning Board was $100,800 but it has grown with added responsibilities.

According to the plan, the Planning Board stimulates and coordinates the programs of the government departments. A major function is related to public works—their regulation, coordination and progress. Through the Governor, legislation is proposed and promoted. The coordinated plan for communities is the basis for decisions on electric lines, aqueducts, industries (both government-organized and private), housing projects, parks, etc. The process of carrying out public-works projects must be in accord with the Economic Program. Recommendations of the Planning Board are presented to the Execu-

---

[4] Robert L. Heilbroner, *The Great Ascent* (New York: Harper & Row, 1963), p. 83.

tive and to the Legislature; they must receive legislative auth- ization and appropriation; the Department of Public Works receives detailed plans, consults the Planning Board, adjusts to the budget and then submits its proposals to the Planning Board for final authorization. In 1957–58 more than 1,000 proj- ects were submitted to the Planning Board, of which 950 were approved at a cost of $46,000,000. The rejection of public-works projects which do not conform to the over-all plan is as impor- tant a function of the Board as approval.

Coordination with municipal government is carried out through local planning commissions made up of nine members, including the mayor, the president of the municipal assembly, three others appointed by the mayor, and four appointed by the president of the Planning Board. Minority parties are represented on these commissions.

A division of the Planning Board coordinates the work of the Economic and Industrial Development Company, the De- partments of Agriculture, Commerce, Government Develop- ment Bank, Port Authority, Urban Renewal, Authorities for Electrification, Water, etc. One example of the value of such cooperation is given in a quotation from Candido Oliveras, when President of the Planning Board (1961):

> In 1957 there was imported $74,000,000 worth of wheat, flour, cattle feed, grains, fertilizer, refrigerated meat, meat products, milk products, flour products and eggs. These imports were for the direct consumption of the people. Some of these, refrigerated products, milk, meat, etc. were sold direct to the consumer. In other cases it went to the consumer by way of shops for bread and other flour prod- ucts. In other areas such as that of cattle feed and fertil- izer, it was used for the production of cattle and poultry. We see that these imports—$74,000,000 represent con- sumption of $129,000,000. We calculate that in the year 1974, we can reduce imports to $15,000,000 due to local production and can increase consumption and exports of these products to $250,000,000.[5]

A second illustration of the coordinating function was shown when the Department of Education planned the construction of schools in a part of the island where the Planning Board sched-

[5] Pico (1961), *op. cit.*, p. 26.

ule had a projected hydroelectric project which would require flooding the area. The result of cooperation between Planning Board and the Department of Education led to a change in the location of the proposed schools to a place which could be used by the inhabitants of the valley when they were moved to a new site.

Roads must be constructed with a view to industrial growth and to the balance in urban-rural planning; they must also be coordinated with the program and financial aid provided by the Federal Government. It is clearly difficult to separate urban and rural planning because of their interdependence.

As in all modern societies, the pull of the cities is felt in Puerto Rico with the corollary that, as mechanization and the application of present-day knowledge in agricultural production become more effective, fewer workers in agriculture will be needed. Although in our opinion planning in and for the rural areas in Puerto Rico is rapidly catching up with urban and industrial planning qualitatively, much still remains to be done in working out a balance between urban and rural communities and their economic interdependence. The fact that the effort has been made, and is continuing, to bring industries to the rural areas shows great foresight on the part of Puerto Rican planners. Throughout the world, as societies modernize, the trend tends to be to migrate from country to city. If, in Puerto Rico, there can be wise decisions on where the balance lies in regional planning it will be a contribution of real dimensions.

The functioning of the Planning Board combines the ideal and the practical. The need to bring ideas into conformity with the budgetary resources makes its actions realistic. The process of presentation of plans from the government agencies, the time schedule set up for preparation for legislative action (eleven months), the provision for public hearings and regard for criticism by the press, consultations with the Governor, the Secretary of State, the Secretary of the Treasury, and the Director of the Bureau of the Budget—all these are the parts of a process that is thoughtful and orderly and that follows a democratic method.

To decide priorities in planning and in the long run for proportions in appropriations is the function of the Planning Board and the Governor. This is recognized. For decisions preliminary to the final action for the over-all plans, however, the heads of government agencies have responsibility not only for practical plans for their own agencies but for value judgments in such planning. Without this the dream would be lost, the inspiration would die. That the parts must be fitted into a whole is accepted with the idea of planning, and growth must come for the organism as a whole. Thus, education cannot exist as an end in itself but must be geared to the needs of the society; some areas of agriculture must be curtailed where it is no longer profitable, no longer able to absorb the number of workers who formerly lived, however inadequately, on the land; schedules for health programs must be selective because they must combine, in the proportions which are practicable, public health and individual care; public works must be used to serve other agencies according to the general plan but must also be a source of jobs in an economy where there is unemployment.

Therefore, in passing any judgment on planning, these considerations are all parts of the whole. General welfare is the purpose, changing as the various parts of the economy move, revised in the plans devised for the periods ahead. Not everything can be predicted, outside forces may influence rates of change.

> It is the destiny of the planning agency to accept, from those who define the general aspirations, their definition of what ought to be, to make this definition precise and practical, to show how much of it is feasible and how that much can be attained—in alternate ways if there are such —and to pass this precis on to the decision-makers with recommendations, taking it back with such modifications, wise or unwise, as the people's representatives suggest or demand and putting it together again as commanded. . . . The planning agency is a coagulator, a putter-together, a conjoiner which brings hope into focus and promises into possibility, a protector of reason among competing imaginative conceptions, a reducer of vague expectations to measured charts, tables and maps, a filler-out of strategies with the stuff of tactical reality. It is sometimes a killjoy; but sometimes a fulfiller of dreams.[6]

To imagine, to coordinate, and to make decisions on priorities—this combines creativity with order and judgment. This

[6] Tugwell, *op. cit.*, p. 38. [*The Stricken Land*. New York: Doubleday, 1947].

process lies at the heart of Puerto Rico's progress; it is a symbol of the dream becoming reality. The fact that mistakes are recognized and changes made, that balance is kept among the many parts, that no goal is regarded as static, make up the ingredients of a remarkable performance. It is, of course, easy —and perhaps sometimes right—that the interested observer finds things to criticize; no doubt one can see areas apparently neglected, individuals who do not benefit directly from the programs now in operation, questions on the priorities selected. But no one can look at the accomplishments without a recognition, and the effectiveness of the planners in Puerto Rico.

Looking back over the last thirty years in Puerto Rico, we find great forces at work which are responsible for both the visible and the invisible changes which have taken place.

Certain accomplishments of the planning program in relation to both short-term and long-term goals can be noted. The following show progress toward goals:

1. Increased employment at higher wages, more security, and greater satisfaction in work.

2. Increased life expectancy and health.

3. Increased comfort in living, through new facilities in electricity, water and housing.

4. New forms of economic development through cooperatives, incentives for both industry and agriculture.

5. Greater freedom for the individual through new kinds of mobility, higher income, education, recreation.

Another category could be set up illustrating programs for temporary or experimental purposes. Illustrations would be:

1. Public welfare for employables (pending the increase of employment opportunities); shoes for school children, school lunches, distribution of surplus commodities—all for the improvement of health and physical well-being.

2. The program of Fomento, with its special incentives to industries.

3. Experimental programs such as the coffee program and certain housing programs.

It was such programs as these, undertaken by Operation Bootstrap, which were concerned primarily with essential means for health and economic improvement. Muñoz Marín, using the expression "Operation Serenity," gives the new purpose for the future: "An attempt to give to economic effort and political freedom objectives that can commend themselves of the spirit of man in its function as leader of, rather that of servant to, the economic processes."[7]

It should be noted that the optimistic view of Puerto Rico's future is not universally accepted. Gordon K. Lewis in *Puerto Rico, Freedom and Power in the Caribbean*, points out the growth of conflicting economic interests, the development of pressure groups—American style—and

> the old cleavage, to take a final example, between the landed gentry and city commercial interests promises to be replaced, as new class lines harden, with a new alliance between land owners and the urban business groups. . . . Industrial society, as Durkheim has pointed out in a well-known analysis, is unique in that it releases in its members voracious and essentially limitless appetites for material goods and satisfactions.[8]

Perhaps this astringent criticism is a useful counteraction to any complacency about current performance and could help to give content to the idea of Operation Serenidad.

We have said little about the political changes which have been so important to the new life of Puerto Rico. This study will not take a position on the question of Puerto Rico's political status vis-à-vis the United States, which is now being studied by a committee over a two-year period before making recommendations to the Congress of the United States and the people of Puerto Rico. But the great inspiration which Commonwealth status brought about is essential to an understanding of the motivation for change. The preamble to the Constitution of Puerto Rico declares:

> The democratic system is fundamental to the life of the Puerto Rican community;
>
> We understand that the democratic system of government is one in which the will of the people is the source of public power, the political order is subordinate to the rights of man, and the free participation of the citizen in collective decisions is assured;

[7] From remarks by the Honorable Luis Muñoz Marín, Governor of Puerto Rico, at Harvard University, June 16, 1955.

[8] Gordon K. Lewis, *Puerto Rico, Freedom and Power in the Caribbean* (New York: M. R. Press, 1963), pp. 256–57.

We consider as determining factors in our life our citizenship of the United States of America and our aspiration continually to enrich our democratic heritage in the individual and collective enjoyment of its rights and privileges; our loyalty to the principles of the Federal Constitution; the co-existence in Puerto Rico of the two great cultures of the American Hemisphere; our fervor for education; our faith in justice; our devotion to the courageous, industrious, and peaceful way of life; our fidelity to individual human values above and beyond social position, racial differences and economic interests; and our hope for a better world based on these principles.

The Popular Democratic Party's program, adopted in 1960, contains a series of commitments which required legislation of a budgetary nature. Among others, the following would be enumerated:

  I. *Education*

  Construction of 2,000 classrooms during the next four years.

 II. *Health*

  To provide 1,800 hospital beds during the period 1960 to 1964; and provide pure water to the thousands of families who are still without this service in the rural zone.

III. *Housing*

  1. Property tax exemption up to $15,000 for owner-occupied dwellings.
  2. Sale of apartments in public housing projects.
  3. Face the problem of the excessive increases in land values.

 IV. *Labor*

  Introduce social measures to alleviate the problems resulting from mechanized agriculture.

  V. *Agriculture*

  1. Provide subsidies for farmers engaged in tobacco cultivation.
  2. Establish credit facilities for small agricultural businesses.
  3. Continuation of subsidies to the sugar cane growers.

VI. *Transportation and Communication*

   Construction of 600 kilometers of highways and the improvement of 500 additional kilometers.

The budgetary procedure is outlined as follows:

We try to determine in the first instance the minimum sum that would be required to maintain the level of development that has been obtained. In general terms we make this determination in the following manner:

a. Examining the situation in the immediate past year and for the current fiscal period, and including the following:

   1. Funds available during each of the two respective years (those left over from previous years and new allocations).

   2. Expenditures during the year (work completed or in the process of construction).

   3. Estimated surplus at the close of the year.[9]

GROUPING OF THE MUNICIPALITIES OF PUERTO RICO FOR PROCESSES OF PLANNING

Puerto Rico has had extraordinary success in its efforts to raise the standard of living. Without doubt, this development, which has to some extent reached all municipalities on the island, has not been carried out with the same vigor and effectiveness in all, and efforts to equalize advantages are the purpose of the long-term regional plan. Certain municipalities, especially those of the metropolitan area of San Juan, have absorbed the greater part of the development, although others have also made great gains. Imbalance occurs in the net increase of income among the municipalities; opportunity for employment varies greatly; concentration of population, particularly in the San Juan area, intensifies differences in the economic level between it and smaller municipalities. The uneven development among municipalities is illustrated by the influx into Bayamón (part of the San Juan metropolitan area) which showed (1950–60) a 341.9 per cent increase in population. The

[9] Commonwealth of Puerto Rico, Office of the Governor, Puerto Rico Planning Board, Eduardo Rivera Rivera, Director Bureau of Public Works, *Methods and Procedures in the Preparation of the Four-Year Financial Plan*, July, 1963, pp. 10–11.

municipality of Arroyo, on the other hand, showed 14.1 per cent while the increase for the whole island was 129.5 per cent. Others actually showed a decrease. Uneven employment opportunity was, of course, the chief reason—San Juan alone providing 19,203 new jobs.

It is natural that private investment should establish new industries, businesses, and services in those areas where development is easiest. It is necessary for industry to share common services and therefore to establish its location with regard to facilities and the availability of labor. But the metropolitan areas face special problems because the resources for the development of good living are not equal to the rapid increase of population. To offset the disadvantages, the Development Company works on a principle of decentralization of industry to relieve this pressure.

The Planning Board, beginning in 1957, has been studying and formulating plans for regional development in order to orient the growth in such a way as to give to the whole island the benefits which accrue from employment and the services which the government can provide as a result of increasing prosperity. The following outline gives the points considered for development:

1. The underlying purpose of the government has been to minimize the socio-economic differences which exist among the municipalities in Puerto Rico.

2. In order to establish a pattern for the location of business, industry and services, the accessibility of the principal ports was the first consideration. This was decided for three basic reasons:

a. The island imports a high percentage of articles for local consumption.

b. Puerto Rico, because of the limitations of its own size, does not constitute a market adequate to absorb its industrial products, and therefore, depends on exterior markets, especially the United States.

c. The type of industry which has been established and has the greatest potentiality of growth in Puerto Rico imports all, or nearly all, its raw materials.

Therefore, based on these criteria, the three chief regions for the island have been established as the cities of San Juan, Ponce, and Mayaguez, where the main ports are located.[10]

[10] Junta de Planificación, Estudio para determinar la Agrupación de los Municipios de Puerto Rico para Propósitos de Planificación.

The setting up of these regions represented, first, the need to formulate plans for the growth of these as urban centers—for social and economic development according to a major urban plan. Following this came the study of possibilities for making certain municipalities in each of the regions surrounding these cities accessible for the other municipalities within the regions —a grouping based on topography, roads, transportation, and the accompanying changes from traditional to modern ways of life.

The subcenters, though showing orientation toward the center, manifest vast differences and become important in the regional grouping as areas for development, as well as in their relation to the main center of the region. For example, one group of municipalities in the Ponce area already has a high degree of industrialization. Here are located the large oil refineries, and other commercial and industrial development, with resulting higher economic levels. The other sector of the Ponce region reaches into the most remote mountains with scattered agricultural population (one of the municipalities in this section is Adjuntas, where one of our study communities is located), and the towns of Jayuya and Adjuntas as centers. The development of two such disparate sections requires entirely different types of planning. Similarly, in the San Juan area, there are isolated municipalities—Orocovis and Barranquitas. Here, agricultural workers represent 46 per cent of the population and the standard of living is among the lowest in the island.

Obviously, then, the plan is not based on homogeneity within these regions, but rather on the functional interaction among the several municipalities within each region and their direction toward the center. As one index of this, the movement of workers from one municipality to another was analyzed: among the residents, those who were employed elsewhere and where they worked; among the nonresident workers, the places where they were employed. The transportation facilities and use were also studied and it was found that the three regions were the logical centers from this standpoint; the most distant places were no more than ninety minutes from one of the centers and were near enough to a subcenter of the region to make each regional division practical as a plan for development.

The following factors are considered significant in the establishment of the three regions:

1. Availability of ports

2. Existing metropolitan areas
3. Political organization
4. Concentration of population
5. Distribution of industrial employment
6. Commercial sales and services per capita
7. Economic levels
8. Number of non resident employees

Taking these factors as a point of departure, the area of influence of each of these metropolitan areas was determined. The most important was the evaluation of the degree of dependence of the municipalities on the center or subcenter and the accessibility of these centers for further development.

The characteristics analyzed were the following:

1. Administrative divisions used by the different government agencies and corporations. These divisions of regions and subregions of the Planning Board cross other established regional divisions of government agencies already in operation. These remain as practical administrative units. The Planning Board must, of course, take into consideration in over-all planning the practical requirements of these agencies in carrying out their respective programs.

2. The movement of employees—i.e., the analysis of the relation between residents and place of work of the workers in each municipality in Puerto Rico.

3. The availability of transportation and the distance in time of each municipality from the center.

4. The geographic location of the municipalities with respect to the urban centers (this included analysis of physical conditions, topography, and whether these limited or furthered the accessibility of each municipality).

The first requirement in the area studies was the specific possibility for maximum development of potentialities, minimizing of isolation in the distant municipalities, and the amelioration of the limitations which interfere with progress.

In setting up subregions, the most prosperous areas were selected on the grounds that these formed the centers within the region. Clearly, the index of prosperity can only be used in a relative sense and is not universally applicable to all municipalities within a region, but each of the subregions has as its center the most prosperous municipality.

One of the tests in analysis of the three centers was the number of residents from other municipalities who travel daily to work in these cities. In 1960, a total of 25,964 workers were employed in San Juan who were not residents of this municipality; and in Ponce there was a registration of 2,892 such persons; in Mayaguez—a total of 2,712.

The comparison of the figures for the three main urban zones, with statistics for the rest of the municipalities of the island, show effectively that San Juan, Ponce, and Mayaguez are the principal sources of employment in Puerto Rico.

REGION AND SUBREGIONS

San Juan Region I,
    Sub Bayamón   —Hato Lejas
    Sub Caguas   —Juncos–Mangó
    Sub Loiza   —Rio Grande–Medianía Alta
    Sub Cayey   —Cidra–Bayamón
    Sub Arecibo   —Sabana Hoyos
Ponce Region II
    Sub Adjuntas   —Yahuecas
    Sub Juana Dias   —Collores
    Sub Salinas   —Lapa
Mayaguez Region III
    Sub Moca   —Voladores
    Sub Aguadilla   —San Antonio

As an illustration of the separate jurisdictions of individual government agencies, the plans of both the Department of Health and the Department of Education may be cited. In each case, the regional plans now considered in these departments represent fresh research, reexamination of old divisions of organization, and a program of decentralization. This shows that the opportunity exists, within the over-all programs of the Planning Board, for the flexibility recognized as a necessary ingredient in the best adaptation of departmental organization to special needs of the population. Decentralization would mean that the regions would become autonomous in certain respects but it would involve also—and more importantly—the coordination of services within each region. As far as the development of new methods of the democratic process within a complex society are concerned, these new forms of organization are striking examples of the ability and the confidence of Puerto Ricans to experiment, to test, and to create.[11]

[11] It should be inserted parenthetically that this comment comes from one of the directors of the present study as a result of her experience in the 1930's when the Department of Education was only beginning

The description of the Department of Health experiment, using Bayamón as the experimental region, includes too much detail for this report, but the general aim was to "assure a higher quality of health services by providing better opportunities for professional growth to medical and allied personnel and by allowing the utilization of their professional skills at the highest possible degree of efficiency." This required new forms of communication, the integration of clinical services, physicians from (formerly) municipal hospitals becoming members of the staff of the base hospital, and chiefs of clinical services in the regional base hospital carrying consultative and supervisory responsibilities for local functioning of health centers. In certain fields of medicine, where use of laboratories and specialists are most necessary, the regional hospital, in the case of the Bayamón region, affiliated with the University of Puerto Rico medical school. The base hospital has special resources to offer but the flow of patients, of education, and of services is a two-way one between local and regional centers. The full organization and administration of the regional idea includes changes in nursing services along lines of community health service, nutrition, etc.; public health, including environmental sanitation, the training of inspectors, control of communicable diseases; health education.

If this program is found good and extended to other regions, it will change completely the present form of administration which is described in the following quotation:

> In the present centralized organization and administration of the Department of Health of the Commonwealth of Puerto Rico (see section on reorganization of the Department of Health) all major and important decisions are made at the central departmental office, by the Secretary himself or by division or bureau chiefs by virtue of authority delegated to them. Personnel working on intermediate or local echelons of the organization have very little, if any, participation in program planning activities conducted at the level of the offices of the Secretary of Health. A two-way communication system is missing.

---

to free itself from the influence of the continental United States' methods in education. The establishment of the Second Unit Schools and various adaptations to Puerto Rican needs began then under the leadership of the Commissioner of Education, Dr. José Padín.

Planning Regions and Sub-regions as Defined by Planning Board as of 1962

LEGEND

—— Region Boundary

- - - - Subregion Boundary

—— Municipality Boundary

A Subregion Fajardo

Thus, the central level issues orders and the intermediate local levels follow orders.

This organizational and operational setup is responsible outside the Bayamón region, and still to some extent inside the region, for the uncoordinated, unrelated operation of health and welfare institutions throughout the island of Puerto Rico. Thus, in municipalities, public health units, public welfare units, and hospital units the services are geographically integrated in a health center, but professionally operate in a vacuum. Although these units serve the same clientele, the by-products of this organizational setup is a situation in which there are overlappings of programs on the one hand, and gaps in programs on the other.

At the regional or district level general hospitals operate as separate organizational units of service. Their only relationship with local health and welfare centers is along one-way avenues of communication by which service is given to patients from these centers on a referral basis. There are no professional relationships between the technical staffs of the health and welfare centers and those of the general district hospitals.[12]

There are five proposed regions for health services. In the Bayamón region Health and Welfare will be integrated; in the others welfare services will continue their own programs and all welfare activities will be under the direction of a Deputy Secretary of Health. The general health care program will be directed by a Deputy Secretary of Health. Both deputy directors will be responsible for the coordination of the two programs.[13]

SUBURBAN PLANNING

A special program for planning suburban development has been started. In these plans it is recognized that closer cooperation is needed between agricultural and urban planning; in this

[12] Puerto Rico Department of Health, *Regionalization of Health and Welfare Services in Puerto*, Progress Report, July 1, 1958-December 31, 1959 (Rio Piedras: The Commonwealth of Puerto Rico), p. 47.

[13] *Ibid.*, p. 59.

CRUV (Urban Renewal and Housing) must be more concerned as suburban communities grow and the separation between urban and rural becomes less distinct. The Planning Board envisages a "green belt" as part of this new suburban development and sees also the changing distinctions among urban, semirural, and suburban. It has the hope that communities may develop, or be developed, in which there will be a mixture of classes in which public housing may be included and where there will be increased opportunity for upward mobility. From an economic standpoint, municipal services—electricity, water, sewage, etc.—can be better provided where population density is greater and adjustments to this need can be made. Those communities or areas which remain truly rural do not at present come within this category.

POPULATION

The problem of population control cannot be adequately dealt with in this study, but neither can it be completely ignored. Its bearing on economic and social improvement is no greater and no less than in other parts of the world; in other words, the danger exists that population increase can offset the advantages of economic growth.

> The implications of the present patterns of fertility and mortality for future populations have great significance, particularly in view of the national aspirations of the less developed areas for improving levels of living. To achieve higher levels of living, income per capita must, of course, be increased. Planners must, therefore, be aware of what the prospects are for future population to be able to set desired economic goals and lay plans for their achievement.
> By the end of the century, Latin America will have the most rapidly growing population, more than trebling to reach a total of 650 million from a level of about 200 million.[14]

This quotation serves as preface to what must be said about the effect of population on the future of Puerto Rico. In the

[14] Philip Hauser, "Man and More Men: The Population Prospects," *Bulletin of Atomic Scientists,* June, 1964, p. 7.

1930's Puerto Rico was a heavily overpopulated island. The actual increase and the rate were both among the highest in the world.

The Planning Board has prepared an elaborate *Analisis de Población* (*Informo Preliminar*), 1940–80. This analysis deals with both quantitative and qualitative factors of the population question and gives the following points of view for its report:

1. We know that population is a field of both quantitative and qualitative data. These data answer for us the when and the where of population. In this phase we are interested in the growth, in the vital statistics, in the quality, composition and distribution of the population.

2. We know that population is a dynamic field of human behavior which requires sociological interpretation. It is in this phase that we are interested in knowing how cultural changes are affected by population and the social interaction with population trends.

3. We know that population is a field of social action and here we ask the following question: What is the significance of the data? What ought to be done and what can be done?

4. The primary purpose of planning is to provide adequate satisfaction for the physical, social, economic and cultural needs of a given population. This makes it evident that the study and understanding of the growth, distribution and composition of this same population is an indispensable element in planning.[15]

Table 1 shows population increase and rate in three cycles— from 1775 to 1960.[16] During the first cycle—1775 to 1881—the decrease is attributed to the high rate of infant mortality.

Estimates since 1960 have been affected by a marked change in the emigration predictions. It may well be that the trend of return to Puerto Rico from the continental United States will actually increase in numbers, bringing the problem of population increase to a critical point and accentuating the difficulties of housing and employment.

15 Puerto Rico Planning Board, Office of the Governor, *Analisis de Población*, translated from Chapter XIV.

16 A. J. Jaffe, *People, Jobs and Economic Development* (New York: Columbia University Press, 1959).

TABLE 1

Population Increase

	Year	Pop. in Thousands	Table of Annual Increase
First Cycle	1775	70	4.61
	1800	155	3.20
	1815	221	2.34
	1832	330	2.42
	1846	448	2.17
	1860	583	1.92
	1877	732	1.32
	1887	799	0.87
Second Cycle	1899	953	1.50
	1910	1,118	1.54
	1920	1,300	1.56
	1930	1,544	1.69
	1935	1,724	1.95
	1940	1,869	1.89
Third Cycle	1950	2,210	1.69
	1960	2,349	.62

TABLE 2

Civilian Noninstitutional Population, the Labor Force, Employment and Unemployment, with an Assumption of Zero Migration, Puerto Rico, 1960–80

Year	Civilian Population (noninst.)	Labor Force	Per cent of Participation	Employed	Per cent of Unemployed
1960	1,379.0	625.3	45.0	542.0	13.3
1962	1,454.0	670.0	46.1	585.3	12.6
1970	1,911.0	916.0	47.9	689.4	24.7
1975	2,189.3	1,082.2	49.4	752.6	30.5
1980	2,526.3	1,250.1	49.5	862.3	31.0

Table 2 illustrates the estimate of the employment situation based on a figure of zero emigration, showing a possible rise in unemployment from 13.3 per cent in 1960 to 31 per cent in 1980.[17]

The birth rate has been decreasing and it may be hoped that this trend will continue. Raw data on reproduction projected for 1960 give a rate of 2.13 and for 1970 of 2.04.

[17] Puerto Rico Planning Board, *Analisis de Población*, Table XXXV, p. 106.

The report of the Planning Board concludes with a series of recommendations dealing with such questions as decentralization as a means of spreading the opportunities for work and the space for living, and recognizes the general tendency toward a lower birth rate where more urban ways of living prevail, with higher levels of education and occupational opportunities.

The remedies suggested for overpopulation are of a socioeconomic nature and there is no doubt that these are of very great importance in population control. However, the specific subject of birth control also deserves most serious attention in Puerto Rico, as in other parts of the world. Its history in Puerto Rico has been an erratic one since its inception, as part of the program of the PRERA. For a full program to be undertaken would require a change in the position of the Catholic Church. If such a change occurs the facilities of Puerto Rico could very quickly put a program into operation due to the groundwork which is already there. The value of such a program is, we believe, of great importance in the lives of individuals as well as in its impact on the population problem.

Certain accomplishments of the planning program in relation to both short-term and long-term goals can be noted. The following show progress toward goals.

1. Increased employment at higher wages, more security, and greater satisfaction in work.

2. Increased life expectancy and health.

3. Increased comfort in living, through new facilities in electricity, water, and housing.

4. New forms of economic development through cooperatives, incentives for both industry and agriculture.

5. Greater freedom for the individual through new kinds of mobility, higher income, education, recreation.

EL DOLAR PRESUPUESTARIO DE 1965
THE 1965 BUDGET DOLLAR

PROCEDENCIA — *WHERE IT COMES FROM*

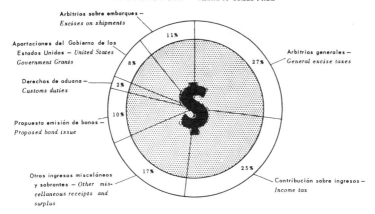

Arbitrios sobre embarques —
Excises on shipments

Aportaciones del Gobierno de los
Estados Unidos — *United States
Government Grants*

Derechos de aduana —
Customs duties

Propuesta emisión de bonos —
Proposed bond issue

Otros ingresos misceláneos
y sobrantes — *Other mis-
cellaneous receipts and
surplus*

11%

8%

2%

10%

17%

27%

25%

Arbitrios generales —
General excise taxes

Contribución sobre ingresos —
Income tax

DISTRIBUCION — *WHERE IT GOES*

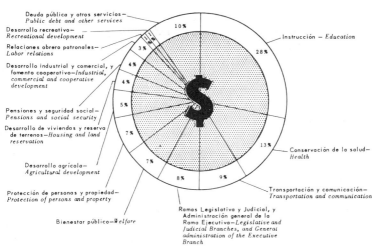

Deuda pública y otros servicios —
Public debt and other services
Desarrollo recreativo —
Recreational development
Relaciones obrero patronales —
Labor relations
Desarrollo industrial y comercial, y
fomento cooperativo—*Industrial,
commercial and cooperative
development*

Pensiones y seguridad social —
Pensions and social security
Desarrollo de viviendas y reserva
de terrenos—*Housing and land
reservation*

Desarrollo agrícola —
Agricultural development

Protección de personas y propiedad—
Protection of persons and property

Bienestar público—*Welfare*

10%

3%

4%

4%

5%

7%

7%

8%

9%

28%

13%

Instrucción — *Education*

Conservación de la salud—
Health

Transportación y comunicación—
Transportation and communication

Ramas Legislativa y Judicial, y
Administración general de la
Rama Ejecutiva—*Legislative and
Judicial Branches, and General
administration of the Executive
Branch*

Sidney W. Mintz

PUERTO RICO: AN ESSAY IN THE DEFINITION OF NATIONAL CULTURE*

Throughout this report, it has been contended that the term "culture" has been used carelessly and unreflectively by many students of Puerto Rico. An attempt has been made here to distinguish between "culture" as a term applying to the esthetic product of an elite, and as an anthropological category covering all of the learned social and symbolic behavior of the members of a society, and its consequences. It is also necessary to differentiate what might be called "national character" or "national characteristics" from the variant sets of behaviors and values typifying different social segments of the same polity. Thus, on the one hand, one must separate out the esthetic products of a literate, historically conscious minority from those of "the people," widely conceived; on the other, one must distinguish those widely held "Puerto Rican" traits from those marking special groups or classes within the total society.

It should be plain enough that, while one may regard the novels of a Laguerre and the "plenas" and "décimas" of the countryside as fitting with equal justification within Puerto Rican culture, they represent very different aspects of that culture, and are to a large extent mutually exclusive aspects. Similarly, while there may be some grounds for claiming that disdain for manual labor, for example, is an historically determined "Puerto Rican" cultural attitude, it must be noted that this would definitely not be true for many, or possibly even most, Puerto Ricans. Finally, what goes by the label of "Puerto Rican national characteristic"—for instance, the speaking of Spanish, or a sexual double standard—may not only fail to hold for everyone, but in all likelihood has very different sym-

* In *Status of Puerto Rico: Selected Background Studies for the United States—Puerto Rico Commission on the Status of Puerto Rico.* Washington: U.S. Government Printing Office, 1966, pp. 380–434.

bolic connotations in different social segments of the national society.

These qualifications should suggest the difficulties that one faces in seeking to treat Puerto Rican culture as if it were some sort of concrete undifferentiated entity. Nor is the problem in any way a uniquely Puerto Rican one; few are the social scientists so blithe and confident as to deal with greater assurance in the case of French culture, Russian culture, or North American culture. The fact is that modern nations do not lend themselves readily to holistic analyses of this sort, and the layman's notions about national character rarely find confirmation in the work of social scientists, no matter how convincing such notions may seem. "German" authoritarianism, "French" romanticism, and "English" doggedness may be delightful conversational counters for many observers, but no one has been truly successful in transforming such imputations into solid social science facts.

If any basis at all is to be discovered for formulations of this sort, I believe it will probably be located in one of four spheres of inquiry: social history; value-categories; socialization and child-training patterns; or "social idioms." Numerous attempts have been made to etch in some national identity—Russian, for instance, or French, or Mexican—by appeals to one or another of these four kinds of data. In the case of Puerto Rico, those few attempts that have been made to spell out the essentially Puerto Rican have not been conspicuously successful, though I have tried in this report to refer to the findings of some studies directed to this end.[1] One is left with the feeling that, if there are genuinely distinctive character traits or values we may confidently call Puerto Rican, they are extremely hard to enumerate and harder yet to corroborate by social science methods.

[1] The late Clyde Kluckhohn, anthropologist, sought to get at what might be called "national character" through studies of group values. In an appendix prepared by Mrs. Jane Collier, a tentative application of the Kluckhohn approach to Puerto Rican materials is offered. It must be emphasized that this work was based on written materials only, and involved no fieldwork. All the same, the findings are of some interest. Wolf's brilliant paper on Mexican group relations (1956b), and Lauria's exploration (1964) of Puerto Rican interpersonal relations deal with "social idiom"; the work of Kathleen Wolf (1952) makes valuable use of child-training data for Puerto Rico; and Steward's associates (1956) employed social history very significantly in their analyses.

We have seen that Puerto Rican society was propelled in a special direction by the lengthy isolation that ensued after the discovery of the Mexican mainland (1519), and that continued almost unabated until the very start of the 19th century. During this period, Puerto Rico was effectively controlled by a small military bureaucracy, Spanish rather than creole in identity, and little involved in the problems of Puerto Rican development. The rural population included persons of heterogeneous genetic and cultural origins, who adapted to life on the island's "internal frontier" by maintaining a substantial detachment from public affairs of any kind. It was because of these rural highland folk that there originated the image of the jíbaro—unlettered, laconic, shrewd, shy to the point of seeming semi-feral, and "unspoiled." Although slavery was important at various times between 1510 and 1815, it did not become the major basis for economic activity as in the non-Hispanic Antilles, nor did race emerge as a basic social assortative device. The insular social structure, however, was marked by a clear separation between the urbanite and the countryman and between the Spaniard and the creole.

It is important to keep in mind at the same time that the bulking rural population did not preserve Spanish folk culture in some state of unchanged 16th-century purity, as has sometimes been suggested. Many features of the Spanish heritage were sloughed off or supplanted in the Puerto Rican rural setting, and other cultures—Amerind, African, and non-Hispanic European—contributed to the growth of a particular Puerto Rican rural subculture. Though certain parallel processes occurred in Cuba, Santo Domingo and elsewhere, Puerto Rico, like any other society, has had its own unique cultural history.

After 1800, the social structure of the island changed more sharply, especially as the development of the slave-based plantation system was accelerated. Slavery and foreign immigration grew, and commercial expansion replaced the military emphasis that had dominated Puerto Rico's position in the Spanish imperial system. Early pioneers in commerce, whose main concern at the start of the 19th century was to win economic concessions from the Crown, soon became more concerned with the extraction of labor effort from the rural population of the island; both slavery and forced labor were encouraged by the concessions of 1815 (Fernández Méndez, 1959). In other words, once the Crown agreed to permit rapid economic development in the island, Puerto Rico entrepreneurs separated themselves ideologically and by identity from their less privileged countrymen, in the quest for higher profits and swifter economic growth. A sense of Puerto Rico nationality, utterly dormant in the 18th century, was stunted anew, as the plantation system expanded, and free but landless countrymen, white and colored alike, were forced into plantation labor.

After 1850, Spanish controls over Puerto Rican economic activities were intensified once more, leading to the growth of a more nationalistic sentiment among national leaders. Divisions in political view had appeared in the struggle over abolition, with the newer hacendado group more anxious to maintain slavery than the older, more powerful plantation owners. Further divisions, between Spaniards and creoles, also became sharper as questions concerning Puerto Rico's future political status began to be asked. Even earlier, in the 1830's, the United States had begun to emerge as an important potential market for Puerto Rican products, and the inescapable presence of the "Colossus of the North" inevitably influenced Puerto Rican political thinking. More and more, after 1850, Puerto Rican political opinion failed to divide simply into two camps—for Spain, or for autonomy—and the political issues were complicated by the differing stakes of various groups on the island. There were those fundamentally loyal to Spain and essentially accepting of Puerto Rico's dependent status under the Crown; there were those others who desired greater autonomy, the abolition of slavery, and a stronger orientation to the United States; finally, there were the separatists, who sought in varying degrees an autonomous or independent Puerto Rico.

In the late 19th century, beginning with the active struggle for abolition, there emerged the first clear expression of political nationalism in Puerto Rico. It was related to the continued dominance of Spaniards in all administrative circles, to the differential favorable treatment accorded Spaniards in contrast to creoles, and to the rapid economic gains in island economic life of capital-holding Spanish mercantile groups. To a great extent, Puerto Rican entrepreneurs and businessmen had been unable to maintain the economic momentum of the early 19th century, since neither sugar nor coffee had been continuously lucrative, and the island had come to depend heavily upon Spanish merchant capitalists and banks. In the closing decades of the 19th century, the barriers between creoles and Spaniards became sharper, and political repression of creole separatists grew. Though the weakening of Spanish overseas strength made possible the political reforms of 1897, these reforms were immediately terminated by North American rule.

The saga of Puerto Rican growth after 1897 is too well known to require much repetition here. Decades of governmental neglect were accompanied by a frighteningly rapid expansion of North American large-scale economic interests. By the onset of the world depression, Puerto Rico had become a plantation colony par excellence, with all of the worst features of absentee imperialism. It is surely worth remarking that no matter how strongly this is stated, very few North American scholars of Puerto Rico will take issue with it, for there is precious little to argue about. Puerto Rico thus became an outstanding example of that rare phenomenon, undisguised North American colonialism and economic imperialism.

The cultural effects of North American rule likewise require no documentation here. Significant institutional changes, most important being the ambiguous political incorporation of the island into the North American system, were accompanied by the introduction of English as the language of instruction, and the growth of transportation, communication, and health systems of a more modern sort. While it is commonly supposed that the cultural impact was felt most sharply in urban centers and among members of the more privileged classes, the plantation system introduced widespread societal and cultural changes in rural areas, particularly along the sugar coasts (Mintz, 1960). To the extent that culture change depended mainly on improved buying power, it was within the urban middle and upper classes that the North American impact might be most easily witnessed, but in some regards, social and cultural change was even more dramatic and thoroughgoing among rural working people. Nor should it be forgotten that continued change among Puerto Rican working folk has often consisted of a taking-on of cultural items and practices already well established among middle class and upper class elements in the cities. (Surely those who most loudly bemoan the extirpation of Puerto Rican culture in the countryside should notice that they themselves are much more Americanized in their styles of life than the country folk—and that the Americanization of the country folk largely consists of taking on the consumption norms of their urban class betters.)

After 1940, some of the most nakedly exploitative elements in the North American hegemony were eliminated or reduced in importance, while the issue of political status was, for most Puerto Ricans, left to one side. The electoral strength of the Popular Democratic Party grew steadily during the 1940's, and to some extent the party ideology and membership changed, as power became more firmly institutionalized. In recent years, the issue of status has been quite vigorously revived, though electoral results continue to give the Popular Party position unmatched support.

Changes since 1940 have clearly brought more and more Puerto Ricans into intimate contact with North America, through migration, expansion of mass media, increasing education, and the implicit acceptance of the majority party's position on continued political association. Not only have many Puerto Ricans settled in the mainland United States or worked there for lengthy periods, thus familiarizing themselves with North American culture and values, but also the number of North Americans who visit or live in Puerto Rico has risen substantially. It can be asserted that the influence of North American culture was less before 1940, even though the exploitative elements in North American control were sharper in those years.

The way Puerto Ricans regard their present cultural status varies significantly, according to the ways in which they participate in all of these recent changes. It is my impression that the problem of cultural identity is not felt acutely by working class persons—an assertion which is not, however, based on reliable up-to-date sociological or anthropological study. Working people in Puerto Rico have been exposed to North American influences for over half a century, but until the 1940's these influences only slowly affected their ability to assimilate new cultural forms. In the highlands of Puerto Rico, North American cultural influences consisted largely of increasing pressure toward migration to the coasts, as the plantation economy expanded and the peasant economy contracted. Traditional highland culture and social forms were "collapsed" by this pressure, however. In coastal areas, such influences were felt through the imposition of the plantation regimen itself: wage labor replaced payment in kind; standardized work rules replaced personalistic affiliations; store-bought consumers' goods replaced homegrown foods; more modern medical services replaced traditional herbal remedies; and so on. But since real incomes remained extremely low, what I would call "consumer-based acculturation" was slow.

During World War II and after, higher worker incomes, electrification, roadbuilding, military service, the rise in emigration, rural industrialization, and a new level of political activity and consciousness began to effect much more basic changes in working class styles of life. Since about 1950, these changes have come with increasing rapidity, and my report on Barrio Jauca (Mintz, 1965), when taken in conjunction with earlier work (Mintz, 1951a, 1953b, 1960; Steward, 1956) suggests, at least minimally, just how rapid and thoroughgoing such changes have become. Nevertheless, I must repeat that, to a very considerable extent, changes in life-style among rural working people seem to consist in large part of a taking-on of forms which have long been standard among the urban middle classes of Puerto Rico, and that "Americanization" or the "destruction of Puerto Rican culture" in this case consists in good degree of a continuation of what is by now an established process in other segments of Puerto Rican society.

It is, of course, a different matter for urban folk and members of the middle classes generally. These are people who, if they have been of middle class status for more than 20 years, have been long practicing those very forms of behavior they may now deplore as they spread among poorer rural folk. To the extent that this is true, I find it difficult to see why it is more tragic for rural workers to give up the décima for rock-and-roll than it is for urban middle class persons to give up the danzas of Morel Campos for either rock-and-roll or the music of Pablo Casals. However, that rock-and-roll is inexorably supplanting the décima is undeniable, it seems to me, and this musical form is American—as any Englishman, Frenchman, or Russian can prove. It is difficult to avoid thinking that certain segments of the middle class, at least, feel themselves better prepared than their lower class compatriots to sift out the "socially good" from the "socially bad" in North American culture. If so, one is tempted to wonder how, were Puerto Rico politically sovereign (as it surely has every right to be, should its citizens so desire), those who know what is better for others would organize a democratic society in which the "socially good" opinions would prevail.

It is clear why cultural ambivalence might be stronger among the middle class elements of Puerto Rican society. Cultural "self-consciousness" is obviously more acute when education serves to deepen one's sense of affiliation to an abstract ideology of identity. Middle class Puerto Ricans, at least in superficial ways, often exaggerate their awareness of the norms, beliefs, and attitudes of their lower class fellow citizens. Though they are sometimes prepared to admit as much—no anthropologist who has worked in the Puerto Rican countryside has missed the experience of having at least one Puerto Rican university colleague admit that he controlled fewer facts about the rural sector than the anthropological stranger—the feeling inevitably persists that only a Puerto Rican can know Puerto Rico, no matter what the individual experiences of the claimant. The assertion is, paradoxically, both true and false. Middle class North Americans would of course react in precisely the same way to the statements of a foreign anthropologist who had worked intimately in the American countryside. Yet any honest North American—anthropologists emphatically included!—would also know that foreign social scientists who had, for instance, worked in an obscure western or midwestern hamlet for a year or two might know at least as much about the culture of the people there, as he himself would know simply by virtue of being North American.

These statements do nothing, however, to diminish the difficulties of presenting a coherent picture of a unitary Puerto Rican culture. It is possible to list a series of adjectives ("docile," "resigned," "tolerant"), of culture traits (décimas, baquines, coffee-drinking, the speaking of Spanish), of institutional subsystems (compadrazgo, noviazgo), of widely-held attitudes and values expressed in language and in social behavior (machismo, personalismo, respeto, relajo), but I do not believe we are able at this time to describe an undifferentiated totality called "Puerto Rican culture."

Puerto Rico's particular history has given rise to a peculiar and unique set of social and economic classes and interest groups. Its political and economic dependence upon the United States has informed and seriously affected the beliefs and behaviors of members of these groups. The processes set in motion by the North American hegemony have continued to operate, and at accelerated speeds in recent decades. Emigration, industrialization, and economic growth have differentially changed the composition of the various groups and classes that make up the society, and have introduced new values and new value-conflicts. Underlying these processes, however, many observers would contend that there exists some ill-defined ideological core that still governs each individual Puerto Rican's characteristic "pitch" or "set" with regard to his identity. In discussing another "Latin" society, Mexico, Eric Wolf has written:

> It seems possible to define 'national character' operationally as those cultural forms or mechanisms which groups involved in the same overall web of relations can use in their formal and informal dealings with each other. Such a view need not imply that all nationals think or behave alike, nor that the forms used may not serve different functions in different social contexts. Such common forms must exist if communication between the different constituent groups of a complex society are to be established and maintained (1956b: 1075).

This suggestion may prove most useful in saying more about what is distinctively Puerto Rican and, in at least some sense, "common" to the Puerto Rican people, than anything else. But the careful research necessary to put it to the test largely remains to be done. One might expect that more work along these lines [one such pioneering paper, I believe, is that of Lauria (1965)], will not so much prove that there is a Puerto Rican identity or national character, so much as analyze how such character or identity works. From this perspective, much that has been said about the problem of identity is largely irrelevant, unless it proceeds from the interpretation of concrete statements and behaviors of the Puerto Rican people themselves. Such an insistence on empiricism will, of course, be regarded by some as a merely inevitable consequence of the writer's North American cultural identity, but surely social science proof will have to consist of more than a series of statements that "sound right."

The issue is complicated by the rapid change that has marked Puerto Rican life in the past quarter of a century. As more and more Puerto Ricans acquire an education, migrate to the United States (often to return), increase their buying power and their consumer choices, acquire new aspirations for themselves and their children, and begin to get a better sense of the wider world, the impact on Puerto Rican culture—however we try to approximate it—is one of inevitable change. The island is not a separate society in the same sense as an independent country with a long sovereign career; United States control and closeness has had the effect, to some degree, of making Puerto Rico a part of itself. The "web of relations" to which Wolf refers in discussing national character now frequently includes North Americans as well as Puerto Ricans. We cannot discuss Puerto Rico as if its relationship with the United States up to this time had had no effect on the Puerto Rican people, or assume that political change can be initiated from a baseline of 1900. Puerto Rico, in other words, is as it is, not as it was a half a century ago. Nothing can restore it to its cultural condition at that time, not even total and thoroughgoing isolation from the United States. Some may bemoan this assertion, but I believe it to be quite inarguable.

The various changes have had different effects on individuals and on socioeconomic groups. For some, they have stiffened the resistance to change and to outside influence, while for others they have heightened the eagerness for yet more change. Probably the more change-oriented persons are to be found principally among highly acculturated upper class groups, and among those of the very poor who have achieved a significantly higher standard of living as a result of recent changes. The growing middle classes, consisting often of service purveyors, government employees, university folk, and small-scale merchants, probably manifest the widest variety of different opinions concerning their culture, and may very well be those most ambivalent about the directions of change. All of this, however, is still in the realm of supposition, since the necessary research to test it also remains to be done.

I have tried here to expose the difficulties implicit in attempting to formulate a picture of Puerto Rican culture as some undifferentiated entity. Where possible, information has been given on some of those features of Puerto Rican life that are commonly regarded as part of a "national culture." At the same time, I have sought to show that our ability to generalize from these features is quite strictly qualified by the social, economic, and ideological complexity of Puerto Rican life. I recognize that this approach has left us without an entirely satisfactory answer to the question of Puerto Rican culture and national identity. I hope at least that it has suggested why, to some extent, the question itself needs to be asked in markedly different ways.

APPENDIX A

The following appendix is, except for a few minor additions and a brief concluding summary, the work of Mrs. Jane Collier, a Harvard graduate student in anthropology. It is an attempt to derive a profile of Puerto Rican values by the application of the Kluckhohn Binary Value Categories to published materials on the Puerto Rican people. Since it is based wholly on such published materials, it is of course no stronger or more consistent than its sources; nevertheless, I felt it would be useful to have Mrs. Collier attempt just such an application.

The Kluckhohn schema was developed in order to obtain general ratings or scores for different societies, based on some weighing of attitude and belief. It consists of a series of polar terms or categories, against which information on a particular society may be checked off. In the following pages, each category is named and described; the derived value imputed by the scorer to Puerto Rican culture is then given in underlined capitals, and comments and quotes are marshalled from the sources employed, to substantiate the scoring. Thus, for instance, the first category is "Determinate-Indeterminate, with reference to the Supernatural." People are believed to see the supernatural world either as primarily orderly and consistent, or as primarily whimsical and capricious. Criteria for these contrasting positions are listed, a value attributed to the Puerto Ricans, and the relevant findings of social scientists who have worked in Puerto Rico are noted.

Mrs. Collier was not able to make a complete survey of the literature; this would have been an enormous task, and the addition of many more materials would not have guaranteed by itself any more reliable result. Still, certain consistencies do emerge. Mrs. Collier also stressed that her work was probably influenced to some extent by her previous experience with the method. All the same, I believe the findings may be of genuine interest.

DETERMINATE—INDETERMINATE: SUPERNATURAL

Description:

Determinate	*Indeterminate*
People see the supernatural world as an orderly world where supernatural events are either	People see the supernatural world as one of chance or caprice, where unpredictability or

predictable to a certain extent, or are consistent with some system of lawful order.

inconsistency predominates.

Criteria:

1. Supernatural beings have clearly defined roles, functions or positions.
2. The religious system is in a highly integrated and internally consistent conceptual scheme.
3. The gods act reasonably, orderly or lawfully. They have regular habits.

1. The positions of supernatural beings or their roles are poorly defined.
2. The religious system is poorly integrated.

3. The gods have irregular habits or act equivocally or are voluntaristic and capricious.

Ranking: Determinate

The supernatural world is basically that of the Catholic church, which is very highly structured. People realize that there is order, even if they do not understand all the theological details. The Protestant sects also see the supernatural world as Determinate. The only major conflicting view is that of the spiritualists, but even the spirits they deal with seem to be subject to "laws." Seda Bonilla (1964: 79–80) notes that at death the spirit of the deceased is left in an innocent and vulnerable state, so that it can be tricked (by magical devices) into performing witchcraft. These spirits do not act by chance or caprice. They are specifically directed by humans to perform the acts they do.

DETERMINATE—INDETERMINATE: SOCIAL

Description:

Determinate

The social world is orderly. Man's roles are well-defined, unambiguous and social behavior is consistent or viewed as consistent.

Indeterminate

The social world contains elements of uncertainty or instability. People sometimes behave inconsistently or are viewed as behaving inconsistently.

Criteria:

1. Prestige, class, wealth, and power roles are clearly defined. The patterns of other

1. Differences of prestige, wealth, class, leadership are variable, or are not clearly de-

roles are stable and unambiguous.	fined. Other roles are flexible, subject to change, or are ambiguous.
2. The society is strongly unified and organized.	2. The society is very loosely organized.
3. People have regular habits. Their living patterns are highly structured.	3. People have irregular habits. They live spontaneously.

Ranking: Determinate

Reuter, 1946. Puerto Ricans are not socially mobile. Traditional ways are deeply embedded. The body of class sentiments lives on.

Landy, 1959: 51. "From birth the child is inculcated with the expectations and duties of his parents' class."

Manners, in Steward, 1956: 144–145. "Since all societies demand specific kinds of reciprocal relationships among their various members, the Tabara infant learns early the kind of behavior which is considered appropriate to him and to other members of the society. He is taught both by precept and example what are the proper responses to other children and to adults of both sexes and all economic and social levels. At the same time he learns the prescribed kinds of behavior required of him toward all other people in most possible situations. * * * He learns, too, that his own position is not inevitably immutable, not forever determined by the accident of birth, but that he or anyone else may actually move up in the social hierarchy and, as he does so, alter the respect relationships between himself and all others."

Seda Bonilla, 1964: 116. Liberty is feared because it is taken to mean chaos where each does what he pleases.

The Puerto Rican world seems basically determinant. Class roles are well defined, and while a person's class may vary with his wealth, there is little ambiguity about what kind of behavior a particular status demands. This may be breaking down now, however, because of a proliferation of statuses as new jobs and positions are created which do not readily fit into the old hierarchy. A man in such a new position may be in doubt as to what type of behavior he should exhibit. But basically the Puerto Ricans seem to want an orderly world in which behavior is regulated by social norms.

GOOD—EVIL: SUPERNATURAL

Description:

Good	Evil
Supernatural beings are mostly supportive and good. They are more benevolent than malevolent.	Supernatural beings are austere, dangerous, or malicious. They are basically evil.

Criteria:

1. Good aspects of the principal supernatural beings predominate over the bad ones. They are more helpful than harmful.	1. The principal supernatural beings are more evil and fear-inspiring than supportive or friendly.
2. Supernatural beings actively intervene to aid humans.	2. Supernatural beings actively intervene to punish or harm humans.
3. Some supernaturals specialize in helping humans and are more prominent than those supernaturals which may specialize in doing harm.	3. Some supernaturals specialize in doing harm to humans, and are more prominent than those supernaturals which may help humans.
4. People have feelings of affection for some supernaturals.	4. People have few feelings of affection for supernaturals.

Ranking: Good

Wolf in Steward, 1956: 214. "The saints are said to guard the household. At regularly spaced intervals the household offers certain goods to the saint, who is expected to reciprocate by furnishing the household with luck and prosperity."

Seda Bonilla, 1964: 79. The spirits of the dead are left innocent right after death.

Mintz in Steward, 1956: 408. ". . . local conversation about witchcraft and sorcery is mainly trivial."

The saints intervene to help men and they are the most important supernatural beings, at least to the lower classes. Even the spirits of the dead which can be manipulated by evil people are good and innocent if left alone. I found no evidence that any emphasis was placed on the devil or on evil spirits.

BUT:

Padilla Seda in Steward, 1956: 308, makes reference to some use of, and belief in, black magic, in the north coast sugarcane community she studied, and relates this to a high local level of insecurity. Steward's other associates found very little supporting material in other communities.

GOOD—EVIL: SOCIAL

Description:

Good	Evil
Human nature is viewed as being basically good.	Human nature is viewed as being basically evil.

Criteria:

1. People are regarded as good until proven evil.	1. People are regarded as evil, until proven good.
2. People prefer to be trusting rather than suspicious.	2. People are highly suspicious, mistrustful, skeptical.
3. People are conceived as responsive and friendly.	3. People conceived of as unresponsive, dishonest, aggressive, predominantly evil or hostile.

Ranking: Good—Evil

Brown, 1964: 49. People distrust others. They have fears of being exploited. Most people doubt that man is by nature cooperative.

Landy, 1959: 246. The male's desire for trust is often frustrated, which leads to a distruct of others.

Seda Bonilla, 1964: 113. People fear being tricked. They learn early not to trust appearances or to trust anybody.

BUT:

Brown, 1964: 48. People "see themselves as being generous, always willing to help their neighbors."

Human nature is conceived of as variable. There is some good because people see themselves as such and in their continual efforts to set up relationships "de confianza" they are trying to find others as good as themselves. Everyday life, however, seems to prove that people are out to exploit and trick one another, but the individual nevertheless goes on trying to find a friend worthy of "confianza" because of his own basic needs. Insofar as others fail to live up to the ideal, the individual is forced back into his belief about the faithlessness of men. Finally, all of these data come only from the lower classes; perhaps the upper classes believe more in the goodness of man.

RETIRING—GREGARIOUS

Description:

Retiring	Gregarious
People can be alone, can withdraw from time to time and do not need the presence of other people. Solitude is valued just as much as sociability.	People like to associate with others as much as possible. Social participation is emphasized. There is a constant desire for company and group activities. The individual may be forced to participate in social activities.

Criteria:

1. Enjoyment of privacy.	1. Avoidance of solitude.

Ranking: Gregarious

Rogler, 1940: 179. "If a Comerieño is alone, he is very likely to be lonesome or, as he describes it, *triste*. If he is not lonesome when alone, he is likely to be considered 'peculiar.' Activities conducted in privacy are unpopular. Comerío is 'full of life,' and public life at that."

INDIVIDUAL—GROUP

Description:

Individual	Group
Emphasis on the rights of the individual.	Emphasis on the duties of citizenship, or on the duties of the individual for the group.
The individual is given priority.	The collectivity is given priority.
Obligations are mainly to the self.	*Obligations are mainly to society,* the extended family, or other groups.
Collectivities are a means to the ends of the individuals, and there is little or no subjugation of self interests.	Individuals are a means to the ends of some collectivity. Subjugation of self interests to group or institutional interests.

Ranking: Individual

Lewis, 1963: 248–9. People in the professions see their new status less as an opportunity to serve the public than as an avenue to personal advancement. They exhibit little sense of social obligation.

Wolf in Steward, 1956: 207. There is a cooperative labor exchange system among poor farmers.

208. "All these relationships take place between equals and demand the exchanges of equivalent values in symmetrical fashion. Their performance is socially valuable, and the man who performs them carefully is rewarded with prestige. The exchange complex has given rise to an image of the ideal neighbor. He is a person who offers his services willingly, who sends meat to his neighbors whenever an animal is slaughtered in his house, who arranges to have the women of his household take care of a neighbor's house when the woman there is in labor and who gives readily of his resources and his knowledges. At the same time, he is expected to be 'shrewd' (listo). He must make sure that he does not give out more in the long run than he receives."

Rogler, 1940: 60. "Mutual aid is an intraclass, not an interclass phenomenon, and its economic importance among the poor cannot be overemphasized."

Rogler, 1940: 61. "The survival of large numbers of families is dependent upon aid received from neighbors."

Mintz in Steward, 1956: 366. "The maintenance of good relationships with one's face-to-face associates is one of the best local guarantees of security, and thrift is not valued highly in the barrio."

Seda Bonilla, 1964: 116. People fear to have anything because others will accuse them of not helping those in need. People try to have nothing, to be nothing.

Landy, 1959: 49–50. "It is not unusual for lower-class persons to perform services free for middle and upper class members because this is their trabajo de compromiso (work of obligation)."

This category shows quite a range of behavior in Puerto Rico, especially among the lower classes. The middle and upper classes seem to be more inclined to be individual, with obligations primarily to the self and the immediate nuclear family. Their emphasis is on getting ahead or at least maintaining position. This is not to say that they don't acknowledge obligations to more distant relatives and to compadres, but such obligations are probably dropped if they become too burdensome or are a social liability.

The situation in the lower classes is far more complex. In very traditional communities such as that described by Wolf, 1956a, the individual forms part of an extensive network of rights and obligations. Proper performance of one's role leads both to prestige and to security. More or less the same thing is true in Comerío where it is recognized that cooperation is necessary to life. But in both these cases there is the strong underlying feeling that cooperation with the group in the end benefits the self. This is even more strongly recognized in Cañamelar, where cooperation is seen as a guarantee of security for the individual. But the situation has been turned upside down in Tipán as seen by Seda Bonilla, 1964. There, the mutual obligations have become a burden to the self, and individuals try to escape from their duties.

There is also a system of rights and obligations between classes, with the upper classes dispensing patronage and the lower classes providing services. Again, proper performance of one's role eventually benefits the self.

Puerto Rico is very interesting in this category because, while there is a great deal of cooperation entailing many obligations which are performed willingly, people nevertheless still see the collectivity as a means to the ends of the individuals.

(I am not very happy with the score on this category. I feel that I was forced into a score of "Individual" by the statements that I quoted above. But I still wonder if the American ethnographers who made the statements were perhaps overestimating the individual advantage derived from cooperation.—J.C.)

SELF—OTHER

Description:

Self	Other
Self concern predominates.	Emphatic concern for other people predominates.

Criteria:

1. Lack of concern over friendships or affectionate relationships.
2. No concern for others in sickness or difficulties.

1. Concern over maintaining or establishing warm friendships and affectionate relationships.
2. Pity, compassion, consolation of others in sickness or difficulty.

3. Extortion from others, exploitation of others, taking advantage of people.

3. Unrequired, unsolicited co-operation.

4. Intolerance of what others believe or do. No attempt to understand their motives.

4. Tolerance shown for what others believe or do. Ability to understand the feelings of others.

Ranking: Self—Other

This is a problem category. Everyone seems to agree that Puerto Ricans are very interested in building and maintaining warm interpersonal relationships.

Petrullo, 1947: 129. Puerto Ricans cultivated the arts of living, among which figured personal relationships, rather than seeking wealth.

Landy, 1959: 168–9. Males are constantly trying to form relationships *de confianza* with other males.

Brown, 1964: 48. "Residents of Viví Abajo see themselves as generous, always willing to help their neighbors."

People even see themselves as capable of being warm and feeling emphatic concern. But the actual state of affairs is apparently quite different. People want trust but they cannot find it. While the individual sees himself as warm and understanding, he fears being exploited by others.

Landy, 1959: 246. "The more he seeks a close relationship with other males, the less the young man is apt to find it. When relationships are established they are brittle and easily fragmented. Thus the male's poignant desires find little permanent gratification, and repeated short-lived relationships lead to a distrust of others. At the same time, however, he longs for nothing so much as to be able to trust the relationship of other men. And so he looks continually for trust, or confianza, relationships. But he looks within a lonely crowd in which confianza relationships are rare because while the demand is great, supply is short."

Brown, 1964: 49. "In general, inhabitants of Viví Abajo are plagued by a distrust of others. They feel that they cannot confide in the majority of people; they never know with utter confidence on whom they can rely in difficult moments. According to them, most people tend to take care of themselves first and worry about others later, if at all. Each person is constantly watchful, for fear of being exploited by someone else. Many in the community believe that no one cares if a neighbor is on the way to failure, but several feel that at least a few people are sympathetic."

AUTONOMY—DEPENDENCE

Description:

Autonomy	*Dependence*
The adult individual tends to be self-reliant and self-sufficient.	The adult individual is dependent on other persons or on the group.

Criteria:

Autonomy	*Dependence*
1. Source of decisions located within the self. A person's behavior is not easily influenced by others.	1. Source of decisions, or basis of decision is external. No reliance on internal judgment. A person's behavior is easily influenced by others.
2. Attempts to do without help when ill, or in other circumstances of need. Feeling that the individual can take care of himself.	2. Dependence on institutions or persons for protection and satisfaction of needs.
3. Teaching of independence and self-responsibility.	3. Teaching of obligations and responsibility to others.

Ranking: Dependence

Brown, 1964: 48. "They are sensitive to other's opinions of them; they would choose to suffer hardship rather than do work which other people would criticize."

Lewis, 1963: 289. "The fear of being exposed to 'what other people will say' inhibits many a person from openly accepting a new solution to an old problem."

478. "In part, it is the terror of ridicule that makes the Puerto Rican adult so conscious of respect."

Petrullo, 1947: p. 128. "In short, there is a greater tendency to lean on someone else for a solution of one's problems than there is in Protestant societies."

I have given very few examples for this category because it is so clear cut. The Puerto Ricans are extremely dependent—on their superiors for favors, on their peers for aid, on their families for support—and they are also extremely dependent on the opinion of others. Little children are born dependent and remain so throughout life, although the character of the dependency changes (see Landy, 1959).

DISCIPLINE—FULFILLMENT

Description:

Some cultures tend to repress spontaneity in the effort to maintain an even tempered social scene, while others prefer to give full expression to spontaneity and are less worried about the consequence of impulsive actions.

Criteria:

Discipline	*Fulfillment*
1. Emphasis on self-control.	1. Emphasis on self-expression.
2. Emphasis on maintaining an even balance of social actions. Social constraint and reserve.	2. No concern with balanced social actions. Lack of social constraint.
3. Moderation.	3. Laxity, pleasure permitting, affirmation.
4. Asceticism, religious fasting.	4. Intoxication or overindulgence.
5. Strictness, austerity, denial, abstinence.	5. Self-realization, orgiastic tendencies.

Ranking: Fulfillment

Rogler, 1940: 181. "There is little social restraint placed upon the overt expression of those moods or sentiments that are called out by social stimuli."

Puerto Ricans seem to emphasize self-expression; however, the amount of freedom is severely limited by the individual's fear of being criticized by others.

BUT:

Seda Bonilla, 1963: 111. Men should not give free reign to emotions. Emotion "means" aggressiveness.

Aggressiveness, if one believes Kathleen Wolf (1952), is strictly controlled in both the middle and the lower classes. This limit on aggressiveness, however, does not seem enough to change the scoring of this category.

ACTIVE—ACCEPTANT

Description:

This category refers to the way man responds to the social world. He may accept it or seek to change it in some way.

Criteria:

Active	*Acceptant*
1. Dissatisfaction with people or society. A desire for improvement or change.	1. Acceptance of people and society.
2. Acts of autonomy sometimes take the form of rebellion in extreme cases.	2. Acts of autonomy sometimes take the form of withdrawal.
3. Social mobility.	3. Little social mobility.
4. Initiative or impatience concerning social actions of others.	4. Tolerance or resignation concerning social actions of others.

Ranking: Active—Acceptant

There is definitely an "active" group in Puerto Rico. The government is clearly active in the changes and reforms that it is trying to bring about. The question remains, however, as to how deeply this value of active permeates, even among the upper classes.

Lewis, 1963: 248–9. Business entrepreneurs and the new middle classes exhibit little sense of social obligations. Professional men see their new status as an avenue to personal advancement.

But this may be regarded as a type of "active" because it is an attempt to improve the position of the self.

The data on the lower classes:

Landy, 1959: 252. "the *mañana* value of the Vallecañeses is reflected in their reliance on the smiles of Fate, in their almost fatalistic acceptance of life as it comes, in their minimal aspirations."

Brown, 1964: 48. "Although a few people assert the impossibility of changing one's destiny, many feel otherwise. To most, the course which one's life follows is the result of personal efforts rather than of forces beyond human control. They firmly reject the concept that some are born to lead and others to follow. In short, the community is not resigned to the fatalistic notion, 'what shall be, shall be.'"

Rogler, 1940: 26. "Resignation, fatalism, and related attitudes that are so prominent in this community, are surely in part the result of this generally low level of health and the all too frequent appearance of death."

It seems clear that the lower class communities vary as to whether they are active or acceptant. The entire lower class cannot be characterized as one or the other.

DOMINANCE—EQUALITY: POWER EVALUATION

Description:

Dominance	Equality
Power over people is a dominant preoccupation in any kind of social interaction.	Power over people is not the main consideration in social interaction.

Criteria:

Dominance	Equality
1. Coercion, restriction, and domination follow lines of relative strength, power, or social position of the adversary.	1. Cases of resisting coercion or restriction, regardless of the relative strength, power, or social position of the adversary.
2. People follow only those who are more powerful.	2. People may follow the nonpowerful as well as the powerful.
3. Accumulation and aggrandizement of social power.	3. Unwillingness to take positions that involve power over others.

Ranking: Dominance

I do not have any quotes on this category, but the value on dominance seems very clear. It has two facets, however. On one side, there are the upper classes, and persons who, through their positions, have power over others. These people are very preoccupied with maintaining their power, and in all interaction they demand the proper respect from their subordinates. On the other side are the people without power. These, far from trying to improve their positions and get power, seem to become almost totally dependent.

Brown, 1964: 50. Everyone prefers receiving orders to giving them.

Lewis, 1963: 476. There is an unwillingness to take responsibility, especially in businesses.

There almost seems to be a fear of presuming on the power of a superior. Both the high and the low seem intent on preserving the present power structure.

DOMINANCE—EQUALITY: ATTENTION EVALUATION

Criteria:

Dominance	Equality
1. Instances of exhibitionism, display of self, of attention-	1. Exhibitionism and the desire for social prestige is absent or

attracting activities. Desire to dominate the attention and admiration of others.

muted.

Ranking: Dominance

To Puerto Rican men life is a continual display of the self. "Machismo" centers around exhibitionism and letting others know how "macho" one is. Even women compete in showing off, but in a far less flagrant manner. Women try to show off through dress, or through having a model family. But in all cases, the individual tries to impress others and gain their approval.

In summing up this appendix, the clear-cut value categories appear to be as follows. Puerto Ricans believe in a determinant (i.e., orderly and consistent) supernatural world. They also believe the social world to be determinant and orderly, though rapid social and economic change, as Mrs. Collier points out, may be affecting this; the growth of new social categories doubtless has produced some ambivalence in values and in behavior. Puerto Ricans regard the supernatural world as not only determinant, but also good. Gods and spirits do not motivate men to do evil, and cannot be readily controlled in order to effect evil results. The social world, however, is by no means taken to be so unexceptionably good. There appears to be considerable doubt that man is "naturally good" and the establishment of social relationships proceeds with the unvoiced expectation that others may trick or exploit one. There appears to be a gap here between what people believe and what they tend to say they believe.

Puerto Ricans are emphatically gregarious. They like (or perhaps better, badly need) the company of fellow men, and appear to regard solitude as bad, and possibly even evidence of badness. Puerto Ricans also stress individuality more than they do the needs or good of the collectivity. This finding may occasion surprise, since much has been said and written of the collectivistic and familistic spirit of the Puerto Rican people. Mrs. Collier finds that individualism (with, of course, very active concern for the needs of one's immediate family) is strong; in the lower classes, this is perhaps less clear. Cooperativeness and group-oriented activity are important and even essential in some lower-class communities, and yet the stress on individual fate seems equally important. Mrs. Collier notes her own reservations about the observers' findings.

A similar lack of clarity marks the self-other category. It seems that Puerto Ricans very much want to create warm interpersonal relationships, and yet greatly fear deception, rejection, and failure in such relationships.

As to autonomy-dependence, the data show that Puerto Ricans are extremely dependent by most ordinary measures. On discipline-fulfillment, the Puerto Rican people seem committed to fulfillment. The active-acceptant value category, like that for determinate-indeterminate (social), seems subject to rapid change in modern Puetro Rico. Mrs. Collier notes that the island possesses individuals or whole groups that are definitely active in their world view—autonomous, impatient, and initiating. Yet the prevailing weight of island values in this regard—especially, perhaps, as revealed in the behavior of lower class folk—is toward acceptance, withdrawal being the most obvious expression of autonomy. One would expect recent changes in island life to affect this characterization somewhat, but there are too few data to prove as much. Brown (1964) and Mintz (1960) offer little to suggest that the change toward activity has been pervasive.

For the dominance-equality (power evaluation) category, Mrs. Collier finds the Puerto Ricans at the dominance end of the scale. She notes, however, that while dominance seems to mark clearly those who have power, dependence marks those who lack it. On dominance-equality (attention evaluation), the Puerto Rican people seem to come out strongly on the dominance side once more. Display to achieve approval seems important for everyone, and suggests that what is approved is subject very much to that of which others approve.

This brief sketch makes clear that the application of the Kluckhohn scale gives only qualified results when applied to Puerto Rico. It does point up some quite firm findings, especially with regard to dependence, gregariousness, and dominance-equality, and it suggests some additional directions in which to search out Puerto Rican values. Since only a part of the available materials on Puerto Rico have been employed in this exercise, it could be readily amplified.

APPENDIX B

This appendix purports to summarize briefly some of the principal books and articles that have dealt, more or less directly, with the theme of Puerto Rican culture. It is written in declarative form, rather than simply as an annotated bibliography, and it is organized under six headings, as follows: 1) community studies; 2) race relations studies; 3) Puerto Rican family structure and attitudes; 4) national culture, national character, national values; 5) studies of change; and 6) summary.

To digest and classify large quantities of disparate data so that they may be read in some orderly and unified fashion is difficult. The classification of particular bits of information can be rather arbitrary, unless one is willing to add on additional new categories along the way. It is rare, moreover, that any two authors write concerning precisely the same thing. Hence each summary tends to be a rather mechanical stringing together of data, not always in satisfactory fashion. Still, it is hoped that some value may be gained from an examination of the different sections of this appendix. In the concluding summary, I make some final comments on "Puerto Rican culture," in the hope that the difficulties in establishing the reality of the national culture will become clearer. The section preceding, on studies of change, mainly suggests our relative ignorance of the cultural derivatives of recent changes in Puerto Rican life.

Community Studies

One of the first such studies was Charles Rogler's "Comerío" (Rogler, 1940), based on sociological fieldwork carried out in the town of that name in 1935. Comerío is a tobacco-producing valley town in the center of the island; at the time of the Rogler study, it was caught up in the world depression, and its class structure and the rhythm of life reflected as much. Rogler gives an informative picture of town life. In ten chapters, varying from five to 25 pages in length, he discusses economic and racial differences, the local economy, social and political structure, education, religion, and recreation. His text is enriched by numerous direct quotations from informants on a variety of subjects, but he does not contend that the commentators speak for their community, or that the community stands for Puerto Rico. In a concluding chapter five pages long, the author contends that the differences between classes in Comerío "* * * were never great enough to undermine an essential interclass unity. To move from an upper class atmosphere into a lower class atmosphere was not equivalent to moving into a different cultural world" (1940: 185).

His findings lead him to assert that the local upper class provided a model or ideal for lower class behavior, and that members of other classes were excluded from equal participation in town life with their class superiors by the exercise of political and economic power. While class differences were more important assortative devices than sexual differences, still the differences between the sexes carry stronger sanctions, "⁕ ⁕ ⁕ because sex mores are more precise and tend to deal with familiar relations between the sexes, while class differences are more diffused and subject to numerous variations" (1940: 186). As class differences reinforce and underlie the differential social participation of Comerío people in local affairs, so, too, do sex differences restrict women to inferior social positions and limit their participation in wider networks, as compared with the men. The primary cause of women's inferior position in the society seems to the author to rest with "limited economic opportunity," and the basic force behind this state of affairs—its primary sanction—is found in the sex mores: "The inferior position of the woman takes most definite form in the sex mores of decency, chastity, and fidelity" (1940: 187).

Though Rogler does not deal with national values or "typical" attitudes, he does conclude that there is an essential unity and consistency in the life of each Comerío inhabitant. The adjustments to the realities of life that each person must make—

> ⁕ ⁕ ⁕ have been of such a nature as to produce such attitudes as complacency, contentment, and fatalism. "I am contented because I make the best of what I have." These attitudes characterize both the nature of his actions and also the underlying tone of his remarks. Religious values approach from another direction and merge themselves into these attitudes, giving them a more exalted sanction and surrounding them with a supernatural atmosphere (1940: 189).

These concluding remarks are the nearest the author comes to a general approximation of Comerío "values" or "philosophy." The study, though lacking the statistical completeness and somewhat self-conscious methodological rigor of later works, is a very useful introduction to Puerto Rican town life. It is as outdated as the changes since 1935 have made it, but when read today by one who feels some familiarity with Puerto Rican values, it makes clear that in many areas, at least, there is some continuity in Puerto Rican life, apparently in spite of all of the subsequent changes.

In the easy 1940's, the late Morris Siegel, an anthropologist, conducted a brief study of a southwestern Puerto Rican coastal town, Lajas, that has never been published. I have been unable to secure a manuscript copy, and my memory of the study is poor, but several of Siegel's findings bear mention here. Siegel had apparently hoped that his investigations would, at least to some extent, stand for the whole of Puerto Rican town life, and he used his findings to formulate several generalizations he believed to be "typically Puerto Rican." Among these were his formulation of the so-called "virginity cult," which Siegel saw as an aspect of nationally-held values. This "cult" or value was an aspect of the institutionalized inferiority of women, an insistence on their purity as a necessary ingredient of masculine values. Its value-significance was paralleled by the idea of the "macho" or "machismo"—the much-discussed concept of maleness, said to permeate Puerto Rican society, as the logical opposite of the cult of virginity. Because I do not have the manuscript at hand, I will not enlarge on this pair of themes, but they will receive additional consideration later.

"The People of Puerto Rico," edited by Steward (1956), has been referred to so frequently in the body of this report that little will be said of it here. This work deliberately by-passed the idea of national values or beliefs, and concentrated instead on creating a picture of Puerto Rican life built up out of four community studies and a study of the national upper class (see also Manners and Steward, 1953). "The People of Puerto Rico" emphasizes differences based on considerations of economics, regional specialization, and class structure, much more than it does any underlying similarities of value or attitude. While it is concerned with the social history of Puerto Rico, as a backdrop to the quality of island society in 1948–49 (when the fieldwork was executed), the book's treatment of change is inadequate. But the reasons lie more with the rapid change that has typified Puerto Rican life over the past 15 years than with the ethnographers or their theory. My own study of the village called "Cañamelar," for example, entirely fails to take account of the changes which were to occur there within a few years of the completion of fieldwork (see Brameld, 1959: 355–359; Hernández Alvárez, 1964). The book also fails to deal with questions of Puerto Rican "character," or "ethos," in accord with the authors' theoretical reservations about this sort of research direction. Nevertheless, "The People of Puerto Rico" very possibly provides the fullest account of Puerto Rican society ever written. In spite of its many defects, it is based on long fieldwork experiences in many settings, and brings together a wealth of data on Puerto Rico of the time.

Edwin Seda Bonilla, an anthropologist who had worked as a field assistant to the Steward group in 1948–49, subsequently returned to the community he had studied and has published some of his findings (Seda Bonilla: 1963, 1964). His work benefits from the contrast provided by years of change; his concern is very much with such change, and I think it would be fair to say that his view is pessimistic and negative. Like many other observers, Seda Bonilla believes that recent changes have eroded some of the positive values of Puerto Rican culture, leaving young people cynical and uncommitted. I will discuss some of his findings in the section on social and economic change.

David Landy's "Tropical Childhood" (1959), though an anthropological community study in its own right, concentrates on personality, socialization and family structure, and will be dealt with mainly in other sections. Landy worked in a southeastern coastal sugarcane community, less fully proletarianized than Mintz' "Cañamelar," or Padilla Seda's and Seda Bonilla's "Nocorá." Perhaps partly for this reason, and partly because of his concern with the "fit" of culture and personality, his study takes on its primary value with relation to questions of personality and child-training.

Two short community studies concerned with comparison and change though they give little depth of observation on attitudes and values, deserve mention here. Ríos and Vásquez Calcerrada (1953) and Vásquez Calcerrada (1953) deal with resettled rural communities, in which former "agregados" were able to make a new and more independent start. The

Ríos and Vásquez Calcerrada study compares a "successful" with an "unsuccessful" resettlement, with the expectation that the successful community would have higher socioeconomic status, more effective "natural leaders," and a higher degree of community integration. Both communities were in the same region, but one was nearer the original settlement from which the "parceleros" had come. Of the three expectations listed, the second and third were confirmed. An unexpected finding was that those migrants who were closer to their former homes were able to make a more successful adjustment. This study, while interesting, tells us little that is relevant to the objectives of the present report.

Vásquez Calcerrada (1953) has more to say about the shift from "agregado" to "granjero" status, though he does not deal at any length with values or attitudes. The extent to which the resettlers participated in the development of their new community was encouraging. The community had considerable stability until World War II, when many people migrated to the United States in search of better work opportunities. Changes in community life incident to resettlement included a somewhat higher level of consumption, more interest in education, considerable use of modern medical facilities, expanded aspirations, and greater participation in community programs. Underemployment, lack of adequate institutional guidance, and lack of job training continued to create difficulties, and apparently the resettlement itself led to some breakdown in community norms of social control. Religious practices were maintained and even intensified in the resettlement; in fact, an active competition among different faiths attended the establishment of the new community. This study, however, while very informative, again bears only limited relevance to the objectives of this report.

Brown (1964) has completed a study of an impoverished highland farming community near Utuado, which has not been published. His findings suggest considerable disorientation and disillusionment among the people with whom he worked: a rather rigid traditionalism (1964: 43), a feeling of helplessness against poverty (1964: 44), a basic distrust of others (1964: 49), and considerable low-keyed quarreling (1964: 49). At the same time, Brown did not find his informants "fatalistic"—they think of their future and believe in hard work (1964: 48), in spite of their difficult situation. People are sensitive to the opinions of others, even while they are distrustful of them, and are inclined to rely mainly on close kinsmen for help in time of need (1964: 45–49). These and other points made by Brown will be referred to once again in the discussion of national character and values.

These few community studies are not all that have been done by any means, nor have I attempted here to deal with works treating urban neighborhoods and slums. The main studies of rural communities, however, forcibly suggest that there is no particular community that can serve as an exemplar for Puerto Rico as a national society—a point Steward made strongly when his associates began their work on the island in 1948. Community studies are valuable for the general information they offer the reader, but they naturally vary considerably in their usefulness as a basis for generalization, depending upon the skills and particular interests of the fieldworker. In the case of Puerto Rico, the most orderly studies were those of Steward's students (Steward, 1956), but I have suggested that much of their work has been outdated by the vast changes of the past two decades.

Several themes seem to appear with suspicious frequency in the works described so far, and they have to do in particular with men's and women's attitudes. Thus, for instance, most findings stress the status differences between men and women, and the culturally accepted status inferiority of women, accompanied by the so-called machismo complex of men. I will return to a consideration of such data in subsequent sections. Also, I have laid little stress here on statistical data, since there is no easy way to bring the disparate bodies of such data from various monographs into any meaningful relationship.

Race Relations Studies

All of the authors who write on race and race differences conclude that Puerto Ricans are very aware of physical differences. "Negro" features are in general regarded as undesirable while "white" features are prized. But there is no "caste system" as there is in the Southern states, nor is there any belief in the biological inferiority of the Negro. The undesirability of Negro traits is social in origin, and stems from the fact that Negroes were once slaves and, even now, are largely concentrated in the lower classes. There is discrimination against people with markedly Negro traits in Puerto Rico, but the degree of this discrimination varies considerably from situation to situation.

Statistics show clearly that Negroes are concentrated in the lower class, and that there are progressively fewer Negroid features in the population as one goes up the social scale. This does not mean that it is impossible for a black man to reach the top, but there are few who make it. The situation is also complicated by the fact that there are many terms to classify Negroes, and the terminology used will vary from situation to situation. Negroes and mulattoes who reach the middle and upper classes tend to be defined as being whiter than their counterparts in the lower classes. It is also true that the defined Negro population is steadily decreasing as more and more people are being classed as white. Gordon (1949) believes that continuing race prejudice will only serve to hasten the decline of the Negro population because all those who can will want to "pass" as white.

Renzo Sereno, in his article on "cryptomelanism" (1947), states that to a white, a Negro has three drawbacks: (1) He is the result of illegitimate union; (2) he is the descendant of slaves; and (3) he is not presentable to North Americans. To these it may be added that he is usually of lower class origin. Given no other indication of status, Puerto Ricans tend to classify persons with marked Negro traits as lower class and to treat them as such. Part of the discrimination that is directed against Negroes is based on social or class prejudice. Most Puerto Ricans, however, are of mixed ancestry. As people rise in the social scale they tend to try to forget their Negro ancestry; but because most are mixed, they are all vulnerable to attack. Negro can be used against someone, even when that person appears to be "pure white."

The degree of race prejudice and the form that it takes varies from class to class. In the lower class, where there is the largest concentration of Negroid features, there tends to be almost none of what we would call "race prejudice." Instead there is an awareness of color as one aspect of an individual, with Negroid traits being considered undesirable. But Negroid traits can be completely outweighed by other more desirable features, such as a secure economic position, good social standing within the community, etc. And as such,

Negroid features are never enough to insure the exclusion of an individual. Instead discrimination takes lesser and more pitiful forms. The child in the family who has the most Negroid features is often the one who is least liked by his parents and most teased by his brothers and sisters. A dark child may not feel free to participate in all of the outside activities of his lighter siblings (Gordon, 1950). Landy (1959) noted that, in the community he studied, the dark girls were the last to be chosen as partners in dances.

The upper class is concerned with "limpieza de sangre" and the perpetuation of special privileges within its own select group. Because of this members tend to exclude any out-group, and Negroes are easily defined in this way because of their obvious physical differences. The upper class maintains select clubs and patronizes the better hotels, which discriminate against Negroes. Even though there are some Negroes who reach high business, professional and political positions, they are still considered to be unacceptable as members of the intimate circles in which the upper class likes to move. These Negroes will be treated as complete equals in business or political encounters among men, but they are never accepted in the home or in intimate social gatherings. An upper class man may marry a mulatto woman without too much censure, but his wife will never be completely accepted and will know that she will be "excused" from many of the functions of the other women of her husband's group. The upper class, however, seems to feel that it is very tolerant, and it actually is, if only because its members do not feel threatened by encroaching Negroes.

The middle class varies tremendously, but probably practices more pure racial discrimination than any other class. (These are the people whom Sereno principally discusses in his article on cryptomelanism.) They know that they themselves may have some Negro ancestry, but they try to deny this by forming exclusive "white" clubs to prove to the outside world and themselves that they are indeed what they would like to be. They have adopted the ideal of "sangre limpia" from the upper classes, while knowing that their own ancestry is actually "tainted." They try to make their insecure position more secure by rejecting everything associated with Negroes and by practicing extreme discrimination. Of course, only a segment of the middle class is able to do this; the middle class does contain some Negroes and many mulattoes. These people often cannot pass as white, and are those who suffer from the discriminatory practices of their fellow members of the middle class. But the middle class is a rising class; its members tend to step on all below them, reflecting a sense of extreme competition. Many middle class jobs, such as that of bank clerk are reserved for "white" people, simply to reduce competition.

Contact with continental racial prejudice has probably had its most far-reaching effect in this class as well; the middle class is trying to modernize itself and most of its ideas about what is modern come from the continent. It is not clear just how much racial prejudice must be blamed on ideas from the United States. It has obviously had some effect in that jobs which involve contact with North Americans are often denied to Negroes; but it is also clear that there was prejudice in Puerto Rico before the United States occupation. The rising middle class probably got its racial prejudice from both sources. This is by no means a complete discussion of the middle class, but it is such a complex and diverse group that the dynamics of racial interaction are very incompletely described in the literature (see also Seda Bonilla, 1961; Williams, 1956).

Rogler (1944, 1946, 1948) discusses the fact that Puerto Rico has ideal conditions for race mixing. The double standard insures that at least middle and upper class men will mate with Negro women and produce mixed children, while in the lower class, marriages take place with little regard to color.

Another interesting aspect of race relations in Puerto Rico is the terminology involved. For instance, the term "negrito" is one of endearment, carrying a sense of togetherness, friendship, and mutual trustworthiness—it is almost a "we're in the same boat together" kind of term. "Blanquito," on the other hand, often carries the opposite meaning. When used by a member of the lower class it implies social distance. It also carries the connotation of "uppity" pretentious, and definitely implies the opposite of togetherness and trust. Rogler, however, also notes that it is a term that may be complimentary, insofar as it does imply the desirable traits of whiteness and higher social class.

Puerto Rican Family Structure and Attitudes

The subject is so vast, and the data on it so numerous, that this account is necessarily brief and extremely summary. I have used Mrs. Collier's scheme in the organization of information under several subheadings; for simple reasons of space, I have omitted many corroborative sources and much specific data, as well as nearly all quoted citations.

COURTSHIP

Puerto Rican girls are carefully guarded throughout their childhood, but this guarding becomes more intense as they reach puberty. Soon after puberty, probably around the age of fifteen or sixteen, most girls are considered eligible for marriage. Upper class girls are introduced to society at this age and lower class girls begin to go to dances. All of the opportunities for young people of opposite sexes to meet and get together are carefully supervised; however, even so, there are few opportunities for a boy and a girl even to get to know each other casually. In the lower class girls dance with many boys, but at least one author recorded that they were not supposed to talk together. (See Mintz, 1960, for autobiographical data on courtship, from the male point of view.) It is on such slim meetings as these that the girls "fall in love," but they are not supposed to fall in love too often. In a study of middle and upper class boys and girls at the University of Puerto Rico, Hill (in Fernández Méndez, 1956) found that most reported only having one or two previous "novios," if they had had even that. In any case, the getting-to-know-each other period is very short and the formal "noviazgo" is established quickly.

Noviazgo is not a trial period to see how the couple get along together—it is a formal commitment to marry. Because of this it is hard to break, and all sides lose face when this happens. But in spite of the closeness of a noviazgo, the couple is still never left alone and Stycos (1955) reports that as it continues, the relations between the couple involve more and more "respeto" and not less, at least in the lower classes.

Charles Rosario (1958) has an interesting interpretation of the function of the noviazgo in Puerto Rico that seems to fit the facts better than those anyone else has offered. He says that noviazgo is a period in which the woman learns to submit her will to that of the man. It is not a time for the couple to get to know each other and set up roots for future compatibility; compatibility does not matter. What matters is that the woman learns her role of submission. This seems to tie in with the fact that after marriage there is little communication between husband and wife. The important thing seems to be that each learns to play his role, and the role of the woman is submission. Throughout life the sexes live in different spheres and even in marriage these spheres barely touch.

Noviazgo often lasts quite a while, and involves visits by the boy to the girl's house, where the couple sit and talk together under the supervision of some member of the girl's family. It may also involve occasional outings by the couple, but always accompanied by a chaperone or a group. This chaperonage pattern may be getting weaker, but it seems doubtful that it will disappear altogether within the foreseeable future. Chaperones not only serve to see that the couple behaves properly but they serve the very important function of preserving the girl's reputation. At marriage a girl should be a virgin, not only in fact but in reputation as well. Even when a marriage is consensual, it is usually preceded by some formal period of noviazgo. It is probably rare that a couple simply get together and elope. Though elopement and consensual marriage are the prevalent forms in a community such as Cañamelar, for instance (Mintz, in Steward, 1956), they involve clear-cut formalities, including more or less overt courtship. There are, of course, always exceptions; there are women with looser morals and families that care less about reputation. But both Stycos (1955) and Rogler (1940) were surprised at the extent to which even the lowest classes observed all the rules of the noviazgo and were careful to preserve their girl's reputation, and Mintz (1960) gives additional detail on relevant attitudes.

HUSBAND—WIFE RELATIONS

Husbands supposedly have complete authority over their wives and children. The outward semblance of this authority is preserved even when it does not in fact exist. Kathleen Wolf (1952) notes that middle class men whose wives worked outside (and who therefore felt that their authority was threatened) would often make arbitrary demands on their wives just to show that they still had control. The actual degree of control that a man exercises over his family varies a great deal, both from class to class and from region to region. The husband's authority seems to be strongest where the family is poor and where the husband controls all the resources. In these families the wife and children work under his direction and submit completely to his demands. Such families are usually found in those rural regions where tobacco and coffee are farmed (see, for example, Rogler, 1940; Wolf, in Steward, 1956). The husband's authority is great and his wife may be reduced almost to the status of a child. She controls no money and so cannot buy herself anything; she is not allowed outside of the house without his permission; and she is expected to submit to his demands without question. She is the one who cares for the children, but even in this job she exercises as little initiative as is conceivably possible.

The authority structure of the family is somewhat more balanced in regions where people live close together and where women have means of earning at least a little bit of money. In these regions the women are not so completely isolated in their homes, they control some money, and they do some of the family shopping. They may also have a chance to earn money by making things at home to sell, such as sweets. The husband's authority is probably still less in urban areas, where lower class women have a chance to work in factories (see also Mintz, 1965).

In some of these cases the wife's income may support the family or at least contribute a large share of it. The husband also loses his authority to dictate his wife's activities when she works outside the home and has a life and friends of her own. The internal strains in these families, given the ideal of strong male authority, are sometimes great (Wolf, 1952; though see Mintz, 1965).

Middle and upper class husbands exercise more authority in their homes than do American husbands, but they do not have the complete control that some lower class men do. In many of the middle class families the women have fewer children and work outside the home. Even if the women do not work, they still have more freedom, as they are not so tied down by childrearing. The middle and upper classes are also beginning to adopt the American idea that children are a woman's job, and husbands are beginning to let their wives make more and more of the decisions concerning the children and how they should be brought up. Along with this goes the attitude that homemaking is a woman's job and that the women should therefore do all the family shopping. In relinquishing the control of money and of the children, middle and upper class men have come a long way from the extremely authoritarian families discussed above. The women have to tread the delicate line between submission to their husbands and exercising their own initiative in running their homes and families.

Almost all of the authors who write on the Puerto Rican family stress the lack of communication between husbands and wives. This lack is really quite understandable, given the childrearing patterns. From babyhood on, boys and girls are kept separate and each is taught to associate only with members of his own sex. Boys and girls share no common activities, and when they finally come together in courtship, the roles played by each are very different. Marriage merely continues the pattern. Husbands and wives each have their own roles and in very traditional families there is no need for communication between them. They share few common activities, and so there is almost nothing to be discussed. When decisions have to be made, the husband dictates and the wife submits. Such a family is, of course, extremely inflexible. It is unable to adapt very well to changing conditions. Because conditions are changing and have changed a great deal in Puerto Rico, it must be surmised that some changes have taken place in the family to make communication (and, therefore, greater flexibility) possible. No author really discusses the extent of these changes in descriptive sociological terms, and so it is difficult to tell just what has been taking place. Probably lower class families in backward areas have maintained more of the old and inflexible patterns (Brown, 1964), while in areas where change has been more drastic or where increased income has raised a family's status, there is now considerably more communication between husbands and wives (Mintz, 1965). But in any case, because of the separation of the sexes, the chances are that communication between spouses will remain at a relatively low level.

Landy especially discusses the power of women in his book "Tropical Childhood" (1959). He notes the inconsistency that, in a culture where the men are supposed to be absolute rulers of their homes, it is the women who are brought up to be stable and responsible. Women supposedly look for stability in marriage and the ideal is to get a man who is "serio" and responsible. But Landy says that such men rarely exist because men are brought up to be insecure and unstable. The women are therefore the anchors of their families and carry a large share of responsibility for the orderly running of society. Women exercise most of their power over their children (Wolf, 1952). There is an extremely strong feeling that a woman should not abandon her children. Fathers may leave, but mothers may not. The children derive their feeling of security from their mothers. In most cases the children are extremely dependent on their mothers, and boys may retain this dependency long after they have become men (Wolf, 1952; Mintz, 1965). But even in cases where men profess dependence on, and love for, their mothers, it is the daughters who end up caring for their old mother. This small area of power that belongs to women is, however, very slight when one compares it to all of the male privileges. Women may be responsible and more secure, but they are decidedly underprivileged. Women—and their roles—are regarded as inferior.

Women are supposed to be virgins when they marry and to remain chaste afterwards. Actually the women use their virginity as a lever against the men. A man who marries a woman and deprives her of her virginity owes her support and reasonable treatment for the rest of her life. The woman, in return, however, must show absolute fidelity in reputation as well as in deed. She cannot do anything which might even hint of infidelity, such as talking with a man who is not her husband. Women are not trusted around men at all. This is understandable, given the fact that women are not brought up to take care of themselves. They are taught to submit to men, and to rely for protection on their fathers, brothers, and later, husbands. It is presumed, and with some accuracy, that if given the chance a woman will fall. This puts a real strain on marital relations. The man can never be completely sure of his wife because he is away all day and he cannot check up on her every moment. The woman, on the other hand, must be extremely careful not to do anything which might arouse her husband's suspicions. The men seem to be the ones who suffer the most, though, because to be cuckolded is to have one's reputation almost completely ruined.

CHILDREARING

Childrearing patterns vary a great deal from class to class and probably from region to region, but there do seem to be some constants. In all classes obedience and "respeto" are the most prized qualities in children. Brameld (1959) cites a male informant who says that children under 10 should "fear," from 10 to 20, they should "respect," and over 20, they should "love" their parents. (Needless to add, the discontinuities in a socialization ideal of this sort are severe.) Love for parents is only secondary. In all classes the sexes are strictly separated. Little girls are kept clothed, are kept nearer home and under closer supervision, and are expected to be more submissive. Little boys are encouraged to be independent and aggressive within certain limits, and are allowed to go about without clothing, at least in the lower class. Boys are not so closely guarded, and in towns are allowed to roam the streets. In all classes children are kept dependent on their parents for quite some time. In the lower class this is fostered by the mother's neglect of the child, who therefore longs for attention; and in the upper class it is often fostered by the fact that the child is overpetted and cared for. In all classes, it also seems that aggression is strongly suppressed. Little boys are encouraged to show aggression in such situations as temper tantrums (Mintz, in Steward, 1956), but are not allowed to direct it against another human. Landy (1959) noted that in his village, children who were involved in a fight were punished no matter whose fault the fight was. Another constant might be that small children are universally loved and enjoyed. Not much is expected of them during the first 2 years and they are the petted playthings of adults. After they begin to talk, however, they are subject to demands for obedience and "respeto."

The lives of upper class children are not at all well described in the literature, but from what little there is it seems that such children are petted and pampered by adults for at least their early years. They have servants to wait on them constantly and are not taught to feed themselves or to do anything. They learn that the way to have their desires met is to order someone to do something, rather than do it themselves (Wolf, 1952). These children also come to see a strict dichotomy in their lives. When they are clean and well behaved they are admitted to the company of their parents and members of their parents' class. When they are dirty or ill behaved they are sent back to the servants. Sereno (1947) suggests that this causes little boys to associate sex with lower class women and "pure" love with their mothers and with women of their own class. When they marry, they allegedly have difficulty establishing adequate sexual relations with their wives.

Lower class childrearing is much better documented, but even there, the variation is notable. In isolated rural areas, children are kept at home and often see only brothers and sisters. Even in areas where families live relatively close together children may be kept isolated by parents who are afraid that their children's behavior might cause them shame (Landy, 1959). In some urban areas, on the other hand, the children run the streets day and night. The little girls are kept somewhat more confined, but they are still in the streets when they can get there. Lower class children are often part of large families and get little care and attention from their parents. The mother of a large family is often too busy to be able to do anything more than just provide food and clothing and a minimum of supervision for her children. In these families corporal punishment is frequent and forms the main means of ensuring obedience in the children. In fact, in some areas, punishment is regarded as a sign of love and the child who is unbeaten is regarded with pity because he is considered to be unloved.

Stycos (1955: 38–39) discusses what his informants listed as the main duties of children toward their parents, and of parents toward their children. Just as children should show obedience and respeto to their parents and love is only secondary, so the parents' main duty is to provide materially for the child, with love again being a minor consideration. Stycos also noted the mother's duty never to abandon her children. Fathers should provide material benefits, while mothers should be around to take care of everyday needs, and for protection. In the lower class families that Stycos studied, the father was always the supreme authority, while the mother was the day-to-day supervisor. Any decision or punishment she carried out, however, was always done in the father's name. Children were found to feel invariably closer to their mothers than to their fathers. The social distance between a man and his children was extreme. It was almost impossible for either to bridge the gap. Fathers were the recipients of fear and respeto but rarely of love.

Landy's entire book was about childrearing, but a few items seem especially interesting. Landy says that children are rarely rewarded for good behavior (1959: 123). Parents believe that if a child is rewarded too often he will lose his respeto for his parents. This ties in with an observation by Seda Bonilla (1964) that parents do not believe in letting their children argue with them because they will lose their "respeto." There seems to be a fear on the part of parents that children will lose their feelings of respect. (But as a part of the normal process of growing up, children have to cut their parents down to size. Children cannot go on forever seeing them as the omnipotent beings that they were during early childhood. One wonders if this normal process of growing up causes real strains in the Puerto Rican family.) Landy also notes in his book that there is very little demand for children to achieve in the community that he studied (1959: 150). Landy concluded with the same observations that others had made that it is much easier for girls to fill the role expected of them than for boys. Girls only have to be submissive and obedient. Boys, on the other hand, are expected to be obedient and show respeto for their parents, while at the same time being independent and aggressive.

National Culture, National Character, National Values

This is perhaps the hardest category of all to summarize usefully. Since I have taken the position that it is very difficult to speak of a common Puerto Rican culture or identity in the body of the report, I feel it essential to sum up what others have said in favor of the existence of some national character structure or value system. The difficulty lies not only with the relative abstractness of the concepts, but also with the many different viewpoints from which the problem has been approached. (I can say parenthetically that, if I had been able to summarize such materials to my total satisfaction at some earlier time, I would have published an article on this subject many years ago.)

Simple lists of traits may be mentioned first, though I have indicated my reserve about them. Reuter (1946) emphasizes the nonsecular and relativistic point of view of Puerto Ricans; the way class sentiments survived in the face of North American preconceptions that political democracy would break down such sentiments; the Puerto Rican predilection for dreams, unrealistic plans, and illusions, and the dependency of attitude of the islanders. I believe his view is ethnocentric and anachronistic.

A far better and more sophisticated enumeration is provided by Saavedra de Roca (1963), who used published sources to document each point. Since it serves no purpose to repeat her presentation wholly, I will simply list here the "prevailing values" in her paper, some of which will be discussed more analytically at a later point in this section. "Dignidad" refers to some powerful inner value concerned with maintaining one's public image or viewed status. It is seen as both a positive value and as a negative one—Cochran (1959) equates it with "sense of integrity," while Tugwell in Fernández Méndez, 1956) feels it may be employed to conceal incompetence, and to substitute fantasy-renderings for the reality of the self. Tumin (1958) stresses dignidad as the source of pride in work, and, with Gillin (1955), sees it as giving a man of any social and economic status the capacity to feel his worth regardless of his worldly success or failure. Individualism is another "prevailing value" of the Puerto Rican, and numerous writers (e.g., Gillin, 1955; Schurz, 1949) see this trait as generally Latin American. This inner quality—be it called soul, or "alma," or "ánima"—is unrelated to the external world. "Whereas the effort of each man on the mainland to be 'as good as the next person' inevitably produced a competitive type of individualism, the possession of a 'unique inner quality' is quite divorced from external contexts" (Cochran, 1959: 123).

Again, personalism or "personalismo" is seen as distinctively Puerto Rican. At least in contrast to the United States. Wells (1955) makes much of personalismo in explaining the special quality of Puerto Rican politics, in particular the emotionally charged adoration of Luis Muñoz Marín. Because of personalism, Cochran (1959: 125–26) tells us, the unification of small businesses into larger entities, the development of nonfamilial commercial ties, the maintenance of a high efficiency in committee work, etc., are hampered. Personalism in effect requires that all social, economic, and political relationships proceed on a basis of known face-to-face contact.

The value put on education is another characteristic of the Puerto Ricans. Tumin (1958), in his study, confirms the findings of Steward's associates (1956) and of Hill, Stycos, and Back (1959), that the desire for education in Puerto Rico burns brightly. Education is both the best marker of class differentiation (Tumin, 1958: 464–66), and the "most effective point of leverage in the total social system."

Family values, especially patterns of familial authority, form another category of the Puerto Rican value system. Saavedra de Roca does little with this theme, except to suggest that class differences are accompanied by differences in paternal authority, using Wolf (1952), Tumin (1958), and Mintz and Padilla Seda (in Steward, 1956) as her sources.

Other familial values discussed by Saavedra de Roca include respect for parents, parental obligations to the children, the position of women, communication between spouses, attitudes toward ideal family size, courtship attitudes, machismo, the woman's role in socialization separation of the sexes, bodily cleanliness, sibling rivalry and cooperation, parental conceptions of childhood, bodily punishment, inconsistencies in socialization, responsibility and dependency. I do not plan to examine these subjects fully here; a number of them are touched upon elsewhere, particularly in the discussion of family structure.

Finally, Saavedra de Roca makes reference to "optimismo" (i.e., as an attitude toward life), which was strongly identified by Tumin (1958: 166), to some extent in contrast to the findings of others. Parenthetically, I would say to this last that the "fatalism" of Puerto Ricans simply made more sense in terms of the realities of 1935 or 1940 than in 1950 or 1960. It would be difficult to contend, for instance, that average North American attitudes in 1935 were not significantly different in this regard from what they would become in 1945 or 1950. Though the Saavedra de Roca article does not employ all of the available relevant sources by any means, though it lacks a historical perspective, and though it gives little on the dynamics of behavior behind these various values or attitudes, it is a very useful preliminary staking-out of areas in which many observers have found common ground in studying the Puerto Rican people.

Figueroa Mercado (1963) covers some of the same ground as Saavedra de Roca, but puts her emphasis more firmly on culture and personality. She attempts to give historical "ori-

gins" for various attitudes—for example, hospitality and generosity are Indian and Spanish in origin, uncertainty
("incertidumbre") and fatalism derive from the disaster-
prone and dependent status of Puerto Rico, and so on—but
such attributions are not completely convincing. The island
is caught up in a spiritual vassalage ("vasallaje espiritual")
that Puerto Ricans must examine if they are to free themselves
from it. Individual and group insecurity, the hope for miraculous good fortune, the unwillingness to make firm decisions,
and other traits have been synthesized by those outsiders
who, not understanding the Puerto Rican collective soul, see
the phrase "A bendito!" as a symbol of the irresolute Puerto
Rican personality. The Figueroa Mercado article shares
much, it seems to me, with the position taken by Pedreira in
his "Insularismo"; it is a good essay, and a moving one. Not
surprisingly, however, it only admits that many changes have
occurred since Puerto Rico fell into North American hands,
and it does not deal at all with what those changes have
meant for "the collective soul" of the Puerto Rican people.

These papers are more than simple trait-lists, but they provide only limited access to any analysis of Puerto Rican character. They go along with such works as Pedreira's
"Insularismo" (though lacking its depths, reflectiveness, and
charm), René Marqués' "El puertorriqueño docil," and other
humanistic approaches to Puerto Rican culture. To some extent "belles-lettres" provide similar insights. As one illustration, César Andreu's "Los Derrotados" (which deals with a
vain nationalist attempt to assassinate an American Army
officer) provides a view of Puerto Rican society that is less
than pure fantasy, and in some ways much more than pure
social science. The class structure of island society is depicted
through the book's characters, and the differences in attitude
and ideology of the protagonists throw real light on island
life. Only two "intellectuals" grace the book's pages. Though
reputable and intelligent, these men are shown as empty, or
hollow, because they could not be true to their own insights.
Fully realizing the need for ideals and for honor (perhaps
an aspect of machismo in this rendering), they simply could
not follow the course they believed to be right. The working
people in the book are factory proletarians, and poor fisher-
men and country folk. They fall into two categories—the
honest but simple people who do the best they can with

what they have (thus embodying dignidad), and the misguided sheep who depend on their class betters as moral guides and get their precepts from the radio. These latter lose their simple peasant culture in a grinding modernization process that gives them nothing better to enhance their lives. Finally, there are members of the middle class and they, too, fall into two categories. Those who choose a nationalist political direction retain their honor, their high ideals, and their status as machos. But the political imperatives deprive them of normal lives, and isolate them from their wives and children; their conflict inheres in the attractiveness of a life that insists on no responsibility except to political principles. The other middle class figures choose to follow North American ideals; moneymaking becomes the be-all and end-all of their lives. They become effeminate as their women become mannish, and their activities make them dishonest and vulgar. Yet they get access to real political power, control money and resources, and thus gain control over others. The climax of the novel emphasizes that—if, indeed, this is the way things are—the thinking man and the principled man have no way out in Puerto Rican society. Obviously, this is a novel, not a sociological tract. But it would be unfair to claim simply that Andreu has given us a picture of what he thinks—much in this book rings true, and articulates real problems in contemporary Puerto Rico. It would be interesting to make comparable sketches of other literary works of this kind, but the rewards are probably tangential to the aims of the appendix.

In the body of the report, I suggested that four sorts of inquiry may give some answers to the question of Puerto Rican identity or national culture: social history, value categories, socialization and child-training patterns, and "social idioms." Something may be said now of each of these categories. Within the category of social history, one thinks of the work of Steward and his associates, the paper by Figueroa de Mercado, and Petrullo's book as examples. Such features of Puerto Rican life as the complex but essentially noncolor-based handling of race differences, the mandatory hospitality, the often illusory hopes for an economic windfall, the attitudes of dependency (especially in the political sphere), the acceptance of rigid class differences, etc., may be traced— though not with conspicuous success, I fear—to Puerto Rico's special history.

Investigations of value systems and reflections on commonly acknowledged values suggest a different direction. Pedreira's book deserves first mention. Some of the papers cited earlier (e.g., Saavedra de Roca) seek greater specificity within the same sphere. Brameld (1959), in an interesting book concerned particularly with the relationship between Puerto Rican culture and education, also makes some attempt to identify a single value system for the Puerto Rican people. He includes in his list of values "* * * the familiar cluster denoted by such terms as friendliness, outreachingness, kindness, sharing, hospitality, brotherliness, and gregariousness. Others that were underscored include devotion to family, personal pride, honesty in government, racial egalitarianism, respect for learning, loyalty to the homeland without fanatical nationalism (the value called nonnationalism), an accent upon being rather than becoming, and love of the Spanish language" (1959: 267). In eliciting responses, Brameld was unable to get clear opinions as to whether Puerto Ricans value esthetic matters above scientific ones, or vice versa; nor was it clear whether cooperation or competition was more important as a typical value of the "average" man (or even whether people felt cooperation was now gaining, at the expense of a more competitive attitude). The difficulties here may lie with the unspecificity of the subject, of course—these are hard things to discuss in the abstract. Brameld did locate two significant areas suggestive of widely held values. His informants largely supported the notion that Puerto Ricans are "* * * relativistic in the sense that they are exceptionally tolerant of attitudes and practices different from their own. Despite the volatility attributed to their modal personalities, they were said to abhor violence of a mass variety; hence they would much rather acculturate and even assimilate foreign values and accompanying practices than militantly resist them" (Brameld, 1959: 271). The author goes on to add:

> Compared with several other Latin American countries, such as Cuba again, it is even possible to say that this "elasticity of accommodation" becomes a value distinctive in several ways—in a lack of chauvinistic quarrelsomeness; in the centuries-old evolutionary rather than revolutionary approach to cultural goals; in the

friendly curiosity with which people listen to while seldom challenging outsiders; in a "purposeful patience";
in respect for the democratic voting process as a slow but
sure way of achieving such goals; in the comparative
success with which migrants accommodate themselves to
a new cultural environment; and in the high regard attached to cultural change (Brameld, 1959: 271).

Another attempt at enumerating values, or at getting at
some value system, is that employed by Mrs. Collier in the
other appendix to this report. Here, written materials were
examined to extract data confirming one or another position
in the Kluckhohn values scheme. Firm answers could be given
in only several categories; for many the data were either con-
tradictory, dealt with different class groupings, or represented
different points in time.

Studies of socialization and child training bulk importantly
in the social science literature on Puerto Rico. Outstanding, I
believe, is the paper by K. Wolf (1952), the book by Landy
(1959), and some of the materials provided by Steward's
associates. Other important data come from the many studies
primarily concerned with birth control and attitudes toward
family size. The difficulties implicit in employing socialization data in order to get at what might be called national
character or a national personality are serious. Among other
things, it is often very hard to establish any wholly convincing linkage between child training and the adult personality,
even when these seem to go together. However, at least something should be said of this, in further elaboration of the data
given elsewhere.

According to Landy (1959: 99, 120), Puerto Rican parents
see children as completely dependent, and also believe that
they have a ready predisposition to be "bad." Little boys are
born with "malicias" (perhaps "malice," but more likely
"shrewdness" or "guile"); girls, though born innocent, are
easily corrupted. Obedience is demanded from children, and
secured. Conformity is deemed more important than achievement; for instance, in spite of the many references to high
values on education, Landy's informants were not overly concerned with keeping children in school (1959: 150–51). Boy
and girl children receive differential treatment and training,
starting at an early age. Wolf (1952: 410–11) points out

how, in the rural highland community of Manicaboa, boys are encouraged toward physical autonomy and movement out of and away from the house, while girls are guarded and protected. Boys continue to go naked much longer than girls, who are clothed almost from the first. At the same time the demands put upon children are much more consistent in the case of girls than of boys; there is generally more for girls to do that needs doing, and success at tasks is an important part of growing up. For boys, the work to be done diminishes in some communities, so that adolescent males may have difficulties in attaching their physical maturation to any worthwhile service to the family. It is not surprising, perhaps, that a 15-year-old girl is ready for marriage while a boy of this age is still seemingly much younger.

Since sexuality seems to be regarded as both inherent and not inherently bad, the separation of boy and girl children, the clear demarcation of male and female tasks, and the strict chaperonage of adolescence, work together in shaping the adult male or female personality. Men cannot control their sexual impulses except through the presence of others, if one is to judge by the way socializing between boys and girls goes on. Girls should not have to resist sexual advances, but should rather have the protection afforded by the chaperone. The lesson seems to be that women are incapable of defending themselves against male sexual aggression, while men are incapable of internally imposed self-discipline. It needs to be understood that such assertions are inferences, rather than clearly stated beliefs or values, and further, that they can hardly be claimed to hold for each and every Puerto Rican.

Much more could be said of child training and socialization, but for reasons of space, I will turn instead to the supposed adult personality derivatives of these and other child training practices. Landy (1959: 168) claims that the Puerto Rican child-training experience leads to an insatiable adult need for intimate social relationships with others. Relations "de confianza" are desired, yet the demands of truly trustful closeness are overpowering, and men are constantly frustrated. Grownups have a "defense," even apprehensive outlook, suggesting that they find their environment hostile and menacing (Landy, 1959: 78). Expressions of salutation response ("Siempre en la lucha," "Ahí luchando," "Siempre defendiéndome," etc.) accompany this alleged attitude. People count heavily on the opinions of others in maintaining their self-images. Landy writes (1959: 194) "The fragile sense of community solidarity, the lack of a strong sense of communal responsibility and duty, and, conversely, a highly developed sense of familism (now somewhat tattered and strained) and individualism in terms of face and dignidad rather than ego-ideals and ego-aspirations" make for a weak superego—and no doubt for considerable dependence on outside opinion. Brown (1964: 56–58) gives a view of men in the rural and impoverished community he studies that builds on these earlier contentions. Here, men value machismo as they do elsewhere in Puerto Rican society. "Defending oneself," gambling, cockfighting, drinking heavily, having many women, and being a "good sport" are all positively valued. Women seek to deflect their sons from these ideals, and mothers are extremely important in perpetuating the curious childish quality of adult manhood imputed to Puerto Ricans; but women, due to their low social and economic status, are unable to keep their sons away from the male view of the world. Such ideals are trenchantly analysed by Wolf (1952), and her contrast of three different community settings suggests that many such values are differently held, and have different symbolic connotations in different class and community groups. Brameld (1959: 192 et seq.) has attempted to synthesize some of these value attributions to adult Puerto Ricans in search of a "modal personality" or "basic personality," but with inconclusive results. The "defensiveness" of the Puerto Rican stands out as an imputed trait or character; it is displayed in guarding oneself against those of higher prestige or more powerful status; in not opposing persons of authority, even when they are regarded with doubt or suspicion; in getting one's way by patient and subtle "killing" of an opposite view, rather than by an open fight; and by the presence of its temperamental opposite, aggressiveness. This aggressiveness may be expressed in self-destructiveness (including suicide), in explosive anger, in homicidal violence (murder viewed as an end point of an adult "tantrum"), and in some features of machismo.

I must admit that I find it difficult to accept any of these statements as describing with total accuracy what is "characteristically Puerto Rican," and few writers on Puerto Rican behavior are so unreserved as to claim this. In a qualified but insightful paper, Albizu and Marty (1958) have attempted to use projective test materials (including Rorschach, modified TAT, and sentence completion tests) to derive a self-image sketch of the personality of lower class Puerto Ricans. Two groups, one in Puerto Rico and another in Chicago, were used as subjects, and the techniques used differed, yet the results show surprising uniformity. The tests revealed much that could be inferred negatively about the personalities of the subjects: A sense of inferiority to non-Puerto Ricans, a lack of resourcefulness and initiative, and a noticeable passivity, among other things. These authors, like many others, emphasize the dependency of the Puerto Rican people, their inability to confront crisis head on, their employment of resignation ("ay bendito") and circumventive aggression ("pelea monga") in seeking solutions, and their docility. Though the results certainly raise doubts and many questions, they are of special interest since they are supposed to originate in the self-perceptions of the subjects, rather than in the observations of naive outsiders.

Numerous other studies might be mentioned in this section, but the materials are too diverse to afford us any unified picture. I wish now to discuss only the notion of "social idiom" as an approach to the study of national character, and to add a final list of traits, before ending this section. Throughout my report I have carefully qualified all judgments about the unity of Puerto Rican culture by emphasizing that culture is a historical product, and is rarely shared (and certainly not, in Puerto Rico's case) by all members of the society. Instead, culture is differentially carried by individual Puerto Ricans, and its symbolic meanings are doubtless differentiated as well. At the same time, I have suggested that the concept of "social idiom" may well provide one of the more fruitful directions for getting at some nationwide value system or "style" that might justifiably be regarded as typically or even uniquely Puerto Rican. The concept rests on the known need for members of different social groups within a single society to interact meaningfully with each other. To do so, they must present images of themselves that are consistent with the social usages and expectations of others. The relational process—or more simply put, the way people carry on behavior in emotionally and symbolically comprehensible ways—requires some basic conventional understanding; Wolf (1956b: 1075),

Seda Bonilla (1957), and others have explored this process usefully, and Lauria (1964) has sought to apply his analysis to one aspect of Puerto Rican social relations. His paper begins with a consideration of the concept of "respeto," and he admits at the outset that the values implied by the term, as well as the term itself, are clichés. It is, he contends, precisely because they are clichés that they say something true and analytically important about Puerto Rican character. Terms such as "hombre de respeto, falta de respeto, hay que darse a respetar antes de ser respetado, hombre de confianza, hombre prócerto, sinvergüenza, de carácter," and many others fall within the area that defines respeto and its opposite, and it is possible to explore this sphere of definition by getting descriptions of acts and feelings from informants. The overfamiliarity of the terminology no more obviates careful analysis than would be true of comparable terminology in the language of another culture. Thus, for instance, in American English, we use such terms as "shame," "self-respect," "no self-respecting person would * * *" "shameless," "conscienceless," "to feel guilty," "to feel small," to be "shown up," to "put up or shut up," "to back down," etc.—and the familiarity of such terms by no means invalidates their usefulness for understanding the characteristic tones of American social life. Lauria contends that, in the Puerto Rican case, proper understanding of such terms and their meanings is typical of the entire society, and not of a single segment of it. Such terms as are understood throughout the society prove their relevance to the social totality because they are clichés, and because they are understood by everyone; they mark the areas in which ready communication among people of different social status require considerable common understanding.

Lauria's exposition deals primarily with two such clusters, "respeto" and "relajo"; he establishes to my satisfaction that these terminologies lie close to the heart of Puerto Rican culture and identity, and give evidence that such identity is a reality. I feel a certain difficulty myself in dealing with these materials though I believe they are extremely insightful and provocative. It seems to me that the terms and their meanings suggest rather more about personality than they do about culture—though I am prepared to admit that they represent aspects of learned social behavior, and not simply "character structure." I also find it difficult to see how such materials can be transformed into a picture of a national culture—something presumably unique, and on a total societal scale. However, I believe the promise of this research is great. Lauria is now working on problems of "social types," with the hope of characterizing Puerto Rican (or Hispanic-Latin American) "social personalities." What is most interesting about the concepts, it seems, is the way they permit one's transcending such basic sociological considerations as differences in class, sex, age, and social status. I believe it is indeed true that, on such values as respeto and its meaning, the Puerto Rican worker and Puerto Rican banker probably share much of their understanding. This is, however, a long way from any satisfactory depiction of Puerto Rican nationhood, and pioneers such as Seda Bonilla and Lauria are well aware of it.

In her work for me, Mrs. Collier attempted at one point to summarize briefly her impressions of the features of Puerto Rican life that figured most importantly in her reading. I have added a bit to her list, but it is admittedly an impressionistic and untested formulation: I include it here for what it may be worth. It should be remembered that these various items are not regarded by Mrs. Collier or by myself as of equal weight or in any sense "proved."

(1) Puerto Rico is not only Spanish-speaking, but bids fair to remain so for as long as one can predict. The Spanish language, while it has different values, no doubt, to members of different groups, is commonly approved of and preferred by nearly everyone. Much of the sentimental speciality of feeling of the Puerto Rican people about themselves and about the island rests in linguistic considerations.

(2) Puerto Rico is a Catholic country; but it is not just any Catholic country, it is Puerto Rico. Puerto Rican Catholicism is much differentiated in class and other terms, and other religions—particularly the nonecumenical Protestant sects—have grown rapidly at the cost of a formal but sometimes empty rural Catholicism. All the same, many of what appear to be widely held or basic values in Puerto Rican life flow from the Catholic spirit; being a "bad" Catholic (consensual marriage, not attending church, not going to confession, etc.) does not signify an absence of Catholicism, but occurs within the context of the presence of Catholicism. The concept of a supernatural order; the belief that objects may possess supernatural powers; the division (implicit, to be sure) of women

into "Marys" and "Eves"; the veneration of Mary and of motherhood; the confirmed use of external sanctions to atone for sins (penance), and of external social devices to control, prevent, and punish behavior; the double sexual standard; the much-used institution of compadrazgo—these, and much else, suggest the underlying power of a Catholic ideology which, in Puerto Rico's case, is less expressed as an aspect of religiosity than as an aspect of national character.

(3) Puerto Ricans continue to accept the idea of a class-structured society in which those with less power and authority owe agreed-upon acts, and attitudes of deference and respect, to others more powerful than they. It is perfectly true that this may well be changing rapidly in Puerto Rico; nevertheless it bears noting that the child-training patterns in many class groupings, and the institutionalized inferiority of women, are behavioral complexes that are probably consistent with this idea of a world ordered into superordinate and subordinate sectors. I will not attempt to substantiate this assertion anecdotally or at length, but examples are very easy to come by (Seda Bonilla, 1957, 1963, 1964; Brown, 1964; Rogler, 1940; Wolf in Steward, 1956; Mintz, 1960; Albizu and Marty, 1958; etc.).

(4) Typically Puerto Rican is the particular complex of attitudes delineated by Gillin (1955) for Latin America, and applied by Brameld (1959) and Cochran (1959) to Puerto Rico: (a) A special image of "the individual"; (b) the acceptance of a stratified social hierarchy (see above); and (c) a transcendental or idealistic view of the world. We have seen that "individualism" signifies here a notion of worth and uniqueness unrelated to the outer world or to worldly success. The idea of the world as a fixed social hierarchy has been raised in the preceding paragraph, and needs no further discussion. As to Gillin's third generalization, it is interesting to note that Steward, though chary of characterological generalization, does write of the Puerto Ricans that (1956: 11) they share "* * * emphasis upon spiritual and human rather than commercial values; interest in poetry, literature and philosophy rather than science and industry; and emphasis on interpersonal relations rather than a competitive individualism." He makes clear at the same time that such dispositions are probably not equally shared by any means by all Puerto Ricans.

(5) The concept of dignidad, and the related concepts of

honor, "respeto, confianza," etc., and their polar opposites, communicated in such terms as "relajón, sinvergüenza," etc. Since I have referred to this material earlier, I will not say more of it here.

(6) The need for interaction in order to define the self. Privacy is neither valued nor desired; the opinions of others seem to weigh more than any internalized abstract code of behavior; dignidad, respeto, confianza, etc., are defined with reference to others. Accordingly, outside sanctions are required to define individual behavior; chaperonage and the overuse of the terms vergüenza and sinvergüenza, are indicators of the powerful ways that outside sanctions function. There is fear of people who are sensitive to outside opinion, and therefore of "sinvergüenzas" fear as well of uncontrolled aggression, and some contradiction between attitudes toward aggression and attitudes toward ideal maleness (machismo).

(7) The double sexual standard. North Americans are hardly in a position to throw stones—but it would be a gross error to suppose that the North American double standard, and that allegedly typical of Puerto Rico, operate in identical or even roughly similar ways. Especially important is the way the double standard concedes no real autonomy to either sex—chaperonage operates as if no man were capable of controlling himself, and as if no woman were really able to say "no." At the same time, it should be noted that the underlying assumption here may make for relatively straightforward and satisfactory sexual relations in marriage. (The ethnographic data, unfortunately, do not confirm such an optimistic inference.)

(8) Together with the double sexual standard, there appears to be a strong belief in the natural inferiority of women —they have five senses compared to man's seven, they are weaker physically, they are more emotional and cannot reason, and they are assumed to have a radically different personality structure. I need hardly add that I am unconvinced that this view is held with equal fondness by members of all social groups, or by members of both sexes.

(9) The cult of virginity, which goes along with the points made above, and conceivably still affects powerfully the quality of social relationships in Puerto Rico.

(10) Consonant with this is the relative lack of communication between the sexes, and their strict separation throughout

life. As in other ways—such as the belief in a rigid social hierarchy, with clear obligations of deference—I believe this aspect of Puerto Rican life is changing rapidly.

(11) Machismo, as a complex of attitudes and values having to do with maleness and male dignidad, and logically counterposed to the points made above. Though machismo as a term has been much used, it has received nowhere the serious analytic and qualifying attention it deserves. Mrs. Collier points out, for instance, that machismo is hinged more to the opinions of a man's peer group than to his inner sense of confident maleness, but much more needs to be done with this idea.

(12) Dependency, as an aspect of social life. Often claimed as a central feature of the Puerto Rican character (see, for instance, Pedreira, 1946; Albizu and Marty, 1958), too little has been done to relate the concept to concrete details of behavior.

To this list might be added, quite provisionally, the emphasis on personal cleanliness as opposed to much lesser concern with the physical environment; an "undeveloped" aesthetic sense; difficulty in deferring gratification; the relativistic tolerance of cultural difference; the unwillingness to rationalize the pleasurable as primarily practical (in contrast to the North American); the reluctance to see guilt as a preferable moral force to shame; and much else.

In concluding, I think it important to emphasize yet again that the kind of view of "the Puerto Rican" or "the Puerto Rican people" provided by arguments of this sort is not one to which I am personally very sympathetic. Though this sketch is brief, I have tried to state the case for such characterizations as fairly as I can. My reservations, once again, inhere in the difficulty, first of all, of proving such assertions; and secondly, in my feeling that class differences and rapid social change both conspire to invalidate these kinds of generalizations almost as soon as they are set forth.

Studies of Change

It may seem paradoxical that so little has been written on social change in Puerto Rico, when few societies seem to be changing so rapidly, or to be receiving so much social scientific attention. Tumin and Feldman (1961) take what may be fairly called an optimistic view of social change in Puerto Rico. Their study, based on questionnaire materials, indicates that Puerto Ricans share a universal desire to educate their children (1961: 123); that people see their society as open because they aspire more for their children than for themselves (1961: 143); that morale is high, and that people do not see present inequalities as insuperable (1961: 164); that those who see their children in the same social class as themselves are culturally conservative (1961: 201); and so on. In fact, there are several methodological difficulties here (not the least, perhaps, being that which dogs all questionnaire studies—the problem of reliability and of comprehension); among them, the disposition to treat informants from the various subcultures of Puerto Rico as if there were no subcultural differences seems particularly shortsighted. In spite of the authors' optimism, and of their confidence in education as the great leveler in Puerto Rican life, the book does not confidently increase our understanding of social change in the island.

Morse (1960), taking a very different tack, strikes out at what he sees as overglib and superficial analyses of the "transformation" of Puerto Rico, and calls this transformation illusory. He wonders whether it is realistic to suppose that the island will really one day have "* * * la piedad católica, las tradiciones afectuosas de familia, el respeto artificial hacia la mujer y el individualismo espiritual y estético, y por el otro lado, el empuje, logro material y 'confort' y la eficiencia organizacional del mundo de los negocios yanqui" (1960: 358). Not only does he doubt the chances for such a hybridization, but he feels called upon to point out that all the United States would be supplying in such an amalgam would be method, technology, and money.

Morse takes issue with the common assumption (as suggested, for instance, by the work of Brameld, 1959, and Cochran, 1959, in their use of Gillin, 1955) that Puerto Rico is but a piece of some single culture sphere called "Latin America," without attention to the special history of the island. That history, he argues, has been poor in national symbols and in national triumphs, and the Puerto Ricans have real difficulty in creating a tough "national self-image" (autoimagen nacional). Puerto Rico cannot be a hybrid of two cultures because Puerto Rico was never really Spanish (in the sense in which much of the South American mainland was). The island society was too fragmented, isolated, dependent, and ignored for this—even the Catholic church had no profound success in establishing itself. Spanish culture was reduced to a framework, perchance a matrix, rather than being the basic structure of the society. Little group identity evolved, perhaps in part because of the isolation of the island, with its internal fragmentation due to limited development, poor communication, rigid class lines, etc. The lack of a group identity may be related, in fact, to the often-imputed "docility" of the Puerto Rican people; they tend to look for help from outside, not trusting their own initiative and suffering when faced with critical decisions. A culture that is docile in this way, Morse contends, has three characteristics: (a) The powers of self-criticism and of self-evaluation are retarded; (b) the people and the whole society are prey to fantasies because they lack a self-image forged in internal conflict; and (c) the members of the society have difficulty in identifying public objects upon which to vent the hostility that all societies possess (1960: 365).

Accordingly, Morse contends, the period of supposed "hybridization" and "transformation" has been one in which wishy-washy policies have developed, which are of no help to the Puerto Ricans in forming a picture of their own identity. Lacking a clear self-image, a clear purpose and a sense of national self, the Puerto Ricans lean too much on fantasy, and their docility hides hostility and frustrations; life swings between the extremes of apathy and frantic activity.

Obviously Morse is not denying that Puerto Rico has changed; he is arguing instead that it has not changed for the better, and that, in the essential terms of a national identity, it is as bemused as ever, if not more so.

An equally pessimistic picture, but somewhat differently, is given us by the work of Seda Bonilla (1964). Based on anthropological fieldwork in a north coast sugarcane community in 1948–49 and a decade thereafter, Seda's study provides an interesting series of insights about change. Seda sees the traditional rural family structure as deteriorating under the impact of higher consumption aspirations, migration, and the resultant inroads on familial and sexual stability. The traditional role of women is crumbling; they seek sexual pleasure for pay, leave their children with their grandparents, ignore the taboo on association with other males besides their spouses, and use their economic independence as a reassurance against the risks of a broken family. Young people admire the easy life of no obligations and little work. They reject the past, and have no use for the idea of the "hombre serio y formal" (1964: 49). They are bored, have little to talk about because they "know so much," and are passive and dependent ("cool"). They do not want manual work, yet lack the education to get clerical or skilled jobs; they tend to emigrate readily, and ridicule tradition and the old "jíbaro" customs (1964:51).

People fear being tricked (see also Landy, 1959; Brown, 1964); they incline to trust no one, and their children are often made promises that are not kept. Generosity is highly valued, but always suspect (1964: 113). People with authority are seen as "good" if they grant special favors. As with a small child, to be denied a favor by one in authority is to be branded as "bad." If a man does not grant a favor, it is because he is holding it back for a relative, or does not like the petitioner (1964: 115). To be denied is to be offended, and so people fear to ask for things; yet they depend on the favors of leaders, and receiving a favor means being in debt. The consolidation and institutionalization of political power, the growth in consumption standards, the easy "out" provided by migration—these have intensified dependency, fear of freedom, and cynicism, while leaving nothing better behind. People fear both being left helpless, and being free, since being free means each can do as he pleases, resulting in a sort of chaos.

Seda Bonilla's work is a fascinating introduction to rural life from a largely "culture-and-personality" orientation, and it contains many sharp insights. However, one has little feeling that the author really controlled in any reliable way his assessment of social change. His pessimism is quite noticeable, and his hopes for communities of the sort he studied are markedly reserved. I will not attempt to examine here the same author's work on attitudes concerning civil liberties in Puerto Rico; but this work does throw some extremely interesting light on the relativistic tolerance imputed to Puerto Ricans. One obvious reservation is that many of these data were collected by questionnaire, with the accompanying problems of confirming reliability.

In a short paper, Maldonado Denis (1963) tackles the question of change, but puts his emphasis on the political implications of such change. In his view, industrialization and "penetración cultural norteamericana" are different streams of influence, not to be confused with each other (1963: 143). People in underdeveloped countries develop a sort of cultural schizophrenia, based on the conflicts implicit in changes away from the traditional culture. In Puerto Rico's case, the culture conflict brought about by North American power has been intensified by industrialization. The economy is largely within the sphere of North American control, and political decisions of a fundamental sort still rest in North American hands. The author sees the solution of Puerto Rico's cultural problems as a political solution—the annihilation or continuity of Puerto Rican culture depends, in effect, on whether Puerto Rico becomes independent, for independence would preserve the culture, while statehood would destroy it. While of interest, this paper adds little that is useful in any weighing of change in Puerto Rico. Though quite different in political outlook, much the same may be said of Fernández Méndez (1955) (also see Benítez and Rexach, 1964). Lewis (1963), in an intimidatingly well-documented study, says much of great interest concerning the Puerto Rican society. I will not attempt its summary here; as in the case of Tumin and Feldman (1961), I have written a review of the book which summarizes my main contentions concerning it (Mintz, 1964).

A short paper by Fernández Méndez (1963) sketches rather superficially the effects of recent changes (particularly economic) on the Puerto Rican family. The description is not based on fieldwork, and the tone is exhortatory rather than objective.

I had hoped that the materials provided by Brown (1964) might give new light on the consequences of change in Puerto Rico, but in fact the materials deal mainly with what could be described as a strikingly conservative and isolated rural subculture. It seems that nothing approaching the Steward-edited work for completeness and detail has appeared on Puerto Rico in the intervening decade, and I am unable to add much that is not impressionistic. I have referred in the body of my report to the study by Hernández Alvárez (1964), and to my own observations on a 2-day visit to a rural community this year (Mintz, 1965), but these data are sketchy, perhaps inconsequential. Given the enormous importance of recent social and cultural changes for any thoughtful analysis of contemporary Puerto Rico, I regret that so little of value can be said here about change.

Summary

The five preceding sections of this appendix enumerate some of the best-known studies of Puerto Rico (with occasional references to "belles-lettres"), and give at least a sketchy accounting of some of their findings. Additional sections—for instance, political life at the community level, life-history studies, and religion—might well have been added, but for the pressure of time. I do feel these materials make clear the difficulties implicit in attempting to draw any single holistic picture of island culture or Puerto Rican identity. While many of the items mentioned under national culture and national values doubtless have a certain validity and generality, I believe it would be hard to make them into a "picture" of the Puerto Rican personality or national culture.

Especially galling is the lack of any suitable factual basis for the interpretation of the impact of change on Puerto Rican culture and values. The obvious consequences are just that— obvious; but these understandings give us neither a full grasp of the society nor any predictive power. If some additional fieldwork were possible, more analytic data would be forthcoming. I should repeat once more my own reservations about holistic analysis of the Puerto Rican case, and admit to the clear incompleteness of the materials assembled here.

Perhaps the major value of such an exercise might be in the extent to which it could provoke additional dialogue concerning island society. It would be most helpful—and I acknowledged my prejudices—were some of the more articulate commentators to attempt ethnographic fieldwork in order to fill out their assertions, both positive and negative, with the words and voices of the Puerto Rican people.

Bibliography

Albizu Miranda, Carlos, and Héctor Marty Torres. 1958. "Atisbos de la personalidad puertorriqueña," "Revista de Ciencias Sociales," 2(3).

Alvárez Navario, Manuel. 1961. "El Elemento Afronegroide en el Español de Puerto Rico." San Juan, Instituto de Cultura Puertorriqueña.

Andreu Iglesias, César. 1956. "Los Derrotados." Mexico, Los Presentes.

Barbosa-Muñiz, José C. 1964. "On Gordon Lewis' Article," "San Juan Review," 1(9).

Benítez, Celeste, and Robert F. Rexach. 1964. "The Puerto Rican identity problem," "San Juan Review," 1(7).

Blanco, Tomás. 1942. "El Prejuicio Negro en Puerto Rico." San Juan, Editorial Biblioteca de Autores Puertorriqueños.

Brameld, Theodore. 1959. "The Remaking of a Culture." New York, Harper and Brothers.

Brown, Jack. 1964. "Subcultures of Isolation in Rural Puerto Rico." Ithaca, N.Y. Mimeographed, pp. 59.

Cochran, Thomas C. 1959. "The Puerto Rican Businessman: A Study in Cultural Change." Philadelphia, University of Pennsylvania Press.

Curtin, Philip. 1955. "Two Jamaicas." Cambridge, Harvard University Press.

Dexter, Lewis A. 1949. "A dialogue on the social psychology of colonialism and on certain Puerto Rican professional personality patterns," "Human Relations" 2(1).

Díaz Soler, Luis. 1953. "Historia de la Esclavitud en Puerto Rico." Madrid, Ediciones de la Universidad de Puerto Rico.

Fernández Méndez, Eugenio. 1955a. "Filiación y Sentido de una Isla": "Puerto Rico." San Juan, Editorial del Departamento de Instrucción Pública.

    1955b. "Reflexiones sobre 50 años de cambio cultural en Puerto Rico," "Historia," 5(2).

    1959. "Criterios de la periodización cultural de la Historia," "Cuadernos," 17.

    1963. "Algunos cambios culturales, económicos, y sociales que afectan la familia en Puerto Rico," "Revista de Ciencias Sociales," 8(2).

Fernández Méndez, Eugenio (ed.). 1956. "Portrait of a Society." Río Piedras. Mimeographed.

Figueroa Mercado, Loida. 1963. "Puerto Rico—cultura y personalidad," "Revista de Ciencias Sociales" 7(1–2).

Gillin, John. 1955. "Ethos components in modern Latin American culture," "American Anthropologist," 57(3).

Gordon, Maxine. 1949. "Race patterns and prejudice in Puerto Rico," "American Sociological Review," 14(2).

    1950. "Cultural aspects of Puerto Rico's race problem," "American Sociological Review," 15(3).

Hanke, Lewis. 1949. "The Spanish Struggle for Justice in the Conquest of America." Philadelphia, University of Pennsylvania Press.

Hernández Alvárez, José. 1964. "Una revisión de Cañamelar después de diez años," "Revista de Ciencias Sociales," 8(2).

Hill, Reuben. 1956. "Impediments to Freedom of Mate Selection in Puerto Rico," in Fernández Méndez, (ed.) 1956, q.v.

Hill, Reuben, J. Mayone Stycos, and Kurt Back. 1959. "The Family and Population Control." Chapel Hill, University of North Carolina Press.

Landy, David. 1959. "Tropical Childhood." Chapel Hill, University of North Carolina Press.

Lauria, Anthony Jr. 1964. "'Respeto,' 'relajo,' and Inter-Personal Relations in Puerto Rico," "Anthropological Quarterly," 37(2).

Lewis, Gordon. 1963. "Puerto Rico: Freedom and Power in the Caribbean." New York, Monthly Review Press.

Linton, Ralph. 1936. "The Study of Man." New York, Appleton-Century.

Maldonado Denis, Manuel. 1963. "Politica y cultura puertorriqueña," "Revista de Ciencias Sociales," 7(1–2).

Manners, Robert A. 1956. "Tabara: Subcultures of a Tobacco and Mixed Crops Community." In Steward, J. H. (ed.), 1956, q.v.

Manners, Robert A., and Julian H. Steward. 1953. "The Cultural Study of Contemporary Societies: Puerto Rico," "American Journal of Sociology," 59(2).

Marqués, René. 1963. "El puertorriqueño dócil," "Revista de Ciencias Sociales," 7(1–2).

Mellafe, Rolando. 1964. "La esclavitud en Hispanoamérica." Buenos Aires, Editorial Universitaria.

Mintz, Sidney W. 1951a. "The Contemporary Culture of a Puerto Rican Rural Proletarian Community." Ph.D. dissertation, Dept. of Anthropology, Columbia University.

——— 1951b. "The Role of Forced Labour in Nineteenth-century Puerto Rico," "Caribbean Historical Review," 2.

——— 1953a. "The Culture-History of a Puerto Rican Sugar-Cane Plantation, 1876–1949," "Hispanic American Historical Review," 33(2).

——— 1953b. "The Folk-Urban Continuum and the Rural Proletarian Community," "American Journal of Sociology," 59(2).

——— 1956. "Cañamelar: The Subculture of a Rural Puerto Rican Proletariat." In Steward, J. H. (ed.), 1956, q.v.

——— 1959. "Labor and Sugar in Puerto Rico and Jamaica," "Journal of Comparative Studies," 1(3).

——— 1960. "Worker in the Cane: A Puerto Rican Life History." New Haven, Yale University Press.

——— 1961a. "The Question of Caribbean Peasantries: A Comment," "Caribbean Studies," 1(3).

——— 1961b. Review of "Slavery," by Stanley Elkins. "American Anthropologist," 63(3).

——— 1963. Review of Tumin, Melvin, with Arnold Feldman. "Social Class and Social Change in Puerto Rico." In "Economic Development and Cultural Change," 11(2).

——— 1964. Review of Lewis, G. "Puerto Rico." In "Social and Economic Studies," 13(4).

——— 1965. "A visit to Barrio Jauca: March 18–20, 1965." Ms., ditto, pp. 95.

Mintz, Sidney W., and Eric R. Wolf. 1950. "An Analysis of Ritual Co-Parenthood (compadrazgo)," "Southwestern Journal of Anthropology," 6(4).

Morse, Richard M. 1960. "La transformación ilusoria de Puerto Rico," "Revista de Ciencias Sociales" 4(2).

Muñoz Marín, Luis. 1924. "Porto Rico. The American colony." In Gruening, E. (ed.). "These United States." New York, Boni and Liveright.

Padilla Seda, Elena. 1956. "Necorá: The Subculture of Workers on a

Government-Owned Sugar Plantation." In Steward, J. H. (ed.), 1956, q.v.

Pedreira, Antonio S. 1946. "Insularismo." San Juan, Puerto Rico, Biblioteca de Autores Puertorriqueños.

Petrullo, Vincenzo A. 1947. "Puerto Rican Paradox." Philadelphia: University of Pennsylvania Press.

Redfield, Robert. 1941. "The Folk Culture of Yucatán." Chicago, University of Chicago Press.

1962. "The Natural History of the Folk Society," "Human Nature and the Study of Society," vol. I. Chicago, University of Chicago Press.

Reuter, Edward B. 1946. "Culture Contacts in Puerto Rico," "American Journal of Sociology," 52(2).

Ríos, José Mariano, and P. B. Vásquez Calcerrada. 1953. "A Social and Economic Study of Two Resettlement Communities in Puerto Rico." Río Piedras, University of Puerto Rico Agricultural Experiment Station, Bulletin 114.

Rogler, Charles. 1940. "Comerío, A Study of a Puerto Rican Town." Lawrence, Kansas, University of Kansas Publications, Social Science Studies.

1946. "The Morality of Race Mixing in Puerto Rico," "Social Forces," 25(1).

1948. "Some Situational Aspects of Race Relations in Puerto Rico," "Social Forces," 27(1).

1949. "The Role of Semantics in the Study of Race Distance in Puerto Rico," "Social Forces," 22.

Rogler, Lloyd. 1965. "A Better Life: Notes from Puerto Rico," "Transaction," 2(3).

Rosario, Charles. 1958. "Dos tipos del amor romántico: Estados Unidos y Puerto Rico," "Revista de Ciencias Sociales," 2(3).

Rosario, José C. 1930. "The Porto Rican Peasant and his Historical Antecedents." In Clark, Victor S., et al., "Porto Rico and Its Problems." Washington, D.C., The Brookings Institution.

Rosario, José C., and Justina Carrión. 1940. "Problemas Sociales: El Negro: Haití—Etados Unidos—Puerto Rico." San Juan, n.p.

Saavedra de Roca, Angelina. 1963. "Algunos valores prevalecientes en la sociedad puertorriqueña," "Revista de Ciencias Sociales," 7(1–2).

Sapir, Edward. 1956. (1924). "Culture: Genuine and Spurious." In Mandelbaum, D. (ed.), "Culture, Language and Personality." Berkeley, University of California Press.

Schurz, William L. 1949. "Latin America." New York, Dutton.

Seda Bonilla, Edwin. 1957. "Normative Patterns of the Puerto Rican Family in Various Situational Contexts." Unpubl. Ph.D. diss. Dept. of Anthropology, Columbia University.

1961. "Social Structure and Race Relations." "Social Forces," 40(2).

1963. "La cultura y el desarrollo económico: el caso de una comunidad puertorriqueña," "Revista de Ciencias Sociales," 7(1–2).

1964. "Interacción social y personalidad en una comunidad de Puerto Rico." San Juan, Ediciones Juan Ponce de León.

Sereno, Renzo. 1947. "Cryptomelanism." "Psychiatry," (10).

Steward, Julian H. (ed.). 1956. "The People of Puerto Rico." Urbana, University of Illinois Press.

Stycos, J. Mayone. 1955. "Family and Fertility in Puerto Rico: A Study of the Lower Income Group." New York, Columbia University Press.

Suttell, L. 1955. "Puertorriqueña ciento por ciento." In Fernández "Mendéz, E. Filiacion y Sentido de una Isla: Puerto Rico." San Juan, Puerto Rico, Editorial del Departmento de Instrucción Pública.

Tannenbaum, Frank. 1947. "Slave and Citizen." New York, Alfred A. Knopf.

Tugwell, Rexford G. 1956. "*Dignidad* and its implications." In Fernández Méndez (ed.), 1956, q.v.

Tumin, Melvin, with Arnold Feldman. 1958. "Social Class and Social Change in Puerto Rico." Princeton University Press.

Tylor, Edward B. 1877. "Primitive Culture." New York, Henry Holt.

Vásquez Calcerrada, Pablo B. 1953. "The Study of a Planned Community in Puerto Rico." Río Piedras. University of Puerto Rico Agricultural Experiment Station, Bulletin 109.

Vientos Gastón, Nilita. 1964. "The Identity Problem: Part Two." "San Juan Review," 1(9).

Wells, Henry. 1955. "Ideology and Leadership in Puerto Rican Politics," "American Political Science Review," 49(1).

Williams, Eric. 1956. "Race Relations in Puerto Rico and the Virgin Islands." In Fernández Méndez (ed.), 1956, q.v.

Wolf, Eric R. 1956a. "San José: Subcultures of a "Traditional" Coffee Municipality." In Steward, J. H. (ed.), 1956, q.v.

1956b. "Aspects of Group Relations in a Complex Society: Mexico," "American Anthropologist," 58(4).

1959. "Specific Aspects of Plantation Systems in the New World: Community Sub-Cultures and Social Class." "Plantation Systems of the New World." Pan American Union Social Science Monographs, VII. Washington.

Wolf, Kathleen. 1952. "Growing Up and its Price in Three Puerto Rican Sub-Cultures," "Psychiatry," 15(4).

Zavala, Silvio. 1964. "The Defence of Human Rights in Latin America (16th to 18th centuries)." Tournai, Belgium, UNESCO.

Kal Wagenheim

PUERTO RICO: A PROFILE*

Despite their vague political status, Puerto Ricans are as ethnically distinct as Mexicans, Frenchmen, or Norwegians. They share a unique Hispano-Caribbean heritage that stretches back nearly half a millennium in time; their language is Spanish, spoken with a Puerto Rican accent and spiced with local idioms. Puerto Ricans share many common traits with their Spanish-speaking neighbors in Cuba and the Dominican Republic, but differences between these three island societies are apparent to all but the most casual of tourists. One might even argue that the long history of colonial dependence has become an integral part of the Puerto Rican "identity," or has, at least, created a curious void in it. Certainly, the last seven decades of association with the United States have caused substantial change in the nature of Puerto Rico's society.

Unlike the new American states of Alaska or Hawaii, which are sparsely populated or lack large "native" populations, Puerto Rico is densely peopled; and of every 100 residents, ninety-six are native-born. Half of the remainder are the U.S.-born offspring of return migrants.

The greatest catalyst for changing the Puerto Rican "identity" is the fact that more than *one-fourth* of all its native sons and daughters live in the United States. And it is not always the same fourth, due to constant in-out migration. Even on the mainland, Puerto Ricans cluster together, resisting efforts to divide them into the black and white racial categories that prevail in the eastern United States. In New York City, the darkest-skinned Puerto Rican will bristle at being called a Negro. "No," he will reply, "I am a Puerto Rican." It is noteworthy that most racial surveys in New York classify Puerto

* Kal Wagenheim, *Puerto Rico: A Profile*. New York: Praeger, 1970, pp. 154–178. Reprinted with permission.

Ricans in a category apart from whites and blacks despite the fact that, in terms of physical characteristics, there is no such thing as a Puerto Rican race.

Puerto Rico's apparently undefinable, but unquestionably singular identity has impelled even those who favor political assimilation with the United States to assure everyone, as Governor Ferré did recently, that "while the United States is our *nación* ("nation"), Puerto Rico is our *patria* ("homeland")." This view is, of course, disputed by autonomists and independence supporters, who insist that Puerto Rico is both the *nación* and *patria* of its native sons, but the fact that Governor Ferré—a staunch opponent of independence—should be concerned with the defense of Puerto Rico's ethnic identity is significant. Even he, as does every other Puerto Rican, refers to the island as *el pais* ("country" or "nation"), which only proves that semantics is a lively sport on this Caribbean island.

Ethnic Roots

Puerto Rico's earliest citizens—some 30,000 copper-skinned Taíno Indians—were killed, frightened off, or absorbed by Spanish colonizers in the sixteenth century. Next came an influx of African slaves. Since the Spaniards brought few women with them, the white, black, and red races were mixed in a stew that has bubbled quietly during five centuries. Today, sizable minorities of *blancos* ("whites") and *prietos* ("dark-skinned") or *negros* ("blacks") occupy the poles of the skin-color spectrum, and they blend gradually into the dominant middle (more than half the population) of the Puerto Rican people, who are either almost-white, or almost-black, or often remarkably Indian, and who fall into a catch-all category known as the *trigueño* ("tan," "swarthy," "olive-skinned," "darkish").

There have been other ingredients in this genetic bouillabaisse. In the late eighteenth and early nineteenth centuries, Frenchmen came from Louisiana when it was bought by the United States, and from Haiti when the slaves revolted. The Latin American wars for independence brought loyalist Spaniards and Venezuelans. As the slave-sugar economy flourished, Scotch and Irish farmers came. When slavery waned, many farmers and laborers came from the province of

Galicia and the Canary Islands. In the 1840's, a labor shortage brought Chinese coolies to Cuba and Puerto Rico where, in the latter, they helped build the Central Highway. Italians, Corsicans, and Lebanese also spiced the melting pot.

North American immigration grew after 1898, but as early as 1873, a small community of *americanos* founded an Episcopal church in Ponce. The North American community numbers more than 20,000 today (including many transients); a growing minority of *continentales*, as they are called here, have intermarried with Puerto Ricans, creating such exotic names as William Smith Gonzàlez, or Roberto Ruiz MacDonald.

The Cuban colony has swelled from 1,000 to 22,000 since the 1959 Castro Revolution. Following the Cubans, in mid-1965, a few thousand Dominicans fled the chaos of Santo Domingo's civil war. There are also small alien communities from different Latin American countries, particularly from Argentina and Venezuela, and a number of families from Spain.

In the United States, the "wretched, teeming masses" of immigrants usually begin at the lower rung of the socioeconomic ladder. But most newcomers to Puerto Rico possess the skills and/or capital that enable them to climb quickly to the upper or upper-middle strata. North Americans are often employed as managers or high-salaried technicians with local subsidiaries of U.S. corporations, or start their own businesses. Many Cuban immigrants have their own firms, mainly in the field of commerce, or are employed as well-paid technocrats. Only the Dominicans, who come from a society poorer than Puerto Rico's, have, in general, begun at the bottom, in factory or service jobs, including domestic work, which many Puerto Ricans no longer seek.

Race Relations

Fuzzy lines between racial groups discourage color prejudice. Slavery's small role (compared with some Caribbean areas), and its peaceful abolition, also contributed to lessen race tension.

A hint of racial harmony came as early as 1770, when Puerto Rico's Governor declared that all free children—white, mulatto, or black—should be educated. Marriage, though, especially in the upper classes, was another matter. Some families endured ludicrous trials, known as *limpieza de sangre* ("blood purification") to prove that no African blood flowed in their veins, thus entitling their members to marry into another "good" family. Folk tunes and idiomatic expressions treated blacks in a pejorative or comic manner. Friendly whites were often, and still are, paternalistic. But there was no government-instituted discrimination. Once slavery was abolished, the law opened public places to all. There were no separate rest rooms, or water fountains, or rear sections of public vehicles for blacks. It was the numbing heritage of slavery that deprived blacks of the tools needed to compete in the "free" society. But even in the nineteenth century, a few black and mulatto Puerto Ricans achieved distinguished places in their community. Outstanding among them was José Celso Barbosa (1857–1921), a doctor who served in the cabinet of the autonomous government (in 1897) as Undersecretary of Education and, later, formed the Statehood Republican Party. Before him was Rafael Cordero Molina (1790–1868), whom one local historian describes as "the Puerto Rican who has come closest to sainthood." A shoemaker, Cordero also had a small school where, for more than half a century, he offered free instruction to poor children.

The U.S. presence has enhanced the awareness of racial differences among Puerto Ricans. Since most American immigrants are white, and wealthier than the average islander, success is equated with whiteness. The Spaniards, too, were white, and, generally, wealthier, but they tolerated—and often engaged in—interracial marriage. Most Americans continue their life style in Puerto Rico, staying to themselves or gravitating toward white Puerto Ricans.

A Civil Liberties Commission in 1958 reported that while racial tension in Puerto Rico is not "critical," intolerance in the United States has negatively influenced the island. It quoted many blacks and whites as saying they would feel "uncomfortable" in a night-club full of people of another race. Some whites complained of colored families moving in next door. When white families were asked the old question, "Would you like your daughter to marry one?" half said no, but only a few said they would forcibly prohibit the marriage.

Prejudice is strongest, says the study, in some private schools, in university clubs, in some private businesses and in some residential sectors. Not a single black employee was visible in any bank office in the entire San Juan metropolitan area when the study was made. Only four black faces were counted in eighty-five San Juan business establishments. Pressure from legislative committees and from the press has now relaxed color prejudice in the business world, although some firms have only "token" Negroes working for them.

But it is ludicrous to suggest that the racial situation resembles that of the United States. The Senate Majority Leader for many years (who nearly became governor in November, 1968,) was the "Indian-ish" *trigueño* Luis Negrón López, who is a wealthy lawyer and gentleman farmer. A dark-skinned mulatto, the late Ernesto Ramos Antonini, occupied the powerful Speaker's post in the House of Representatives. The head of the island's Manufacturer's Association is a black economist. The poor comprise people of all colors. While few white Puerto Ricans marry blacks, those in the larger "tan" population mix freely with either extreme. Puerto Rico's police force is probably darker than the populace as a whole. Thus, many factors required for racial tension are absent. When "Black Power" advocate Stokeley Carmichael visited Puerto Rico in 1967, he soft-pedaled the racial issue and spoke out against United States "colonialism." On the other hand, Roy Innis was able to found a small CORE chapter in the nearby Virgin Islands, where black-white racial divisions are more marked.

Religion

In the year 1928, when the crops thirsted for rain in a certain rural *barrio* of southeast Puerto Rico, the citizens resorted to an old ritual known as the *rogativa*, or group supplication. They marched up and down the dusty road, praying for rain. Two weeks later, Hurricane San Felipe devastated the *barrio*. One oldtimer who recalls the catastrophe says, "They haven't celebrated a *rogativa* there since."

Many Puerto Ricans regard spiritual affairs in the same eclectic manner.

At the turn of the century, when the U.S. Army invaded Puerto Rico, an Army chaplain remarked, "Puerto Rico is a Catholic country without religion." More recently, island writer Pedro Juan Soto refined the thought somewhat when he observed, "Puerto Ricans are a religious people in search of a religion."

Well over 99 per cent of the population is Christian, with about 80 per cent Roman Catholic. The remainder are Protestants: Baptists, Methodists, Lutherans, Episcopalians, and Pentecostals. The Jewish Community Center in San Juan has a few hundred member families, most of them nonnative residents. There are also small groups of Mennonites and Mormons, and San Juan has a Salvation Army and a Watchtower Bible and Tract Society.

But the prevailing mood is a kind of "womb to tomb" Roman Catholicism, with little practice in between. The average Puerto Rican has been baptized, confirmed, and—when the time comes—will receive the last rites of the Catholic Church.

Christianity permeates even daily conversation. It is common in the countryside for a child, when entering or leaving the home, to request a *bendición* ("blessing") from the father, who will respond, "May God and the Virgin bless you." In planning a matter as casual as meeting for lunch the next day, many Puerto Ricans will add, *"Si Dios quiere"* ("God willing"). Common expressions of surprise are *"Ay virgen!"* and *"Ave Maria!"* both of which refer to the Virgin Mary. Even more frequent, to express or plead for compassion, is *"Ay bendito!"* which is short for *"Bendito sea El Señor"* ("Blessed be The Lord").

Almost all homes in Puerto Rico, from mansions to shacks, are adorned with pictures of Christ, crucifixes, or figurines of saints. Children are taught to fear *el diablo* and to respect *Papa Dios* ("Father God"). People often cross themselves when passing in front of a church. Each year, towns and villages celebrate festivals honoring their patron saint. Periods such as Holy Week, or between Christmas and Three Kings' Day (Epiphany) feature many masses and processions. When a new business opens, be it a mammoth bank building or a humble laundromat, the ubiquitous priest appears, with holy water and a blessing.

But Puerto Rico's Catholicism is hardly orthodox; it is often mixed with personalistic saint worship, spiritism, and superstition. Protestantism, especially the "swinging" revivalist variety, is a growing force.

Catholic church attendance (and participation in confession) is low, with prayers at home to a favorite saint often substituting for going to mass. Consensual marriage—ignoring both church and civil authority—is common among the poor. It is mainly among the rich and in the growing new middle class that one finds frequent church attendance and confession. Even here, a study of 200 wealthy Catholic families shows that while 142 wives and 91 husbands attend church often, only half the women and one-seventh of the men confess regularly.

While Holy Week is generally solemn, the annual patron saint festivals are times for merrymaking, with gambling and dancing in the plazas, which are full of ferris wheels, merry-go-rounds, and penny-pitching booths. Christmas is also a time of party-going and fun. In San Juan, during the annual festival to honor St. John the Baptist, the traditional midnight dip in the ocean (in which even the mayor participates) is a mere punctuation mark in a long night of partying.

To illustrate the mixed attitude toward the church, though many poor couples live in consensual union, they will usually have their children baptized.

Religiosity is more common outside the church. In rural villages, a person near death will be visited by friends and relatives, who maintain a night-long *velada* ("vigil"); the women pray inside the home; the men, after paying their respects, will often sit outside chatting, where they are served black coffee, soda crackers, and cheese. The night after death, a *velorio* is held, and much the same ritual is celebrated, although the men outside may down a nip of *cañita* ("clandestine cane rum") to combat the cool night air. Drunkenness or loud talk on such occasions is deplored, and imbibing rarely, if ever, evokes the bonhomie of the proverbial Irish wake. In some regions of the island, rosaries are recited for nine nights after the funeral.

The Catholic Church has had a long, checkered history since its establishment on the island in the early sixteenth century. On the positive side, it was a pioneer in opening new territories. Many pueblos were founded by priests, whose small, thatched-roof missions in remote zones served scattered rural settlers. In a few years, a town plaza was marked off, with a permanent church building at one end and the municipal hall at the other forming the nucleus for a new community.

The church also maintains medical services and schools, including Catholic University in Ponce and a number of good primary and secondary schools. Its religious festivals and activities, often the only recreational outlets in isolated communities, help foster a sense of community cooperation.

On the other hand, the church preached loyalty to Spain, even under the tyranny of military rule. Despite early church resistance to enslavement of the pre-Colombian Indians, the church opposed the abolition of slavery in the nineteenth century.

In 1969, Padre Salvador Freixedo, a Jesuit priest who wrote a book *(My Church Sleeps)* criticizing church dogma and voicing compassion for divorcees who wished to remarry, was banned from exercising his priestly functions. The crisis was headlined in daily papers for two weeks, as pickets for and against the priest marched in front of the archbishop's home in Old San Juan. Many felt that Padre Freixedo, a Spanish-born liberal who for years has supported prolabor causes, may have been rash in some of his statements, but they also felt that the church was far too harsh in its reaction. His book sold about 10,000 copies in Puerto Rico, making it one of the island's all-time bestsellers.

The Catholic Church's distance—spiritual and geographical —from the rural masses has led to the evolution of an unorthodox creole Catholicism; as well as a flowering of Protestant sects and various spiritualist groups. Many members of the growing middle class do not relate to the deterministic image of Catholicism, which prizes humility and promises paradise in the after-life. They are more drawn to the Protestant ethic of hard work and material achievement, of man's ability to change his fate. Many poor people, on the other hand, find solace in the catharsis of the revivalist wing of the Protestant religion.

Protestantism was long considered heresy in Puerto Rico. Not until the 1800's did the Spanish Crown permit Protestant churches to be built in Ponce and Vieques, after Queen Victoria transmitted the plea of several English families who had settled there.

After 1898, American religious groups looked southward to the Caribbean and saw over a million potential converts. To avoid needless rivalry, the U.S. Methodists, Baptists, and Episcopalians "divided up the cake" beforehand and created exclusive territories for proselytizing. By 1919, a Protestant

Evangelical Council was formed, and some Puerto Rican ministers were trained. But little impact was made on the rural, poverty-stricken island. By 1942, the American Protestant hierarchy reported with some chagrin that its ministry was "middle class . . . alien to Puerto Rican society and to the economic structure and life of the community." Sunday collections were so scanty that the American parent body was obliged to pay large subsidies.

The creation of a Puerto Rican middle class, more than a change in the nature of the Protestant Church, has attracted new adherents. There were enough on Easter Sunday, 1967, for Billy Graham to pack a baseball stadium in San Juan, where he addressed the throng with the help of a Spanish interpreter standing at his side.

But of an estimated 300,000 Protestants on the island, only about 70,000 belong to the major sects.

The rest belong to the revivalist movements such as the Pentecostals, the Seventh Day Adventists, or to the home-grown church opened in 1940 by a near-legendary woman named Mita, who died in 1970. She also opened Mita churches in the Spanish-speaking sections of Chicago and New York and in Santo Domingo. At one of her packed revival meetings, held the same week Billy Graham came to town, she referred to him as "the gringo with the big white teeth, who has come to steal away my parishioners."

The poor found it easy to identify with Mita, a woman whose thoughts may have been in the heavens, but whose words and methods were down-to-earth. The Mita sect has its own business and provides needed services to its followers; membership sometimes results in upward social mobility. After Mita's death, members of the sect continued its operation. The poor also identify with Pentecostal lay pastors, who have usually emerged from their own ranks and who offer living proof by their example of one's ability to advance by faith and hard work. Churches are usually storefronts in working-class districts or converted small suburban homes.

The Pentecostal faith, which offers group singing and emotional public testimony, also demands the discipline of exemplary dress and behavior, including abstinence from tobacco and alcohol; this helps the poor withstand the apparent hopelessness of their existence.

The sometimes traumatic migration to New York's hostile environment is ameliorated, too, by joining a revivalist group.

A 1948 survey showed that 5 per cent of New York's 300,000 Puerto Ricans were Pentecostals. Today, with nearly 1 million islanders in New York, about one family in ten belongs to, and helps support, a small church, which receives no subsidy. Led by pastors from their own *barrio*, singing the old biblical hymns, in Spanish translation, to the rhythm of maracas and tambourines, the Puerto Rican poor have, in effect, created a church of their own.

Espiritismo ("spiritism") is frowned upon by the church, but attracts many Puerto Ricans, who feel that it does not conflict with more orthodox religious practices.

There are different types of spiritist beliefs. Some practices, such as the use of certain herbs to remedy real or imagined ills, rest on the fringe between superstition and common sense folk medicine. Some of the herbs have no real therapeutic value; others are dangerously toxic; but some are used as active ingredients in "store bought" medicines. These herbs are found growing wild in the countryside or bought in urban stores known as *botánicas*, which feature a bizarre variety of merchandise. Herbs, such as mint and rue, are prepared as teas for intestinal disorders. Others are mixed with alcohol into *alcoholado* and rubbed on for aches and pains. The *botánicas* also sell incense, candles, and powders of different colors, which have alleged magical properties, and figurines of Christian, African, and Oriental symbols. Several *botánicas* flourish in New York City, where they attract a mixed clientele of Puerto Ricans, Cubans, Dominicans, Haitians, other West Indians, and some North Americans.

The spiritualist medium, who contacts the dead or analyzes a visiting stranger's troubles and offers advice, is another popular branch of the occult in Puerto Rico. Nathan Leopold, who researched this field on the island, writes that spiritualism had its roots among uneducated country people but the remarkable thing has been "the rapid spread, both geographic and social . . . [it] flourishes in the big cities as well . . . it has spread to the learned professions . . . many doctors, lawyers, and professors are firm believers." He tells of a small town near San Juan where one medium, a garbage truck driver who is also a brilliant conversationalist, holds *consultas* on Saturdays and general services on Sundays. People line up at 5 A.M., to be attended two hours later.

In some remote villages, semiliterate peasants harbor be-

liefs in witches and spirits; there are occasional touches of
African witchcraft culture in coastal areas inhabited by de-
cendants of slaves. Expanded medical services in the countryside have reduced the use of folk cures, but superstitions
associated with love and hate prevail. These are gradually
waning, however. People who swear to the existence of spirits
will often say that "they existed years ago, but not nowadays."

There is still considerable fear among the uneducated of
el mal del ojo ("the evil eye"). The greatest concern is for
attractive infants, who are the object of stares from covetous
strangers. To ward off this threat, some parents adorn the
child with a bracelet known as the *"asabache,"* which is
usually a jet-black bead or piece of plastic. It is said that this
practice dates back to ancient Egypt.

Perhaps the most powerful religious-mystical tie in Puerto
Rico and in other Latin American cultures is the *"compadrazgo,"* which, literally, means coparentage. It resembles
the concept of god-parentage among Christian North Americans, but is far more solemn. Parents will select *compadres*
("godfathers") and *comadres* ("godmothers"), generally,
when a child is baptized. This has strong practical reasons;
in times of crisis, which are frequent among poor families,
compadres can be counted upon to lend a helping hand. In
some cases, a poor family may seek out a rich *compadre*,
whose wealth or influence may at some time in the future
provide crucial aid to the godchild. The wealthy *compadre*
will usually accept, often out of friendship, sometimes to tap
the labor of his poorer *compadre*, who may be a worker on
his farm.

But the *compadrazgo* is more than a system of improvised
social security. It has a definite mystical quality. Two unrelated men who cultivate a deep friendship may wish to "seal"
it by becoming each other's *compadre*, without any baptism
being necessary. This is tantamount to adopting a new
brother. In some cases, even, a man fearing that a neighbor
friend is covetous of his wife, will try to neutralize his rival's
lust by making the potential rival his *compadre*. Cuckoldry
in such a case would be considered doubly treacherous and
evil. (This recalls the case of a promiscuous woman, a prosti-
tute, in one of Oscar Lewis' studies, who remarked that she
could not bring herself to make love to a man who was her
compadre.)

Casual acquaintances will sometimes call each other *compadre*, or *compai*, to express friendship, but the formal *compadre* relationship implies deep respect.

Language

One afternoon, an American resident of San Juan drove up to a gas station to have the spark plugs of his car changed. Having consulted a Spanish-English dictionary beforehand, he asked the attendent to put in new *bujías* and, in return, received a puzzled gaze. Finally, after the car owner lifted the hood and pointed, the attendant smiled and said, *"Ah! Los espares!,"* which is an Hispanicized version of "the sparks."

After seven decades under United States stewardship, Puerto Rico's Spanish is liberally sprinkled with English "loan words." English is a required second language in the schools. There are English-language publications and radio and television stations. Since the United States is the hemisphere's main producer of new technology and also dominates commerce, the island's Spanish vocabulary has had to stretch to accommodate words that describe new tools, processes, and products.

The degree of impact of the English language depends upon geography and economics. One hears less English in the countryside than in San Juan—and less among the poor, who have limited contact with schools and white collar jobs, two sources of English usage. One encounters more English (and often better Spanish) among the wealthier classes, who are involved in commerce or the professions and who may have studied at U.S. universities. Return migrants who have spent their formative years in the United States, may speak a tangle of both tongues, known as "Spanglish."

Spanish was the only language of any prominence used in Puerto Rico during the 400-year Spanish colonial period. But when the United States took over in 1898, it tried to use English instruction as a political tool to absorb Puerto Rico into the American governmental system. English was established as the official language in the schools, when neither the teachers nor the students understood a word of it. This was called the Clark Policy, after Education Commissioner Victor Clark. Two years later, a new commissioner, Martin Brum-

baugh, made Spanish the medium of instruction in the first
eight grades and English, from the ninth through the twelfth.
In 1905, Commissioner Roland Falkner went back to the
Clark Policy; but in 1916, Commissioner Paul Miller com-
promised and made Spanish the teaching language in grades
one through four, Spanish, and English in the fifth grade
and English in grades six through twelve.

In 1934, José Padín, a Puerto Rican, returned to the Brum-
baugh policy of 1900; and in 1937, José Gallardo began a
series of changes that, by 1942, made Spanish the teaching
medium in grades one through six. English was emphasized
in junior high school, and both English and Spanish were
used in the senior high schools.

In 1948, Puerto Rico's first native elected Governor appointed Commissioner Mariano Villaronga, who made Spanish the medium of instruction in all grades, with English as a
required second language, to be taught in special daily
classes.

Adrian Hull, an English-language specialist in Puerto Rico
notes that "practically every type of language policy for the
teaching of English in the public schools of Puerto Rico has
been tried with the exception of having English and Spanish
as the language of instruction on alternate days." And, he
adds, this possibility was suggested.

Although Spanish now prevails, English enjoys prestige
because of its monetary value. "Improve your personality,
learn English," was the sign of one adult night school in
Hato Rey. "Secretary: must be bilingual" is frequently seen
in newspaper want ads. An occasional ad will say that "Only
English is essential."

International teen culture also peppers local Spanish with
anglicisms. Urban youngsters talk about *jipis* ("hippies") and
memorize the song lyrics of the Supremes, the Beatles, Tom
Jones, and other pop music stars. The second most popular
radio station in San Juan features American pop music for
tineyers ("teenagers").

But, except for Spanish-speaking islanders who lived in
the United States, one senses that Spanish in Puerto Rico has
great resilient strength. External currents may add new
words, and even alter syntax, but it is highly unlikely that
Puerto Rico's "new Spanish" will be English.

Most educators agree that if Puerto Rican children were

better trained in Spanish they would more readily learn English, too, without any loss in the richness of the vernacular. But language instruction continues to be viewed as a political tool by all sides. Late in 1969, Governor Ferré flew back from Washington and announced that he was seeking Federal funds to expand English language instruction—to speed Puerto Rico on the way to statehood. The anti-English language reaction of the *independentistas*, following the Governor's nonpedagogical statement, was as inevitable as sundown following sunrise. Thus, Puerto Rico's language problem is much more than one of mere communication.

University of Puerto Rico philologist Rubén del Rosario does not think that the Spanish language here is in grave danger of disappearing, ". . . unless we should become a state of the Union, whereupon English would most certainly prevail within one hundred years."

He believes that the Spanish spoken in Puerto Rico, Cuba, and Santo Domingo are "basically alike, and the same as the rest of Latin America." As for frequent word mixing; there are many words such as *bar, coctel, record, standard,* and *ticket* which are used in almost all Hispanic nations. In Puerto Rico, only a few hundred English words are used; these in no way affect the basic structure of our language. Most of these foreign words refer to new ideas and new objects for which there was no traditional equivalent.

He notes that the common Spanish word for "rum"—*ron*—was imported from the British Antilles some hundred years ago. The word "*fohtró*," based on the American dance (foxtrot) of the 1920's, has evolved here into an idiom for "fight" or "tussle." The word "*plei*" (from the English "play") describes a party among friends or a romantic episode. "This type of word," he says, "is absorbed into our language and enriches it."

Puerto Rico's Spanish has also been enriched by at least 500 Indian words, most of which relate to flora and fauna. Some are used throughout Latin America, but others are 100 per cent Puerto Rican, such as "*guajana*," referring to the white tips of the sugarcane stalk. Puerto Rico has twenty-nine cities, including Arecibo, Guayama, Mayagüez, and Yauco, which have Indian names. Some African words—*bembe* ("big lip"), *quimbombó* ("okra"), and *guineo* ("banana") hark back to the epoch of slavery.

Puerto Rico has many other words, such as *agallarse* ("become ruffled and angry"), *chévere* ("great," "well-done") and *pon* ("hitchhike"), which are local inventions, resulting from the addition of prefixes or suffixes to existing words.

Population and Birth Control

Hormigueros, a small town in southeast Puerto Rico, has no space left to bury its dead. The few empty gravesites are reserved, and urban sprawl prevents expansion of the cemetery. Until new land is found, the dead of Hormigueros are taken to nearby Cabo Rojo, San Germán, or Mayagüez.

Hormigueros is a microcosm of the island's spiraling population problem. It took over 400 years after Columbus discovered Puerto Rico for the population to reach 1 million. Only forty years later, a second million was added. Today, there are 2.8 million people and a population density of 800 per square mile; at the present 2 per cent growth rate, the population will double within thirty-five years. Public health measures have cut infant mortality and stretched life expectancy. Each day, 190 infants are born and forty-four persons die, leaving a natural increase of more than 50,000 persons a year.

Were it not for the mass migration of Puerto Ricans to the mainland in the past two decades, the island would already have over 3.5 million people.

What looks like a population explosion is really, says one local writer, a "poverty explosion." The family whose parents graduated from high school has an average of 2.2 children. But parents who have not attended school bear an average of 6.3 children. Some poor families have as many as 15 or 20 children. Today, more than one person in three is under fifteen years of age. With relatively few wives working, this means that the male breadwinner must feed a large household.

Until 1939, it was a felony to offer birth prevention information in Puerto Rico. And just ten years ago, the Catholic Church declared such teachings a mortal sin. But pressed by reality, more and more Catholic-born politicians are listening to the views of Catholic-born doctors, economists, and planners, who, almost unanimously, favor some form of family planning.

As one of his first acts, Governor Ferré named a high-level committee to study the population problem, and its conclusion was that "drastic steps are necessary." While rejecting enforced birth control, it recommended a vigorous program of birth control education and cheap government supplies of contraceptives.

Such a program has already been successful on a smaller scale in the past three years. Close to 50,000 women have been included in "family-planning," or "family-spacing," programs. Without fanfare, the Health Department opened sixteen clinics in one of the island's five regions, the Northeast, which includes the metropolitan San Juan area. New mothers were told about "family spacing" and, "after consulting with their husbands and their own conscience," could choose from a variety of birth control methods. The new program will expand services to the island's other four health regions. Health Department officials predict a 6,000 drop in births the first year, which will relax some of the future pressure on schools and other social services.

The pioneer in Puerto Rico's population control program is the privately run Family Planning Association, which, since its establishment in 1948, has been strongly attacked by the church. The Association has offices in sixty of the island's seventy-seven towns, serving over 30,000 mothers with free information and contraceptives. As government clinics expand to all regions, this organization will be gradually phased out.

Patterns of Living

A generation ago, when most Puerto Ricans lived in the countryside *"el pueblo,"* the nearest town, consisted of a plaza surrounded by a church, the municipal hall, a few stores, and a scattering of homes.

As Puerto Rico became industrialized, one-family homes cropped up around the cities. Pastures gave way to tidal waves of new "bedroom communities," a short drive from town.

More than twenty thousand new dwellings are built each year, three times as many as in 1950; of these, one fourth are low-cost homes for the poor, built by the government. Private housing investment has quadrupled in a decade, and home-building represents 8 per cent of the gross product, twice the United States ratio.

The new executive elite has created a demand for lavish suburban homes and luxury high-rise apartments in San Juan. The housing boom is felt everywhere, but mostly in the 70-square-mile San Juan area, the core of a megalopolis that creeps westward along the coast to encompass Bayamón, eastward to Carolina, and south to Caguas. Many of the "suburbs," known as *urbanizaciones*, have their own shopping centers, churches, and schools. Whatever planners neglect to include is quickly added by the residents. Corner homes, or those on main avenues, are soon converted into barber shops, beauty parlors, real estate offices, grocery stores, bars, and auto parts dealers. Open-air carports are soon walled in, or second floors added, to accommodate a newborn child, an elderly parent, or as a rental unit. Thanks to year-round summer weather, muddy tracts soon blossom forth lawns, palm trees, and flowers.

Housing costs climb so rapidly that the moderate-income family must buy at the fringe of the suburbs. The poor cannot afford urban homes built by private enterprise. The cost of housing has gone up 7.2 per cent a year. The kind of home sought by the average American family costs over $30,000 in Puerto Rico. Condominium apartments near the beach start at $40,000.

Land costs now represent 34 per cent of a new home's cost, which is nearly double the U.S. average. By 1972, the cheapest private homes in Puerto Rico will cost $16,300; a family will need a yearly income of $6,000 to quality for a mortage. Only one family in five earns that much today.

Housing Conditions

Puerto Rico's young, fast-growing populace assures a continued demand for housing. In the next four years, over nine thousand new homes will be needed just to absorb the new population, without denting the large backlog of substandard homes.

In Puerto Rico's cities alone, over 40 per cent of the 393,700 dwellings are classified as "inadequate," or "deficient." Many of these are shacks on the edge of town, built on marshland or creek bottoms, or on steep hillsides, and lacking in sanitary facilities. They often consist of scrap lumber and metal, although some owners improve them with concrete blocks. The number of urban shacks continues to grow as the poor flow in from the hills and procreate at high levels.

Nine out of ten urban families who live in "inadequate" homes cannot afford to buy a home built by a private developer. Some of these families, who earn from $2,600 to $5,000 a year (considered the "moderate income range" in Puerto Rico; quality for low-cost homes with long-term government financing. But most of the poor earn less than that, and qualify only for the low-rent apartments called *caseríos*, which now house 40,000 families. Over 11,000 families are on the waiting lists for *caserío* dwellings, and it appears that many of them have a long wait in store. In fact, if the current rates of slum growth and public housing construction continue, the number of slum houses—although they will represent a smaller portion of all housing—will not diminish within the next half century.

The Slums

In Puerto Rico, a slum is called an *arrabal*. Thousands of island families still live in *arrabales* in the midst, or on the edge, of the cities.

Despite the hardship of urban poverty, some slum founders displayed a sense of humor in naming their communities. "La Perla" means The Pearl. One of the worst-smelling slums is called Buenos Aires ("Good Airs"). Other slums are called—in translation—Good Advice, Black Ass, Boston Braves, and Vietnam.

Puerto Rico's worst slum belt is located along the banks of the Martín Peña Channel, which begins at San Juan Bay and flows eastward for a few miles, emptying into the San José Lagoon. In this area of marshes and stagnant water, 71,000 people live in 14,000 tightly packed homes. The Martín Peña slum has the city's highest infant mortality rate, the greatest number of welfare cases, the highest rates of tuberculosis, pneumonia, delinquency, and violence. The slum emerged during the Depression years, and experienced startling growth in the 1950's. Most of the homes were built illegally on public land, of scrap wood and metal, with flimsy partitions for walls. Late arrivals built closest to the water, sometimes driving wooden piles into the black muck of contaminated water. The people use outdoor privies, and sidewalks consist of crude plank bridges above the water, which is full of garbage and human waste; much of the area is inaccessible to garbage pickup trucks. A few of the Martín Peña residents own their shacks, which have an average value of $1,400, but most families rent them, for an average of $23 a month. Newcomers may buy a crumbling shack for $100, to gain the land beneath it. After paying a $25 fine for clandestine construction (which, by now, is considered part of building costs), they will slowly fix it up. Municipal authorities, in a dilemma between obvious legal violations and the plight of the poor (who also vote), provide building materials, such as planks and roofing paper, as well as light and water outlets.

La Perla slum on the Atlantic Coast in Old San Juan is elegant by comparison with Martín Peña. Located on steep seaside banks, separated from the city by thick Spanish colonial fortification walls, La Perla is a labyrinthine Caribbean Casbah of 900 houses, with a population of 3,300. The beach is filthy, strewn with driftwood and garbage, an ideal site for the pigs that some families raise there. But a constant sea breeze eliminates the stench, which overwhelms the newcomer in some parts of the Martín Peña area. Despite poverty and high levels of violence, the general mood in La Perla is one of gaiety. There is constant noise from radios, jukeboxes, and television sets. Some homes are so closely packed together, that one may see an elderly woman gazing out her window and into the window of a neighbor to watch an afternoon soap opera on television. Most of La Perla is served by electricity and water, and the narrow streets permit garbage trucks to descend from the city above for regular pickups.

A recent study of 100 "multiproblem" slum dwellers gives a profile of the slum resident who lives in extreme poverty. Most were born in the country and migrated to San Juan between 1939 and 1951; 22 per cent are unemployed; nine out of ten are Catholic, but also practice spiritualism. Many own TV sets and refrigerators, but few own cars. They spend half of their limited income on clothing. All buy on credit and owe about 10 per cent of their income to installment debts. They have only tenuous contact with rural relatives. Half the 100 persons studied did not visit their relatives even once a year. Two-thirds of those with relatives in New York—sometimes a mother, father, or brother—did not know their New York address. If asked, most slum dwellers want to "get out." But few know how.

Puerto Rico has high hopes for the Model Cities Program,

an ambitious federally funded plan to rehabilitate slums in several American cities. San Juan was chosen because the low income and poor housing of many of its residents qualify it as a socioeconomic "disaster area."

The program aims to improve the lives of five thousand families in the Martín Peña slum belt and in the nearby Nemesio Canales public housing project. Unemployment is about 40 per cent, and monthly income averages $200 in these areas.

The multimillion dollar Model Cities Program will spend an average of $13,000 per family in services to provide health, welfare, employment, education, and job sources.

But, according to Howard Stanton, a social scientist who worked on parts of the plan, hundreds of millions of dollars more "will be spent on quite different programs," such as express highways and swirling intersections, requiring the relocation of perhaps half the families. Stanton feels that this uprooting, plus the services administered by well-paid middle class technicians to the poor may cause more trouble than it solves. He suggests that, while it might not be the best approach, giving each poor family its $13,000 in cash "might work better."

Income and Welfare

Income in Puerto Rico has multiplied tenfold since 1940, but is still far below U.S. levels, and is less equitably distributed.

Between 1953 and 1963, for example, personal income went up by 65 per cent. But the "lower class" (the 45 per cent of the families who earned $2,000 or less a year; received only 16 per cent of the island's total wages, compared with 18 per cent a decade before. The "middle class" (the 45 per cent of the families who earned from $2,000 to $6,800 a year) had increased their share from 47 to 49 per cent. The "upper class," (the 10 per cent of the families earning over $6,800 a year) still earn about 35 per cent of total income.

Unemployment (without mentioning thousands of persons who are underemployed, working less than thirty-five hours a week, or who are permanently out of the labor force) has wavered between 10 and 13 per cent for many years. The average jobless male has only six years of schooling; one-eighth of the island's adults have had no schooling at all, which guarantees that at least that portion of the populace will, for a long time to come, be marginal to the society and depend upon some form of welfare.

The standard of living has risen sufficiently, and items of clothing are reasonably enough priced for even the poorest man to wear shoes, a clean pair of slacks, and sportshirt. But many of these "well-dressed poor" walk around with empty pockets, and stomachs much the same.

Welfare Payments. The Commonwealth Government, with limited funds of its own, plus meager supplements from Washington, must spread welfare payments thin. For the 86,502 people (aged, blind, disabled, and dependent children) who received aid in 1966, the average payment was about $3 a week.

There is a widespread impression that most health and welfare benefits come from Washington. But in 1966, Puerto Rico spent $86 million of its own funds ($59 million on health and $27 million on welfare), compared with only $15.8 million from the U.S. mainland treasury. The U.S. contribution was only .5 per cent of the total Federal outlay of $3.19 billion that year. On the basis of population size, without even mentioning need, Puerto Rico should receive three times as much. But ceilings established by Congress, in 1950, severely limit the total amount of aid that Puerto Rico may receive. The island must also usually match Federal aid on a 50–50 basis, while the U.S. states pay as little as $.17 for each Federal aid dollar and have no ceiling limits.

In 1966, while Washington spent $15.8 million in Puerto Rico, it sent $45.9 million to Mississippi and $112 million to Oklahoma, states which have less people than Puerto Rico and higher per capita income. While Puerto Rico's aged, blind, and disabled get about $13.25 a month, recipients in the nine U.S. states at the bottom of the scale average $50 monthly, which was called "woefully inadequate" by President Johnson in his 1966 message to Congress on older Americans.

Since residents of Puerto Rico do not pay Federal taxes, many Congressmen feel that the island should not share in programs to which it does not contribute.

However, Santiago Polanco Abreu, who was Puerto Rico's Resident Commissioner to Washington until 1968, claims that this argument has "little relevance." He says that Puerto Rico contributes to the U.S. general welfare "in many ways," by being a major U.S. export customer, by sending its sons to fight in the U.S. Armed Forces, and "besides, welfare residents cannot pay taxes anyway. It would be a strange system, that determined welfare eligibility by the amount of Federal taxes the perspective recipients were fortunate enough to be paying."

Puerto Rico was totally excluded from a 1966 amendment to the Social Security Act, which pays monthly benefits to uninsured persons age seventy-two or over. Puerto Rico was again excluded in 1967, when the amendment was re-amended, to increase monthly payments up to $75 a month.

In 1969, when President Nixon announced plans for a new type of guaranteed income plan for the poor, no mention was made, at first, of Puerto Rico. When officials in Washington were pressed, they said the island would participate, but that Puerto Rico's poor would get "somewhere around 55 per cent" of the benefits per capita compared with the mainland poor.

On the basis of its per capita income, Puerto Rico devotes a large portion of its resources to welfare. It spends $6.64 per $1,000 of personal income, compared to a U.S. mainland average of $4.86. But since it is working from such a small base, its payments are scanty, especially in the San Juan area, where the cost of living surpasses that of most American cities.

A not untypical case of the meager help provided by public welfare in Puerto Rico is that of Agripina Carrión, a forty-year-old woman, interviewed recently in a local newspaper. Agripina Carrión lives in a public housing project with five children; her husband abandoned her eight years ago. Her lone source of income is a $37.25 monthly welfare check. One son, eighteen years old, dropped out of school after the sixth grade and is jobless. Another son, nineteen, who is an invalid and confined to a wheelchair, suffers from calcium deficiency and is getting worse. Their home is a three-bedroom public housing apartment, which is virtually bare, except for some scattered pieces of torn-up furniture. Mrs. Carrión pays her $6.50 monthly rent without fail. She pays $4 a month for electricity. The rest goes for food and clothing. She also receives a Federal food package, which includes rice, butter, wheat and corn flour, beans, and canned meats. She buys the rest at a nearby *colmado* (grocery store) on credit and usually owes $20 by the time the check arrives. Neither she nor her invalid son eat lunch. They awaken late, have coffee, bread and butter, perhaps an egg. That is all until suppertime. Her three young daughters eat a free lunch at school, provided by another Federal program. Her typical supper is rice, beans, and, perhaps, some canned meat or sausage. Once or twice a month they have a treat of fresh meat, usually chicken.

Surplus Food Program. The food Mrs. Carrión receives comes from surplus commodities distributed by the U.S. Department of Agriculture, in a program costing about $20 million yearly. Twenty-two different food products are given out monthly to nearly 500,000 people at seventy-nine distribution centers throughout the island. This program reaches people on relief, patients in medical and mental clinics, and children in day care centers. The food packages rarely last the entire month, but the items are appreciated by the poor. Many complain, however, that they cannot stomach the canned powdered milk (a number of poor in the country, or in the slums, feed this milk to pigs they raise in their backyards). Other recipients have picketed welfare offices, showing cheese, beans, corn meal, and rice that was infested with worms and maggots.

Michael Myerson

PUERTO RICO,
OUR BACKYARD COLONY*

Citizens of San Juan were not surprised when they awak-
ened one morning early this February to find that the Selective Service office, the local branch of General Electric and a
portion of the El San Juan Hilton Hotel had all been bombed.
Such attacks, carried out by a group calling itself Armed
Commandos for Liberation (CAL), have become a fact of
daily life in Puerto Rico. As the movement for independence
from the U.S. has gained in momentum, more than a hundred
bombings, the majority aimed at American corporations, have
shaken the island over the past year alone. Of all the targets
for this assault, one of the most obvious has been the popular
image of Puerto Rico as the "happy commonwealth"—a sultry
playground for American tourists and the showcase of U.S.-
guided progress in the Caribbean. While the dust from the
first pro-independence explosions was still settling, more and
more Puerto Ricans, especially the young, were beginning to
see how this tourbook rhetoric was used to conceal the bitter
fact that their island was and is the only classic colony in
the American experience.

[I]

For Puerto Ricans, colonial status is nothing new. They
have spent the last five centuries under the rule of one Western country or another. Puerto Rico came close to achieving
independence in the late 1800s, winning an autonomous constitution from Spain, only to lose it a year later when the
island was "ceded" to the U.S. as part of the spoils of victory

* Michael Myerson, "Puerto Rico, Our Backyard Colony." *Ramparts*
(June 1970). Reprinted with permission.

in the Spanish-American War. Ruled first by the U.S. military, then by presidential appointees and only recently by an elected governor, Puerto Ricans have had little power over the fate of their island; they were even made U.S. citizens over the objection of their one elected body.

Today the island legislature's powers are limited to traffic regulations and the like. Real political power resides in the U.S. House Committee on Insular Affairs and the Senate Committee on Territorial and Insular Affairs, both of which meet in Washington, D.C., some 1500 miles from San Juan. Appeals from Puerto Rican courts are decided in Boston and final jurisdiction rests with the U.S. Supreme Court.

U.S. federal agencies control the country's foreign relations, customs, immigration, post office system, communications, radio, television, commerce, transportation, maritime laws, military service, social security, banks, currency and defense —all of this without the people of Puerto Rico having a vote in U.S. elections.

The extent of U.S. military control of the country is particularly striking. One cannot drive five miles in any direction without running into an army base, nuclear site or tracking station. Green Berets were recently discovered in the famed El Yunque National Rain Forest, presumably using the island as a training ground.

The Pentagon controls 13 per cent of Puerto Rico's land and has five atomic bases, including Ramey Air Base. A major base for the Strategic Air Command, Ramey includes in its confines everything from guided missiles to radio jamming stations which prevent Radio Havana from reaching Puerto Rico and Santo Domingo. In addition to the major bases, there are about 100 medium and small military installations, training camps, and radar and radio stations.

In the late 1940s, Puerto Rico became the target of Operation Bootstrap. Hailed as an economic "New Deal" for the island, Bootstrap bore the kind of name that encourages Americans to believe unquestioningly in their country's selfless generosity to other peoples. In truth, the new program was a textbook-perfect example of imperialism, guaranteeing tax-free investment to U.S. firms developing the island as a market for U.S. goods. (As the Wall Street Journal put it: "Two million potential customers live on Puerto Rico, but the hopeful industrial planners see it as the shopping center for the entire Caribbean population of 13 million.") While it fed America's sense of self-righteousness and brought profits to U.S. investors, Bootstrap left untouched the misery of the majority of Puerto Rico's 2.5 million inhabitants. In fact, by limiting the development of the island's economy and forcing continual dependence on the U.S., Bootstrap deepened the cycle of poverty in Puerto Rico.

Over one million *boriqueños* have left their native land for the *barrios* of East Harlem and South Bronx. That one-third of a nation would escape into exile to the slums of New York testifies to the living conditions in the Caribbean "paradise."

Four out of every five Puerto Rican families earn less than $3000 per year; one half receive less than $1000 annually. Oscar Lewis puts unemployment at 14 per cent; knowledgeable Puerto Ricans insist that a figure as high as 30 per cent is more realistic. That is a permanent condition twice as bad as the depths of the Great Depression in this country. Per capita income in Mississippi, our poorest state, was 81 per cent higher than in Puerto Rico in 1960. Whereas wages are a fraction of those on the mainland, the cost of living on the island is higher. Most statistics place island costs at 25 per cent higher than those in New York, Chicago or Boston.

Housing for most Puerto Ricans is abominable. In many a rural town, the only livable building is the town jail. Even government agencies consider 46 per cent of Puerto Rico's housing to be inadequate. Not atypical is the Los Chinos district of Ponce (Puerto Rico's second largest city), one of several slum areas, made up of thousands of one-room dirt-floor shacks inhabited by eight- and ten-member families. Groups of these families share a single outdoor toilet.

To most tourists, San Juan *is* Puerto Rico, and the Condado district (the strip of luxury hotels that accommodate tourists in increasing numbers each year) *is* San Juan. But within walking distance of the Caribe Hilton and the Flamboyan Hotel on the Condado are some of the worst slums in the Americas. Their picturesque names throw into bold relief the horror of their reality—La Perla (The Pearl), Los Bravos de Boston, etc. One slum, El Fangito, stretches for five miles along a rat-infested swamp which seeps with San Juan's sewage.

On a walk through Los Bravos de Boston, I met a woman standing outside what can only euphemistically be called a house. Made of bulletin board, sealed together with bailing wire and topped by a sheet of tin, the shack would have been blown over by a healthy gust of wind. The wretched home, six by six feet, housed the woman, her husband and two babies. As we spoke, an infant slept outside at our feet, his bed the basket of a rusty shopping cart. The mother, in a state of despair, had learned only that morning that the government was going to move the shack elsewhere that day, and there was no way to contact her husband, a construction worker, to tell him where to come when his day ended.

If it does little to improve the lot of the poor, Bootstrap has by any standards been a bargain for investors. Offering U.S. firms cheap labor and tax "holidays" of 10 to 17 years, Bootstrap was hailed by Hubert Humphrey as the "miracle of the Caribbean."

As the colonial government reports: "Manufacturers average 30 per cent on their investment—thanks to the productivity of Puerto Rico's three-quarter million willing, able workers. Profits in electronics run 10.8 times those of the mainland industry's average." Every dollar invested has brought a profit of 30 cents during the first year. U.S. investments in Puerto Rico are the highest—after Venezuela—in all of Latin America.

For every dollar produced in the island's industrial system, only 17 cents is left in Puerto Rico. Only Britain, Canada, Japan and West Germany import more U.S. goods. This island of les than three million people buys more from us than do Spain, Portugal, Austria, Ireland and the four Scandinavian nations combined.

Sugar and petroleum account for most of the country's industry. The sugar industry, controlled by three U.S. companies (the Central Aguirre Sugar Company, owned by the First National Bank of Boston; C. Brewer & Company; and the South Puerto Rico Sugar Company of New Jersey, the largest owner of cane plantations in the world), is a classroom model of neo-colonialism. It accounts for half the island's agricultural income—a fact determined not by the agricultural needs of the island but by the U.S. sugar quota. Impoverished Puerto Rican plantation workers chop the cane for tax-free U.S. companies, ship the raw product to the States where it is refined, packaged and taxed, and then buy back the finished product at exorbitant prices.

Only the petrochemical industry has seen a bigger growth in Puerto Rico, with heavy investments from every major U.S.

petroleum corporation—Phillips, Union Carbide, Texaco, Standard, etc. Virtually ringing the Caribbean coast of the island in search of offshore oil, they have caused severe pollution in some of the best fishing waters in the world. This, together with the fact that the federal government prohibits Puerto Rico from maintaining its own fishing fleet, has resulted in the island's being forced to import 95 per cent of the fish it consumes.

Early in the 1950s, huge copper deposits were discovered in the interior. American Metal Climax and Kennicott Copper, operating through subsidiaries, moved in, taking exclusive rights to the deposits. Comparable in size to the largest deposits in this country, their ore value is higher than any in the United States. The deposits are worth at least $1.5 billion; American Metal Climax paid Puerto Rico just ten dollars for an exploration permit.

News of the deposits and of the negotiations between the two companies and the government was kept secret until the Pro-Independence Movement got word of the talks and began a public campaign. Through picketing, diplomatic protests and local organizing, the independentists have for four years successfully prevented the companies from starting production. Although the contract has not been signed yet, speculation is that with 64-year-old millionaire industrialist Luis Ferré as the new governor, the signing is imminent.

Washington propaganda has always held that Puerto Rico has no riches, that it needs the United States, hence independence is unreasonable. Now Japan has offered the country a better deal on its copper than have the U.S. companies, but its colonial position prohibits Puerto Rico from engaging in foreign trade. Undoubtedly, its oil, sugar, tobacco and coffee could also attract better prices if offered competitively. There seems no way to check or reverse the depletion of Puerto Rico's riches other than independence. The major argument against independence, aside from lack of natural wealth, has been the size of the country. But Puerto Rico has more people than the island nations of Cyprus and Jamaica; than eight Latin American countries, including Paraguay, Costa Rica and Panama; than some 32 member states of the United Nations, including Laos, Israel, Jordan, Albania and Lebanon.

[II]

Leading the drive for independence from U.S. domination is the Movimiento Pro-Independencia of Puerto Rico (MPI). A prominently displayed painting dominates the offices of the MPI in San Juan. The picture, depicting the Ponce Massacre of March 1937 when police beat and killed nationalist demonstrators, was painted by Fran Cervoni, one of Puerto Rico's most important artists and a member of MPI's Political Commission. Only part of the painting remains as the artist rendered it, the canvas having been salvaged from the fire which destroyed the MPI headquarters in November 1965. Nobody one encounters has the slightest doubt that the arsonists were agents of the U.S. Central Intelligence Agency.

Today, new fires are being set in Puerto Rico, but this time the flames are spreading in a different direction. Since New Year's Eve 1967, at least 75 fires aimed at North American properties have caused damage ranging in estimates from 25 to 75 million dollars. No one has been caught; no evidence has been found; no witnesses have come forth. But a group calling itself the Armed Commandos for Liberation (CAL) has taken credit for the action. To the chagrin of the propertied, no one can prove who belongs to CAL, although the press has attempted to tie the group to MPI. Police have even arrested local MPI leaders in connection with the bombings, but were forced to release them for lack of anything resembling evidence.

The island, already blanketed by CIA and FBI agents, has practically suffocated with the massive invasion of reinforcements from those two agencies. The Wackenhut Corporation, a Miami-based security firm, boosted its guard force by 40 per cent in less than a year, the bulk going to watch over U.S. holdings in Puerto Rico. Bargain Town, one of whose stores was fire-bombed, now has Burns Agency guards, equipped with fire masks and with fire-fighting equipment, both inside and outside its stores 24 hours a day. Still the bombings continue.

The goal, says CAL leader Alfonso Beal, is to make it so costly to stay in Puerto Rico that they leave. "We are in the first stage of operations," he says, "and in this phase we intend to cause $100 million worth of damage to U.S. concerns. Our idea is to inflict such heavy losses on these enterprises that the insurance companies will have to pay more money in indemnity than they have received in payment, thus upsetting the economy."

On September 23, 1968, the centenary of the Grito de Lares, the rebellion against Spanish colonialism, CAL issued a statement declaring the tourist strip of Condado a "zone of war" and asking Puerto Ricans to stay out, "especially in the evening hours." At an open-air ceremony commemorating the Grito de Lares that same afternoon, attended by some 20,000 *independentistas*, Juan Mari Bras, MPI general secretary, paid tribute to those who have begun to engage in the highest form of struggle, armed struggle. The crowd took up the chant: "Fuego! Fuego! Fuego! Fire! Fire! Fire!"

The cadres of MPI are serious revolutionaries. They are dedicated, committed to the long-range struggle, have very few illusions about their "objective reality" and are terribly energetic. This is true both of the top leadership and of the activists.

In Aguadilla, a town 60 miles west of San Juan, in the northwest corner of the rectangular island, MPI has established the José de Diego Mission. There are some two dozen such central missions scattered throughout Puerto Rico supported by twice as many "partiotic missions." A central mission is one with its own headquarters, the facilities to print leaflets and the organization to distribute literature. Patriotic missions are groups of cadres in the surrounding towns who, working out of the central missions, strive to expand their organization to the point that they have strength enough to become central missions themselves.

The Aguadilla mission has, in addition to the familiar posters of Latin revolutionary heroes, the slogan in large black letters: "Diablos, No! No Iremos!" (Hell No, We Won't Go!) The town is located on the coast, and the shacks pile on top of one another, ascending to the peak of the hill overlooking the Atlantic. The slums get poorer as the landscape rises. At the top stands the pride of the Diego Mission—the first *zona libre* (free zone) of Puerto Rico. Made up of clusters of the worst shanties in Aguadilla, the zone's official name is Cerra Villa Nuevo. It has been organized by MPI, which now has the near-unanimous backing of the people there. Today, the police no longer venture into Cerra Villa Nuevo.

Many hundreds of families populate the free zone (the

total population of Aguadilla is placed at around 50,000).
The dirt paths that pass for roads are filled with mangy,
limping dogs, pigs and goats. Due to the continuing expansion
of U.S. military bases, tracking stations and radio intelligence
centers, land is becoming scarce and the rural poor are being
forced off their land and herded into already overcrowded
city slums. Aguadilla is faced with massive unemployment
and the figures extend far above the estimated 30 per cent
for the whole of the island.

On the day I met him, Julio Alvarez, one of Cerra Villa
Nuevo's most active MPI cadres, was on trial for burning the
U.S. flag. In contrast to the severe penalties dealt out to
Julio's contemporaries in the States for similar offenses, the
young man only received a fine of $25. The courts apparently
fear to tread on Puerto Rican national feeling.

Julio's shack in the free zone, perhaps a dozen feet square,
contains a "kitchen with a mini-stove and an outdoor sink
which one must stretch out of the window to reach. Boiling
on the stove was a pot of yucca root, Julio's dinner. One wall
features a half-dozen water colors painted by Julio. His book-
shelf, a made-over produce crate, contains Dostoyevsky's
House of the Dead, The Idiot and *The Brothers Karamazov;*
some works of Cervantes; and books on Monet, Manet and
Turner. Whatever else life denies him, Julio Alvarez's intellectual pursuits will continue. It is Julio and hundreds of his
neighbors who comprise the population of the island's first
zona libre.

Women are conspicuously few in the movement's leadership, not an uncommon situation on the Latin continent. One
of the exceptions is Lucila Andino, the 25-year-old director
of the Carolina Mission. Her district stretches perhaps 25
miles east to Luquillo, the town surrounding Puerto Rico's
most famous and luscious strip of beach. Included in the area
is the village of Loiza Aldea, which must be reached by raft.
Loiza is populated almost entirely by black Puerto Ricans,
and the origin of this ethnic make-up is a subject of constant
speculation. Consensus generally holds that a slave ship cap-
sized off Loiza's coast and the slaves that made it to shore
settled in the area; it then became a haven for runaway slaves.

Lucila is one of two female mission directors of MPI; the
second heads the organization in Mayaguez. Puerto Rico's
fourth largest city. Perhaps a major reason for this lack of

women cadres in the movement, aside from the obvious one of the general status of women in Puerto Rican society, is that much of the recent growth of MPI has come through its anti-draft activities. In 1966, a young worker named Sixto Alvelo became the colony's first draft resister. Within a year, MPI's newspaper *Claridad* printed a full-page advertisement listing the signatures of 1000 Puerto Rican youths who joined the Resistance. They stated their refusal to recognize what they consider to be a colonial draft, to serve in a foreign army, and they expressed their solidarity with the South Vietnam National Liberation Front. (In 1965, MPI had established a fraternal relationship with the NLF.) The ranks of the thousand have since been swelled much beyond that. Rarely does a day go by when a young resister is not arrested.

                    ✿   ✿   ✿

One of MPI's most encouraging recent developments is the success of FEPI, the high school independence movement. The high school organization serves not only to radicalize the hundreds of thousands of young people (half the island's population is under 25); it is also provides the movement with a major wedge into the working class and peasantry.

Ponce is Governor Ferré's town and main base. In addition to his cement factories and his newspaper, *El Dia*, he has uncounted real estate holdings, foundries and much of the most costly land in the city. Yet here too the MPI is extremely active.

In the slums of Los Chinos, and in La Playa near the Caribbean, as throughout the city of Ponce, the MPI mission conducts nightly "ciné-meetings." In the twilight hours, portable bulletin boards filled with news, posters and photographs are set up at a given intersection. As night falls, speakers make a brief presentation of the movement's program and ask for support, and then projectors show films, imported from Cuba and Vietnam, projected onto the wall of a windowless building. As many as 600 neighbors come to these meetings, even though chances are good that they will be interrogated by the FBI the following day.

                    ✿   ✿   ✿

MPI insists that social justice and independence will not be achieved through the established electoral process, for whatever laws are passed in San Juan are subject to approval by Washington. At election time, the movement is actively engaged in promoting the boycott as a political weapon. There are the remnants still of the independentist electoral party, PIP, but it has pretty much deteriorated as MPI gains strength and as the reality of the colonial situation becomes ever more apparent. Little more than 40 per cent of the eligible voters are registered and of that number only perhaps half bother to cast their ballots.

While MPI is firm in its principled opposition to the colonial establishment, it maintains active supporters within the establishment. These are referred to as its *segundo nivel*, its second-level membership. In the political parties, the government and the press, the second level acts as a source of intelligence for MPI, letting it know of impending arrests or shady government dealings. In 1967, for example, *Claridad*, the movement's weekly paper, broke the story of the hitherto undisclosed discovery of copper in the center of the island.

It is the work in the copper areas and the slums, and similar organization among the petroleum workers, that has brought about the radicalization of MPI and the search for fundamental social change, say movement spokesmen. In April 1968, Juan Mari Bras announced that MPI would uphold the right of Puerto Rico to use any methods, including armed struggle, to achieve its independence. In the midst of a press campaign to determine who was behind the recent wave of bombings, and attempts to tie MPI to CAL, the announcement caused a sensation.

MPI calls itself the "Patriotic vanguard" of Puerto Rico. That is to say, it is the nationalist cause and urge that gives it life. But it is internationalist in outlook. Besides its pact of solidarity with the NLF in South Vietnam, the movement has representatives on the executive committees of the Organization of Solidarity with the Peoples of Asia, Africa and Latin America, and the Latin American Students' Organization, both based in Havana.

As Mari Bras says, "Puerto Rico is battling against time in its struggle to save its nationhood." Only a crisis in the U.S. colonial system will force independence. The sort of crisis MPI speaks of in this regard is a massive unified demand by the island's people that makes their outright colonial status an embarrassment to the United States. The only force that can create the crisis, MPI believes, is the working class when it is organized. The development of workers' cadres is to be a main focus of the organization from now on.

The United States does not want a Puerto Rico free and

independent to determine its own course. Nor, says Mari Bras, does it want a state with its own nationality. But the Yankees too see the possibility of a crisis developing in its system. So it attempts to destroy the Puerto Rican nationality through its military-economic-cultural penetration of the island. If the United States should succeed in its offensive, it could then grant Puerto Rico statehood at the point of crisis.

Meanwhile, the Movimiento Pro-Independencia organizes in the slums of the cities and the hovels of the countryside, among university and high school students, and in the growing industrial working class. They are, they say, a patriotic vanguard leading a national struggle of survival. While nationalism is the cause and self-reliance the urgent need, MPI is by no means unaware of the role of anti-imperalist North Americans. In fact, they see it as our responsibility to fight with them for independence. Ultimately, says one MPI leader, "What you do in the United States may well determine the fate of Puerto Rico's nationhood."

PART II:

THE MIGRATION

Eva E. Sandis

CHARACTERISTICS OF PUERTO RICAN MIGRANTS TO, AND FROM, THE UNITED STATES[*][1]

According to the 1960 Census, there were 617,056 first-generation Puerto Ricans living in the United States.[2] Although they made up less than one per cent of the total population of the United States, the migrants and their 275,457 United States-born offspring equalled 27.5 per cent of all Puerto Ricans—those on the Island plus those on the mainland—in 1960.[3] Since they constitute such a large proportion of the total population of Puerto Ricans, the selective characteristics of the migrants have significant implications for their own adjustment in the United States and for Puerto Rico's future.

A steady stream of return migration has complemented the migration stream to the United States. Although the return migrant stream is smaller in size, at least 145,000—or five per cent—of the Island's inhabitants in 1965 were return

[*] Eva E. Sandis, "Characteristics of Puerto Rican Migrants to, and from, the United States," *International Migration Review*, vol. 4 (1970), pp. 22–42. Reprinted with permission.

[1] This research was supported by a grant from the United States Office of Education to the Center for Educational Research at The University of Puerto Rico, Rio Piedras. The author is indebted to Joseph P. Fitzpatrick and Nathan Kantrowitz of Fordham University, Robert J. Havighurst of the University of Chicago, and José L. Vázquez Calzada of the University of Puerto Rico, for their comments and criticisms of earlier drafts of this paper.

[2] Although technically, Puerto Ricans are United States citizens and Puerto Rico is politically a part of the United States, the term United States is used here to refer only to the mainland, or continental United States.

[3] According to the 1960 Census, the Island population comprised 2,349,544 inhabitants.

migrants, according to a reliable estimate.[4] The socio-economic and motivational characteristics of the return migrants also may have significant implications for Puerto Rican society. It is important, then, to determine what these characteristics are. The injection of an occupational and educational elite back into the Island, for example, will create specific demands for jobs, housing, schools for children, and other institutional facilities. In addition, such return migrants may have considerable influence on the rate and direction of social change.

This paper presents a resumé of available data on the socio-economic and motivational characteristics of Puerto Rican migrants to the United States, as compared with the Island inhabitants; and a resumé of the characteristics of Puerto Rican return migrants, as compared with those who remain on the mainland. Presentation of these comparisons will reveal substantive gaps in our knowledge, as well as methodological weaknesses which affect the reliability of the data on which the comparisons are based. Hopefully, this discussion will lead to a renewed effort to fill the substantive gaps, and overcome the methodological difficulties, which currently exist in this field of research.

DATA SOURCES

The main source of information about the socio-economic characteristics of Puerto Rican migrants living in the United States is the U.S. Census of Population. Data on the migrants is contained in the subject reports on Puerto Ricans in the United States.[5]

There is no equivalent Census volume on Puerto Rican return migrants living in Puerto Rico. However, Hernández made special tabulations of original data from the Puerto Rican Census of 1960, to obtain data comparable to those for Puerto Rican migrants living in the United States. For purposes of his analysis, return migrants were defined as "persons born in Puerto Rico, residing in the United States in 1955, and

---

[4] José Hernández Alvarez, *Return Migration to Puerto Rico*. Institute for International Studies, University of California, Berkeley, 1967, 17.

[5] The most recent data are contained in: U.S. Bureau of the Census, *U.S. Census of Population, 1960, Subject Reports, Puerto Ricans in the United States*, Final Report PC (2), Washington, D.C.: U.S. Government Printing Office, 1963.

returning to the island and resettling there prior to April 1, 1960."[6]

The main advantage of Census data for investigating the socio-economic characteristics of migrants is their wide coverage and comprehensive scope. Their greatest drawback, for this purpose, is their static nature. In dealing with such variables as the educational and occupational characteristics of migrants, one cannot determine, from Census data, whether they are selective—differentiate migrants from nonmigrants prior to their departure to the United States—or the result of assimilation, upon arrival on the mainland.

Two surveys are complementary sources of information about the socio-economic characteristics of Puerto Ricans migrating to, and from, the United States.

Beginning in December 1955, the Bureau of Labor Statistics of the Commonwealth of Puerto Rico Department of Labor, conducted a "ramp" survey, of passengers arriving at, and departing from, the San Juan International airport.[7] Although technical and administrative difficulties forced its discontinuance in 1964, this survey was a pioneer attempt to obtain information about the incoming and outgoing population on a continuing basis.[8]

A major drawback of the ramp survey, from the standpoint of obtaining information about migrants, was that it sampled flights and passengers, rather than migrants. In reporting on the characteristics of resident and nonresident passengers who travelled by air between the United States and Puerto Rico, the survey did not distinguish between migrants and those who travelled for other purposes. The greater the volume of air traffic became, as a result of increased travel between Puerto Rico and the United States by businessmen, visitors, etc., the less likely it became that the characteristics of the passengers accurately reflected those of the ever diminishing proportion of migrants among them.

[6] Hernández, op. cit., 9.

[7] The reports were published cumulatively by year, from 1955 to 1964, by the Bureau of Labor Statistics of the Commonwealth of Puerto Rico Department of Labor, under the title of Characteristics of the Passengers Who Travelled by Air Between Puerto Rico and the United States.

[8] A short history of the ramp survey is contained in an unpublished paper of the Bureau of Labor Statistics, Commonwealth of Puerto Rico Department of Labor, Some Notes about the History of the Migration Survey, San Juan, Puerto Rico, June 1968.

In addition, technical difficulties in interviewing passengers resulted in overinclusion of young adult males in the ramp survey. This produced biased estimates of the demographic and social characteristics of the passengers.[9]

In 1964, the Bureau of Economic and Social Analysis of the Commonwealth of Puerto Rico Planning Board, initiated an annual "household" survey of migrants, utilizing the household sample of the Department of Labor.[10] Members of the sampled households are asked about persons in their household who have left for the United States during the preceding year ("out-migrants"), and about persons living in their household now who returned from the United States during the preceding year ("in-migrants").

One consequence of utilizing this method is that emigrating *households* are lost to the sample. The procedure tends to underestimate the actual number of migrants to the United States, and to give a biased picture of the characteristics of those who migrate.[11]

The Census, the ramp survey, and the household survey are the three major sources of information about the socio-economic characteristics of Puerto Rican migrants to, and from, the United States. Although each source provides valuable information bearing on migration, each has methodological limitations which hamper an evaluation of the socio-economic selectivity of migrants. The ramp survey does not distinguish clearly between migrants and other air passengers. The household survey does not include information on migrating households. And the Census provides only static data on the characteristics of migrants.

Information needed to evaluate the motivational characteristics of migrants is equally difficult to obtain. The one comprehensive study of the motivations of Puerto Rican mi-

[9] Critiques of the ramp survey can be found in Hernández, *op. cit.*, 17; and José L. Vásquez Calzada, *The Demographic Evolution of Puerto Rico*, unpublished Ph.D. dissertation, The University of Chicago, 1964, 114–116.

[10] The sample used by the Department of Labor is described in: Bureau of Labor Statistics, the Commonwealth of Puerto Rico Department of Labor, *Redesign of the Household Sample for the Labor Force Survey*, March 1963.

[11] A critique of the household survey can be found in: José L. Vázquez Calzada, *Las Causas y Efectos de la Emigracion Puertorriqueña*, unpublished paper, University of Puerto Rico, School of Medicine, October 1968, 2–5.

grants in the United States is the survey by Mills and associates, whose findings are reported in *The Puerto Rican Journey*. Between January and May 1948, the researchers conducted 1113 semi-structured interviews with Puerto Rican-born adult migrants. The study was conducted within an area sample of households, in two core areas of New York City—Spanish Harlem and Morrisania.[12]

The Mills study provides data on the content and directional pull of migrants' motivations, and on the migrants' information sources about New York.

In addition, the study provides data on the occupations of the migrants, both at the time of their departure for the United States, and at later stages, during their stay on the mainland, thus permitting an analysis of mobility trends.

The greatest drawback of the Mills study, from the standpoint of analyzing the socio-economic and motivational characteristics of today's migrants, is that the investigation is over twenty years old. The study needs to be replicated, to see how socio-economic developments in Puerto Rico and in the United States since that time are affecting the motivations and experiences of migrants.

One change in the pattern of Puerto Rican migration since its early post-World War II days, is the increasing dispersion of Puerto Ricans throughout the United States. Whereas in 1950, 85 per cent of all migrants lived in New York, in 1964, only 60 per cent were living there.[13] It would therefore be interesting to compare the socio-economic and motivational characteristics of migrants in New York with those settling in, or returning to Puerto Rico from, other parts of the United States. Perhaps there are differences with regard to initial selectivity, or subsequent assimilation, or both.

A valuable source of information about the motivations of prospective return migrants are the recently published data of Myers and Masnick.[14] The findings are derived from a

[12] A detailed description of the research design is presented in: C. Wright Mills, Clarence Senior, and Rose K. Goldsen, *The Puerto Rican Journey*, New York: Russell and Russell, 1967 reissue, ix and 218 ff.

[13] Migration Division, Commonwealth of Puerto Rico Department of Labor, *A Summary in Facts and Figures*, New York, N.Y., 1964–65 edition, 16.

[14] George C. Myers and George Masnick, "The Migration Experience of New York Puerto Ricans: A Perspective on Return," *International Migration Review*, Spring, 1968, 80–90.

subsample of native-born Puerto Ricans living on the lower east side of Manhattan obtained from a Cornell University Medical School study of air pollution. 234 male and female respondents from 136 households were interviewed during the last six months of 1965.

The study provides data on differences between migrants who plan to remain in the United States, and prospective return migrants, regarding their attitudes towards, and social ties with, Puerto Rico and the United States. As Myers and Masnick themselves observe, it would be useful to complement their investigation with studies of other differences between the two groups, in areas outside the scope of their present study, such as the differential assimilation of the two groups to the United States.

THE SOCIO-ECONOMIC CHARACTERISTICS OF PUERTO RICAN MIGRANTS LIVING IN THE UNITED STATES, AS COMPARED WITH ISLAND INHABITANTS AND RETURN MIGRANTS

This section examines the data on the educational, occupational, and income characteristics of three groups: Puerto Rican migrants living in the United States, Island inhabitants, and return migrants. This makes it possible to study the extent to which a socio-economic selectivity characterizes the two groups of migrants, and the possible implications of such selectivity for Puerto Rico, and for the migrants themselves.

Educational Selectivity

According to the 1960 U.S. Census of Population, first generation Puerto Ricans residing in the United States had completed more median years of schooling than the Island inhabitants, but less median years of education than return migrants. These findings held both for males and females. The figures are given in Table 1.

Two additional surveys corroborate the Census findings of educational differences between migrants living in the United States, and return migrants. Even though the three data sources vary somewhat in the precise medians for the three groups, the direction of the differences is the same.

According to the 1964 ramp survey conducted by the Commonwealth of Puerto Rico Bureau of Labor Statistics, "return migrants" (nonresident airline passengers arriving in Puerto Rico from the United States) had completed 12 median years of schooling, as compared with 9 median years for "migrants" (resident passengers) leaving Puerto Rico for the United States.[15]

TABLE 1

Median Years of School Completed, for Puerto Rican Migrants Living in the United States, Inhabitants of Puerto Rico, and Return Migrants, Aged 25 Years and over, by Sex, 1960

	Males	Females
Return Migrants	8.6	7.6
Puerto Rican Migrants		
Living in the United States	7.9	7.1
Inhabitants of Puerto Rico	4.8	4.3

SOURCES: U.S. Bureau of the Census, U.S. Census of Population, 1960; Volume 1, Characteristics of the Population, Part 53, Puerto Rico; Subject Reports, Puerto Ricans in the United States, Final Report PC (2), Washington, D.C., U.S. Government Printing Office, Washington, D.C., 1963; and special census tabulations of return migrants by Hernández, *op. cit.*

Similar findings were obtained from the 1964 household survey conducted by the Commonwealth of Puerto Rico Planning Board. According to this survey, the median years of schooling were highest for return migrants, who had completed 8.5 years, followed by the migrants leaving Puerto Rico, with 7.3 years, and lastly, the inhabitants of Puerto Rico, with 5.8 median years of school completed.[16]

The question may now be asked: Do these educational differences represent educational selectivity of migrants,

[15] Bureau of Labor Statistics, Commonwealth of Puerto Rico Department of Labor, *Characteristics of Passengers Who Travelled by Air Between Puerto Rico and the United States*, 1964, 9 and 14.

[16] Junta de Planificacion, Estado Libre Asociado de Puerto Rico, 1964 *Informe Economico al Gobernador*. Primera Parte, Enero de 1965, 166. The survey does not always distinguish between Puerto Rican-born and foreign-born in-migrants. The "in-migrant" category includes not only return migrants, but Americans and foreigners—chiefly Cubans and Dominicans—who live in Puerto Rico. However, the return migrants constitute approximately four fifths of all in-migrants.

rather than differential educational mobility upon arrival in the United States? This question has to be answered before the process of migration and return can be identified as one of upward mobility. To answer the question, it is necessary to know *where* the migrants acquired their education. For selectivity implies that the migrants differed from the non-migrants in educational status *prior* to their arrival in the United States.

Unfortunately, the Census does not provide this information. The household survey asked household members about the educational level of migrants prior to their departure from Puerto Rico. According to these findings, it appears that the educational differences exist at the time of departure, and do represent a selective characteristic of migrants. Therefore, the higher educational status of Puerto Rican migrants living in the United States, shown by the Census, is the result of the educational selectivity of migrants, rather than of their educational mobility in the United States.

The educational selectivity of Puerto Rican migrants probably is not a guarantee of good job opportunities when they come to the mainland. For the important fact, as far as their potential socio-economic mobility in the United States is concerned, is not so much their higher educational status as compared with the Islanders, but their lower educational status as compared with the inhabitants of the United States. According to the 1960 Census, the median years of school completed for males 25 years and older are 10.4 for United States inhabitants as compared with 7.9 for the migrants. The respective figures for females are 10.8 and 7.1 median years.

Not only are the median years of schooling of Puerto Rican migrants living in the United States lower than those of the U.S. inhabitants, there is a much smaller proportion of migrants with either high school diplomas or college experience, which are increasingly important for obtaining even minor white collar jobs on the mainland. Whereas 41.4 per cent of the U.S. inhabitants 25 years old and over, have at least a high school diploma, this is true of only 14.3 per cent of the Puerto Rican-born residents in the United States. This probably means that although the migrants' higher level of education as compared with Island inhabitants may help the migrants get jobs when they come to the United States, it is definitely not high enough to assure their occupational mobility.

Several studies investigating *generational* mobility among Puerto Ricans in the United States have found that there is an upward movement, both educationally and occupationally, among second generation Puerto Ricans.[17] A needed complement to these studies is an investigation of the extent of generational mobility among U.S. inhabitants, which may or may not be proceeding at a more rapid rate.

To summarize, there is some evidence that the educational differential between Puerto Rican migrants in the United States and the Island inhabitants represents educational selectivity, prior to their migration. It is questionable how much difference the educational selectivity makes for the kinds of jobs the migrants can get on the mainland, since most do not have a high school diploma or any college experience, and they are competing against a labor force where the educational level is higher than theirs.

It should also be noted that the higher educational median of the migrants as compared with the Island inhabitants reflects the fact that they are concentrated in the middle, rather than at the bottom, of the educational ladder, and not their educational superiority to non-migrants all the way up. While there are proportionately fewer migrants than Island inhabitants aged 25 years and over who have less than five years of education (29.4 per cent as against 54.6 per cent), there are also proportionately fewer migrants than Island inhabitants who have been to college (4.6 per cent as against 7.5 per cent).

This finding is even more compelling when one considers that adult migrants living in the United States are concentrated in the younger age groups. Seventy three and a half per cent of the migrants 25 years and over are less than 35 years old, as compared with 28.3 per cent of the Island inhabitants. A comparison of the educational level attained by migrants and Island inhabitants in this 25 to 34 year age group shows that the migrants are less likely than the non-migrants to have either very little, or very much, schooling. The data are presented in Table 2.

These data suggest that it is more difficult for those in the

[17] Nathan Kantrowitz, "Social Mobility of Puerto Ricans: Education, Occupation, and Income Changes Among Children of Migrants, New York, 1950–1960," *International Migration Review*, Vol. II, Spring, 1968, 53–71; and John J. Macisco, Jr., "Assimilation of Puerto Ricans on the Mainland: A Socio-Demographic Approach," Idem, 21–38.

middle educational range to find satisfactory jobs in Puerto Rico, than for either those at the top or bottom of the educational ladder.

TABLE 2

Years of School Completed by Persons Aged 25 to 34 Years, for Inhabitants of Puerto Rico and Puerto Rican Migrants Living in the United States, 1960

Years of School Completed	Inhabitants of Puerto Rico	Puerto Rican Migrants Living in the U.S.
	%	%
1 or more years college	12.8	5.0
4 years high school	13.9	12.7
1 to 3 years high school	12.4	20.8
5 to 8 years elementary school	24.5	39.6
less than 5 years elementary school	36.1	21.9
Total (per cent)	99.7*	100.0

* No information available for .3 per cent.
SOURCES: Same as for Table 1.

It is also possible, as some have suggested, that those who decide to migrate are the more apt and the more highly motivated, as indicated by their educational selectivity. Although this is a plausible conjecture, it needs to be demonstrated, by obtaining independent data on the aptness and motivation of migrants as compared with the Island inhabitants.

Data from the Census, the ramp survey, and the household survey all indicate that the educational status of return migrants is higher than that of both Island inhabitants and first generation Puerto Ricans who live in the United States. This higher educational status of the return migrants may be due mainly to selectivity, prior to their departure from Puerto Rico, or to differences in educational mobility during their stay in the United States. Again, data are needed on the educational history of these persons prior to their initial departure from Puerto Rico, and during their stay in the United States, to determine the extent to which educational selectivity is involved.

One must also consider the consequences of the return of an educational elite to the Island for Puerto Rican society. It

TABLE 3

Occupational Distribution of Employed Puerto Rican Migrants
Living in the United States, Inhabitants of Puerto Rico, and
Return Migrants, Aged 14 years and over, by Skill Level, 1960

Occupation According to Skill Level	Return Migrants	Inhabitants of Puerto Rico	Puerto Rican Migrants Living in U.S.
	%	%	%
White Collar (Professionals, Farmers, Managers)	22.6	18.6	6.0
Minor White Collar (Sales, Clerical)	21.4	14.3	10.7
Skilled (Craftsmen)	12.6	11.2	8.0
Semi-Skilled (Operatives, Service*)	36.4	29.5	66.9
Unskilled (Farm Labor, Other Labor)	7.0	26.4	8.4
Total (per cent)	100.0	100.0	100.0

* Includes private household workers.
SOURCE: Same as for Table 1.

would be useful to determine to what extent the return migrants could be utilized to spur planned social change on the Island. Discussing the utilization of return migrants as catalysts of social change in developing countries, Myers and Masnick have argued that "careful training of, and planning for, return migrants should be a concern of governmental and private agencies in both the country to which migrants come, and to which they return."[18]

Occupational Selectivity

The next characteristic to be examined is the extent of occupational selectivity among Puerto Rican migrants in the United States, in comparison with Island inhabitants and return migrants. Table 3 gives the occupational distribution by skill level for the three groups, according to the 1960 Census.

The data indicate that the occupational distribution of migrants is quite different from that of either the Puerto Rican

[18] Myers and Masnick, *op. cit.*, 80.

inhabitants or the return migrants. Only 16.7 per cent of the migrants are in white collar occupations, as compared with 32.9 per cent of the Island inhabitants and 44.0 per cent of the return migrants. The pattern is similar in the skilled occupations. On the other hand, substantially more migrants are in semi-skilled work than are Island inhabitants or return migrants. Finally, there are fewer unskilled—especially farm laborers—among both the migrants and the return migrants than among the inhabitants of Puerto Rico.

But are the occupational characteristics of the migrants a selective trait, or rather, a product of their stay on the mainland? If the distribution represents occupational selectivity, it means that the migrants come from the middle sector of the skill scale. They are less likely to be drawn from either the white collar sector, or from the unskilled labor sector in Puerto Rico. On the other hand, if the occupational distribution of migrants is a product of their stay in the United States, it suggests that white collar and skilled workers have been downwardly mobile, whereas there has been some upward mobility among the unskilled.

In order to see whether there is an occupational selectivity among migrants, data are needed which indicate their occupation at the time of departure from Puerto Rico. Unfortunately, the Census data do not give this information. Furthermore, since the Census gives the occupational status of migrants at only one point in time, one cannot trace, by means of these data, the occupational shifts of the migrants during the course of their stay in the United States.

Although changes have taken place in the occupational distribution of both Island inhabitants and migrants since the 1940's, the Mills study throws some light on the question of occupational selectivity of migrants. Mills collected data about migrants' occupations before they left Puerto Rico, when they first came to the US, and at the time of the interviews. The data are presented in Table 4.

First, a comparison of the occupational distribution of Island inhabitants and migrants at the time of their departure from Puerto Rico indicates little difference between them in the proportion of white collar workers; some selectivity of migrants in the direction of skilled labor; and substantial selectivity in the direction of semi-skilled work, and away from unskilled work.

TABLE 4

Occupational Distribution of Employed Puerto Rican Inhabitants,
1940, and of Puerto Rican Migrants to the U.S. for Last Job
in Puerto Rico, First Job in the U.S., and Job in the U.S.
at Time of Interview

Occupation, by Skill Level	Puerto Rico Inhabitants	Last Job in Puerto Rico	Migrants First Job in U.S.	Job in U.S. at interview
	%	%	%	%
White Collar	25	20	11	12
Skilled	5	18	18	15
Semi-Skilled	20	41	25	53
Unskilled	50	21	46	20
Total (per cent)	100	100	100	100

SOURCE: Mills, et al., *op. cit.*, 35, 66.

Second, a comparison of last job in Puerto Rico with migrants' job in New York at the time of the interview, indicates that there was a drop in the proportion of white collar workers, and an increase in the proportion of semi-skilled workers. This picture remains essentially unchanged when one examines the occupational distributions separately for males and females. One specification is that the drop in proportion of skilled workers is limited to females. Furthermore there is a slight decrease in the proportion of unskilled among the males.[19]

Actually, however, the comparison of these marginal distributions understates the amount of mobility—especially downward mobility—which has occurred as migrants moved from Puerto Rico to the United States. A cross-tabulation of migrants' occupations at the time of their interview in New York, by their last occupation in Puerto Rico, showed the following occupational mobility patterns for males and females:

About one fifth of the male migrants were upwardly mobile, but almost twice as many experienced downward mobility. Among female migrants, the same proportion were downwardly mobile, but even fewer moved up. No cross-tabulations are presented on the extent, and direction, of mobility by former skill level in Puerto Rico; but Mills notes

[19] Mills, et al., *op. cit.*, 66.

TABLE 5

Direction of Occupational Mobility, from Last Job in Puerto Rico to Job in New York at Time of Interview, by Sex

Direction of Mobility	Males	Females
	%	%
Upward	21	17
Stable	39	43
Downward	40	40
Total (per cent)	100	100
	(N = 261)	(N = 142)

SOURCE: Mills, et al., *op. cit.*, 71, Table IV-10.

that upward mobility was "largely restricted to the climb from unskilled to semi-skilled wage work."[20]

It is clear that the Mills survey needs to be replicated, to ascertain whether the mobility pattern found in 1948 still holds in 1969. If so, it suggests that Puerto Rico is losing its more highly (though not most highly) trained workers, while the United States is not making full use of the occupational training they have. For the migrants themselves, this may involve frustration and disappointment, and may lead, in some instances, to a decision to return to Puerto Rico.

The occupational characteristics of return migrants have already been noted. Table 3 indicates that over two fifths of the migrants who have returned to Puerto Rico are concentrated in white collar occupations, as compared with only 16.7 per cent of the first generation Puerto Ricans living in the United States. Furthermore, substantially fewer return migrants than migrants living on the mainland, are to be found in semi-skilled jobs.

Although little is known about why migrants return, it is important to investigate the possible relationship between their return to Puerto Rico and their occupational mobility in the United States. Perhaps these migrants are persons who held white collar jobs in Puerto Rico, lost these in the U.S., became dissatisfied with their changed job status, and returned to Puerto Rico to resume white collar careers. On

[20] Mills, et al., *op. cit.*, 69. The Mills study may have underestimated, slightly, the extent of upward mobility, since the sample was restricted to households in two low income, "core" areas of New York City, from which the more successful Puerto Ricans may have moved out.

the other hand, the return migrants may be persons who were upwardly mobile in the United States, and having achieved white collar status, decided to return to Puerto Rico. If the first hypothesis is true, return migration is an indication of failure to achieve the goals which motivated the migration; if the second hypothesis is correct, it is a sign of success. Since there are no data on the jobs held by the return migrants either at the time of their departure from Puerto Rico, or during their stay in the United States, it is impossible to determine, at this time, which hypothesis is correct.

Whatever the reason for their return, one must also consider the possible impact of the influx of such an occupational elite on Puerto Rican society. To an unknown extent, they are filling manpower needs, or creating a labor surplus, in specific industries.

TABLE 6

Median Personal Income, for Puerto Rican Migrants, Living in the United States, Return Migrants, and Puerto Rico Inhabitants, 1959

	$
Puerto Rican Migrants Living in the United States	2513
Return Migrants	1560
Puerto Rican Inhabitants	819

SOURCES: Same as for Table 1.

In this connection, it is relevant to note the extremely high unemployment rate among return migrants in the Puerto Rico labor force: 18.8 per cent of the males, and 14.0 per cent of the females, aged 14 years and over, are unemployed.[21] This is substantially higher than the unemployment rate of Puerto Rican migrants living in the United States, and of the Island inhabitants.

Income

Whereas occupationally, first generation Puerto Rican migrants in the United States appear to exhibit more downward than upward mobility, their earnings in the U.S. appear to increase substantially. Table 6 gives the median personal

[21] Hernández, *op. cit.*, 43, Table 2.2.

income for Puerto Rico inhabitants, Puerto Rican migrants living in the United States, and return migrants.

Information is not available about the earnings of the migrants prior to their departure from Puerto Rico. But it seems likely that they earned more than the Island inhabitants; this can be inferred from their educational selectivity. Nevertheless, since the median annual income for migrants in the United States is more than three times that for Puerto Rico, it seems clear that the migrants have considerably improved their earning capacity subsequent to their move to the mainland.[22] Financially, they are probably better off in the United States, despite the fact that their living expenses are also greater.

The median income for return migrants is substantially less than for the migrants living in the United States, particularly when their differential occupational concentration is taken into account. This could mean that other reasons than income are important in the decision to return. It is also clear, however, that despite a drop in absolute earnings, the income of the return migrants in Puerto Rico is still high, relative to the rest of the Island population.

So far, this study has examined the socio-economic selectivity of Puerto Rican migrants in the U.S. and return migrants, to determine the significance of the migration for Puerto Rican society, and for the migrants themselves. Despite the methodological limitations of the data, it seems safe to conclude that a socio-economic selectivity characterizes migrants prior to their departure from the Island. Educationally, occupationally, and with regard to income, they are better off than the rest of the Puerto Rican working class. Upon arrival in the United States, many migrants experience downward occupational mobility, whereas the earnings of most increase substantially.

Return migrants in Puerto Rico are characterized by higher educational and occupational status, and lower income, than migrants who remain in the United States. One possible explanation is that return migrants are persons who were downwardly mobile on the mainland, and returned to Puerto

[22] Mills reported that the Puerto Rican migrant's first job in New York doubled his former earnings. Mills, et al., *op. cit.*, 74.

Rico to resume white collar, or skilled blue collar, careers. A second possibility is that the return migrants were upwardly mobile in the United States, and then returned to the Island. Data on the educational and occupational history of those who return are needed to sort out which hypothesis is correct.

THE MOTIVATIONS OF PUERTO RICAN MIGRANTS IN THE UNITED STATES, AS COMPARED WITH THE INHABITANTS OF PUERTO RICO AND RETURN MIGRANTS

Why do Puerto Ricans decide to migrate to the United States? And why do some of these migrants decide to return to Puerto Rico? Implicit in the preceding discussion was the assumption that Puerto Ricans migrate to the United States mainly to improve their lot. If so, it suggests that the migrants are dissatisfied with at least some aspects of life in Puerto Rico, and see life in the United States as better satisfying some of their needs.

The fact that they migrated to the mainland does not necessarily mean, however, that the dissatisfactions the migrants experienced in Puerto Rico differentiate them from those who remain on the Island. To some Islanders, alternatives to their present lot simply may not be visible; or migration to the United States may not be the accepted mode of coping with their dissatisfactions.

Furthermore, many Puerto Ricans on the Island do migrate, but internally, from the rural areas to the metropolitan centers of Puerto Rico.[23] It would be important to know why some Puerto Ricans choose to migrate internally, while others decide to come to the United States. No study has investigated this question so far. Perhaps the motivations of the two groups of migrants are similar, but the locus of their social and communications networks is different. Internal migrants may have heard about job openings from relatives in San Juan, while migrants to the mainland heard about jobs from relatives in New York.

Earlier, this study has alluded to the motivations of return

[23] Vázquez, *op. cit.*, 1964, 144–145; and George C. Myers, "Migration and Modernization: The Case of Puerto Rico, 1950–1960," *Social and Economic Studies.* Vol. 16, No. 4, Dec. 1967, 425–451.

migrants. We suggested that the migrants' decision to return to Puerto Rico may be motivated either by success or failure in achieving the goals for which they migrated to the mainland. But the migrants' return, or plan to return, to Puerto Rico does not necessarily mean that in their success or failure they differ from those migrants who remain in the United States. The two groups simply may differ in their perception of the economic opportunities awaiting them in Puerto Rico, or the strength of their social ties with the Island.

The dearth of data on the motivations of Puerto Ricans who come to the United States is surprising, especially in the light of the sizeable literature on the Puerto Rican migration to the United States. The 1948 Mills study is the only comprehensive survey of the attitudes of Puerto Rican migrants on the mainland. However, as already noted, the survey was done twenty years ago, and needs to be replicated.

According to Mills, only 54 per cent of the migrants reported that they themselves had made the decision to migrate to New York. The remaining 46 per cent had followed the decision of others.[24] This suggests that the migratory movement as a whole is determined by only slightly more than half of those who migrate. These 54 per cent, then, are a "strategic" public, on whose decisions the movement of the remainder depends.

More men than women are deciders—72 per cent as compared with 42 per cent. Perhaps the male followers are adult sons coming at the request of parents, or fathers coming at the request of their grown-up children.

Among the deciders, the main reason given for migrating was economic. Mills reports that 89 per cent of the male deciders, and 69 per cent of the female deciders, said they migrated for economic reasons. The study does not present a breakdown of the content of the economic motivations, although Mills illustrates typical responses, such as "getting a job," or "making money."

The second major reason for migrating to the United States, according to Mills' respondents, was their family situation. Sixteen per cent of the male deciders, and thirty-six per cent of the female deciders, gave family reasons in response to questions about why they moved to the mainland. Again, no breakdown is presented of the content of the

---

[24] The Mills data on the motivations of migrants, cited in the following paragraphs, can be found in Mills, et al., *op. cit.*, Chapter 3.

family-related motivations. The study notes that the migrants either were drawn to New York by relatives already settled there, or less often, they "wanted to escape or void family situations on the island."

In addition to asking respondents why they left Puerto Rico and came to New York, Mills also attempted to determine whether the decision was subjectively experienced as a "pull" or a "push."[25] The study reports that 67 per cent of the deciders answered only in terms of pulls, 27 per cent in terms of pushes, and 14 per cent reported both pushes and pulls. Economic reasons were more likely to be described as pushes than family or other reasons, but despite this, more reported economic pulls (60 per cent) than economic pushes (30 per cent).

Mills' data demonstrate conclusively the primacy of economic motivations in migration to the United States. But any attempt to understand fully the "economics" of the migratory movement, requires a more detailed inventory of the economic dissatisfactions in Puerto Rico and the economic attractions of the mainland which ultimately lead to a decision to migrate. In addition, one has to determine the *cumulative* impact of specific attractions and dissatisfactions, balanced against each other, as compared with any one pull or push, in precipitating the move.

The Mills study reveals *salient* economic motivations, and apparently these tend to be of the "pull" kind. But it must be remembered that salient reasons in response to open-ended questions about "why" a person moved[26] need not be the only reasons or the most important ones, in determining the move. As Peter Rossi has observed, in his study, *Why Families Move*, a general "why" question usually produces "a congeries of answers, each kind of answer corresponding to a different interpretation of the general 'why' question by the respondent."[27] The analytic difficulties in the interpretation

[25] Senior has suggested that the push-pull approach to migrant's motivations may be too mechanistic a conceptual framework. See: Clarence Senior and Donald O. Watkins, "Toward a Balance Sheet of Puerto Rican Migration" in *Status of Puerto Rico: Selected Background Studies Prepared for the U.S.-Puerto Rico Commission on the Status of Puerto Rico*, Washington, D.C., 1966, 731 ff.

[26] The question was: "Can you tell me, in your own words, why you left Puerto Rico and came to New York?"

[27] Peter H. Rossi, *Why Families Move*, Free Press, Glencoe, Illinois, 1955, 124.

of reason frequencies, point up the necessity for having an a priori frame of reference, outlining the kinds of data considered necessary for the interpretation of migratory shifts, and the necessity of collecting from respondents information on all the relevant points—in other words an "accounting scheme." Each respondent has to be asked whether, and to what extent, specific kinds of dissatisfactions in Puerto Rico and specific kinds of attractions of the mainland, were operative in forming his decision to migrate.

Also needed, as already noted, is a comparison of the motivations of those who leave the Island, with those who do not. Among the latter, it would be useful to distinguish between the motivations of Island inhabitants who have migrated internally, and those who have not.

It is possible that the difference between internal and external migrants, on the one hand, and those who have not moved at all, on the other, is not one of economic motivations, but rather, of visibility of alternatives to their present lot, or the acceptability of migration as a way of coping with their dissatisfactions. Differences between internal migrants, and those Puerto Ricans who migrate to the mainland, may also have less to do with economic motivations than with the extent to which their respective social networks are anchored in Puerto Rico, rather than in the United States.

Many of the gaps in our knowledge about the motivations of migrants as compared with non-migrants, also exist about the motivations of migrants who settle down in the United States as compared with those who return to Puerto Rico.

No comprehensive study has been done, so far, about the motivations of migrants who have returned from the United States to Puerto Rico. Myers' and Masnick's recent investigation of prospective return migrants is the only existing study which compares the attitudes of prospective return migrants with migrants who plan to stay in the United States.

According to this exploratory study, 33.5 per cent in the sample of New York Puerto Ricans say they will definitely return to Puerto Rico. The remainder either plan to stay in the United States, or are not sure whether they will return to Puerto Rico eventually.[28]

28 The data cited in the following paragraphs are from Myers and Masnick, *op. cit.*, 81 ff.

The respondents were asked why they were thinking—or not thinking—of returning to Puerto Rico. Both those who planned to stay and those who planned to return to Puerto Rico reported pulls rather than pushes as influencing their plans.

Sixty-seven per cent of those who planned to stay in the United States gave retentive or "pull" factors as most influencing their plans. Among the pulls the respondents referred to were their friends in New York, having a good job and a good home there, and the wish to educate their children on the mainland. Only 13.9 per cent gave repulsive factors as most influencing their plans to remain in the United States.

Similarly, eighty-eight per cent of the prospective return migrants mentioned attractions of Puerto Rico as most important in influencing their plans to return.

As with the Mills study, these responses may indicate that the respondents interpreted the question to refer to pulls, rather than to pushes, or that the "pulls" were more salient, rather than reflecting the unimportance of specific pushes. Again, the need is evident for an accounting scheme, according to which all respondents are asked about specific dissatisfactions with life in the United States, and specific attractions of life in Puerto Rico. This will make it possible to gauge their influence, individually and cumulatively, on the decision to return.

To summarize, Myers and Masnick's findings show that the stronger the migrants' social and psychological ties to Puerto Rico, the more predisposed they are to return to Puerto Rico. Future studies need to examine upon which contingencies, such as job opportunities in Puerto Rico, the activation of these predispositions to return depends.

CONCLUSION

In order to ascertain the socio-economic selectivity of migrants, data are needed about their educational, occupational, and income history, both before their departure from Puerto Rico and during their stay in the United States. Census data are inadequate for this purpose, since the Census only provides information about the socio-economic characteristics of migrants once they are in the United States, and at one particular point in time. One alternative method would be cross-sectional surveys, which rely on the recall of migrants about their educational and occupational careers. More desirable would be a panel study, which follows the careers of the same group of migrants (perhaps beginning with a group of prospective migrants) over a protracted time period.

According to the currently available data sources, an educational and occupational selectivity appears to characterize the migrants. They are drawn mainly from the middle educational and occupational strata in Puerto Rico. Most have at least some schooling, but relatively few have a high school diploma. Most are drawn from the skilled and semi-skilled occupations, rather than from the unskilled labor sector.

For Puerto Rico, therefore, the migration involves the loss of its more highly trained workers. But the migrants' higher educational and skill level, as compared with the average Puerto Rico inhabitant, appears to be less important for their socio-economic status in the United States, than their lower level as compared with the average U.S. inhabitant. Occupationally, there are strong indications that the movement is downward, more often than upward. Their income, however, seems to go up substantially upon arrival on the mainland.

Return migrants living in Puerto Rico have more years of schooling completed, a larger proportion of persons in white collar occupations, but lower incomes, than Puerto Rican migrants who settle down in the United States. However, data are needed about the educational, occupational, and income history of these return migrants, to determine whether they are different in this respect from migrants who stay in the U.S., already prior to departure from Puerto Rico, or whether these differences are the result of their varying careers in the United States.

It is also important to assess the impact of such a group of return migrants, characterized by a relatively high educational and occupational status, on the institutional facilities of Puerto Rico, and on the tempo and direction of societal change.

This study has also examined the extent of current knowledge about the motivational characteristics of Puerto Rican migrants in the United States and return migrants. Although economic motivations clearly have played an important part in the migration of Puerto Ricans to the United States, the paucity of contemporary data on the motivational characteristics of migrants is striking.

In the existing literature, evaluations of migrants' motivations in leaving Puerto Rico and coming to the United States have tended to rely on salient responses to open-ended questions about "why" the migrants came. Future studies should provide a uniform frame of reference for respondents, in accordance with an "accounting scheme." All respondents must be asked about the extent of their dissatisfactions with specific aspects of their life in Puerto Rico—steadiness of employment, income level, chance for occupational advancement. Similarly, all must be asked about the extent to which particular aspects of life in the United States served as attractions in deciding to come.

Furthermore, the motivations of the migrants should be compared with those of Puerto Ricans who do not migrate to the United States. This would allow an investigation of whether such migrants are indeed more motivated to improve themselves socio-economically than Puerto Ricans who remain on the Island. Among the Island inhabitants, one should distinguish between those who have migrated internally, and those who have not. Internal migrants may be much more similar, motivationally and in their socio-economic background, to Puerto Ricans who migrate to the United States, than to Island inhabitants who have not migrated at all.

No study so far has systematically explored the motivations of migrants who have returned from the United States to Puerto Rico. Data on the motivations of prospective return migrants indicate that pulls, rather than pushes, influence those who plan to return. Return-predisposing factors, such as strength of social ties with Puerto Rico, differentiate between the prospective return migrants, and those who plan to remain in the United States.

Clarence Senior and Donald O. Watkins

TOWARD A BALANCE SHEET OF PUERTO RICAN MIGRATION*

It has been made obvious that migration is a complex phenomenon. However, at the risk of oversimplification, an attempt will now be made to summarize the debits and then the credits of our balance sheet. This effort is difficult only in part because of the complexity of migration, which is one important consideration. Second, it is difficult because many of the factors which should be spelled out in detail are still largely unstudied or are highly resistant to quantitative treatment. Third, and closely allied with the second, is the highly subjective nature of individual reactions to discussions of migration. The subject is liable to lead to quite volatile reactions. An outstanding example is the peroration to a speech on migration at the conference on the subject organized by the University of Puerto Rico in 1956:

> I would rather see Puerto Ricans die in the jungles of Ecuador than in the asphalt jungles of New York City!

Migration undoubtedly is strong medicine! Courage is needed to pull up one's roots, sever the ties of neighborhood, of village, even perhaps of family. Granted that the courage is sometimes that of desperation, it must still be present.

"I miss my family," was the number one reason for unhappiness about life on the continent among the War Manpower Commission recruits, and "I miss my friends and relatives" was the top reason given for dissatisfaction by those who had

* Clarence Senior and Donald O. Watkins, "Toward a Balance Sheet of Puerto Rican Migration," in *Status of Puerto Rico: Selected Background Studies for the United States—Puerto Rico Commission on the Status of Puerto Rico.* Washington: U.S. Government Printing Office, 1966, pp. 743–758.

migrated to St. Croix. The fieldworkers in the farm labor program of the migration division of the Puerto Rico Department of Labor year-after-year have reported family reasons as the major factor in noncompletion of work agreements.

The literature of migration includes many moving accounts of the disorganization of family life which has so often accompanied migration.

A good deal has also been written on the deleterious influence on the family of migration to New York City. Two factors must be considered in this connection. The urbanization process itself has a disruptive effect on family life; migration from the country to the city in Puerto Rico itself may well have more or less the same consequences as migration from Puerto Rico to New York City. Second, it is seldom noticed that migration may be one consequence of family disruption. The Columbia study found, for example, the following contrasting proportions of divorced and separated persons among the migrants as compared with persons residing on the island:

	Men (percent)	Women (percent)
Migrants	4.0	16.0
Islanders	1.4	6.4

No matter how the issue is qualified, however, migration, especially of working class persons, has led to a good deal of personal suffering and family disruption. No one can put a dollar sign on loneliness and heartache; any attempt to quantify this debit item would be doomed to failure.

The drama of the so-called "Puerto Rican problem" put the group in the headline of New York City newspapers in the late 1940's and early 1950's. The newcomer often was treated as if he were the cause of the difficulties of which he was the victim.

Personal difficulties varied, of course, with age, sex, education, previous occupational history and training, color, religion, marital status, rural or urban origin, whether accompanied by family, size and age distribution of the family, etc. Probably more influential than any other single factor is ability to understand and speak English. The Columbia University study concluded "that language proficiency is the most important factor" in its index of adaptation. Sixty-five percent of all Puerto Ricans interviewed during a study of Lorain, Ohio, in 1954 mentioned language as the source of their greatest difficulty.

Studies in New Haven, Conn.; Buffalo, N.Y.; Jersey City and Perth Amboy, N.J.; Philadelphia, Pa., and New York City varied in their emphasis on the needs of the newcomers. That of the Welfare Council of New York probably is the most inclusive:

> The difficulties of these congested Puerto Rican areas may be listed as: (1) need of houses, (2) need of care for children, (3) need of recreation centers, (4) need of more special teaching and handling of school children, especially of the older ones, recently arrived in the schools with many Puerto Rican students, (5) need of training in occupational skills, (6) need of prenatal care and of health care generally, (7) need of education as consumers in the continental environment, and especially in regard to foods, (8) need of information, in Spanish, as to the rights and responsibilities of citizens and the services available to them in New York, through governmental and voluntary agencies, (9) need to build up local understanding of Spanish culture. Finally, (10), in order to meet the non-English-speaking applicant halfway and understand his needs immediately, agencies need Spanish-speaking personnel.

Many agencies tried to carry out the numerous recommendations of the Welfare Council report. Several years later, the Brooklyn Council for Social Planning surveyed the difficulties of the Puerto Ricans as they reported them, to all the social, civic, religious and welfare agencies of that Borough. The 24 organizations answering reported the following:

> *Language.*—Listed by 19 agencies in first place, by 3 in second place.
>
> *Housing.*—Listed by 15 agencies in first place, by 7 in second place.
>
> *Health.*—Listed by only 6 agencies in first or second place, but 18 agencies listed bad health as a prevalent handicap.

Employment.—Listed by only 1 agency in first place, but 13 agencies found that Puerto Ricans have some difficulty in obtaining employment.

Family relations.—Listed by 4 agencies in first place, 12 agencies mentioned this as a difficulty but gave it slighter weight.

Government relations.—Listed by all agencies as a minor difficulty.

Other difficulties.—Three agencies mentioned financial difficulty and two listed "cultural patterns," without specifying which ones.

Many of the agencies were willing to help, but one of the fundamental factors found by the Columbia University study was that "Even in time of need, the migrant is generally reluctant to approach an institution for help. He is accustomed to depending on his friends or relatives, whether the problem is unemployment, lack of funds or family troubles. Even Puerto Ricans who have been in New York a relatively long time continue to rely most strongly on family and other informal assistance, although some do learn to seek agency help."

The schools, as always with newcomers with families, bore a large share of the responsibility for helping integrate the newcomers. A special study was conducted from 1953 through 1957 of the Puerto Rican children, their relations with the other children and their progress in school. The report is a veritable mine of information and suggestions and has resulted in dozens of curriculum bulletins and interpretive materials.

How were the children adapting? A study of 162 pupils in 1 Manhattan school in the 12 months April 1953 to March 1954 brought the following proportion of ratings:

	Percent
Rapidly adjusting	18
Normally adjusting	62
Poorly adjusting	20

One of the problems encountered by the Puerto Rican is that of the widespread discrimination against persons of dark complexion. A whole book would be required to do justice to the theme. Let us here simply quote the Rev. Father Joseph P. Fitzpatrick of the Fordham University sociology department who has been following Puerto Rican affairs and participating in "human relations" efforts on behalf of better understanding of the newest newcomers for many years. Interviewed by *Time* he said he saw the Puerto Rican migration as a real boon to New York and the United States. Unlike previous immigrants, the Puerto Ricans bring with them a history of racial tolerance and a tradition of social intermingling that lets them marry people of other skin colors, from Negroes to whites. "I did a study last year of the behavior of Puerto Ricans in six Catholic parishes in New York." Father Fitzpatrick reported:

> I found that 25 percent of all the Puerto Rican marriages involved people of noticeably different shades of color. It is my own hope that they will make explicit the principles of human brotherhood, of universal respect for men and women, that have been implicit in their culture. If they do, they will have brought a priceless contribution to the life of the mainland.

One problem in dealing with attempts to evaluate an ethnic group in its early days in a new community is that "everybody knows" the pathology of the group and, of course, the entire group is characterized by the attributes of its most visible persons, i.e., the ones who have the most difficulty adjusting to the new environment. While a minority of the Puerto Ricans may have had serious troubles, the consensus of the social workers, teachers, ministers, labor leaders and others who have worked closely with the Puerto Ricans in New York City is probably found in the words of a veteran of 50 years of work in the settlement house movement who said she was encouraged by the fact that her Puerto Rican neighbors "are being assimilated into the life of the city faster than any previous group, partly through their own impressive efforts and partly because we're learning better how to help the process."

Next, let us look at some of the debit side so far as Puerto Rico is concerned.

Some years ago the senior author attempted to deal in monetary terms with another debit factor: "The cost of raising a man," who was then relinquished to another economy. Using techniques suggested by Louis J. Dublin and Alfred J. Lotka, an estimate was made of the cost of food, clothing, shelter, light and fuel, household equipment, medical care, personal attention, entertainment, transportation, education and vocational education, gifts and contributions which a working class family might have to meet to raise a male child to the age of 18. This, in the 1925–43 period was calculated at around $2,500 in rural areas and about $3,000 in cities. The social costs appeared to total about $500 more.

Obviously this cost would be much greater today, because of (1) an increase in the social costs; (2) an increase in price levels, and (3) a rise in the standard of living as well as in levels of living. It was pointed out at the time that:

> it must be noted that we are not here dealing with the personal intrinsic value of a man as a husband, father, son or friend but solely with the value which may reasonably be assigned him as a factor in the economic life of the island. Data are lacking with which to make an estimate of possible future earnings, which would be a more efficient method of computing value. We must therefore fall back on "cost of production" as a rough measure of the value of a man. Obviously, if future earnings were capitalized, the figure in most cases would be considerably higher than the present estimate.

It has recently been pointed out that the concept used by Dublin and Lotka is a static one which does not take the demographic situation into account. It is suggested that the concept of marginal value be applied in the process of assessing the money value of a man. This would mean that:

> In a society with underemployment and relative scarcity of consumer's goods, an additional person will exert further pressure on the supply of such goods and possibly increase even their price, if he can afford to pay it; as, at the same time, it will not be possible to take advantage of his labor in view of the prevailing underemployment, he will become a liability rather than an asset to society.

This dynamic concept probably is more meaningful than the Dublin-Lotka approach, although obviously it would be exceedingly difficult to apply. The condition described comes uncomfortably close to being that obtaining in Puerto Rico.

Another item on the debit side undoubtedly is the loss by the Puerto Rican economy of initiative and skills which are qualities of a large proportion of the migrants. One can hear repercussions of this loss in meetings of businessmen, especially those connected with recently organized plants. Again and again one has been told over the past 20 years about the "best mechanic we had" who used a bonus payment to buy his airplane ticket to the States, where he went to work immediately at twice or three times his hourly rate in Puerto Rico. Here again it would be extremely difficult, if not impossible, to quantify the movement, but there is no doubt of its existence nor of the general need for more and higher level skills as the economy becomes more highly developed.

There is one debit factor which can be demonstrated quantitively: the effect of migration in increasing the dependency ratio, i.e., the proportion of those in the population who are employed to those who are below and above the productive ages. Comparison of Puerto Rico in 1950 and 1960 and comparison between Puerto Rico and the United States will both be helpful in understanding this. There were 2.7 dependents per worker in Puerto Rico in 1950; this had increased to 3.3 in 1960, a rise of 22 percent. The 1960 ratio is almost double that of the United States, which was 1.7. This means that a given increase in productivity must be shared in Puerto Rico with 4.3 persons; in the United States with only 2.7 persons.

Furthermore, the age distribution of the dependents makes the Puerto Rican ratio more expensive to its economy than is the dependency ratio of the United States to its economy. The proportions over 65 years of age are approximately equal: 23 percent in Puerto Rico and 25 percent in the United States. The most expensive dependents are children under 15. Puerto Rico has 185 such children for each 100 employed workers, the United States 84. The heavy concentration of migrants in the young adult age categories plus the high birthrate and low death rate combine to bring about this result.

Finally, it has been charged that dependence upon migration as a solution to the problem of overpopulation exposes the Puerto Rican economy to the risk of a wave of return migration when depressions hit the economy of the United States. This has been true historically, as has been seen. It seems clear, however, that length of residence on the continent has reduced the return flow when unemployment rises. First, the unemployed man now has greater possibilities of local support than in any of the pre-1935 days. Second, the knowledge which he can use in judging whether or not to "stick it out" or return to Puerto Rico is more readily available than ever before. Third, the facilities of the United States Employment Service and of the Migration Division of the Puerto Rico Department of Labor enable him to judge whether another labor market in the United States would afford better opportunities than "going home."

How much each adverse factor sketched above will weigh will depend to a considerable extent on personal predilections. Obviously, judgment on the positive factors also will be subject to the same subjective weighing process. It is somewhat easier to quantify some of the credit factors, however.

B. THE BENEFITS OF MIGRATION

Migration usually benefits the migrant economically. Data gathered in the 1948 study indicate the process. The average weekly cash income of those migrants who came to New York City during the post-World War II period from the island's labor force was:

> Last job in Puerto Rico, $14.60.
> First job in New York, $28.05.

Average earnings for those who came during the war years were:

> Last job in Puerto Rico, $14.00.
> First job in New York, $31.43.

Earnings of those who came during the 1930's, the depression years, averaged:

> Last job in Puerto Rico, $12.00.
> First job in New York, $22.62.

Corresponding earnings for those who came in the prosperity years prior to 1929 were:

Last job in Puerto Rico, $13.00.
First job in New York, $19.04.

Regardless of the period in which they came to New York, the migrants consistently earned more money on their first job in New York than they had earned in Puerto Rico. Those who came prior to 1929 got jobs which paid them about 50 percent more than the jobs they had left in Puerto Rico. Those who came during the depression years increased their income 89 percent. Those who came during the war years more than doubled their Puerto Rican earnings on their first job in New York. Those who came in the immediate post-World War II years did not quite double the wages they had earned on their last job on the island. Data with which to compare living costs are lacking, but personal experience indicates that those in Puerto Rico are not far below those of cities on the Mainland.

The distribution of jobs in New York City among Puerto Rican employed males is given as follows by the 1960 census:

	Percent
Semiskilled (operatives)	41.0
Service	19.2
Clerical and sales	11.5
Craftsmen and foremen	10.5
Professional, managerial, technical, and proprietors	5.4
Unskilled	5.4
Miscellaneous	7.0

Women, of course, are highly concentrated in the operatives category (65.3 percent); followed by clerical and sales (15.3 percent); and then by service trades (7 percent). However, there were only 514 Puerto Rican domestic servants in the entire area. On the other end of the scale there were 2,721 Puerto Rican women listed in professional, technical, managerial, and related fields.

Unfortunately, census data for comparisons of 1950 and 1960 occupational figures for New York City are not available. We do have data, however, for the United States as a whole for first and second generation male Puerto Ricans in 1960. They are given in the following table:

Occupational groupings	Puerto Rican born	Puerto Rican parentage
	Percent	Percent
Professional, technical, managerial, etc.	5.3	12.4
Clerical and sales	9.3	18.4
Craftsmen, foremen, etc.	10.1	16.7
Operatives	40.0	26.4
Service (except domestic)	17.7	10.6
Laborers (except farm and mine)	8.3	7.4
Farm and mine laborers	3.1	1.3
Miscellaneous and not reported	6.2	6.8

It will be noted that the first two groups, which make up the "white-collar" occupations, more than doubled as a proportion of those employed between the first and second generations (from 14.6 to 30.8 percent).

The increase in the white-collar occupations was much sharper among the Puerto Rican women than among the men: first generation, 16.4 percent; second, 57.4 percent. This is slightly above the average for all employed women in the United States, 54 percent. There was a drop of about two-thirds in the "operatives" category: from the first generation's 66.3 to 22.6 percent for the second generation. These data, especially those for the needle trades, will sound familiar to all students of our immigration history.

What incomes do the Puerto Ricans get for their work? Here again, we find increases varying in much the same manner as do those of other workers. Income reported in the 1960 Census was $2,533 for the United States as a whole, compared with $1,654 reported in the 1950 census. Those who were farmers reported incomes of $1,434; rural nonfarm dwellers received $1,857 and urban dwellers averaged $2,555.

First- and second-generation differences between 1950 and 1960 incomes reported are as follows:

	Puerto Rican born	Puerto Rican parentage
1950	$1,664	$1,526
1960	2,513	2,868

But there is the factor of age to be taken into account. Earnings increase toward "middle age" and then, except in the case of highly educated professionals, tend to decline. But the average age of the Puerto Rican-born persons in the States is 27.9; that of second generation is 5.9. Obviously, if we are to compare first- and second-generation earnings fairly, we must offset the age factor. This we can do by using the same age group. Let us compare the 25–34 category for the United States as a whole and the four States for which the 1960 census furnishes income data:

	1st generation	2d generation
United States	$2,687	$3,519
California	3,183	3,944
Illinois	3,208	4,042
New Jersey	2,782	3,677
New York	2,631	3,466

Another answer to the question, "Are the Puerto Ricans climbing the economic ladder?" is found in the 1960 Census data for median family income for New York City's five counties and three "next door" counties:

New York (Manhattan)	$3,459
Kings (Brooklyn)	3,868
Bronx	4,108
Westchester	4,890
Richmond (Staten Island)	5,136
Suffolk	5,594
Queens	5,756
Nassau	6,665

The median family income in Puerto Rico, as shown by the 1960 Census, was $1,082. Since price levels do not vary greatly between New York City and the cities of Puerto Rico for comparable levels of living, the economic advantages are clear.

Consumer goods data from a 1957 marketing survey indicate that in that year 80 percent of the Puerto Rican households in New York City had at least one radio, 79.9 percent owned a TV set, 93.3 percent had an electric refrigerator, and 41.2 percent had their own telephone.

The 1960 census showed 7,396 homes owned by Puerto Ricans in New York City; 18 percent of those in Philadelphia owned their homes.

Of course, "Man does not live by bread alone." There are many indications that life in their new homes is a fruitful, happy one for many thousands of Puerto Rican families. Interviews under many different circumstances and with many different groups indicate that new sights and sounds, new experiences, parks, playgrounds, music, opera, theater—all the advantages of an urban culture—are greatly appreciated. "Maybe I am not going to do so well, but my children will have greater chances for a secure and prosperous future." These words in one form or another are repeated thousands of times. And the children of those who return, having become accustomed to life in a big city, are now freely expressing their loss when they return to Puerto Rico to live. They miss, according to teachers who have discussed the matter with them, "the parks, the playgrounds, the gymnasiums, as well as specific schoolteachers with whom they had become friendly."

It would be easy in attempting to draw up a balance sheet of the migration, to do what prejudiced and bigoted persons in the United States usually do—judge the entire Puerto Rican population in the United States by the small minority which gets into trouble with the formal institutions of the receiving communities. Relief and crime are generally the two areas in which the greatest misunderstandings arise. Report after report has showed that the proportion of Puerto Ricans on relief has varied from around 6 percent to about 11 percent, depending on the business cycle. The past few years have seen the percentage on relief rise to one out of five. Sixty percent of the 20 percent are receiving "supplementary" relief; i.e., they are employed but their income does not suffice to support their family.

Time (June 23, 1958) summarized official information on the New York City situation in the second area as follows: "Puerto Ricans form 8 percent of the population and their share of the crime rate is only slightly more than 8 percent." So far as juvenile delinquency is concerned, a few years ago a broad-scale study of Puerto Rican children in New York City schools found that in two Manhattan school districts which were studied intensively, the court appearances for Puerto Rican children ran 12 per 1,000 pupils compared with 14 per 1,000 for non-Puerto Ricans. Similar studies have showed that in general the *Time* statement applies to juvenile delinquency as well as adult crime.

Migration is likely to benefit the one who moves to a more complex, more highly productive economy because it enlarges his scope of action, gives him greater opportunities to grasp if he is capable of grasping them. This is obvious in the case of most moves to the United States. There is another factor which plays an important but still largely unanalyzed role in migration. A study in St. Croix found that the Puerto Ricans who had moved to that island were much in demand as more productive workers than the local people. Here there was no question of a more highly developed economy. There was apparently a higher "mobilization" of the energies and abilities of the newcomer since he was facing a crisis in his life and was impelled to put forth greater efforts than his customary and habitual efforts in his former environment. Most people usually operate on a lower level of mobilization of energies than their maximum level, or even of their optimum level, as William James pointed out years ago. In the language of the man on the street, "getting out of an old rut peps you up!"

Closely related to the economic advancement of the Puerto Rican living in the States is the benefit to the entire Puerto Rican economy of their remittances to family and friends. Official figures seriously underestimate the amount of money flowing into the island since they are based on check and money order flows and do not include money sent in bills through the mails or carried in the pockets of those who return, either to visit their old home or to stay. Still, the official figures are most impressive: For the 15-year period 1947–63 such remittances totaled $553,700,000 (see table XV).

Two other sources of income arising out of the migration now contribute sizable sums to the Puerto Rican national income: Social security and unemployment insurance payments. It would require a separate study to determine what proportion of the former payments arise out of accounts built up only in Puerto Rico and what arose out of economic activities on the continent. It should be noted that social security payments in Puerto Rico increased from $7.4 million in 1950 to $69.1 million in 1961. By 1963, OASI and disability payments totaled $68,485,000 and unemployment insurance payments were $11,755,000.

No estimates were found of the total of unemployment insurance payments in Puerto Rico on accounts built up in

TABLE XV.

Personal remittances to Puerto Rico, 1947–63
[In millions of dollars]

1947	8.3	1956	33.5
1948	9.2	1957	38.4
1949	12.9	1958	34.7
1950	12.6	1959	40.3
1951	17.0	1960	50.7
1952	21.5	1961	59.3
1953	27.9	1962	61.0
1954	29.3	1963	66.0
1955	31.4		

SOURCE: Puerto Rico Planning Board.

the States, but judging by the experience of some of the Southern States to which workers return when recession strikes, it could run into quite a few million dollars annually.

These direct economic benefits obviously might be considered as repayments on the "cost of production of a man" if we wish to use that concept. There are also some important economic benefits which are not quite so direct in their repercussions. Demographic pressures have been seen to be directly reflected in the high rate of unemployment. Let us see what would have been likely to happen if there had been no out-migration between 1950 and 1960. The population in the latter year would have numbered 2,970,000, instead of 2,350,000 or about 620,000 more inhabitants. It would have been necessary to create 310,000 new jobs more than were created during that period. Otherwise the unemployment rate would have soared far past the extreme danger mark, since only about 100,000 new jobs were created in the entire period 1947–61.

The effect on the per capita income of Puerto Rico would have been most depressing. There are few indications of scarcities of workers serious enough to interfere with production. It would, therefore, seem clear that the removal of the migrant in the labor force would not have affected the level of the national income. This means that if the population had grown by 620,000 more persons during the decade than it actually did, there would have been a proportionate reduction in the per capita income, rather than an increase.

The migration not only removed an average of about

47,000 persons per year in the 1950–60 decade; it also reduced the rate of natural increase. Janer's calculations give
birth and death rates and rates of natural increase as follows:

	Birth rate	Death rate	Rate of natural increase
1950	40.0	9.9	30.1
1960	33.5	6.7	26.8

Net out-migration caused shifts in the age and sex structure
and reduced the number of women with spouses present.
Janer estimates that otherwise the birthrate would have declined only to 38.6. This would have meant a rise in the rate
of natural increase from 30.1 in 1950 to 31.9 in 1960, instead
of a reduction!

The school system is already striving desperately to keep
up with the number of children it must teach as a result of
the high rate of natural increase. It can readily be seen what
a burden it would have had to carry if it had not been for
the out-migration of some thousands of children during recent years. New York City alone received a net of 44,464
children from Puerto Rico in the 10 years, 1953–54 to 1962–
63. Some indication of the addition we should have to make
if we included children born in the States to those who left
Puerto Rico to live and work in the States is given by the
New York City public school system report that in the 1964–
65 school year it was teaching 190,465 children born in
Puerto Rico or born of parents who had been born in Puerto
Rico.

We might estimate the number of such children in private
and parochial schools in New York City and those attending
school in the 100-some towns and cities with Puerto Rican
communities as at least 90,000. This would give us a total of
approximately 280,000 more children who would probably be
attending school in Puerto Rico if it had not been for the
migration of recent years! This would require an expansion
of over one-third in the capacity of the school system of
Puerto Rico. Furthermore, at a per-pupil expenditure of $150,
it would mean either an increase of $42 million a year in the
education budget or a reduction in school services.

Obviously, the same type of calculations could be made
for the additional strain on the economy in the fields of

health and welfare, in the absence of migration. The point will not be further labored.

One final point must be listed on the credit side of migration. The U.S. economy and society has served as a vast training school for many Puerto Ricans who have gone to work in its factories and shops. Those who have returned to their homeland are in thousands of cases trained in skilled and semiskilled work and experienced in the industrial disciplines so that they make a real contribution to "Operation Bootstrap."

A comparison of the occupational distribution of returnees for 1960–64 and of all employed persons in 1964 indicates how the two populations compare (see table XVI).

TABLE XVI.

Occupational distribution of returnees 1960–64 and Puerto Rican employment, 1964: percentages

Occupational grouping	Returnees 1960–64	Puerto Rican employment
Total workers	100.0	100.0
Professionals, technicians and related workers	9.7	7.6
Farmers and farm administrators	1.4	6.6
Other managers, administrators, ond owners	10.6	8.7
Office and sales personnel	22.8	15.6
Craftsmen, foremen, machine operators and related workers	34.7	29.2
Domestic workers		2.6
Other service workers	8.7	9.0
Farmworkers and foremen	8.2	13.8
Laborers, except farm and mine	4.2	6.9
Others	.6	

SOURCE: "1964 Informe Económico al Gobernador," op. cit., p. 163.

That the returned migrant ranks higher than the resident workers is not surprising in view of their more extended education, already noted. Are they being put to work in Puerto Rico? An attempt to quantify the answer to this question has been made by the planning board. It compares the increase in employment between 1960 and 1964 and the employment of the immigrants by job categories. The results are shown in table XVII. It will be seen that the potential of the returnee is being used: 18,900 workers occupy jobs in the white collar fields, of the 37,000 created in the 5 years studied.

TABLE XVII.

Increase in employment and utilization of returnees, 1960–64

Occupational groupings	Increase in employment	Employment of returnees
Professional and technical	15,000	4,300
Managers and owners	7,000	4,700
Clerical and sales	15,000	9,900
"White collar" jobs	37,000	18,900
Craftsmen, foremen, and machine operators	50,000	15,600
Farmers, laborers, service workers, domestic, and others	6,000	9,500
"Blue collar" jobs	56,500	25,100

SOURCE: "1964 Informe Económico al Gobernador," op. cit., p. 162.

The less-skilled returnees are not being absorbed so readily: only 44 percent of the new jobs in the bottom two categories were filled by them as compared with 51 percent of the "white collar" jobs thus filled.

Again, on their return, the migrants find by experience that education and training are crucial in Puerto Rico as they are in the United States. Academicians can write articles and books proving that this is so; the less educated worker discovers it for himself at the cost of the shoe leather he wears out "pounding the streets."

C. SUMMARY

The elements of a balance sheet involving human beings are obviously less subject to quantification than are those of business accounting. They are similar in one important respect: double-entry bookkeeping always is present. Each move which means a given move toward the credit side involves a present or potential item on the opposite page. And the credits and debits vary in importance depending on who reads the books and what his interest is in the transaction. It is also important whether the interest is longrun or short-run; whether it is public spirited or strictly for personal power or profit; whether it is informed or uninformed; whether it arises out of reasoning based on facts or out of deep-seated prejudices.

The authors have attempted in this balance sheet to state those facts which seemed to them to be relevant. But relevance is determined by one's outlook on life, by one's philosophy, if you will. Our philosophy is based on faith in man. We believe that man can, by taking thought, add more than a cubit to his stature as a social being. And, of course, thought must involve action to become socially relevant. We believe that social institutions exist to serve man's goals in life and not vice versa. We believe that the struggle to achieve one's goals helps strengthen the person and that groups which are formed by men to aid them in their struggle perform an indispensable social function in building a stronger culture and an indispensable function for their members in enriching their personalities.

We believe that men living in isolation from the main currents of world thought and world action begin to deteriorate, to vegetate. The major centers of cultural growth have always been those which have been involved in the meeting and mixing of diverse peoples; in the exchanging of ideas; in the debating of new concepts; in the learning of new ways while holding to the verities of the past. Contacts between people of differing languages, of differing cultures—especially when they take place on a nonexploitative basis—will enrich all the participants. Knowledge is one of the human values which grows with sharing.

It is on the basis of these beliefs that we concluded that, in general, the migration from Puerto Rico has tended to benefit:

1. the migrant and his family;
2. the area in which he comes to live; and
3. the area from which he migrates.

1. We believe our data indicate that the migrant goes where he believes opportunity exists and that usually he is correct in his belief. If he is wrong, he usually returns or

moves on to another area. He moves, specifically in the case of the Puerto Rican, not only to assure a more satisfactory life for himself, but a more rewarding future for his children. Life is no "bed of roses," nor does he expect it to be. He is used to working hard and wants an opportunity to secure an adequate reward for his work, now and in the future.

2. The area from which a man migrates may well be inconvenienced in many ways, but if it suffers from an excess of workers capable of doing the kind of jobs which need being done, if it cannot quickly furnish sources of employment, and if another area needs men to do such jobs, it is economically and socially sound for them to leave.

3. The area which requires the workers obviously benefits because commodities and services are being produced which would not have been. It is not enough to say that perhaps it would be just as well if those foods and services were not produced. It is the responsibility of the social, political, and economic structures of an area to decide such matters. If an area wants to abolish an industry or a service, such a decision should be made after full and free discussion of all the costs and benefits. But if an industry is allowed to exist, it will need personnel. And if the local population does not produce the manpower needed, the alternative to abolition of the industry is in migration of the needed personnel.

The alternative to freedom of movement, within national boundaries, is to adopt the totalitarian system of internal passports. Central direction of where workers can move and which industries can hire or fire might possibly be more efficient. It is certainly not consonant with our democratic way of life. And it might produce more efficient robots for factory jobs. It might even be less troublesome for areas into which newcomers move. But our goal, in our opinion, is not the production of robots but of men who are increasingly more capable of efficient, economic, and social aspects.

PART III:

LIFE ON THE MAINLAND:

CONFLICT AND ACCULTURATION

Francesco Cordasco and Rocco Galatioto

ETHNIC DISPLACEMENT IN THE INTERSTITIAL COMMUNITY: THE EAST HARLEM [NEW YORK CITY] EXPERIENCE*

Frederick M. Thrasher's definition of a so-called interstitial community is typical of the sociological thinking of the 1920's, which was influenced strongly by the University of Chicago school headed by Park and Burgess. Thrasher, loyal to the concentric circle theory of cities, maintained that an *interstitial* area, an area that would be called today a *ghetto*, is typified by deterioration, shifting population and cultural isolation.[1] The work of William F. Whyte and Herbert J. Gans points out that such areas are not necessarily disorganized socially and are not deteriorating in terms of social organization and integration;[2] indeed, the term *deterioration*

* F. Cordasco and R. Galatioto, "Ethnic Displacement in the Interstitial Community: The East Harlem [New York City] Experience," *Phylon: The Atlanta University Review of Race and Culture*, vol. 31 (Fall 1970), pp. 302–312. Reprinted with permission.

[1] See Thrasher's classic study, *The Gang* (Chicago, 1927); for general orientation, see David R. Hunter, *The Slums: Challenge and Response* (New York, 1964); and Marshall B. Clinard, *Slums and Community Development* (New York, 1966).

Most of the data used for this study was made available by Dr. Leonard Covello, the curator of the newly formed American Italian Historical Association (AIHA), an organization made up of social scientists who are interested in studying the Italian experience in America in a scientific manner. Special thanks go to Rabbi Goodman of the Jewish Welfare Center of New York at 145 East 32nd Street, New York City, for making available much needed material on the Jewish population of East Harlem.

[2] *Cf.* William F. Whyte, Jr., *Street Corner Society* (Chicago, 1943, 2nd ed., 1955); and Herbert J. Gans, *The Urban Villagers: Group and Class in the Life of Italian Americans* (New York, 1962).

171

is too crude and value ridden for serious sociological purposes. Yet Thrasher was correct in stating that slums are plagued by shifting population and are essentially isolated from the rest of society. In these two respects, the sociologically complex and fascinating area of the upper East Side of Manhattan known as East Harlem is an interstitial area, or a slum. East Harlem is and has been a poor area and has had its share of social pathology. But it is the isolation of a slum from the rest of society simply because its subculture does not conform directly to the culture patterns of a dominant group that causes it to be known by "outsiders" as a pathological and decadent area.

East Harlem is an interesting area. Most minority groups have lived there at one time or another; however, the ideal melting pot never melted substantially. The immediate scope of this paper is to trace the movement of the largest ethnic groups through this area from 1900 to 1960. These groups are Italians, Jews, Puerto Ricans and Negroes. The aim of this paper is to document and establish probable reasons for the change in East Harlem from a "Little Italy" to a so-called Spanish Harlem, and eventually to an extension of Negro Harlem. East Harlem housed during the 1920's the largest Italian immigrant community in the United States. We will attempt to explain and trace the growth of the Italian population and its replacement by Puerto Ricans and Negroes, with some notice of the Jewish subcommunity which slowly withdrew from the area.

Geographically, East Harlem is defined as the area from

TABLE 1

Health Areas and Their Equivalent Census Tracts for East Harlem

Health Areas	Census Tracts
16	198, 196, 204, 206, 210
17	192, 194, 202
20	182, 184
21	180
22	178, 188
25	172, 174
28	160, 168
29	158, 166
30	164

96th Street north to the Harlem River. This area is divided statistically in terms of Health Areas, each of which is subdivided into Census Tracts.

Although culturally isolated, the area is serviced by several surface line buses and several subways. The main subway that passes through the area is the Lexington Avenue Line, but it must be noted that at one time the Third Avenue "L" and the Second Avenue "L" also served the area. There are some physical barriers that act also as social barriers: the tracks of the New York Central Railroad run elevated from 96th Street to 110th Street along Park Avenue, and at one time they separated middle-class Central Harlem from lower-class East Harlem. However, as Central Harlem began to change into a Negro ghetto, the Jewish and Protestant middle classes moved out, and today these tracks serve only as physical barriers that separate the low-rent housing projects west of Park Avenue from the low-rent tenements on the East Side that appear to be doomed because of the bulldozer ideology.[3] Another physical barrier is Mount Morris Park and there is, of course, the limiting effect of the Harlem and East Rivers.

The most important street in East Harlem is 116th Street. This has been traditionally the most desirable residential area, and it still houses what remains of the professional offices of doctors, lawyers, and brokers. This street signified to the Italian population a sort of main street—equivalent to the *il corso* of their native towns and villages. It is then not surprising that old-timers remember when their dream was to move to 116th Street where the rents were high, but where prestige was achieved. East Harlem today is predominantly Negro and Puerto Rican. A few Italians, mostly elderly, remain in some "pockets," but they are slowly disappearing. East Harlem is a typical urban slum, a kind of necessary evil that will be part of the industrial city until all discrimination and class differences are rooted out.

It is erroneous to conclude that the slum resulted from the ethnic immigrations. Anderson, in his thorough study of the

---

[3] See Patricia C. Sexton, *Spanish Harlem* (New York, 1965), particularly, "The Bulldozer and the Bulldozed," pp. 35–46; and Jane Jacobs, *The Death and Life of Great American Cities* (New York, 1961). For commentary on Sexton, see F. Cordasco, "Spanish Harlem: The Anatomy of Poverty," *Phylon* (Summer, 1965), 195–96.

history of the slum, shows that slums existed before the great ethnic immigrations. He observes that "As a social phenomenon, the slum seems to resist most attempts to abolish it. Whether opposed by movements of reform or rising land values, it only yields to change its locale or modify its appearance. This has been at least the characteristic of the slum in New York. . . . Whether tent or tenement, the slum in this city is as old as the segregation of the poor."[4] This is even more true today. With the building of so-called housing projects, an entire area is destroyed and many of those displaced settle in contiguous areas, thus enlarging the slum. Also, low-rent housing areas usually "become worse centers of delinquency, vandalism and general hopelessness than the slums they were supposed to replace."[5]

EAST HARLEM AT THE TURN OF THE CENTURY

A census taken by the New York Police Department in 1895 based on political districts roughly equivalent to what is today known as East Harlem released the following figures:[6]

TABLE 2

Political District	Male	Female	Total
31	22,503	28,499	51,002
32	32,064	30,930	62,994
33	28,362	27,749	56,111
34	35,614	34,919	70,533
Totals	118,543	122,097	240,640

In the period 1902–03, according to the most reliable source of ethnic enumeration, *The Report of the Tenement House*

[4] Nels Anderson, *The Social Antecedents of a Slum: A Developmental Study of the East Harlem Area* (unpublished Ph.D. dissertation, New York University, 1930), p. 16.

[5] Jacobs, *op. cit.*, p. 4.

[6] Reported in Salvatore Cimilluca, *The Natural History of East Harlem from 1880 to the Present* (unpublished M.A. thesis, New York University, 1931), p. 44. The significance in terms of absolute data of Table 2 is questionable because of poor eumeration, and because the political districts of the period do not correspond exactly to what is known as East Harlem today.

Department of New York City, East Harlem was predominantly Irish and German: "The Italians who predominate today [1930], in 1903 were in the minority. This point serves to illustrate that the Italians did not settle in East Harlem until the first decade of the new century. The nucleus of Italians was located along Second Avenue from 102nd to 116th Streets. They were more densely located in the vicinity of Thomas Jefferson Park."[7] Between 1900 and 1910, ethnic trends in East Harlem were creating an Italian subcommunity which was to become the largest Italian settlement in the United States.

WHY EAST HARLEM?

Around 1900, the number of Italians who came to the United States increased steadily, but this immigration did not reach its apex until 1914.[8] Because of the economic conditions of these early immigrants (conditions aggravated by the *padrone* system),[9] they were forced to live in "pockets" of extreme poverty and squalor. The first Italian slum was in notorious Mulberry Bend of lower Manhattan. The conditions of this slum are best outlined by Jacob Riis in *How the Other Half Lives*.[10] This original "Little Italy" was so unfit for human habitation that "the only remedy was demolition."[11] In the late 1890's demolition was a rare phenomenon, and the proposal made in 1884 by the Tenement House Commission to demolish the Bend was unusual and quite courageous. After a long battle, the area was ordered evacuated and made ready for demolition by 1895.[12] But after many houses had been demolished, some people continued to live in the Bend under even worse conditions. If the qualitative terms used

[7] Cimilluca, *op. cit.*, p. 46.

[8] See generally Robert F. Foerster, *The Italian Emigration of Our Times* (Cambridge, Massachusetts, 1919; reissued with an Introductory Note by F. Cordasco, New York, 1968).

[9] See Marie Lipari, "The Padrone System," *Italy American Monthly* (April, 1935), 4–10.

[10] Jacob Riis, *How the Other Half Lives* (New York, 1890).

[11] Stephen Noft (ed.), *Gli Italiani di New York*. Works Projects Administration (New York, 1933), p. 14.

[12] See Jacob Riis, *The Battle With the Slum* (New York, 1902).

above to describe the Bend are too imprecise, one should turn to Riis for vital statistics which show that the Bend's rate of infantile mortality was 139.83 per thousand births, as compared to the rate for New York City as a whole of 26.27.[13] The general mortality for the Bend was 10 percent higher than for the city as a whole.[14]

It is little wonder that some Italians left this area and settled where they formed core communities that were to grow as additional immigrants joined them. As soon as these core communities were established the number of Italians living in them grew, not necessarily because of an exodus from the Bend but because of the large number of Italians who were entering the United States during this period and settling near their relatives and *paesani*. The demolition of the Bend and the moving out of Italian families who had been able to free themselves from their status of virtual indentured servants had an effect on the ethnic make-up of East Harlem. We believe that a core community was established in East Harlem which acted as a magnet in attracting others who were arriving from Italy. There is evidence that at the turn of the century there was indeed a small Italian community in East Harlem. In talking to some old-timers, we found that some of their relatives had come from the Mulberry Street area at the turn of the century. So far we have answered why the Italians might have moved from Mulberry Bend but not why they settled in East Harlem. That in East Harlem the houses were already old and transit facilities were accessible to the area is important. It would appear to be accurate to say that East Harlem was only one of the many core communities in New York but that because it was in Manhattan where dwellings were less expensive than in newer boroughs like Brooklyn, it became a "Little Italy" by 1910.

But during the following decade a turning point was reached since East Harlem saw a total decrease of 7,224 persons between 1910 and 1920.[15] This may seem small, but it must be seen in conjunction with the fact that the influx of Italians in this area was increasing. This decrease is impor-

---

[13] *How the Other Half Lives*, p. 65.

[14] Riis' major writings against the tenement slums are assembled in F. Cordasco (ed.), *Jacob Riis Revisited: Poverty and the Slum in Another Era* (New York, 1968).

[15] Cimilluca, *op. cit.*, p. 50.

tant sociologically since it shows that the German and Irish elements were moving out very rapidly because of the influx of Italians. This influx must have been traumatic to the older residents of the area and there is no doubt that the "there goes the neighborhood" syndrome became widespread. The Jews were a group that also responded to this pressure by moving out, and their exodus will be outlined below. During this time, the Negro population began to increase in Central Harlem and gradually squeezed out the middle-class element in this area.

By 1920, the Italian immigration had become smaller as a result of the legal curtailments of migration from eastern and southern Europe; but the moving out of the older groups from East Harlem continued and a net decrease in population is recorded. Of course, it must be noted that some more mobile Italians also left the area. Cimilluca shows that in the 1920 to 1930 period, many Italians left New York City.[16]

THE 1920-1930 PERIOD

The period 1920–1930 is characterized by a Jewish exodus, by a further drop in the total population, and by the stabilization of the Italian segment. By this time Italians were the largest group in East Harlem, and, for the first time, some Puerto Ricans—a very small number—began to settle near the northeast corner of Central Park. Another interesting development during this period was the increasing pressure that Negroes were beginning to exert eastward.

The increase in the Negro population can be dealt with first because it was the most obvious development in East Harlem. By 1931, there were 164,566 Negroes in East Harlem, or 38 percent of the total population. This number has continued to increase up to the present.

The most interesting ethnic population trend during this period is the decline of the Jewish population. The 1937 *Welfare Council Report* tabulated the decline.[17]

[16] Cimilluca, *ibid.* See, also, Noft, *op. cit.*, for Italian demographic shifts during this period.

[17] Welfare Council of New York, *Report on East Harlem Population* (New York, 1937).

TABLE 3

Jewish Population in East Harlem from 1919 to 1937

1919	128,000
1923	122,000
1927	52,000
1932	15,500
1937	4,000

The decline is significant, and interesting to study in some detail. The exodus of the Jewish group is of great sociological importance insofar as it shows that when a minority group has reached a certain middle-class status it regards other minority groups as a threat to the well-being of its neighborhood. This tragic but true pattern operates among most groups and signifies, perhaps, the point at which a minority "arrives." According to the Jewish Welfare Board Study of 1931, the total Jewish population in East Harlem had decreased from a high of 213,209 in 1920, to 159,927 in 1930, a total decrease of 28 percent.[18] This study goes on to note that "The influx of Puerto Ricans (among whom there is a considerable Negro element) and Negroes into East Harlem has been a significant factor in displacing the Jewish population which is moving largely to the Bronx and Brooklyn."[19]

It may be true that the rapid Jewish exodus of the 1930's is attributable to the Puerto Ricans; but, as we have seen from Table 3, The Jewish exodus began in 1919. And, as we shall see below, the number of Puerto Ricans in the 1920's was nominal; and even in 1930 there were few Puerto Ricans in East Harlem. As an hypothesis of why the Jews moved out of this area we propose a kind of socioeconomic thesis. First, the Jews were responding to a new middle-class ethic. The 1920's

[18] Jewish Welfare Center of New York, *Study of Changes in the Population of East Harlem* (New York, 1931); see also the Center's *Supplementary Study of the Federation Settlement* (New York, 1932), and an earlier study of the Jewish Welfare Board of New York, *Preliminary Study of the Institutional Synagogue* (New York, 1924). Note a large discrepancy between the Jewish studies and the Welfare Council *Report*. The Jewish studies are probably more accurate since the Welfare Council relied on Census data where Jews were enumerated by nationality. The Jews knew who their co-religionists were.

[19] *Ibid.*, p. 1. The Jewish studies are available at the Jewish Welfare Center of New York (145 East 32nd Street, New York City).

had been years of prosperity and the developing Bronx was becoming increasingly attractive. Second-generation Jews, responding to the demands of the middle-class ethic, were the first to leave. The old-timers at first refused to go, but as time went on their ideas about East Harlem began to change. We have noted already in passing that at this time the Jewish population was being pushed by growing Negro Harlem from the west and on the east. This threatened the older Jewish community and the exodus to the Bronx was slowly completed. What we discern is a succession of new ethnic groups in East Harlem: Negroes and Italians pushing out Jews while Italians were in turn to be pushed out by Puerto Ricans who in turn would be pushed out by Negroes.

Although our hypothesis differs from the explanation given in the Jewish study, the wealth of information in the study is of great value. Moreover, the study is extremely useful because it outlines in detail the last large Jewish community in East Harlem. This was specifically in the area bounded by 112th Street, 98th Street, Fifth Avenue, and Third Avenue. This area in particular saw a decrease in total Jewish population from 48,000 in 1923, to 11,000 in 1930, a drop of 400 percent.[20] By 1940, most Jews had moved out of East Harlem, although many instead of selling their houses became landlords whose houses were rented to Negroes. Many of the old Jewish merchants also remained. Jews thus became the only white men accessible to Negroes, and many of the problems involving Negroes and Jews are to be explained by this fact.[21]

THE GROWTH OF THE PUERTO RICAN POPULATION

It is interesting to note Cimilluca's statement that the East Harlem area, "at the present [1930] is being invaded by Puerto Ricans; these people speak their native language which is Spanish, and they are commonly called 'spicks.' "[22] This

[20] *Ibid.*, pp. 1–2. *The Supplementary Study* (*op. cit.*) includes a detailed block by block account of the remnants of the Jewish Community.

[21] See generally, Nathan Glazer and Daniel Patrick Moynihan, *Beyond the Melting Pot: The Negroes, Puerto Rican, Jews, Italians, and Irish of New York City* (Cambridge, Massachusetts, 1963).

[22] Cimilluca, *op. cit.*, p. 30.

is a most important statement because it heralds things to come. As we shall point out below, although in 1930 there was no "invasion," the term *spick* was widely used among Italians as a derogatory label for Puerto Ricans they believed to be "invading" their neighborhood. Italians, who had been called by a variety of derogatory names, for the first time could transfer some of their frustration to the Puerto Ricans, and the word *spick* was a good vehicle for this transfer. The sociological significance here is obvious. It is an observed fact that in the United States one minority tries to benefit at the expense of another—even if this benefit is purely psychological.

The growth of the Puerto Rican population in East Harlem was slow. Chenault's pioneer work, *The Puerto Rican Migrant in New York City*, is the best source of data for the study of this growth. At the time of Chenault's writing there was no separate enumeration for Puerto Ricans in the Census. Chenault cites data accumulated by the United States Department of Labor, and the following table can be constructed from the data assembled.[23]

TABLE 4

Number of Puerto Ricans in the United States
at Census Dates and in 1935

Year	Number	Increase
1910	1,513	—
1920	11,811	10,298
1930	52,774	40,943
1935*	58,200	5,426

* Estimate, December 31.

Chenault noted, "because the movement of Puerto Ricans in the United States is technically one of internal migration, there are no legal restrictions against his [sic] coming to the United States."[24] This made the enumeration even more difficult. However, from Table 4 it was obvious that the United

[23] Laurence Chenault, *The Puerto Rican Migrant in New York City* (New York, 1938). Considerable documentation on the Puerto Rican mainland experience is in F. Cordasco and Eugene Bucchioni, *Puerto Rican Children in Mainland Schools: A Source Book for Teachers* (New York, 1968).

[24] Chenault, *op. cit.*, p. 53.

States was hardly being invaded by Puerto Ricans. But this term, once applied to most of the more visible groups, was to be attached to the Puerto Ricans and was to make their problems more difficult.

The bulk of the immigration from Puerto Rico into New York City came after World War II, and before the war, "the major part of the movement of Puerto Rican people took place in the decade 1920–1930."[25] We have already pointed out that this was still an insignificant migration numerically but a

TABLE 5

Movement of Persons Between Puerto Rico and the United States

Fiscal Year	Arrivals from Puerto Rico	Departures to Puerto Rico	Excess of: Arrivals	Departures
1921	9,480	7,694	1,786	—
1922	6,576	7,059	—	438
1923	9,036	6,829	2,207	—
1924	11,512	7,231	4,281	—
1925	1,279	8,136	3,143	—
1926	14,055	9,212	5,243	—
1927	19,161	9,728	9,433	—
1928	17,034	10,808	6,266	—
1929	15,911	9,462	6,449	—
1930	18,617	9,290	9,327	—
1931	11,517	12,625	—	1,108
1932	9,683	10,385	—	702
1933	8,700	9,953	—	1,253
1934	11,569	7,466	4,103	—
1935	13,174	10,214	2,960	—
TOTAL	177,304	136,092	55,198	3,501

significant one sociologically. The Italian immigration over, the need for an explotable "green horn" group was met by the Puerto Ricans. The Depression, with its high rate of unemployment, put an end to the demand for cheap labor after 1930; thereafter, the number of migrants from Puerto Rico dropped and did not increase until the late 1940's, as Table 5 shows.[26]

[25] *Ibid.*, p. 54.
[26] *Ibid.*, p. 37. Chenault constructed his table from data available in the United States Department of Labor reports.

Chenault defined the first Puerto Rican settlement as the area from 110th to 97th Streets. The increase in the number of Puerto Ricans in East Harlem caused the area to begin taking on Hispanic characteristics.

This section on the Puerto Ricans must be concluded with some additional data on other changes which were taking place in East Harlem in the 1930–1940 decade. Regarding the total population of the area, the decline that began in 1910 continued. This shows that the Puerto Ricans were unable to replace all of those who were moving out as a result of the "Puerto Rican scare" first reported by Cimilluca. East Harlem during this period remained predominantly Italian, and in 1937 the *East Harlem Study* states that, "This area houses what is probably the largest Italian colony in the Western Hemisphere and also contains a major portion of the largest Puerto Rican colony in the world."[27] This was the largest Puerto Rican colony because there were of course not many Puerto Rican colonies outside the New York area.

FROM 1950 ONWARD

At a glance, three trends characterize the period of the past 20 years. First, there is the sharp increase in the Puerto Rican element, an increase which gave the area the unofficial name of *Spanish Harlem*. Second, there is the disappearance of the Italian group. Only some "pockets" remain. The bulk of these inhabitants of Italian descent are older persons. They live for the most part on East 116th Street from Second Avenue to the river and along Pleasant Avenue near Thomas Jefferson Park. Third, there is the increase of the Negro population. Also, as a continuing trend, the decline in total population continues. Table 6 shows the population drop from 1950 to 1957.

According to the *Town Hall Report*, part of this drop is a result of pending housing and school construction; however, in view of the fact that this represents an almost chronic loss of population, we disagree with this report. The population loss is in keeping with a pattern of continuing decline. The area of East Harlem is in a state of decline. Furthermore, the

[27] Mayor's Committee on City Planning, *East Harlem Community Study* (New York: East Harlem Council of Social Agencies, 1937), p. 16.

TABLE 6

Total Population of East Harlem*

| Ethnic | 1950 | | 1957 | |
Composition	Total	Percentage	Total	Percentage
White	88,829	49.15	59,264	39.71
Nonwhite Non-Puerto Rican }	31,498	17.43	26,575	17.69
Puerto Rican	60,380	33.42	63,575	42.60
Total population	180,707	100.00	149,414	100.00

* The 1950 figures are from the United States Census of 1950, the 1957 figures are from a special New York City enumeration. The table comes from the *East Harlem Town Report,* June 6, 1969, p. 2.

number of old people in the population of the area is on the increase. These facts point to two important demographic factors. Foreign immigration into East Harlem is ending (we consider Puerto Ricans as foreigners in this respect). A migrant population is usually a young population, especially when the migration is from a distant place. The increasing age of the East Harlem inhabitants supports this observation. These facts, however, apply to only the white East Harlem population because the movement of Negroes into this area is largely from Central Harlem and because the number of Negroes coming from the South (technically internal migration but it can be classified as long distance migration) has declined substantially in recent years.[28]

According to a recent report made by the East Harlem Committee on Aging, "a breakdown of the white population [of East Harlem] shows 65 percent of it to be comprised of Puerto Ricans, 14 percent of Italian stock and 2 percent of various other ethnic origins."[29] The total population of the area is estimated as 170,000, of which 63 percent is white, 35 percent is Negro, and 2 percent falls under the catch-all category of "other races."[30] The report breaks down the white population in terms of age, and one interesting fact is that 11 percent of this group is 60 years old or over. This corrob-

[28] HARYOU, *Youth In The Ghetto* (New York, 1964), p. 124.

[29] The East Harlem Committee on Aging, *Older People in East Harlem* (New York, Department of Labor, Migration Division, Commonwealth of Puerto Rico, 1964).

[30] *Ibid.,* p. 26.

orates the statement above that the white population in East Harlem is becoming an old population.

Today, East Harlem looks like any other slum in New York. It has a Puerto Rican dominance, but this is slowly vanishing as the area becomes increasingly Negro. Among the whites, only the poor and the elderly remain, while the more mobile go to live elsewhere. The net effect is to make the area even poorer.

SOME SOCIOLOGICAL IMPLICATIONS

By analyzing the changes in ethnic groups in East Harlem, we have noted several sociological points that need elaboration. The most important concerns the movement of groups. One ethnic group pushes another. This shows that, no matter what the nation's ideological tenets are, the importance of ethnicity in American inter-group life cannot be denied. Robert E. Park could not have been more wrong when he formulated his "race relation cycle." He stated optimistically that "The race relation cycle, . . . takes the form, to state it abstractly, of contacts, competition, accommodation, and eventual assimilation."[31] The "melting pot" concept is obvious in his thesis; but judging from the empirical reality in East Harlem, this cycle never had a chance because the cultural differences among the various groups in the area were so strong that there was no possible way for any meaningful contact and eventual accommodation to take place.[32]

This brings us to the problem of the role of contact as a conflict-reducing agent. There is little doubt that inter-group contact reduces stereotyping and misunderstanding. But if cultural forces block contact, there is no hope that the cycle can be operative. Applied to East Harlem, this would mean

[31] Robert E. Park, "The Race Relation Cycle" in Amitai and Eva Etzioni (eds.), *Social Change* (New York, 1964), p. 377.

[32] Leonard Covello, principal of East Harlem's Benjamin Franklin High School for almost a quarter of a century, strove valiantly to effect community participation in the social institutions of the area (presaging the community-control conflicts presently attending the Intermediate School #201 complex in East Harlem) but without long-range success. See Leonard Covello, "A High School and its Immigrant Community: A Challenge and An Opportunity," *Journal of Educational Sociology*, IX (February, 1956), 333–46.

that the various ethnic groups were and are completely isolated from each other. There is the continuing isolation and lack of understanding that are normal for any such situation, but we disagree with Sexton's analysis of the East Harlem Italian community as an example of extreme isolation. The journalistic statements made by Sexton are unfortunate and show the difficulty of studying an area as complicated as East Harlem.[33]

Another consideration is the role that each group has played in the elevation of the group just above it. It appears that a group will try to advance at the expense of a group just below it. We have already pointed out that this may have psychological rewards for a group that has been the target of discrimination and which seeks another group to which to transfer some of its frustrations. This takes us to the role of the Negro group as the "last mover." Negroes are helping push Puerto Ricans out of East Harlem. The question is who, if anybody, will push the Negroes out. It seems unlikely that another ethnic group will ever migrate in sufficient numbers to help Negroes break the vicious cycle which Myrdal calls "The Principle of Cumulation."[34] Negroes will find exits from the ghetto only through the resolve of society as a whole to break the vicious cycle.

[33] See footnote 3, *supra*.
[34] Gunnar Myrdal, "The Principle of Cumulation" in Etzioni, *op. cit.*, pp. 455–58.

Juan A. Silén

WE, THE PUERTO RICAN PEOPLE:
A STORY OF OPPRESSION
AND RESISTANCE*

The imposition of North American citizenship on Puerto Ricans in 1917 must be understood within the framework of a military government issuing military orders. An order of February 6, 1899, issued by the military governor, Gen. Guy V. Henry, reorganized the government, reducing it to four office secretariats, and did away with the autonomous cabinet, pronouncing it "incompatible with American methods and with progress." An order of May 9, 1899, by the then military governor, Gen. George W. Davis, replaced the office secretaries with a civil secretary—a job which went to Dr. Cayetano Coll y Toste of the Republican Party.

The Foraker Act of 1900 permitted the U.S. Congress to establish a regime without authority on vital questions and created a political climate of limitations. It made commerce subject to U.S. coastal trade laws; it installed a customs system with regard to imported products and a monetary system in which the U.S. dollar became the currency of the country. All the U.S. laws which were locally applicable were to be imposed, and a judicial system whose employees and functionaries had to swear fealty to the U.S. Constitution was set up. There was also to be a Supreme Court and a federal court. The post of Resident Commissioner was instituted, and federal and military authority was established over everything not otherwise specified.

With the establishment of a legal and constitutional framework, the door was opened wide for absentee businessmen

* Juan A. Silén, *We, The Puerto Rican People: A Story of Oppression and Resistance*. New York: Monthly Review Press, 1971, pp. 36–45 and pp. 55–60. Reprinted with permission.

and capital to impose their economic dominion. On foundations that began to signal absentee economic penetration a political scaffolding was erected to "legalize" the system and fortify the conservative structure of parties which lacked any ideology and were guided by strictly electoral perspectives. These parties operated under a system of alliances between the top leader, the local machines, and a coalition of factions and interests. Starting with the Foraker Act and followed by the Jones Act of 1917 and Public Law 600 of 1950, which established the Free Associated State, the whole procession of laws imposed on Puerto Rico was nothing but a U.S. operation to assimilate and permanently dominate the island.*

Compulsory U.S. citizenship for Puerto Ricans was debated as early as 1900. It was opposed by Senators Henry M. Teller from Colorado, S. M. Cullon from Illinois, and J. C. Spooner from Wisconsin, who at the same time opposed statehood for the island. Teller is quoted as having said: "I don't like the Puerto Rican. They are not fighters like the Cubans. They were under Spanish tyranny for centuries without showing enough manhood to oppose it. Such a race is unworthy of citizenship."

But by 1905, when American economics had progressed, Theodore Roosevelt said: "I earnestly advocate the adoption of legislation which will explicitly confer American citizenship on all citizens of Puerto Rico." In the discussion of the Olmsted Bill in 1910 the possibility of imposing citizenship was again raised, and in 1912 this discussion was resumed in the U.S. Senate. On March 12, 1914, the House of Delegates, at that time the only body elected by the Puerto Rican people, sent a "Memorandum to the President and Congress of the United States," rejecting the imposition of U.S. citizenship and the elimination of Puerto Rican citizenship (which the Foraker Act of 1900 had retained): "We firmly and loyally oppose our being declared, against our express will or

---

* A long struggle was involved in this legislative process. The U. S. government sought to assimilate what we might call the "nationalist rearguard," and made concessions to Puerto Ricans to undermine the independence movement. Thus we must differentiate between the directly assimilationist laws representing the Yanqui offensive and the autonomist laws representing the Puerto Rican counteroffensive. The Free Associated State had a dual nature: on the one hand, it was a step toward statehood and a permanent union; on the other, a step toward independence because it revived the debate within our nation.

without our express consent, citizens of any other than our own beloved country which God granted to us as an inalienable gift and incoercible right . . ." However, the document was distinctly timid: the major concern was the prospect of losing customs income and of having to "impose a 4 or 5 percent tax on the value of property . . ."

In a speech before the U.S. Congress on May 5, 1916, Muñoz Rivera, then Resident Commissioner in Washington, said: "For sixteen years we have endured this system of government, protesting and struggling against it, with energy and without result." Of the action Congress might take, he said: "It can, by a legislative act, keep alive the hopes of the people of Porto Rico or it can deal these hopes their death blow." Faithful to the line he pursued all his life, Muñoz Rivera made this plea to the assembled Congressmen: "In Porto Rico no blood will be shed. Such a thing is impossible in an island of 3,600 square miles. Its narrow confines never permitted and never will permit armed resistance. For this very reason Porto Rico is a field of experiment unique on the globe . . . Our behavior during the past is a sufficient guaranty for our behavior in the future. Never a revolution there, in spite of our Latin blood; never an attempt to commercialize our political influence; never an attack against the majesty of law. The ever-reigning peace was not at any time disturbed by the illiterate masses, which bear their suffering with such stoic fortitude and only seek comfort in their bitter servitude, confiding in the supreme protection of God. (Applause.)"

The Jones Act was passed, removing the last obstacle to U.S. economic penetration. The people, 60 percent illiterate, didn't understand, or didn't care, what was happening. The incapacity and vacillation of the petty bourgeoisie and the traditional parties was responsible for the imposition of U.S. citizenship—which included the obligation to serve in the U.S. armed forces. Themselves bereft of an ideology, those groups had no moral banner to raise that could have aroused the masses to militant rejection.*

* The law was so important for U. S. domination that in 1952, when the Free Associated State (Estado Libre Asociado—ELA) was introduced, it was kept along with the ELA Constitution. Thus were reserved to the U. S. government decisions that were vital to the people's sovereignty.

In the fight against the Jones Act, José de Diego emerged from his temporizing stance toward independence to become its chief spokesman. Replying to people who muttered about our "lack of combativeness," he said: "The Puerto Ricans made a Puerto Rican revolution and helped in three Cuban revolutions. We sent two militia companies to Santo Domingo in the seventeenth century to fight the British . . . and in the nineteenth century more than 1,000 Puerto Rican soldiers fought for Cuba's freedom." He stated his position bluntly: "No person of average mental capacity can fail to grasp that citizenship collectively imposed on Puerto Ricans would raise a new obstacle to the ideal of independence and to its preservation and propagation."

In this spirit de Diego became a campaigner for the Caribbean ideal of a confederation. He called the Jones Act what it was—an imperialist project—and armed the Word by defending our language against U.S. plans for cultural assimilation. To those who accused him of "inconsistency" in himself accepting U.S. citizenship he replied: "If the citizenship decree had not been compulsory . . . I would have taken refuge in the maternal warmth of my own citizenship. I needed U.S. citizenship to raise my voice and fight for restoration of Puerto Rican citizenship, for the creation of our Republic . . ." Thus he saw it as a fight "within the regime against the regime," in the framework of loyal opposition but with possibilities of greater radicalization. His death in 1918 cut short the process to which he had committed himself and left on the nationalists' shoulders the heavy weight of continuing the struggle.

De Diego represents an era, a historical task, and some contradictions. He was the first great orator of the *independentista* masses.

THE LITERATURE OF DOCILITY

The literature on the theme of Puerto Rican "docility" has emerged in periods of crisis, when our collective life suffered from hunger, political subordination, and colonial pessimism. Our isolation from the world has made us try to idealize our real situation as a formula of escape. The educated classes have been the most guilty of portraying the Puerto Rican as

subordinate to nature and the soil, thus glorifying determinism in all its phases—natural, biological, social, psychological,
and political.

It is in José Gautier Benítez (1848–1880) that we meet
the first manifestation of this attitude. Regarded by many
as our national poet, he was both the product of a "bitter
colonial experience" and of the romantic tendencies of his
period, "one, aristocratic and feudal . . . ; the other, petty
bourgeois, revolutionary in appearance but utopian and conservative in reality . . ." Thus in his poetry the utopian gives
place to the unreal:

> All that is in you is voluptuous and light
> Sweet, gentle, caressing and tender,
> And your moral world owes its enchantment
> To the sweet influence of your external world.

So, too, the struggle to free the Negro is deformed into a
conservative concept which hides all the historical drama:

> when the yoke of the captive was destroyed . . .
> we saw Redemption without Calvary.

All of Gautier Benítez' poetry is oriented toward the soft,
the sweet. Utopianism determines the patriotic sentiment,
but then denies the reality of a society submitted to the
feudal exploitation of a decadent European monarch.

From Gautier Benítez' romantic-aristocratic-feudal lean-
ings we proceed to the petty bourgeois, seemingly revolutionary attitude of Louis Muñoz Rivera (1859–1916). Honored
by the colonial government through its Department of Public
Instruction and the Institute of Puerto Rican Culture, Muñoz
Rivera displays his pseudo-revolutionary stance in what his
biographers and defenders have called his "pragmatic politics." Behind this phrase is concealed the lack of faith in the
people that characterized his life, a lack of faith which was,
as Aníbal Ponce has said, "the emphatic affirmation of the
man who thinks over the man who lives; the scorn for struggle
and action; the arrogance of the intellectual elite with their
proud conviction that, outside of their world, there is nothing but agitation without importance." Here is Muñoz Rivera
the revolutionary expressing himself in a newspaper article
entitled "The Insult" in 1892:

Thus they repay our four centuries of *loyalty;* thus they respond to our *meekness* and provoke our anger. With Cuba, which can launch its brave *macheteros* into the virgin forest and offer itself to the North American Union, it is one thing. With Puerto Rico, which has never denied its *affection* for the motherland [Spain], it is the traditional ten of the best with the lash. For Puerto Rico's history is not stained with bloodshed and violence [does he forget that the *Grito de Lares* occurred in 1868, and that 1887 was the terrible year of the *componte?*]; Puerto Rico *never unfurled* the banner of rebellion. What bitter irony! The Cubans, who ask with catapults in their hands, are thrown a crust of bread. The Puerto Ricans, who come with humble petitions rather than taking to the woods, are scorned and slapped.*

All this to propose nonparticipation in the forthcoming elections.

In his poetry, Muñoz Rivera's conception of the people comes out more clearly. He writes of the people in his *Retamas* (1897):

> Decadence is coming,
> You can feel it already:
> The once-proud people
> Has degenerated.
>
> Don't you feel on your withered brow
> The accursed footprint
> That the idea left at parting?
> This people doesn't want to save itself.
>
> If it calls, if it dies,
> It's that it longs to fall and die.

In the poem *Paris* he expresses his humanist credo, similar to that of Erasmus' in *The Praise of Folly:* "True prudence for a mortal consists in correctly judging the dose of wisdom

* We emphasize certain of Muñoz Rivera's words because they illustrate the idea this "apostle" had of the Puerto Rican people and of the meaning of autonomy.

compatible with *human nature,* and *dissembling his senti-ments about the errors of the multitude,* if he cannot share them." What seems to be a song to the people is a rejection of the people who might threaten ruling-class stability and peaceful transition from bureaucratic colonial power:

> I condemn revolt; yes, I condemn
> Unbridled rebellion
> Which kills and robs, burns and annihilates:
> I know that men abandon reason
> When they learn to fight
> From behind a rough barricade.

Again, in the poem *El Paso del Déspota,* in which the terrible year of 1887 and the excesses of General Palacios are referred to, the people are a "poor acacia which bends in the storm." In *Nulla Est Redemptio* they are a "humble and meek" creature who "lovingly kisses his chains . . ." And in his testament, *Minha Terra,* his whole ideology is reflected in the position of the petty bourgeoisie under Spanish domination:

> Puerto Rico, you pallid Puerto Rico
> You cannot break out of your jail,
> Because you lack—long live Christ!—
> Much nerve in your character,
> Much lead in your hills,
> And much steel in your valleys;
> Because in your fields there is no people;
> Because in your veins there is no blood.

With the depression of 1929, in a climate of discontent and social deterioration and under the influence of nationalism though not linked to it, there arose a movement described in our literature as the "generation of the 30's." A new genera-tion of intellectual youth called for an examination of con-science; they wanted answers in order to find their identity. They were concerned with two key questions: Who are we? Why are we? It was a generation with the courage to set down its preoccupations in black and white. Its greatest mis-take was seeking our roots not in the people themselves but in Spain: it suffered under the same difficulties as the Spanish generation of 1898, with its fragmentary and partial interpretation of the world and of the Puerto Rican. Its chief tendency was the Hispanic one of abstract creation, and in the words of Margot Arce de Vázquez, "Hispanism . . . is a reflexive mood of patriotism" for those who "deny that economic liberation and social security programs are enough; also, and above all, the spirit must be liberated."

This generation marched beside other great ideological movements, distinguishing between spirit and matter and seeking liberation in a "Puerto Rican affirmation" which could not be proclaimed behind the people's backs. It expressed itself in the journals *Isla, Indice,* and *Brújula,* and had Antonio S. Pedreira as its ideological mentor and his *Insularismo* as its bible. Its guilt before history was propagandizing for a whole determinist interpretation which weighed like lead upon later generations.* It saw Puerto Rico as a "hodgepodge" with gloom as part of our personality: the "landscape" had helped shape our character as a people, our geography was "soft" and "feminine."

Ideology is a combination of theory, system, at times simply state-of-mind, forming a whole: "An ideology necessarily includes feelings, sympathies, antipathies, hopes, fears, etc." Within this aggregation we can observe the feelings of a class, the antipathies and hopes and fears of a class. And thus we will find the ideology of the dominator and dominated, the exploiter and exploited, the colonizer and the colonized.

But in studying the Puerto Rican character we cannot take off from only *one* typical idea. As Richard Levins says, "Puerto Rican political ideology is not uniform in all its sectors. Nor is it something homogeneous . . . For us, national

---

* To justify ruling-class ideology, determination was developed into a science, a metaphysical doctrine which made all phenomena conditional on the circumstances in which they were produced. Theoreticians and scientists sought to explain a world where the individual or the collective is conditioned by geography, by race, by economic, social, or political development. Thus they defended exploitation on the basis of social Darwinism and established racial categories of backward or "underdeveloped" peoples, with race or geography determining national character, and even behavior. At the beginning of the twentieth century this was called the "white man's burden," and imperialism hid itself behind the mask of a "civilizing" mission. This mission was supposed to bring the benefits of Western, Christian civilization to subject peoples. A whole theory of the Nordic peoples' superiority over tropical peoples emerged, and a whole system of colonialist exploitation based on Christian ethics was developed.

character is a set of ideas, contradictions, and their interrela-
tions." We cannot accept as our heritage from this generation
that consumed itself in its own "creative fire" the determinism
of many of its ideas, the error of many of its concepts of
man, the soil, history, and struggle as the process of liberation.

And while the chief aim of these writers of the 1930's was
to rescue the mind of a community damaged by colonialism
through certain Hispanic—and purportedly universal—values
(hence their need to examine their own consciences in order
to assert themselves), their social aggressiveness was no more
than a leaning toward a timid agrarian reform which fell far
short of the militant agrarianism of the Mexicans. Their *inde-
pendentismo* spirit fed on a utopian socialism which made
them first cousins of the autonomists. Their political affiliations, with some exceptions, remained within the limits of
the traditional parties. They saw some hope in the *jíbaro*, but
their fatalistic vision made their view of him incorrigibly
romantic. Antonio S. Pedreira's *Insularismo*, Manuel Méndez
Ballester's *Tiempo Muerto*, Enrique Laguerre's *La
Llamarada, and* Vicente Géigel Polanco's *El Despertar de un
Pueblo* are the works of a generation within a particular historical framework. They are the products of *one* conception of
man, the land, and history.

When we seek an explanation of the attitudes of the Puerto
Rican of this period, when we try to understand his answers
to the questions "Who are we?" "Why are we?" we come upon
Insularismo. This interpretive essay on our reality contains
influences of all the determinist theories fashionable when it
was written in 1934. No other book has had such repercussions among Puerto Rican intellectuals or enjoyed more popularity and publicity. Thus a whole series of misconceptions
has been transmitted from generation to generation, without
their harmfulness ever being categorically challenged.
Pedreira is hoping to find a definition of our reality by means
of a regional analysis. His aim, he says, is "to point out the
disparate elements that can make sense of our personality."
So he plunges in and finds that the mixture of races creates
a confusion in our character—and that "our rebellions are
momentary, our docility permanent." The climate "melts our
will" and makes us *"aplatanados."** Our history is that of a

---

* *aplatanados*: an indigenous peasant word implying a lack of
strength, spirit, or the will to resist.

"rudderless ship" vacillating between incompetence and fear. Absence of originality is a feature of our character, and rhetorical pill-gilding is a national disease which no one of us escapes.

Why did *Insularismo* become the book of the hour? Why the popularity of Pedreira's definition of the Puerto Rican? To understand, one has to see Pedreira as only one of several exponents of the literature of docility. The definition of our character he produced was adapted to the interests of the ruling class; its view of our people followed the current of the end-of-nineteenth-century intellectuals and was cut to the measure of the "pragmatic politicians." Above all it was a justification of the colonialism to which we have been submitted, for the racial and geographical premises on which Pedreira relies to define the Puerto Rican's character have been discredited by the history of humanity in recent decades. Examples are the Africans' fight for independence; the establishment in the Americas of the first socialist state, Cuba; and the continuing resistance of the Vietnamese people to North American aggression.*

The "literature of docility" did not die with the generation of the 1930's. In 1962, René Marqués published "El Puertorriqueño Dócil," an explanation of the failure of the nationalist movement of the 1950's which reflected the pessimism of the intellectual elite of that decade.† Marqués defines himself as both pro-independence and pessimistic, as Puerto Rican and docile. He re-masticates the pseudo-scientific hash of Pedreira, but what Pedreira sees as geographical factors, Marqués sees as psychological. His theory of "docility" de-

* Another source of justification for the colonial situation came from José Colombán Rosario, a self-styled sociologist who in 1935 insisted on defining the *jíbaro* in the same terms which Pedreira had defined the Puerto Rican. For Colombán Rosario the *jíbaro* was "suitable material to be guided by a *cacique*." He was lazy, weak, and characteristically spiritless, and his docility could be counted on. See Colombán Rosario, *Desarollo del Jíbaro de Puerto Rico y su Actitud Presente Hacia la Sociedad* (San Juan: Bureau of Supplies, Printing & Transportation, 1935).

† The Ateneo Puertorriqueño awarded the book a prize in 1960, and the author read parts of it before the Sixth Congress of Puerto Rican Psychologists on August 26, 1961, at the University of Puerto Rico. Mexico's *Cuadernos Americanos* reproduced it in 1962 and the University of Puerto Rico's *Revisia de Ciencias Sociales* in 1963. See René Marqués, *Ensayos, 1953–1966* (San Juan: Ediciones Antillana, 1967).

noted only an aristocratic attitude which brought the writer's class prejudices and fear of the people to the surface. To prove the Puerto Rican's docility Marqués took contemporary literature "as a springboard for the examination of psychological realities." He had previously explained the docility *à la* Pedreira as an "historical inheritance": "Puerto Rico was colonized by a handful of faintly industrious or frankly lazy people who had learned their docility in Spain, where they were of low social rank . . . With them would be fused, without much effort, two primitive ethnic groups that had been made docile by forced labor and slavery, Tainos [Indians] and Africans."

Marqués aimed to show that free-state-ism was the psychological synthesis of the Puerto Rican personality, and that its two aspects, nationalism and annexationism, are characterized by a self-destructive drive. And so he submitted to us his novel "proof" of docility. One notes with interest that much of the "proof" is in his own works, his short stories, plays, prologues, essays, and novel. If we followed his "logic" we could conclude that the docile one is the author. In fact he represents the continuation of the ideology of the pseudo-scientific writers, best expressed by Pedreira: the belief in our *inability* to take action and the *lamenting* of colonial reality. Marqués' is the pessimistic ideology of a writer who has been overcome by colonialism, of which he is a part. He rigs up a theory on scholastic foundations to reach a spiritual level from which he loses sight of the economic, political, and ideological struggles raging in the heart of human societies.

As Marqués himself says, he speaks for those who "seem undisposed to let themselves be trapped in the net of a concrete ideology." We find that he is the prototype of the writer who uses the patriotic theme not to attack a system, a structure, an ideology, but to recreate a state of mind produced by assimilation into the colonial medium. He is the standard-bearer of a theory of antipathies which serves well to garner plaudits from the middle class and the bureaucrats, postulating a so-called independence which will not "trap one in the net of a concrete ideology." This position has parallels with that of the native bourgeoisies and with humanists who carry the word "democracy" in their mouths while reserving their heart's core for the aristocracy. The docile Puerto Rican is essentially a colonialist's construct based on a determinist concept.*

Thus we have two types of docility: the one that is applauded and the one that is deplored. The applauded docility serves the interests of imperialism and the ruling classes, and establishes as a "social value" an alleged characteristic which permits the exploitation of Puerto Ricans. The deplored docility, the docility of a Muñoz Rivera, is the self-justification of certain reformist positions.

* The weakness of our bourgeoisie toward imperialism is a fact. It arose from the class interests linking it with the North American power structure, in which it assumed the junior-partner role in exploiting the Puerto Rican masses. It responded to a phenomenon of a political, not a psychological, nature. When, however, the bourgeoisie confronted the far-from-docile workers it used violence to repress the labor movement whenever it thought it necessary.

Pete Hamell

COMING OF AGE IN NUEVA YORK*

Here, examine the baggage, with the great jets screaming in behind us and the glossy girls staring from the counters of the San Juan airport and the signs blinking at us from every space and the horde of strange cold faces coming through the arrival gates and the cold wind of New York starting to blow within them across the darkened airfield. Quickly: while the children run to the candy machines and the girl from Trans Caribbean argues with the passengers on the outgoing flights and the cop lolls against the wall swinging the bat of authority and you check the ticket again and hope that nobody knows that you have some pages of La Prensa *in your shoes and some yames for your aunt in Brooklyn. Quickly: it is getting cold.*

The luggage: new undershirts bought in the Pueblo supermarket on the road to Bayamón. Some slacks, and shirts, and the suit bought for Belen's wedding two years ago to that guy from Caguas who left her later. That luggage, and the other kind. The way the flags of the Popular party blow in the sea breeze in spring over the tarpaper roofs of La Perla; children playing in those mud streets; tourists with peeling faces gawking over the walls of the old city; the sea beyond, foaming at the shore, and then green, and then turning dark blue away out where the Atlantic conquers the Caribbean. Up in the hills, the road turning, chickens cawing in the damp morning, an old jíbaro with a lined face walking on homemade sandals with a machete on his hip, the flamboyan trees exploding against the hillsides, a flock of white birds against the blue roof of the sky. That luggage: nuns in white habits walking along the Avenida Ponce de Leon, and the tourist ladies in bikinis on the beaches of the Condado, and the Cuban

* Pete Hamell, "Coming of Age in Nueva York," *New York*, vol. II (November 24, 1969), pp. 33–47. Printed with permission.

*whores along the waterfront in San Juan Antiguo, and the
way the sidewalks in El Fanguito were made with rubber
tires and there was no electricity and no toilets and you
drank water from a common pump. One summer the ticks
came like a plague and attached themselves to the skins of
children, and the public health people sprayed and made
everyone sicker. That luggage: the yellow eyes of old men,
women gone crazy with the spirits, the man who used to wear
silk suits in the afternoons and play piano in the bands and
who was found dead one morning with a needle in his arm.
That luggage: but the sweet part more than the bad, with the
sun climbing in the sky, and the sound of laughter, and the
distant swelling roar of the sea, and music.*

*New York, mon. Check the luggage. I've got some Don Q
in the overcoat, and when I sit down, I'm going to start drinking. It's dark out, but I've made this trip before. I don't want
to see the swells around El Morro, or the lights of fishing
boats, or the garish light-blinking spread of San Juan. I don't
want to see it vanish behind me. I might never see it again.*

The Puerto Ricans came to New York to live better. It was
as simple as that. It was a trickle at first, in the 1920s and
1930s, because the ticket on the Bull Line cost more than a
man could earn in a year, and the trip was long and dangerous and the city was a mean, hard place then, if your skin was
dark and your language was Spanish. Some of the earliest
worked on the Brooklyn piers, unloading bananas, with the
spiders large enough to play baseball with and the old Bull
Line captains keeping the men in line. A few drifted into the
South Bronx and the Lower East Side to the places that
were being abandoned by the Jews and the Irish who were
starting to make it. But most went to East Harlem, El Barrio,
where 110th and Lex was the center of the world, and you
could buy *plátanos* at the Park Avenue market and rice and
beans from people you knew.

They came here because the island they left behind was the
sinkhole of the Caribbean, with a life expectancy of 32, a
place where the American rulers would sit around the palace
in white duck while *jíbaros* died in the mountains from yaws
and parasites. Even today, with conditions changed radically
from the dark years of the 1920s and 1930s, the population
density of Puerto Rico is 11 times that of the United States,
unemployment runs at a constant 13 per cent, and the per

capita income is still only about $1,000 a year. New York might have been a strange and alien place to those early arrivals, but it was better than dying young.

And then the migration started to build. Puerto Ricans were different from others who had come to New York from the slums of Europe. Most importantly, they were citizens and had been so by act of Congress since 1917. So they were not immigrants, they were migrants. They fought in the First World War and all the wars after, and if there were large numbers of Puerto Ricans then who wanted independence from the United States, it was only because the United States had treated them so shabbily. The *independentistas* followed in the footsteps of Muñoz Rivera, and later followed a brilliant man named Albizu Campos, who died finally of heartache and insanity. Muñoz' son, Luis Muñoz-Marín, made the journey in those years, and sat around the Village writing poetry and Socialist tracts and enjoying himself more than he ever would again.

And through all those years, before the explosions of the years after the Second World War, the dream remained the same: to come to New York, make money, learn a trade, and go home to Puerto Rico. Muñoz-Marín went back and became the most important politician in the history of the island. For others it wasn't so easy. I remember once, a few years ago, sitting around one afternoon in Luis Cora's barbershop in East Harlem, talking to a man who had settled in New York in 1921. He was a seaman who had given up the sea because his wife was lonely, and who had come to New York because he had no job back in Puerto Rico.

"I always thought I would go back," the old man said. "But it was too expensive, too long a trip. I finally went in 1958, with my son, who paid for the airplane ticket. In three days I was ready to come home. I had been away too long and I was a New Yorker, not a real Puerto Rican anymore. It was sad."

A Puerto Rican was something strange and exotic in those days. There weren't enough of them to be a threat to anybody, not enough of them to be identified as a group. The word "spic" came later (most common theory: from the phrase "No spik Inglis"). It came with the wave after the war. It came with the airplane.

And it was the airplane that changed everything. The ships

started shifting to freight (and I knew a woman who had been torpedoed in one off the Bahamas during the war and lived to put double locks on her home in Williamsburg and lose a husband to alcohol). The airplane changed it all. The hustlers moved in with the charter flights and created a kind of airborne steerage, with shaking aircraft, packed with women and screaming children, skimming out over the Atlantic, pushing against the headwinds of the North, moving on, leaving it all behind, heading for New York. A lot of the planes never made it, falling into the sea with their cargoes of people doomed to hope, until the charter flights were banned and the big lines took over.

Every day the planes unloaded, and the people were pathetic to look at. Their suitcases were cardboard, tied with rope, holding everything they possessed. They did not understand the cold; they had seen snow only in the movies; they arrived in January in sports shirts, with vague addresses scribbled in pencil on the backs of envelopes, and hardly any money. The cold overwhelmed a lot of them. "After that first winter," a friend told me, "I was never warm." Somehow they would make it from the airports to town, and there were jokes among them later, when they had the luxury of laughter, that the Puerto Ricans were the only people in New York who knew how to get to Idlewild by public transportation.

There was no place to go except to the slums, of course: to the dark spiky landscapes of fire escapes and mean streets and doors covered with metal. There was never enough heat, and they plugged towels into the cracked windows to keep out winter, and bought a hundred thousand miles of felt tape to tack around doors, and made blankets from leftover clothes, and carried drums of kerosene up to the stoves in the parlor, and kept the gas ovens going at night. It was never warm enough, and every time you picked up a paper then and saw a headline that said SEVEN PERISH IN TENEMENT BLAZE, you knew it was Puerto Ricans and that they had died of the cold.

That New York cold killed a lot of them. The cold made a man a "spic" instead of a man. The cold that sent women off to work in sweatshops for more money than their husbands were making cleaning the slops in the cellar of the Waldorf. Myths were growing up then, in the late '40s and early '50s, especially after the outbreak of the Korean War brought jobs and the Puerto Rican trickle became a flood. They were here to go on welfare. They had come here because Vito Marcantonio, the old leftist congressman, had bought their votes. It didn't seem to matter that the Puerto Rican migration coincided almost exactly with the increase or decrease in jobs or that the Puerto Ricans had arrived at a time when automation was starting to eliminate the jobs which were traditionally the first rung on the immigrants' ladder. The myths grew up, part of the New York cold, part of everything that is mean-spirited and ungenerous in us.

The cold broke things apart among those who were not prepared to resist it. I remember one man I knew in East Harlem, sitting alone in his kitchen, while platoons of roaches scurried across the walls, his wife gone off, the house smelling of feet and long-burnt bacon, talking quietly over a can of Schaefer about how it had all gone wrong. "We should not have come here," he said. "This is an evil place. There is no respect, not for people, not for fathers." His daughter had not been home for two nights. She was 15 and he didn't know what to do about her. He talked about her, and about how he would like to go back to Puerto Rico, and how if he could find his wife he would bring her back with him and they could put the thing together again. His tone said that his mouth was lying. The city had broken him, and he sat there while a parakeet he had bought for his wife's birthday whistled in the other room. It was August and the cold came through the rooms, damp and threatening and triumphant.

But the Puerto Ricans have done what all the immigrants did. They have endured. They turned out to be long-distance runners, not sprinters, and now they are a very important part of this town. There are, to begin with, their numbers. The latest count shows that there are 1,586,397 Puerto Ricans in the United States (up from 855,724 in the 1960 census), with 977,832 of them in New York (up from 629,430 in 1960). In 1950, Puerto Ricans were only 3 per cent of the city's population; today they are almost 11 per cent. About one-third are second generation. One recent set of figures showed that there are 244,458 Puerto Rican students in the public school system, an increase of 75 per cent over a 10-year period.

The Puerto Ricans have spread to all parts of the city

(although Richmond still does not have any sizable population). Brooklyn now has the most—a symbol, I suppose, of the trend of migration; in this town a lot of the old immigrants went from the Manhattan slums to the Bronx and on to Brooklyn. The Puerto Ricans, who once were most heavily concentrated in East Harlem, were forced into the slums of the South Bronx by the swinging ball of urban renewal, and are now making it into the greener glades of Brooklyn. In addition, the number of Puerto Ricans outside the city has increased from 30,000 to 51,200, a 70 per cent jump. Suffolk County, with its Puerto Rican population increase of 4,700, leads the other 62 counties in the state.

More important is the fact that the Puerto Ricans have been accepted. It has been a long time since I have heard the word "spic" around this town. (The Spanish-language papers continue to use the word *boricua*, which derives from the pre-Spanish name for the island, Borinquen. A lot of the second-generation kids just refer to each other as "P.R.s".) In my white-middle-class neighborhood, the Puerto Ricans open grocery stores and put starched collars on their children in the mornings before sending them off to school.

The Puerto Ricans have followed the old routes: some 10,000 of them run small businesses in this town, and some are expanding into larger things. There are people like José Rojas, who is now the president of Puerto Rican Steel Products Incorporated at 4 Whale Square in Brooklyn. He and eight others have started their own steel plant, with the help of private business interests and the United Puerto Rican and Spanish Organizations of Sunset Park. Or someone like Pablo Morales, who got a $2,000 loan from the Banco de Ponce several years ago to buy a truck, and now owns five trucks in his own garage on Westchester Avenue and Southern Boulevard in El Bronx. The Puerto Rican banks themselves are an important part of the story, ever since they were allowed to operate in New York after changes in the state banking laws in 1961; Banco de Ponce now has four branches in the city, as has the Banco Popular, and the Banco Crédito is now breaking into this lucrative market.

The Puerto Rican Homeowners Association has plans to build a $2.7 million low- and middle-income housing development in Brooklyn, and the Puerto Rican Community Development Project has instituted programs which in one year led to 402 members of the community's receiving high school equivalency diplomas. Everywhere the mood is one of energy and movement; it is a long way from the desperate days of the early arrivals, when you would see thin, shivering girls in spring coats in winter walking 14th Street with guys in plastic-visored yacht caps, going to S. Klein on Christmas Eve to buy their kids the scraps. The great Puerto Rican neighborhoods are still solid blocks in the town: East Harlem, the South Bronx, Williamsburg, Red Hook, the Lower East Side. But there are Puerto Ricans scattered now throughout the city, in Bay Ridge and Corona and Inwood and out into the suburbs. They've purchased through grief and work and endurance that special thing which the sociologists work so hard at dehumanizing: mobility.

That mobility has freed the first brigades of the emerging Puerto Rican middle class in this town (with the same set of conflicts over loyalties to those left behind which afflicts the black middle class). But there are still hundreds of thousands living in desperate situations, and the Puerto Ricans are in fact still at the bottom of the city's economic ladder. One recent study (by Leonard S. Kogan and Morey J. Wantman) estimated that the median annual income for all city families was $6,684. The Puerto Ricans earned $3,949, nonwhites $4,754, and whites $7,635. The Puerto Ricans had gained only $49 in two years, while whites gained $927. Puerto Ricans receiving relief rose more in percentage than any other group—from 29.5 per cent of the welfare rolls in 1959 to 33 per cent in 1967—they are now about 35 to 40 per cent. Some estimates state that some 40 per cent of the city's Puerto Ricans are receiving some form of public assistance, most of it supplementing the low wages paid to Puerto Rican fathers.

In East Harlem last year, according to Herbert Bienstock, the regional director of the Bureau of Labor Statistics, 36.9 per cent of Puerto Rican workers were unemployed or subemployed. The general rate was 33.1, indicating that blacks there fared slightly better. In Bedford-Stuyvesant, 29.7 per cent of Puerto Ricans were unemployed, compared to 27.6 per cent of the blacks. In Harlem itself, 12 per cent of the Puerto Ricans are unemployed, and 8 per cent of the blacks.

In some respects, the situation is not encouraging at all. White-collar employment of Puerto Rican men actually declined from 17 to 12 per cent from 1960 to 1965, according to Richard Lewisohn of the Economic Development Administration, while—in the familiar pattern—white-collar employment of Puerto Rican women increased (from 18.7 per cent to 24.9 per cent). In a report released last year by the federal government's Equal Employment Opportunity Commission, we learned that only .9 per cent of these employed in radio-TV and newspaper white-collar jobs were Puerto Ricans. (On the three major New York dailies, only 2.5 per cent of *all* employees were Puerto Rican or of Latin background.) In the banking industry, only 5.1 per cent of white-collar employees were Puerto Rican. The government queried 4,239 firms with 100 employees or more, or with more than $50,000 in federal contracts; some 1,926 firms did not employ a single Puerto Rican in a white-collar job. A survey by the State Human Rights Commission showed that of 25 of the city's 41 major advertising agencies, only 1.6 of their 18,000 employees were Puerto Rican.

Some of this can be attributed to the problem of education. An analysis by the Puerto Rican Forum shows that of those Puerto Ricans who finish high school, 90 per cent have been getting a general diploma, 8 per cent a vocational degree, and only 1.2 per cent the academic diploma leading to college. In the elementary schools, there is still an insistence on teaching kids in English, which they sometimes do not know, with the result that ordinarily bright kids are stunned and humiliated before they have much of a chance to learn anything at all.

Another factor is that the Puerto Ricans are the youngest people in the city, with a median age (according to a 1966 City University study) of 19.1, compared to 38.6 for whites and 26.1 for nonwhites. This indicates a group in flux, and the educational statistics at present might be quite misleading; there might be an explosion of academic diplomas any year now. It is one indication of the way the Board of Education sees the students, however, that despite the fact that blacks and Puerto Ricans make up more than one-half of the city's public school population, only 30 of the more than 900 schools are named after distinguished blacks and only five after Puerto Ricans.

And yet, just because the Puerto Ricans are so young, and just because they are starting to make their move, we have to deal with their presence in a rational way. Anyone who understands New York will understand that their presence is a good thing for us, perhaps the most fortunate piece of luck we have had since the end of the Second World War.

To begin with, the Puerto Ricans have brought an element of stability to New York. When the white middle class started its mass stampede to the suburbs, lamming like units of a defeated army across the frontier, the Puerto Ricans stayed on. They stayed on because they had to stay on. You simply do not have a choice if you can't ever imagine yourself having $2,000 for a down payment on a house. They stayed on, too, because they wanted to. More than the white-middle-class refugees, the Puerto Ricans understood early that this could be a mean and nasty and vicious town, but it was also a great one.

"I tried living in the country," my friend José Torres, the former light-heavyweight champion of the world, once told me. "It was beautiful. There was grass and trees and clean air and birds. People were friendly. It was healthy. The schools were not crowded. The trouble was that I started going crazy. I needed noise."

Noise. Not the noise of jackhammers and ripped sidewalks and coughing trucks. What Torres means is the noise of streets, to be able to walk along Smith Street in Brooklyn and hear people shouting back and forth at each other in greeting and guys coming out of saloons on Saturday afternoons to stop friends and whisper *piropos* to girls ("Ah, *mi vida*, it must have been a fine and splendid mother to have produced such a beauty as you"). The noise is at a party in my friend Cocolo's house on Dean Street, the bathtub packed with ice and beer, babies crying in the kitchen, the table groaning with *pulpo*, and arguments in English and Spanish over the Mets and Mario Procaccino and the cost of cigars and Fidel Castro and the best way to seduce a Swedish girl. Cocolo has hit the number for the third time that year, and all his friends are there, and his relatives. "Hey, you better eat all this stup, mon, because you doan hit the number three times in a year every year." Cocolo is beaming, and on his wall he has a picture of Jack Kennedy and a poster from the O'Dwyer campaign and a smaller picture of Robert Kennedy, and later in the night, all of us slowed by beer and food, and the children asleep, and not much more to travel to daylight,

Cocolo points up at the picture of Bob Kennedy and says, "Hey mon, you explain this goddam country. What kine of a sum-of-a-bitch would shoot that guy? Huh? You explain that to me, mon." And the other three guys start to sing, because they've seen this happen before, and they don't want Cocolo, who is 38 years old and weighs 240 pounds, to start crying all over again.

That kind of noise: and nights in Otero's on Smith Street, eating *pernil* in the back room, and talking boxing at the bar, and how one night we all came in late and the place was empty and Junior, the bartender, had a big bandage on his face. "What the hell happened?" someone said. "You get in a fight with your girl?" And Junior said, no, it wasn't a fight, it was a car accident. Pedro Ortiz, the meanest-looking man in Brooklyn, leers: "Hey, Junior, you don't have to lie to us." And Junior gets mad and goes into the back room and comes back with the door from his car, the whole goddam door, smashed and crumpled, and everyone starts to laugh, and Pedro Ortiz falls off the stool, and we order another round.

That's what José Torres means by noise. Noise and life. Travel around a little and look at it: the Jefferson Theatre, with the children crying in the audience and guys selling ice cream right in the middle of the movie, and a great comic like Johnny El Men making jokes on the stage about being a Puerto Rican in New York. Move around: to the Broadway Casino, or Carlos Ortiz' place in the South Bronx, or the Club Caborrojeño, and make a Saturday night. Who's on? La Playa, or Tito Puente, or El Gran Combo, with the music thundering down, the musicians making bad jokes, and lights sly and romantic, the girl singers with impossibly narrow waists above implacable swelling hips. And on the dance floor, girls with soft fleshy faces doing hammering mambos with their shoes off, series after series, the guys weaving baroque steps around them, the floor itself starting to groan from the pounding, the single guys lined against the walls, the people from the community clubs sitting in private parties at the tables, an occasional older woman chaperoning her daughter or niece. Ten years ago, Torres and I spent a lot of time in those places, and maybe he would have been a better fighter and I would have been a better writer if we had stayed home. I doubt it. We certainly wouldn't have had as much laughter.

The problems remain terrible. Nine out of 10 Puerto Ricans over the age of 25 have never finished high school. There are still large sections of the community which do not read or speak English, which depend for news and information on the Spanish radio and TV (UHF) stations and upon *El Diario-La Prensa* (the other Spanish-language paper, *El Tiempo*, is a right-wing sheet directed to the community of Cuban exiles and other non-Puerto Rican Spanish-speaking people in the city: *El Tiempo* supported Mario Procaccino over Herman Badillo in the Democratic primary). There are still many Puerto Ricans working for unconscionably low salaries in sweatshops and factories run by gangster unions; a union like the International Ladies Garment Workers Union still does not have real representation of Puerto Ricans at its highest level despite the overwhelming number of Puerto Ricans in its rank and file. Narcotics remains a poison, with some communities, like Hunts Point in the Bronx, practically devastated by the problem. Heroin addicts were practically unknown in Puerto Rico itself until those who were contaminated started coming home from New York. The Puerto Rican street gangs, which were so prominent in the 1950s (the Enchanters, the Dragons, the Latin Gents, etc.), have largely disappeared, not because of especially enlightened social workers, but because a junkie doesn't have much time for gangbusting. ("It's not cool anymore to be in the hitter's bag, man," one kid told me last year.)

In the 1950s and early 1960s, there were still so many broken marriages that they seemed to a casual outsider to be almost a majority. Every day's issue of *El Diario* carried stories of guys who would visit their estranged wives and throw wives, kids and selves out the fourth floors of tenements. The pressures were intolerable: women who worked and made more money than men offended the Puerto Rican male's occasionally exaggerated sense of *machismo;* the resort to welfare was humiliating; the disgraceful conditions of the tenements themselves did not exactly make for the most encouraging belief in a happy and rich future. But that seems to have lessened with the breakthrough the Puerto Rican men made into the town itself. If a man does not feel he is being supported by his wife he can find it a lot easier to live with her, whether he is a Puerto Rican or not.

The younger generation of Puerto Ricans are also making

the whole thing move in another way. They don't feel sorry
for themselves, they have been here all their lives, they have
a sense of what must be done and how to go after it. Some
are starting militant Puerto Rican organizations, like Barrio
Nuevo in East Harlem. Others are going the college route.
Many of them have been made aware of the obscene distor-
tions in American life which let blacks, Puerto Ricans and
poor whites fight unjust wars while the children of the middle class have the luxury of protesting it from the sanctity of
the college campus. Some have gone into a rather romantic,
nostalgic Puerto Rican independence bag, which might work
if the Puerto Rican in Puerto Rico could only believe it was
the best thing for him. (The various independence parties
have never fared well at the polls in Puerto Rico, which, if
it ever gives up its present semi-colonial commonwealth status, would more likely opt for becoming a state.) Increasingly,
the younger generation is political, and if that has set up a
generation gap of sorts, it is only because the Puerto Ricans
are finally part of something larger. For one thing, they have
a sense of laughter now that just wasn't there 15 years ago; I
think of the group of Puerto Rican high school girls on the
F train, coming back from Coney Island singing: "We all live
in a yellow submarine, eating rice and beans, eating rice and
beans . . ."

The young people are throwing over some of the things
their parents believed in. The ones I've talked to are not ter-
rified of Communists (despite all the horror stories passed on
to them about Fidel). They certainly don't listen much to
the spiritist heresy, in which *brujas* (witches) can be hired
to cast spells, or win women, or whatever else one might
want, at a price and with the purchase of the right herbs at
the *botánica:* Religion itself doesn't seem very strong anymore, either. Some 85 per cent of the Puerto Ricans in Puerto
Rico are Catholics, but until very recently the church there
was run by outsiders, by Irish bishops or Spanish bishops, by
anyone but Puerto Rican bishops. In New York this meant
that not many Puerto Ricans ever went to church, and those
that "got religion" generally ended up in a more lively, less
authoritarian, but somewhat more puritanical form of Christianity like the Pentecostal.

The younger people seem more interested in specifics. I
remember going to a meeting in East Harlem the day after

the 1967 riots took place. Ted Velez and Andrew Segarra and Torres and a lot of others had worked long into the night trying to cool the riots, and this meeting, in a school auditorium, was held to try to make sure that that trouble would not flare up again. There were representatives from the city and from the police to listen to the grievances of the young people who had done most of the fighting and bottle-throwing. Their initial grievance, as it had been in other circumstances in other sections of the city, was with the Tactical Patrol Force. The TPF, these kids felt, was an armed guard of cops from outside the district, cops who could not possibly know who was who in East Harlem, who probably did not know much about Puerto Ricans, and who had reacted brutally and without sensitivity to the first outbreak of trouble. That was predictable. But when that had been cleared out of the way, they got down to the real issues. One kid got up, his voice laden with emotion, and said very loudly: "All right, to hell with that for a minute. I want to know *why* in the goddam hell you can't get the garbage off 112th Street? Just get the garbage and we'll believe you." It is a measure of how the bureaucracy cannot seem to unwind itself that in August of this year there was almost a second East Harlem riot. It was over the failure of the Sanitation Department to pick up the garbage on 112th Street.

When there was trouble on the Lower East Side the year before last, I went down there to talk to the people on the streets. One guy ran up to his apartment. "I got to get our demands, mon." The demands were again familiar: get the TPF out of the neighborhood, clean the garbage more frequently ("We got big families, mon, and we make more garbage"). But the demands that interested me were the ones that seemed most Puerto Rican. One was "a place to play dominoes." The other: "dancing once in a while."

Politically, the Puerto Ricans are certainly on the move. The near victory of Herman Badillo in the Democratic primary has probably removed "the Puerto Rican thing" the way John F. Kennedy's 1960 victory changed the myth about Catholics running for President. This was not supposed to be the year for a Puerto Rican, and Badillo was supposed to have been better off running for the controller's office or as president of the City Council on somebody else's ticket. When he almost won (he lost by 38,000 votes), he established himself *and* the Puerto Ricans as an important political force in New York. On the other hand, there still remains a problem of apathy to be overcome. The Puerto Ricans are still the hardest people in the city to get registered, because of a combination of factors (distrust of politicians, uneasiness about the language, and fear of anything resembling an agent of the government are some of the factors; among older Puerto Ricans, there is still some feeling that they aren't from New York, that their political candidates are an airplane ride away).

The streak of conservatism in the Puerto Ricans also seems to be widening as more of them make it into the middle class. Many of them join regular Democratic clubs, because they see those clubs as the safest way to make it politically; a man like Tony Mendez, the regular boss of East Harlem, remains a powerful man politically, and some of the less radical or adventurous younger Puerto Ricans don't want to take any chances on blowing a career by playing Don Quixote. Rivalry among Puerto Rican politicians is rather strong, and sometimes leads to bizarre situations: next year there will not be a single Puerto Rican serving on the City Council, despite the fact that there are more Puerto Ricans here than in San Juan. In those councilmanic districts where a Puerto Rican might have been elected, Puerto Ricans ran against each other and non-Puerto Ricans slipped through the seams.

Despite that, the Puerto Rican community seems more together now than it has ever been. "Up until a couple of years ago," a pretty young schoolteacher from the Two Bridges district told me, "I was ashamed to say I was a Puerto Rican. I would say I was Spanish, or something like that. Today I'm ashamed for being ashamed. We P.R.s are really going to take this town."

They might just do that—politically, at least—and it might not be such a bad thing. They have already added things to New York which have made it a better place: their music and their food and their sense of the outrageous. No matter where you want to go, if you travel with a Puerto Rican cab-driver, he'll take you there: he'll say: "Hey, I don't know where it is, but you show me, mon, and I take you." The rocky decade with the marriages seems over, and the stable family unit is there again, the way it is in Puerto Rico. There is still a feeling among those who came here from

Puerto Rico that they don't really belong to this town, but in that sense they belong nowhere. My friend Johnny Manzanet, who is a boxing commissioner now, once said to me: "You know, I sit here in New York, and I'm homesick for Salinas; I go home to Salinas and I'm homesick for New York. I don't know what the hell I am."

What seems to be forming is a special breed: the New York Puerto Rican. One who listens to La Lupe and the Beatles, who reads the *Times* and *El Diario*, who can move around the East Side pubs and still make it up to the Broadway Casino. He is a baseball fan, because of Orlando Cepeda and Roberto Clemente and a dozen other stars who came up from the island; but he probably does not look for the score of the Ponce-Caguas game anymore; he more than likely roots for the Mets (I have yet to meet a Puerto Rican who cared for pro football or rooted for the Yankees). But he no longer needs to go to prizefights to identify vicariously with heroes. He seems to be breaking down between two New York cultural traditions, with a touch of the third: the Puerto Rican with a can of beer in a paper bag playing dominoes on the street is the Irish Puerto Rican; the guy selling the beer in the *bodega* is the Jewish Puerto Rican; the guy starting to move into numbers and narcotics in East Harlem is the Mafia Puerto Rican. Ah, give me your tired, your poor . . .

Here, compadre, put the luggage in the rack. I'll be in the bar having a Scotch and soda. It will be warm soon enough. I have to tell my friends about snow, and the lights of Broadway, and the way the kids wear their hair in the East Village, and that crazy night I spent at the Electric Circus with the newspapermen. That, and hard afternoons looking for work, and the time we had to grab the landlord and push his face against the wall to make him listen to the rats scratching behind us. That, but the good things too: theatres, and the Big A, and fight night at the Garden, and hanging around the corner on Degraw Street, and playing ball in the weekend leagues in Central Park, and the great shows coming through at the San Juan and the Puerto Rico. That, and how the skyline looks coming across from Jersey at night, and the way the girls swagger down Fifth Avenue on the first warm day of spring. It will be warm soon enough, and I want to see the pastel houses in the sun and the palms blowing in the breeze and the dead calm before the hurricanes. And music.

Joseph P. Fitzpatrick

TRANSITION TO THE MAINLAND*

TRANSITION TO THE MAINLAND

The institution which faces the most direct shock in the migration to the mainland is the family, and the progress of Puerto Ricans can be measured to a large extent by a study of the family. First a statistical description of Puerto Rican families can be presented, followed by an analysis of the effect of migration on the family.

It has long been recognized that the migration of Puerto Ricans is a family migration, in the sense that they either come as families, or expect to stay and found their families here. This is reflected in the percentage of the population on the mainland which is married. According to the 1960 census, of all Puerto Rican males over 14 years of age, 70 per cent were married; of females, about 80 per cent.[14] Age at marriage shows a sharp decline from first generation to second generation, indicating an adaptation to mainland patterns.

Type of Ceremony

Another indication of change can be found in the type of religious ceremony of Puerto Rican marriages on the mainland. As indicated before, this varies considerably from one area of Puerto Rico to another. Comparison of type of religious ceremony for all marriages in Puerto Rico for 1960 with type of religious ceremony for Puerto Rican marriages

* Joseph P. Fitzpatrick, "The Family: Transition to the Mainland," *Puerto Rican Americans*. Prentice-Hall, 1971, pp. 92–100. Printed with permission.
[14] J. P. Fitzpatrick, "Intermarriage of Puerto Ricans in New York City," *Amer. J. of Sociol.*, 71, 4 (1966), 401, Tables 4 and 5.

in New York City for 1959 brings results as shown in Table 6–4.

Two things are evident from Table 6–4. The pattern of marriage ceremony differs considerably between Puerto Rico and New York, and the pattern in New York, as in Puerto Rico, changed greatly between 1949 and 1959. The increase in Catholic ceremonies can be explained by the widespread efforts of the Catholic Archdioceses of New York and Brooklyn to develop special programs for the religious care of Puerto Rican people between 1949 and 1959. In addition,

TABLE 6–4

Type of Religious Ceremony for All Marriages in Puerto Rico and All Puerto Rican Marriages in New York City for Selected Years

	Civil (%)	Catholic (%)	Protestant (%)
Puerto Rico, 1949	24.3	61.4	14.3
Puerto Rico, 1960	36.2	45.8	17.6
New York City, 1949 (n. 4514)[a]	20.0	27.0	50.0
New York City, 1959 (n. 9370)	18.0	41.0	38.0

SOURCE: J. P. Fitzpatrick, "Intermarriage of Puerto Ricans in New York City," *Amer. J. of Sociol.*, 71, 4 (1966), 403.

[a] A small number of other types of ceremonies are included in this total.

ceremonies in Pentecostal and Evangelical Churches declined from 1949 to 1959, particularly between first and second generation. If the Protestant marriages performed by ministers of Pentecostal and Evangelical sects are taken separately, the decline is very evident. In 1959, 38.4 per cent of first generation grooms were married by Pentecostal ministers, but only 33.3 per cent of second generation grooms; among brides, 37 per cent of first generation, but only 30.1 per cent of the second generation were married by Pentecostal ministers.[15] The implications of this for religious practice will be discussed in Chapter Eight. The consistent drop from first to second generation tends to confirm the theory that association with sects

[15] *Ibid.*, 404, Table 10.

and storefront religious groups is a first generation phenomenon. When the second generation becomes more familiar with American life, they tend to withdraw from the sects.

Out-Group Marriage

The most significant evidence of adjustment to life on the mainland has been the increase of marriage of Puerto Ricans with non-Puerto Ricans. In his study of New York marriages, 1949 and 1959, Fitzpatrick established that there is a significant increase in the rate of out-group marriage among second generation Puerto Ricans over the first. The data are presented in Table 6–5.

The increase in the rate of out-group marriage among Puerto Ricans in both 1949 and 1959 between the first and second generation was as great as was the increase for all immigrants in New York City in the years 1908 to 1912.[16] It is legitimate to conclude from this that, if out-group marriage is accepted as an index of assimilation, the assimilation of Puerto Ricans in New York is moving as rapidly as the assimilation of all immigrant groups during the years 1908–1912.

Changes in Values

Much more important than the statistical description of the Puerto Rican families in the United States or in New York City is the study of the changes in values which they face. Probably the most serious is the shift in roles of husband and wife. There is abundant evidence that this is a common experience of immigrants. It is provoked by a number of things. First, it is frequently easier for Puerto Rican women to get jobs in New York rather than Puerto Rican men. This gives the wife an economic independence which she may never have had before, and if the husband is unemployed while the wife is working, the reversal of roles is severe. Second, the impact of American culture begins to make itself felt more directly in New York than on the island. Puerto Rican women from the poorer classes are much more involved in

[16] The data for marriages of immigrants, 1908–1912, which were used in the Fitzpatrick study were taken from Julian Drachsler, *Intermarriage in New York City* (New York: Columbia University Press, 1921).

TABLE 6–5

Rate of Out-Group Marrage of Puerto Ricans in New York City, 1949 and 1959, by Generation; and of All Immigrants in New York City, 1908–1912

	First Generation		Second Generation		Increase in Second Generation
	%	No.	%	No.	%
Grooms:					
Puerto Rican, 1949	5.2	3,079	28.3	378	23.1
Puerto Rican, 1959	3.6	7,078	27.4	638	23.8
1908-1912	10.39	64,577	32.4	12,184	22.01
Brides:					
Puerto Rican, 1949	8.5	3,077	30.0	523	21.5
Puerto Rican, 1959	6.0	7,257	33.1	717	27.1
1908-1912	10.1	61,823	30.12	14,611	20.02

SOURCE: J. P. Fitzpatrick, "Intermarriage of Puerto Ricans in New York City," *Amer. J. of Sociol.*, 71, 4 (1966), 398.

social, community, and political activities than they are in Puerto Rico. This influences the Puerto Rican wife gradually to adopt the patterns of the mainland.

Even more direct and difficult to cope with is the shift in role of the Puerto Rican child. Puerto Rican families have frequently lamented the patterns of behavior of even good boys in the United States. Puerto Rican parents consider them to be disrespectful. American children are taught to be self-reliant, aggressive, and competitive, to ask "why," and to stand on their own two feet. A Puerto Rican child is generally much more submissive. When the children begin to behave according to the American pattern, the parents cannot understand it. A priest who had worked for many years with migrating Puerto Ricans remarked to the writer: "When these Puerto Rican families come to New York, I give the boys about 48 hours on the streets of New York, and the difference between his behavior and what the family expects, will have begun to shake the family."

The distance which gradually separates child from family

is indicated in much of the literature about Puerto Ricans in New York. In the autobiography of Piri Thomas, *Down These Mean Streets*,[17] it is clear that this family—and it was a good, strong family—had no way of controlling him once he began to associate with his peers on the streets. The sharp contrast of two life histories, *Two Blocks Apart*,[18] also demonstrates the difficulties of a Puerto Rican family in trying to continue to control the life of a boy growing up in New York. His peers become his significant reference group. A considerable number of scholars and social workers attribute much of the delinquency of Puerto Ricans to the excessive confinement which the Puerto Rican families impose in an effort to protect their children. Once the children can break loose in the early teens, they break completely. When Julio Gonzalez was killed in a gang fight on the lower East Side in reprisal for the murder of a Negro girl, Theresa Gee, in 1959, he was buried from Nativity Church. Julio's father, a poor man from a mountain town in Puerto Rico, was like a pillar of strength during the wake. He was a man of extraordinary dignity and self-possession. After the funeral Mass, he went to the sacristy of the Church, embraced each of the priests who had participated, and thanked them. Here was a man who sought to pass on to his son the qualities of loyalty, dignity, and strength. But when the son reached the streets, different definitions of loyalty and dignity took over. As Julio was dying, after the priest had given him the last rites of the Catholic Church, he fell into unconsciousness, mumbling: "Tell the guys they can count on me; tell them I'll be there."[19]

Probably the most severe problem of control is the effort of families to give their unmarried girls the same kind of protection they would have given them in Puerto Rico. When the girls reach the early teens, they wish to do what American girls do—go to dances with boys without a chaperone, and

[17] Piri Thomas, *Down These Mean Streets* (New York: Alfred A. Knopf, 1967).

[18] Charlotte Leon Mayerson, ed., *Two Blocks Apart* (New York: Holt, Rinehart and Winston, Inc., 1965).

[19] For a lengthy discussion of this change of values and its relation to delinquency, see J. P. Fitzpatrick, "Crime and Our Puerto Ricans," in *Catholic Mind*, LVIII (1960), 39–50. This is reprinted in Gus Tyler, *Organized Crime in America* (Ann Arbor: University of Michigan Press, 1962), pp. 415–421.

associate freely with girls and boys of the neighborhood or school. For a good Puerto Rican father to permit his daughter to go out unprotected is a serious moral failure. In a Puerto Rican town, when a father has brought his daughters as virgins to marriage, he can hold up his head before his community; he enjoys the esteem and prestige of a good father. To ask the same father to allow his daughters to go free in New York is to ask him to do something which the men of his family have considered immoral. It is psychologically almost impossible for him to do this. This tension between parents and daughter(s) is one of the most difficult for Puerto Rican parents to manage. It is frequently complicated because Americans, including school teachers and counsellors, who are not aware of the significance of this in the Puerto Rican background, advise the parents to allow the girls to go out freely.[20]

Finally, the classic tension between the generations takes place. The parents are living in the Puerto Rican culture in their homes. The children are being brought up in an American school where American values are being presented. The parents will never really understand their children; the children will never really understand the parents.

Weakening of Extended Kinship

Apart from the conflict between generations, the experience of migration tends to weaken the family bonds that created a supporting network on which the family could always rely. To a growing extent, the family finds itself alone. This is partly the result of moving from place to place. It is also due to the fact that the way of life in mainland cities is not a convenient environment for the perpetuation of family virtues and values. The Department of Social Services provides assistance in time of need, but not with the familiar, informal sense of personal and family respect. Regulations in housing, consumer loans, schools, and courts create a requirement for professional help, and the family is less and less effective.

[20] Protection of the girls generates its own problems in Puerto Rico, a form of "cloister rebellion" which may lead to escape from the home or elopement. It is well described in Stycos, *Family and Fertility, op. cit.,* Chap. 5.

Replacement of Personalist Values

Closely related to all the above difficulties, and creating difficulties of its own, is the slow and steady substitution of impersonal norms, norms of the system rather than norms of personal relationships. The need to adjust to the dominant patterns of American society requires a preparation to seek employment and advancement on the basis of merit or ability. To people for whom the world is an extensive pattern of personal relationships, this is a difficult adjustment.

This process of uprooting has been described before in the extensive literature about immigrants. It leads to three kinds of adjustments. The first involves escape from the immigrant or migrant group and an effort to become as much like the established community as possible in as short a time as possible. These people seek to disassociate themselves from their past. They sometimes change their name, they change their reference groups, and seek to be accepted by the larger society. They are in great danger of becoming marginal. Having abandoned the way of life of their own people, in which they had a sense of "who they were," there is no assurance that they will be accepted by the larger community. They may find themselves in a no man's land of culture. In this stage, the danger of personal frustration is acute.

A second reaction is withdrawal into the old culture, a resistance to the new way of life. These people seek to retain the older identities by locking themselves into their old ways of life.

The third reaction is the effort to build a cultural bridge between the culture of the migrants and that of the mainland. These are the people who have confidence and security in their own way of life, but who realize that it cannot continue. Therefore, they seek to establish themselves in the new society, but continue to identify themselves with the people from whom they come. These are the ones through whom the process of assimilation moves forward.

PRESENT SITUATION OF PUERTO RICAN FAMILIES

In view of the above discussion, it is important to discover at what level of assimilation the Puerto Rican family now stands, and how it is affected by the problem of identity. In terms of intermarriage, the data indicate that the increase in the rate of out-group marriage between first and second generation is as great as it was for all immigrants to New York, 1908–1912. Replication of the study for 1969 which is now in progress at Fordham University, New York, will involve many more first and second generation marriages, and will give a much more reliable indication of the trend. In this regard, Puerto Ricans are simply repeating the consistent pattern of immigrants who preceded them.

Second, in view of the character of the migration from Puerto Rico (i.e., the return of many Puerto Ricans from the mainland and the continuing movement of large numbers of new migrants to the mainland), there continue to be large numbers of Puerto Rican families in the early and difficult stages of adjustment to New York, struggling for a satisfactory cultural adjustment as defined by Gordon and Eisenstadt.

The increase in the number of second generation Puerto Ricans indicates that the classical problems of newcomers, the problems of the second generation, are very likely at a serious level and will continue to be so for a considerable length of time. In Chapters Nine to Twelve, some problem areas as they affect the Puerto Ricans will be reviewed— problems of education, mental illness, need for public assistance, and drug addiction. It is not clear just how family difficulties contribute to these larger problems, but it is certain that these problems contribute immeasurably to family difficulties. In the early 1960's, a group of Puerto Rican social workers founded the Puerto Rican Family Institute in an effort to assist Puerto Rican families in New York. The objective of the Institute was not simply to provide family casework, but rather to identify well established Puerto Rican families in New York and match them as *compadres* to newly arrived families which showed signs of suffering from the strains of adjustment to the city. This was an attempt to use the traditional forms of neighborhood and family help which were characteristic of Puerto Rico. Where families could be matched, the program has been very helpful. But recently the Institute has found that the percentage of families with serious and immediate problems has been increasing. This may reflect the fact that, as agencies around the city learn of a Puerto Rican Institute, they refer their Puerto Rican problem cases to it; it may also reflect the shock of uprooting upon the newly arriving families, or the disruption which occurs as the numbers in the second generation increase. The growth of militancy among the young will be another factor which will increase tension. However, in the demonstrations at City College of New York in the Spring of 1969, in which militant Puerto Rican students played a major part, observers commented that the parents of the Puerto Rican students were very much on hand supporting their sons and daughters, bringing them food, clothing, and supplies.

In the period during which the Puerto Ricans struggle for greater solidarity and identity as a community, the family remains the major psychosocial support for its members. In many cases it is a broken family; in others it is hampered by poverty, unemployment, illness; but it remains the source of strength for most Puerto Ricans in the process of transition. In the turbulent action of the musical *West Side Story*, when Bernardo, leader of the Puerto Rican gang, sees Tony, a youth of another ethnic group, approaching his sister Maria, Bernardo pulls Maria away from Tony to take her home; he then turns to Tony in anger and shouts: "You keep away from my sister. Don't you know we are a family people!"

During 1966 the first presentation in New York of *The Ox Cart* took place. This is a play by a Puerto Rican playwright, René Marqués, which presents a picture of a simple farm family in the mountains of Puerto Rico, struggling to survive but reflecting the deep virtues of family loyalty and strength. Under the influence of the oldest son, the family moves to a slum section of San Juan in order to improve itself. But deterioration sets in as the slum environment begins to attack the solidarity and loyalty of the family members. The family then moves to New York, where the strain of the uprooting becomes worse, the gap between mother and children more painful, and the virtues of the old mountain family seem even more distant. After the violent death of the son, the play ends with the valiant mother setting out to go back to the mountains of Puerto Rico, where she hopes to regain the traditional values of Puerto Rican family life which were destroyed in San Juan and New York.

This is an ancient theme, and it may be as true for Puerto Ricans as it was for earlier newcomers. But if the Puerto Ricans make it on the mainland, it will be through the same source of strength which supported the immigrants of earlier times—the solidarity of the family.

Manuel Maldonado-Denis

PUERTO RICANS:
PROTEST OR SUBMISSION[*]

ABSTRACT: The situation of Puerto Ricans in the United
States cannot be seen as abstracted from that of those living in
Puerto Rico. Puerto Rico has been a colony of the United
States since 1898, and the most pervasive characteristic of its
population—both in the Island and in the Mainland—is its
colonialist mentality or world view: hence, the attitude of submission and acquiescence characteristic of the Puerto Ricans.
The only forces in Puerto Rico that represent Puerto Rican
protest against the perpetuation of colonialism in Puerto Rico
are the proindependence groups. In this respect, their goal is
similar to that of the Black Power advocates in the United
States, because both groups are faced with a similar situation.
Only when Puerto Ricans have achieved decolonization, both
psychologically and politically, will they be able to come of
age as a true protest movement. Otherwise they run the risk of
a total destruction of Puerto Rican nationality, and cultural
assimilation by the United States.

Among the minority groups in the United States, Puerto
Ricans are the latecomers. In what constitutes an impressive
mass exodus after World War II, nearly a half-million Puerto
Ricans emigrated to the United States between 1945 and
1959. As a noted demographer has indicated, from 1940 to
1960 the Island lost nearly a million persons as a result of
this mass migration.[1] The majority of these Puerto Rican emi-
grants have settled in New York City, where an estimated

[*] Manuel Maldonado-Denis, "Puerto Ricans: Protest or Submission,"
Annals of American Academy of Political and Social Science, vol. 382
(March 1969), pp. 26–31. Reprinted with permission.

[1] José Luis Vásquez Calzada, "La emigración puertorriqueña:" ¿solu-
ción o problema"? *Revista de Ciencias Sociales*, Vol. VII, Núm. 4
(Diciembre 1963).

hree-quarters of a million live at present. They are concentrated mainly in East Harlem or Spanish Harlem—"El
Barrio," as Puerto Ricans are fond of calling it. A recent study
has pointed out that since the mid-1950's there has been a
reverse flow of migrants to Puerto Rico, estimated to number
at least 145,000.[2] Ease of communication with the Mainland,
the absence of immigration requirements (Puerto Ricans have
been American citizens since 1917), and the spur of economic necessity help to explain the reason why "at least one
out of every three persons born in Puerto Rico has experienced living in the United States at some time in his life."[3]

Furthermore, it is the declared policy of the Commonwealth's government to foster this mass migration as an "escape
value" that will help to ease the pressures of a population
growing at an annual rate of 2.1 per cent (as of 1966). This
migration tends to be among those age groups whose economic productivity is greatest. According to Dr. Vázquez
Calzada, in the decade from 1950 to 1960, 70 per cent of the
migrants were persons ranging from 15 to 39 years of age.
The Island's labor force faces an acute unemployment problem. Government economist Hubert C. Barton has estimated
it at 30 per cent, while other economists estimate it at around
14 per cent. But the situation facing the Puerto Rican migrants in the United States is hardly any better. An Associated Press dispatch, quoted in *The San Juan Star*, May 22,
1968, points out that Labor Department official Herbert
Beinstok indicated that a 1966 survey had shown that the
subemployment rate for Puerto Ricans in slum areas in New
York is 33.1 per cent, while the unemployment rate is 10 per
cent. In this respect, one need only read Patricia Cayo
Sexton's *Spanish Harlem: Anatomy of Poverty* or Helena
Padilla's *Up from Puerto Rico* to understand that the lot of
the Puerto Rican ghetto-dweller in New York is hardly any
better than that facing the "lumpenproletariat" in the slums
of San Juan, so vividly described by Oscar Lewis in his con-
troversial book *La Vida*. But, notwithstanding Puerto
Rican participation in the Poor People's March on Washington, and some sporadic outbursts of rebellion, it can hardly be
said that Puerto Ricans in the United States—as a group

[2] José Hernández Alvarez, *Return Migration to Puerto Rico* (Berkeley:
University of California, 1967), p. 40.

[3] *Ibid.*, p. 40.

that faces the prejudices and hardships of a nonwhite group in a racist society—have achieved, in their struggle for liberation, a level of consciousness and of militancy similar to that of Afro-Americans.

ISLAND AND MAINLAND PUERTO RICANS: SIMILARITY OF PROBLEMS

It would be a grievous mistake, however, if the problems facing the Puerto Ricans in the United States were to be seen as abstrated from the situation of the Puerto Ricans who live in Puerto Rico. The essence of the matter really lies in the relationship that exists between Puerto Rico and the United States.

Puerto Rican Nationality and United States Colonialism

It is my contention that Puerto Ricans are a colonial people with a colonial outlook, and that, as such, they have not been able, so far—as the Afro-Americans groups are increasingly doing—to achieve a true "decolonization," either in the political or in the psychological sense of the word. This holds true for Puerto Ricans both in Puerto Rico and in the United States. All the problems faced by Puerto Rico as a colony of the United States are found—and magnified—in the American metropolis: the question of identity, the problem of language, and the achievement of political power commensurate with numerical strength. And, yet, an attitude of acquiescence, of passive submission, seems to characterize the Puerto Ricans both here and in New York City, with the exception of those groups within the Puerto Rican population which have mounted a persistent protest against the perpetuation of colonialism in our country ever since 1898. I refer in this instance to those sectors of our population which have carried on the struggle for independence from American domination.

Puerto Rico exhibits a distinct nationality. And Puerto Ricans—including those who live in the Mainland—are a people with a culture, a language, a tradition, a history. Nevertheless, the colonization of Puerto Rico under the American flag has meant the gradual erosion of our culture nd the slow but persistent destruction of the Puerto Rican's ense of identity. This means, in effect, that, as the late ationalist leader Pedro Albizu Campos stated on one occasion, the essential goal of any colonial regime is the cultural ssimilation of the colonized people. The process is not yet complete because Puerto Rican culture has shown a certain esilience, a certain capacity for survival and resistance, that as forced the colonial legislators and administrators to pause before continuing in their course.

As Frantz Fanon—the most perceptive and articulate writer speaking for the colonized, not the colonialists—has pointed out, colonialism creates in the minds of colonial peoples a sense of inferiority, a feeling of impotence and self-destruction, a desire to negate themselves by becoming more like the colonialist. Thus, aggressiveness tends to take the orm of internal aggressiveness, an aggressiveness against one's own group. The situation is very similar to that of the black people living in a white man's world. They are faced squarely with the problem of either asserting their own "négritude" or assimilating to the ways of the whites. Accordingly, one of the responses to colonialism may be, not liberation, but submission to the colonizer: assimilation, not the struggle for identity. This, I submit, has been the case of the Puerto Ricans. It is only because there are groups within our society which fight for the survival of our nationality that it has survived to the present day. Otherwise, Puerto Rico would have disappeared as a nationality, to become another ingredient within the American melting pot.

Proindependence Movements

American occupation of the Island in 1898 dealt a grave blow to those Puerto Ricans who believed that the United States would not impose upon the Puerto Rican people a colonial regime similar to that which had governed the Island during the four centuries of Spanish rule. And, in 1904, independence was adopted—together with statehood and autonomy—as one of the definitive solutions to Puerto Rico's political status by the Partido Unión de Puerto Rico, the most powerful political party at that time. However, the struggle for Puerto Rican independence reached its highest peak in this century during the decade of the 1930's, spearheaded by the Puerto Rican Nationalist party, under the leadership of Pedro Albizu Campos. Proindependence sentiment was strong in Puerto Rico at the time, and both Albizu Campos and Luis Muñoz Marín (who later was to reject the ideals of his youth) were outspoken in the defense of independence. After several violent encounters with the police, and the killing of the chief of police (an American) by members of the Nationalist party, all of its top leaders were jailed under a "conspiracy" statute of the federal government (1936). On Palm Sunday of 1937, the police carried out—under orders from Governor Blanton Winship—what is known as the "Ponce Massacre," in which the police shot unarmed demonstrators of the Nationalist party in the City of Ponce. With their leaders jailed, the Nationalist movement entered into a state of disarray, and official repression gained momentum.

Repression reached its peak in 1950 and 1954, as a consequence of the Nationalist uprising of October 30, 1950, the attempt to kill President Truman, and the shooting of several congressmen by four Puerto Rican Nationalists in 1954. As a result, Albizu Campos spent the rest of his life in prison, or under police detention in the hospital where he was interned following a stroke, until he was released by Executive order shortly before his death. Many of his followers were jailed or killed as a result of these acts, and there are, at present, seventeen political prisoners in Puerto Rican and American jails, some of them serving sentences of up to 460 years. It is fair to say that police persecution of Nationalist party members and the jailing of the leaders of the party were successful enough to blunt the effectiveness of the Nationalist party as a political force in Puerto Rico.

It was also in the 1930's that the Popular Democratic party (PDP) was founded by Luis Muñoz Marín. Although originally committed to independence, social justice, and the liquidation of colonialism, the PDP, once it achieved power in 1940, veered its course in such a way that it is, at the present moment, the archenemy of independence. As a result, a group of the disenchanted founded the Puerto Rican Independence party in 1946, a party devoted to the search for independence through the ballot box. This party reached its greatest strength in the 1952 elections and then started to decline to its present all-time low. Dissidence within its ranks led to the creation, in 1956, of the Pro-Independence Movement (PIM), at present the most militant and radical of all proindependence groups in Puerto Rico. Although there are at least three other proindependence groups—the Puerto Rican Independence party, the Nationalist party, and the Socialist League—the PIM is undoubtedly the one which, by its policy of confrontation, exhibited through resistance to the military draft, alliance with United States New Left groups, and attendance at the Organization for Latin-American Solidarity (OLAS) Conference, as well as through political activism guided by a radical ideology, has been able to carry on the protest movement in Puerto Rico most successfully at the present time.

Contemporary Conflicts

Puerto Rican youths are compulsorily drafted into the United States Army, as a result of the fact that, in 1917, Congress imposed American citizenship on the Puerto Rican people. A movement has emerged, particularly among university youth, for the purpose of refusing to serve in the United States Armed Forces. About a year ago, more than a thousand Puerto Rican youths signed a public statement declaring that they would refuse to enter the United States Army under any circumstances. The United States District Attorney in San Juan has already indicted about fifty youngsters, but the number of opponents to the draft keeps increasing. So far, the policy of the United States government seems to be one of intimidation, but none of the cases have come up before a court. The matter is generally disposed of by means of a technicality.

University students have also expressed their protest by battling the police on the campus at the University of Puerto Rico on October 28, 1964 and, more recently, on September 27, 1967. In May of 1967, more than a thousand students successfully disrupted a parade of the Reserve Officers Training Corps (ROTC) at the University of Puerto Rico, as a means of demonstrating their protest against militarism. The leaders were suspended as a result. Many of them now face indictment for the events of September 27, 1967, when the police shot at the students on two occasions, killing a man who happened to be on campus at the time as an innocent bystander.

"Repressive Tolerance" and the Colonialist Syndrome

As an American colony, Puerto Rico illustrates very clearly what Professor Marcuse has called "repressive tolerance." The Puerto Rican is allowed to express his views about "the System," insofar as the does not endanger it. Indeed, "the System" itself fosters the kind of dissent that can be shown as a confirmation of its members' own "generosity" and sense of "fair play." In this respect, the colonial elite that rules Puerto Rico on behalf of the American power elite has been successful, so far, in muting Puerto Rican discontent or in suppressing it altogether by incorporating or assimilating it within the existing structures. The same holds true— with rare exceptions—with Puerto Rican leaders in New York. The Puerto Rican youngster is taught an official interpretation of our history that denigrates or ignores the independence movement and its tradition. Private schools in Puerto Rico—out of which come the future numbers of the colonial elite—indulge in the antipedagogic practice of teaching everything in English. The mass media are almost totally controlled by Americans. Indoctrination to imitation of American mddle-class values is constant in the mass media. Add to these factors the influence of absentee ownership of most of our industry (78 per cent is owned by Americans), commerce, and financial institutions; the occupation of more than 13 per cent of our tillable land by American Armed Forces; and the drafting of our youth into the United States Armed Forces, and the picture will emerge more clearly. Puerto Rico is a country that is threatened at its very roots by the American presence here, the rhetoric of "a bridge between two cultures" and "bilingualism" notwithstanding. After seven decades of American colonial rule, what is really surprising is that there is still a hard core of Puerto Rican culture and identity that holds out against the American culture's penetration.

And yet, the most pervasive, the most significant, tendency that one finds among the Puerto Rican population, both in the Island and in the United States is what one might call the "colonialist syndrome": that aggregation of attitudes, orientations, and perceptions which magnifies the power, wisdom, and achievements of the colonizer while minimizing the power, wisdom, and achievements of the colonized. No one illustrates this attitude better than the completely "Americanized" Puerto Rican, who, in his quest to be more "American," seeks to identify as closely as possible with the patterns of culture of the metropolis. The grotesque aspect of this syndrome may be found in the "men" (as he is called), or cultural hybrid, resembling the Mexican "pachuco," whose sense of identity is so blurred that he—like his Mexican counterpart described so brilliantly by Octavio Paz in *The Labyrinth of Solitude*—has no roots and no bearings: a cultural schizophrenic who does not know what he is.

The colonialist "syndrome" is, of course, played down by the elite that helps it on its way, but it is nurtured by an almost complete dependence on the United States Congress as the main source of legislation for Puerto Rico, as well as by other federal aid programs extended to Puerto Rico and administered directly by the federal bureaucracy. As long as Puerto Ricans themselves do not control the decision-makers who determine their fate on a day-to-day basis, the attitudes and orientations characteristic of colonial subservience to the wielder of power will continue to prevail in Puerto Rico and among Puerto Ricans in the Mainland. Today, the Puerto Rican protest is limited to a minority of the population, while the majority remains acquiescent, perhaps more out of a sense of impotence than out of approval of the present situation.

A Puerto Rican protest will only be effective when Puerto Ricans free themselves from the mental bonds that, more than anything else, hold them in submission. The real problem now is how to crystallize the Puerto Rican protest effectively, so that more and more groups within the population, here and in the Mainland, will come to understand, at the conscious level, that their true interest lies, not in assimilation and dissolution, but in assertion and identity. "Puerto Rican power" should be a welcome complement to Black Power, to the extent that it sees Puerto Ricans—as the Afro-Americans are increasingly seeing themselves—as a nationality that is faced with the threat of extinction within the framework of a colonial situation. This can only mean—as the one fruitful way of achieving "Puerto Rican Power"—that charity begins at home, that is to say, that Puerto Ricans must achieve total power in Puerto Rico.

Independence versus Assimilation

The definitive triumph of colonialism would be the total assimilation of our population into the American union. Insofar as the Puerto Rican protest movement is an anticolonialist one—and so it has traditionally been—it will have to be attuned to the currents that are at present shaking the world with the demands of "the wretched of the earth." This means no more, and no less, than that the only way in which a protest movement can be successful in Puerto Rico is through the espousal of independence as a first step towards the achievement of economic independence. This struggle is at present being carried out by the Pro-Independence Movement of Puerto Rico, but also by other proindependence groups in the Island. The message is being carried to the ghettos of New York and elsewhere. Colonialism as an institution is dead the world over. Puerto Rico cannot—will not—be the exception to this rule. Otherwise, we may be faced with a situation similar to that of New Mexico: cultural hybridization and eventual assimilation to American culture. This prospect—insofar as Puerto Ricans achieve consciousness of its real implications—should be enough to deter them from committing cultural suicide by becoming the fifty-first state of the American union.

Frank Browning

FROM RUMBLE TO REVOLUTION:
THE YOUNG LORDS*

Ceil Keegan is 27 years old, a widow, the mother of two
small children. Deep brown circles appear under her eyes
where the bones were crushed during one of the three beatings she has suffered since Christmas. Several months ago Ceil
was walking near her home in Westside Chicago when three
men drove up, forced her into their car and took her to a
party a few blocks away. She was slapped around and beaten
for three hours. The three men were plainclothes cops. They
stood by smiling. Later they dumped her back at home,
nearly dead. A few weeks after that, just a block from her
home six kids from a white gang beat her and left her
crumpled in the street, unable to move. Ceil is a target because she works in the headquarters of the Young Lords Organization, a Puerto Rican street gang-turned-political movement.

Today Ceil is probably safe from the intergang warfare
which left her lying in the street. Not because she's dropped
her work for the Young Lords, but because of the way the
Lords are working with street gangs all over Chicago.

The Lords, until 1967 just another gang, have become the
most potent revolutionary organization of Puerto Rican youth
in the United States. The Lords are not prodigal sons, returned from suburbia to organize the ghetto. Less roman-
tically, they started out operating in fundamentally the same
style as in *West Side Story*. That history sets them apart from
the vast majority of radical organizations around the country.
They have negotiated peace pacts among nearly all of Chicago's white and Latin gangs, convincing them to fight, not

* Frank Browning, "From Rumble to Revolution: The Young Lords,"
Ramparts (October 1970). Reprinted with permission.

against each other, but against the system which oppresses them. Influenced by the Lords, the 3000-member Latin Kings, the city's largest Puerto Rican gang, have begun to organize themselves politically and have started their own breakfast-for-children program. At the same time, the Lords have battered constantly at West Lincoln Park's established institutions to make them serve poor people.

In the fall of 1968 they took over the Armitage Street Methodist Church—now the People's Church—to found their headquarters and begin a day-care program.

In the spring of 1969 they led hundreds of their Puerto Rican brothers down the street to an empty lot which was to be made into $100-membership private tennis courts, and transformed it into a children's park.

By summer they had built a coalition with several other community organizations to fight an Urban Renewal plan that envisioned West Lincoln Park as an "inner-city suburb" for midde-income whites. That battle still wears on as the Lords and their allies have joined with architects and lawyers to present their own plans for poor people's housing.

Last winter they opened a free health clinic in the basement of the People's Church, initiating the first attack on the health problems of the entire Puerto Rican community.

The Chicago YLO has inspired the formation of similar groups in Puerto Rican communities in other cities. By far the most significant of these is the New York City Young Lords. A political split between the two organizations which occurred in June has so far been free of the usual acrimony. The two groups, as is clearly revealed in their parallel development, are in any case bound together by common roots—a bond which they now express with the phrase "revolutionary compañeros."

[GANGS AND REVOLUTION]

Once their political conversion began, it took no more than six months to establish YLO's revolutionary outlook. Dennis Cunningham, one of several Movement lawyers in Chicago who have handled cases for the Lords and the Latin Kings for several years, points to the Lords' early and continuing affiliation with the Black Panthers as fundamental to their political development.

Like the Panthers, YLO is organized into ministerial divisions, with specified lines of authority and levels of responsibility. So far the structure has not become highly rigid. The sense of personal loyalty and friendship which pervades the whole collective is probably stronger than the machinery of organizational discipline.

YLO's Field Marshal is a young man named Cosmo. In his job he hangs out on the street, jiving with other gang people. Cosmo recognizes that the Chicago YLO in an important way still is a gang: "You have to understand, man, that even *before,* we were in some ways already revolutionary. Dig? It's not that we were a gang one minute and the next we were all Communists. What we had to realize was that it wasn't no good fightin' each other, but that what we were doing as a gang had to be against the capitalist institutions that are oppressing us."

Up to about six months ago the YLO was completely dependent upon José (Cha Cha) Jimenez, chairman and head of the gang since long before its politicization. Cha Cha is 21 and has been in the gang since 1959; as soon as he began to move into the leadership he was shuttled in and out of jail on all the usual charges stemming from "rumbles," petty theft, possession of drugs, disorderly conduct. Now he faces a one-year sentence on a charge of stealing $23 worth of lumber last summer. A companion convicted on the same offense was given 30 days. His YLO brothers are trying desperately to raise money for appeals, but they do not sound optimistic. Besides, Cha Cha went on trial again early in August on a mob action charge stemming from demonstrations against the city's Urban Renewal plans. When that trial is over he faces seven more charges.

While serving time earlier, Cha Cha discovered how full the jails were of Puerto Ricans—not just gang members, but old and middle-aged people, workers and welfare mothers. It became clear to him that the real enemy was not the Latin Kings or the Paragons or the Black Eagles; the real enemy was Daley's Chicago Urban Renewal, local Alderman George McCutcheon, and the U.S. government, whose imperial colonization policy had so mangled Puerto Rico that he and his family had been forced to leave just to survive.

A year ago last spring, Brother Manuel Ramos was shot to death by an off-duty Chicago cop. The cop crashed a YLO party and when he started badgering one of them, Ramos tried to clear it up. The cop drew his gun and fired dead-on into Ramos's left eye. "I think it was at that point that I became a real revolutionary," Cha Cha says. "Instead of going out and killing a pig, I saw the need to sit down and analyze the ways of getting even. Not with a gun. It wasn't the right time. It still isn't. We have to educate the people before we think about guns."

Cha Cha characterizes most of the early demonstrations as being like gang fights because of their diffuse political character. April 1969 was a real turning-point for the Lords' political demonstrations. Just as a national conclave of Presbyterian ministers opened in Texas, the Lords moved into Presbyterian McCormick Theological Seminary. "Blacks were going down to demand money," Cha Cha reflects, "so we sent a Latin to get money for building houses. At the same time we felt we should do an action here to back him up and make them understand that if they didn't give poor people houses, we were going to take over the offices at McCormick.

"We went into the place, barricaded the doors and set up security with walkie-talkies. At first there were only 40 people.

"We had a press conference and by morning the place was full of poor people and guilty middle-class people. Food was always supplied to us by the people of the neighborhood. People outside tried to make trouble between us and other gangs, and the gangs would come to the gate, but we would rap with them and then they stayed to help and saw that they were political too. Dr. Arthur McKay [president of McCormick] told people he was going to call the police. It was on the news.

"We went back and held a press conference and said no warrant to leave, no piece of paper, was going to evict us anymore. McKay talked to the Board and dropped the charge, and we got a call from Texas saying we had got $600,000 for low-income housing in Lincoln Park. The Board agreed to meet our demands for housing, that their financial records be open, that McCormick join to help community groups, that it publicly oppose the racist policies of Urban Renewal, and that it open its facilities to the use of the community. We were in the building for five days before we got that decision."

If the Lords' activities get results, they also reveal their enemies. The YLO occupied the Armitage Street Methodist

Church in November 1968. For six months they had asked the congregation for permission to use the basement as a day-care center. They had the support of the church's minister, Rev. Bruce Johnson. Nevertheless, an exodus of about 15 per cent of the primarily middle-class membership followed the occupation. Those who have remained with the church—now the People's Church—have transformed it into a center for dialogue on the theology of liberation.

The Lords realize that while their old image as a street gang helps identify them to other street people, older people in the community remain fearful. Local power-brokers like District Alderman George McCutcheon and the right-wing Chicago Tribune try to dismiss the Lords as just a bunch of rabble-rousing vandals.

The Lords never had much hope of winning the hearts of the landowners and city bureaucrats. Still, for the rest of the community—even for those middle-aged or older working people and welfare mothers who have been forced to move from one tiny apartment to another, one jump ahead of the Urban Renewal bulldozer—the Lords' history as a gang is cause for ambivalence.

But there are signs that the Lords are also reaching out more effectively into the entire community. At least two of their projects have had a profound impact on the whole of Lincoln Park and, if they can maintain organization solidarity, could make them the most important political force in Chicago's Puerto Rican community.

[GETTING IT ON]

For the last 15 years, Lincoln Park has been on the urban planners' maps as an ideal spot to create a middle-class enclave, a suburb in the heart of the inner city. Entire blocks on Armitage, Halsted and Larrabee streets now lie bare where Urban Renewal has leveled the homes of Puerto Ricans and poor whites.

Last June the Lords and several other local groups formed a Poor People's Coalition to fight Urban Renewal plans to have the Hartford Company construct middle-income housing. The Lords asked a young architect, Howard Alan, to develop plans to be entered as a contract bid before the

Urban Renewal board. (A $3000 architect's fee was paid by McCormick Seminary.) Community Urban Renewal Director George Stone led them to believe that if the Coalition submitted technically adequate plans, they would get the job.

Alan designed a building, working closely with the Poor People's Coalition and various members of the community. There would be three stories, each set back so that the roof of the floor below formed a play terrace for the apartment above. The front walls were all glass, and workrooms were placed next to them so that mothers would be able to work while watching their children play. "The terraces were designed," says Alan, "for poor people's interaction in response to an existing way of life whereby poor people could rely on each other."

The Lincoln Park Establishment seemed not to take the Coalition's project too seriously until the local Daley-appointed Conservation Community Council—a (supposedly representative) local community board selected to participate in Urban Renewal planning-came through with an 11-2 recommendation favoring the Coalition's bid.

No Community Council recommendation on a construction bid had ever been reversed by the Department of Urban Renewal (with one exception—which was overturned by the Chicago City Council). Furthermore, there has always been a policy that DUR meetings provide ample opportunity for public discussion.

As soon as the chairman opened the meeting last February, he asked all those in the packed audience opposed to the Hartford Company to stand. All but about 10 rose. Just then, a member of the five-man DUR board moved that the bid go to a private contractor. An immediate unanimous vote supported his motion, and by the time the crowd realized what had happened, the board members were clearing away their papers and were on their way out. One man jumped from the audience to grab a microphone and was immediately surrounded by a phalanx of police. Next day the Chicago Tribune headlined, in six columns, "Renewal Hearing Disrupted."

Under the plan approved by the DUR, 15 per cent of the new housing will go to poor people. The Coalition's plan called for at least 40 per cent.

YLO Minister of Information Omar Lopez refers to the

Coalition's defeat as only a skirmish in what is really a war against Urban Renewal. He promises that the Urban Renewal buildings will never go up until they are designed to serve poor people.

Since February, however, the Lords have done little on neighborhood housing—to the dismay of Howard Alan, who is anxious to work up other bids. Mio Villagomez, a lieutenant in the YLO Health Ministry who came to the Lords last winter, sees this as one of the organization's serious problems, stemming mostly from a lack of internal discipline. And he says it shows up elsewhere, when members—perhaps because of the close relationships that grew out of their long association in the gang—fail to concentrate on their own jobs, show up late for meetings, spend too much time bullshitting instead of talking to new people in the streets, or let old programs lapse when a new one has caught their interest.

It is a pattern that will not be easily abolished. One of the things Cosmo notes about street gangs, which has both helped and frustrated the Lords in winning over other gangs to cooperative political work, is a faddish attraction to new styles. For though they may dig what the Lords are doing, it's really hard to develop the tenacity to follow through on organizational detail. That kind of periodic excitement which moves from one new program to another is what Mio criticizes as a lack of self-disciplined democratic centralism.

As long as it was dependent on Cha Cha's gentle-but-tough charismatic style, YLO seemed unlikely to solve this problem. But he has steadily shifted much of the leadership responsibility to his ministers. Friends of the organization believe it is now strong enough to stand without him, should the city's efforts to imprison him succeed. He resigned as chairman in mid-July so that full responsibility for YLO would devolve upon the Central Committee, and "in order to allow the second generation of Lords to assume the burden of responsibility and pleasure of serving the people."

Of equal importance to YLO strength are two new people who have come into the Lords during the last year: Omar Lopez and Alberto Chivera. Their personal warmth and serious efficiency have brought them into powerful positions as Ministers of Information and Health, respectively.

Alberto, a third-year medical student at Northwestern University, runs the health clinic, a program of free medical service to the community staffed by doctors, medical and nursing students and professional health workers. The clinic, which opened in February with a handful of patients, now receives nearly 50 people each Saturday afternoon, with services from prenatal care to eye examinations.

At first many women were afraid to go to the clinic. They were wary of the old gang image and frightened by what they had read in the city's newspapers. Then health workers started canvassing door-to-door, asking people if anyone needed medical care and making arrangements for them to come to the clinic. If they failed to appear, they were sent a personal letter inviting them to come in the next week. Sometimes members of the Health Ministry and doctors go to the homes of people who can't come to the clinic.

Alberto expects that eventually the clinic will be run entirely by the community, with only occasional help from the Lords—a real People's Clinic freely offered to and freely run by the people it is designed to serve. There is, of course, a tendency of such programs to deteriorate into the piecemeal style of government welfare: patching together one project here and plugging up another there. But the health clinic can also be a stepping-off point for further action.

The fact that the clinic does work primarily in the neighborhood means that it is tying itself very effectively into the social structure of the community. If the Lords can continue that direct relationship with the Puerto Rican women, who form one of the strongest sources of traditional stability, then their chances of growing into an effective community-wide political organization are greater than ever before.

On the surface the Health Ministry appears to offer nothing more than a slightly better version of the city's welfare program. But the camaraderie and sensitive care that the clinic has come to offer have probably become the Lords' most successful organizing tool. Not only does it go a long way toward eroding their traditional gang image, but it doesn't take too many trips to the clinic—where treatment comes free—for the poeple to realize that their frustration is rooted in the medical system, especially as it is embodied by Grant Hospital.

When the clinic first opened, Grant had agreed to provide free follow-up examinations upon referral by the clinic's doctors. For a while it worked. Then the hospital started billing patients and initiating collection procedures. By that time, though, enough people were behind the Lords that they could escalate their service demands beyond what Grant would concede while still staying well within the community's reasonable expectations. One especially important demand was that the hospital remove police from the emergency room (police regularly interrogate patients before and during emergency treatment). Grant's intransigence on both counts has in the process heightened older community people's awareness of its inadequacy both as a medical and as a social institution.

Through the health clinic more than any other program, the Lords have been able to strengthen their bonds to the community and stimulate some political awareness of how the established social service institutions work. In addition, local shopowners and businessmen have begun to support the Lords' programs. Most of the food for the breakfasts is given freely by local grocers. One record store owner, a staunch supporter of the Puerto Rican Independence Movement, has given recordings of the Puerto Rican national anthem to be played each morning at the breakfast program.

The Lords, though strong opponents of an apolitical "cultural nationalism," are deeply committed to the liberation of Puerto Rico. They consider themselves revolutionary nationalists and maintain many ties with revolutionary leaders on the island. Before he came to Chicago last February, Communications Deputy Tony Baez was active in the Movement on the island, escaping to Chicago for fear of imprisonment. The Lords see their role as one of making Americans realize that the U.S. government has its own resort colony in just the same manner as the 19th century European empires. [See RAMPARTS, June 1970]

"We feel it our duty to see that 'Free Puerto Rico Now' will be an issue in the next year, second only to getting out of Vietnam," one Young Lord explains. "Why the stress on a nationalistic feeling for an island so far away? For a Puerto Rican living in Chicago who was forced to come here as a cheap laborer, that rallying point gives a sense of pride and identity. All were brought here because of the systematic destruction of the Puerto Rican economy and the death of jobs and promise."

It is above all this common heritage of continuing oppression which binds the Puerto Ricans living in Chicago or New

York, not only to their countrymen in Puerto Rico, but also to each other and to those in other cities around the country.

[THE LORDS IN NEW YORK]

The New York Young Lords (who since last June's split with the Chicago YLO have constituted themselves the Young Lords Party, or YLP) come out of a community whose conditions and concerns parallel the Chicago group's. Guided by the immediate needs of the people, the YLP has focused on the problems of inadequate health care and housing, malnutrition, institutions refusing to serve the community—the same issues around which the YLO organized in Chicago. At the same time, however, sources of divergency in their development can be seen, especially in organizational and tactical style and in strategic priorities, and perhaps also in the personal backgrounds of the two groups.

The New York Lords' first action was in July 1969. Unable to obtain brooms from the Sanitation Department to clean 110th Street in *El Barrio*, they got together with people in the neighborhood and built a barricade of garbage across Third Avenue at 110th. In the days that followed, the action spread to 111th and 112th Streets. At each location, the Lords held a rally and signed up some of their first recruits. The garbage offensive lasted until September 2. The Lords played a hit-and-run game, block to block, talking and spreading politics as they went. Thousands of Puerto Ricans fought the police that summer. Many joined the Lords or at least became friendly to the struggle.

That fall, the Lords began to work with welfare mothers. In October they started door-to-door lead poisoning detection tests. They found that cases of lead poisoning—due to the illegal use of cheap lead paint by tenement landlords—reached epidemic proportions in their community.

As the health work continued, the Lords themselves learned how to do simple blood tests for iron deficiency anemia, another poverty disease widespread in the community. The lack of proper nutrition convinced them to undertake a free breakfast-for-children program.

For weeks, the Lords visited the First Spanish Methodist Church on 111th Street and Lexington Avenue, trying to convince Humberto Carranzana, the Cuban refugee who ran it, to open the large basement facilities for the breakfast program (the church was in use only a few hours a week, on Sundays). On Sunday, December 7, when the Lords attemped to address the congregation, police were called in and beat and arrested 13 Lords. The women who were in the church fought back just as hard as the men, and the Party points to this as the awakening of its struggle against male chauvinism. The Lords returned to the church on December 28, 1969. This time they took it over, renamed it People's Church and began an 11-day occupation. They established an embattled communal enclave with free breakfasts, free clothing and health services, a day-care center, a liberation school, community dinners, films, and on New Year's Eve a revolutionary service to herald "The Decade of the People."

Over a hundred thousand people passed through the doors of the church during those days. The Lords explained their programs. They invoked the teachings of Jesus as a people's gospel of helping those in need.

The barricaded, barred and chained door of the church gave way to police hammers and chisels at 7:15 A.M., Wednesday, January 7. The occupation ended peacefully—as the Lords had promised, for their part, that it would. All of those busted were charged with civil contempt of a January 2 court injunction against remaining in the church. In March all of the charges were dropped.

Since January, support for the Young Lords in the community has continued to grow rapidly. This was made unmistakably clear at the Puerto Rican Day Parade on June 7: As the Young Lords passed by in their purple berets, hundreds of thousands of people greeted them with cheers and the clenched-fist salute.

Community support was demonstrated in a different way a week later with the arrest of the YLP Chief of Staff, Juan "Fi" Ortiz, 16 years old, on charges of kidnapping, armed robbery and assault. The next day four different newspapers provided four implausibly differing versions of Fi's supposed crime; all of them were variations of the theme that 21-year-old Jack McCall of Newark, New Jersey, was kidnapped on an East Harlem street, forced into a car at knifepoint, driven to Brooklyn, struck on the head and robbed of $40. McCall escaped and reported the car's license number to police, who within the space of a few hours checked it, located the car and Fi and arrested him.

Fi's bail was set at $1000. The judge apparently found the police story less than convincing for the bail must approach a record low for charges of kidnapping, armed robbery and assault.

The night of the arrest, hundreds of people gathered to protest at a rally called by the Lords in front of the People's Church, which since the occupation had become a symbol of the struggle in El Barrio. YLP Chairman Felipe Luciano told the crowd: "We will not allow the brutalization of our community to go without any response. For every Puerto Rican who is brutalized, there will be a retaliation."

The Lords left the rally to return to their Bronx office to work on the current issue of their paper, *Palante*. The crowd raised YLP banners left over from the Puerto Rican Day parade the previous Sunday and marched through the streets of El Barrio chanting. *"Despierta, Boricua. Defiende lo tuyo"*—"Awake, Puerto Rican. Defend what is yours."

Suddenly, small groups of people broke from the march and fanned out north and south on Third Avenue. The gates of the A&P supermarket were pulled down and people filled up bags of groceries. Men and women gathered merchandise from other stores on the avenue; barricades went up to keep the cops—now with guns drawn—away from the people in the stores. Poverty program offices and welfare centers were also targets. Rocks and bottles pelted patrol cars. A cop was beaten when he tried to make an arrest. A car belonging to the Housing Authority, New York's Municipal Slumlord, was found abandoned on 113th Street. People covered it with garbage and crowned it with trashcans.

[THE PEOPLE'S MEDICINE]

Lincoln Hospital is located in an industrial sector of the South Bronx, the edge of one of the largest, most run-down Puerto Rican ghettos in the City. At 5:30 on the morning of July 18, a group of about 200 Puerto Rican men and women from the YLP, the Health Revolutionary Unity Movement (a city-wide group of Third World health workers), and the

Think Lincoln Committee (made up of workers and patients at Lincoln Hospital), walked into Lincoln with the aim of turning the hospital over to the community. Among their demands were door-to-door health services for preventive care, sanitary control, nutrition, maternal and child care, drug addiction care, day care and senior citizens' services, a 24-hour-a-day grievance table, and a $140 minimum weekly wage for all workers.

Hours later, hundreds of people streamed in through the front door to get free tests for tuberculosis, iron deficiency anemia and lead poisoning. Passersby looking up at the ancient, grimy building that could easily pass for a warehouse were surprised to see the Puerto Rican flag flying and banners in the window proclaiming: *Bienvenido al hospital del pueblo*—"Welcome to the People's Hospital."

At 10 A.M. there was a press conference. Yvette Trinidad of Think Lincoln answered a question: Why use take-over tactics? "There was garbage piled on the corner of 142nd Street and Cortland right outside of this hospital. We complained, we petitioned, we called the Mayor's office. Nothing was done. Addicts from all over town came over here to search for dirty needles in the rubble. One day we decided to act. We moved the garbage into the office of Dr. Antero Lacot, the hospital administrator; that same day the garbage got removed."

At a political education class at the hospital run by Denise Oliver, YLP's Minister of Finance, three Puerto Ricans, all under 12, told of their experience with medicine.

"My brother broke his arm and had to wait two hours in the hall before a doctor came out."

"My aunt died of a wrong blood transfusion."

"My friend's mother died of hepatitis from a dirty needle."

Negotiations with the Mayor's office over the demands broke down after four and a half hours. By afternoon's end, Tactical Patrol Squad and "Special Events" cops pulled up and parked in front of the hospital. But groups of the Lords and sympathizers, many from gangs like the Bones, the Skulls and the Savage Seven, were leaving the hospital unobtrusively, a few at a time. By the time the 150 helmeted cops marched in formation into Lincoln, there was no one inside except hospital employees. The police captain, paunched and pompous, led his 150 men back out, still in formation. They had removed the Puerto Rican flag from the hospital roof.

The hospital occupation lasted a little over 12 hours. New York radio and TV news broadcasts flashed stories of the terrible conditions at Lincoln all day long. Newspapers across the country carried the story. The AP quoted Hospital Administrator Lacot as saying that the Lords did a service to the community by dramatizing conditions at Lincoln.

[ACTIONS AND IDEOLOGY]

In discussing the difference which led to the New York-Chicago split in the Young Lords, Omar Lopez, Tony Baez and others in Chicago point to the backgrounds of the individuals involved. The Chicago group is made up largely of high school dropouts and some who didn't finish grammar school. The New York chapter evolved out of a political organization called the Sociedad Albizu Campos, most of whose members had either graduated from or dropped out of college in or around New York. The Chicago people feel that the New Yorkers were preoccupied with ideological refinement, whereas they had neither the time nor the educational background to concentrate on theoretical work.

"Here in Chicago we're more concerned with the immediate needs of the people, but we still understand that the real struggle is not a local one," says Omar. "That's why we entered a coalition with the Panthers and the Young Patriots on a national and international level. Yet if we talk of being the vanguard, we need to be up ahead and still have something behind us too. We're better able to analyze when we're out on the streets talking with the people. Ideas must come after actions, not just from reading Marx, Lenin or Mao."

The New York group does not consider its concerns abstract. In their view, a lack of ideological clarity in Chicago was part and parcel of a number of related problems: lack of organizational discipline, leading to inconsistency in ongoing programs; inadequate internal political education; frequent changes in leadership; erratic publication of the national paper—shortcomings that are to a large extent acknowledged by the Chicago group.

The New Yorkers felt that Chicago YLO was not up to

leading a sustained, closely-knit national organization. Last May, after several unsatisfactory meetings, the New Yorkers proposed that the Chicago leadership come East for an extended period to join in forging a new national structure and program. The Chicago people refused. Like the New Yorkers, they were unwilling to leave their local work. The split followed, even though relations remain amicable and Chicago members are "hopeful" that they can continue to "work in a way that will enable us to come together again."

The Lords are trying to confront the problem of how to sustain organizational continuity—a perennial problem on the left. The most long-lived organizations are often the most irrelevant sects. The most vital movements—in campus struggles, for instance—are often plainly ad hoc and ephemeral. Clearly a synthesis is needed, and the experience of the two Young Lords groups will be instructive.

It is no accident that episodic organization is endemic to the left. Not only are groups like the Lords and the Panthers subjected to increasingly ruthless repression, but the left also lacks the access to money, power and friendly media that sustains the established institutions of society. The continuity of radicalism is at bottom a continuity of the suffering and outrage that give rise to it. In time these may find their expression in many different organizations or actions.

At the Lincoln Hospital press conference, a reporter asked how the Lords could go on taking over one thing after another. And Minister of Information Yoruba replied, "Because we serve our people. That's why we could move from People's Church to a TB truck to Lincoln Hospital—and you-all don't know where we're gonna be tomorrow."

Young Lords Party

PALANTE*

Many people ask us, "How did you begin?" A few people have the idea that "some foreign power" organized us, or that we are a gang. This is our story:

In New York City, in January of 1969, some Puerto Rican college students got together because they felt something had to be done to connect them with the people they had left behind in the ghetto. The intentions these people had were good, but vague. They didn't quite understand which was the best way to proceed. As the months wore on, the group met many times in *El Barrio*. People came and went, the group kept changing, and those who stuck around felt things were going nowhere.

Yorúba came into the group in late May (by this time it was called the *Sociedad de Albizu Campos* [SAC]). He was a student at the State University of New York at Old Westbury, and had just returned to the States from a stay in Mexico, which was part of his schooling. He was eighteen at the time. Most of his life before going to Mexico was related more closely to the struggle of Black People in Amerikkka than to that of Puerto Ricans. This was because his dark skin and Afro hair made it difficult for Puerto Ricans to relate to him, especially light-skinned ones.

However, Yorúba's stay in Mexico had made him aware of his Latin roots, so when he returned to Amerikkka he was looking for something to get into. A friend of the brother's who also went to Old Westbury was one of the people who stuck it through with the SAC from the beginning. He introduced Yorúba into the group.

Two weeks after the first meeting he attended sometime in May, Yorúba met David Perez. Old Westbury needed more ghetto spics to maintain its image of a "with it" institution,

* *Palante.* New York: McGraw-Hill, 1971, pp. 8–13; pp. 73–83; and 150–151. Reprinted with permission.

and it sent people out all over the country looking for these strange animals. They had found David in Chicago, where he was hustling an anti-poverty group. Whereas Yorúba was born and raised in New York, David was born in Lares, Puerto Rico. At ten, he came to Chicago, because his family, like hundreds of thousands of other Puerto Rican families, nearly starved due to the effects of "Operation Bookstrap."

When David arrived in New York, he was nineteen years old. He and Yorúba quickly got along, and they went to stay at Yorúba's mother's house on David's first night in the city. They stayed up all night rapping about the SAC in particular, and politics in general. Their points of view on a lot of things were similar, and one thing was especially agreed on: the SAC had to stop meeting and get into the street.

On June 7th, the Black Panther newspaper had a story about an alliance in Chicago called the Rainbow Coalition which the Panthers had formed with two other organizations and a story about one of the groups in the Coalition—the Young Lords Organization (YLO). The Young Lords were Puerto Rican revolutionaries!

The Lords had entered into an alliance with the Young Patriots Organization, a street gang of white youths that had also turned political, and the Black Panther Party. This was called the Rainbow Coalition.

The Rainbow Coalition sent representatives to the annual Students for a Democratic Society (SDS) convention in Chicago, held in May of 1969. An SDSer from Florida, José Martinez, who was looking to get back to his Latin people, met Cha Cha, one of the founders of the YLO, at the convention. Martinez told Cha Cha he was going to New York, and wanted permission to start a Lords chapter there.

When Martinez got to New York's Lower East Side, he soon managed to start a group that met regularly. This group heard that there was another group doing what they were doing—except in East Harlem. These young street bloods would clean up the streets of *El Barrio* at night and leave the garbage in the middle of the street the next morning. In this way, the Garbage (Sanitation) Department was forced to clean it up so traffic could get by. José met with this group's leader, Pickle, and the two groups became one, with the intention of getting recognition from Chicago. It was decided that the new group would work out of *El Barrio*.

At its June 7 meeting, the one where we discussed the

Lords, the SAC talked about both New York groups. We felt that it was important for all the little groups that kept popping up to form one national party, and we felt the Young Lords Organization was that party. The SAC met with the group that had just merged, and a new merger was made. This merger represented the uniting of the street people with the students of working-class background.

Together, this new group, already calling itself the Young Lords, cleaned up the streets of *El Barrio*, rapping to people as they went. On July 26, the group was recognized by Chicago as the New York State Chapter of the Young Lords Organization.

On Sunday, July 27, the Lords of New York blocked the avenues of *El Barrio*. This action grew in size through the summer, as the frustrated, forgotten mass of Puerto Ricans joined in barricading the avenues and streets. Soon the garbage action turned into a confrontation with police, and the YLO became experienced in street fighting, in basic urban guerrilla tactics, the hit and run. For the first time in years, the pigs came into the ghetto with respect and fear in their eyes. This period of the summer of 1969 is referred to by us as the Garbage Offensive.

By September, we felt that our people had accepted us, and that we were now a part of people's lives. We opened an office in a storefront at 1678 Madison Avenue, between 111th and 112th Streets. The leadership of the organization at that time consisted of David Perez, Deputy Minister of Defense; Felipe Luciano, Deputy Chairman; Pablo "Yorúba" Guzmán, Deputy Minister of Information; Juan Gonzalez, Deputy Minister of Education; and Juan "Fi" Ortiz, Deputy Minister of Finance. This was the Central Staff.

Juan Gonzalez joined the *Sociedad de Albizu Campos* just before we merged with Pickle's and José's group. He had just come out of jail, having done thirty days for contempt of court arising from the 1968 student uprisings at Columbia University. Born in Ponce in 1947, Juan came to the States at an early age. His parents felt that they should always "do better," and Juan's family kept moving from place to place, one step before the Puerto Ricans, two steps before the Blacks, and three steps after the whites.

Juan entered Columbia on a scholarship. To support himself, he took a poverty program job on the West Side of

Manhattan. Here, as a community organizer, Juan would go from house to house, getting to know people, and seeing all that his parents kept moving away from. This led him to junk the books his professors would give him for books on how to change the people's conditions, books on revolution. He joined SDS and became a leader of the 1968 uprising.

Fi was a member of Pickle's group, stayed with the merger of José's group, and wound up a Young Lord. He was fifteen at the time of the merger. His father is a preacher who managed to save enough to buy a house in Queens. Most of Fi's time was still spent in *El Barrio*, and he rarely visited the house in Queens.

The brother refused to accept the nonsense taught in school, and he had been tossed out of practically every high school in Queens, until, in 1969, he wound up at Benjamin Franklin in *El Barrio*. Fi is a brilliant photographer whose work of the street scenes has been exhibited in museums. Many of the people in the photo workshop in 117th Street that he belonged to were also with him in Pickle's group. Although he was not a part of the central leadership in the beginning, the Central Staff soon saw the level he was on, and in September he was promoted to Deputy Minister of Finance.

The Central Staff decided that we would shift the Organization's tactics from street fighting to programs which served our people and which would also build the Organization's theoretical level. We began Free Breakfast and Lead Poisoning Detection programs, supported the struggle of the welfare mothers that year, began organizing hospital workers, and studied revolutions in other countries.

In October of 1969, we wrote the Thirteen Point Program and Platform (revised May, 1970) and Thirty Rules of Discipline (revised December, 1970).

That same month, we went to a Methodist church on the corner of 111th Street and Lexington Avenue, and asked if we could use some space to run a Breakfast Program. We couldn't even get in the front door. We wrote letters, began attending services, and talked with the congregation, but the church's Board voted no. December 7 was the church's testimonial Sunday, when people from the congregation spoke. Felipe rose to speak, and twenty-five uniformed pigs, in addition to the plainclothes pigs that had been going to church with us for six weeks, ran in, attacking the Lords and our supporters. The ambush netted thirteen Lords and supporters. They and others who got away were treated for broken arms and heads.

For the two following Sundays, we went back to the church and interrupted services again. The fact that blood was spilled in the church showed us the level the pigs wanted to go to. On December 28, we took the church, renamed it People's Church, and for the next eleven days, we ran free clothing drives, breakfast programs, a liberation school, political education classes, a day care center, free health programs, and nightly entertainment (movies, bands, or poetry). Three thousand people came to the church. This was our Second Offensive, the People's Church Offensive, and the action spread our name around the world.

Two things happened: our membership increased rapidly, and we were now seen as a legitimate threat to the enemy's balance of power.

It was obvious that we were no street gang; as Socialists and revolutionary nationalists, we had become a political force to be dealt with. Those in power knew, perhaps better than we, what could happen if Socialist, revolutionary nationalist Puerto Ricans in Amerikkka hooked up with the other two-thirds of our people living on the island. The explosion would be tremendous.

Our intention after People's Church was to build our organization, to get back in regular touch with our people through our daily organizing programs, which had been suspended for the eleven days of the church. From January through March we did this; during this period there was a series of street battles with the police around drugs. We attacked the police for allowing the drug traffic to come into the neighborhood, and then busting junkies instead of the big pushers. The YLO became involved in getting junkies to kick and in having them serve our people.

In October of 1969 we opened our second office, in Newark, New Jersey; the fact that we managed to run an office there, plus the success of People's Church, prompted National in Chicago to recognize us as the leadership for the East Coast Region, with the responsibility for organizing that area. The Central Staff moved up in rank and became the Regional Central Committee with the titles of Regional Ministers.

The Bronx Branch was opened in April of 1970. This was

also the location of our Information Center. The leadership for the East Coast now noticed that Chicogo was not providing guidance or example; a few things that bothered us were that the newspaper, *YLO*, was not coming out regularly; that there was no political line to follow (which meant that we developed on our own—the Thirteen Point Program and Platform is an example), and that the only branches of the Organization were in Chicago, *El Barrio*, the Bronx, and Newark, while our people were calling for us everywhere. There was also a branch in Heywood, California, but they were in less contact with Chicago than we were. They are now disbanded.

To offset the problem of not having a newspaper which regularly gave our position to the people, in October, 1969, we began publishing a mimeographed packet called *Palante*, the voice of the YLO-East Coast. On May 8th it came out for the first time as a full-size newspaper. The paper has grown in content and circulation. We also have a weekly New York radio program called "Palante" that went on the air on WBAI–FM in March.

In May of 1970, the East Coast Regional Central Committee went into a retreat. We discussed where we had been, and where we hoped to go. We knew that we could not continue to run an effective organization on our own personal dynamism, that definite political principles would have to be laid down for others to follow. As a group, we started studying more, and formulated methods of work that would develop other leaders. One of the main areas that we attacked was *machismo* and male chauvinism. If we wanted to have power in the hands of the people, it would be necessary to have *all* the people fighting *now*. The attitudes of superiority that brothers had toward sisters would have to change, as would the passivity of sisters toward brothers (allowing brothers to come out of a *macho* or chauvinist, superior bag).

It was felt that the vague relationship with Chicago would have to be cleared up. We went deeply into what we felt were the responsibilities of a National Headquarters, responsibilities that Chicago was not fulfilling. After the retreat, we went out to Chicago. After a series of meetings, we felt that we had to split from the YLO and move ahead with the work that was urgently needed. We had now become the Young Lords Party.

Since October of 1969 we had been active in the field of

health, both from the patient's point of view and the hospital worker's. Our work in lead poisoning detection led to deep investigations in New York City that uncovered epidemics; we did the same for tuberculosis.

Ninety per cent of the hospital workers in New York City are Black and Puerto Rican. To meet their demands for better conditions, and to serve the needs of patients, the Health Revolutionary Unity Movement (HRUM) was created, made up of these hospital workers, in the early fall of '69. HRUM has the ideology of the Young Lords Party. It became involved in several health struggles, like Gouverneur Hospital on the Lower East Side.

The Young Lords Party and HRUM, along with the Think Lincoln Committee, a patient-worker group, took Lincoln Hospital in the South Bronx in July of 1970. This was our Third Offensive; we ran programs, like TB and lead poison detection services, and a day care center, in a building the hospital was not even using. This highlighted the oppressive conditions in Lincoln (the building was condemned by the city), which could have been found in any ghetto hospital. Just before Lincoln was taken, a city-run TB x-ray truck was liberated in *El Barrio*. This was a good education for our people as they saw the difference between what the government did and what we did: whereas the city was lucky if it tested 300 people in a week, we examined 300 people in one day.

On July 26, 1970, the Party celebrated its first anniversary. Soon afterward, in August, a branch was opened on the Lower East Side.

In August of 1970, Felipe Luciano was demoted from the Central Committee to the position of cadre in the Party. He left the Party in October. This was one dramatic example of a series of internal problems, and the Central Committee met in early September to get the Party moving again. One of the results of this was the establishment of a definite system of work and responsibility within the Party. This is called democratic centralism; briefly, it means that there is a top-down, centralist chain of command in the Party, and that at each level (central committee, branch staff, etc.) democracy is practiced.

For this series of meetings there was a new minister, Denise Oliver; afterward, there were some changes on Central Committee, and also, another minister was added, Gloria

Gonzalez. Juan was now the Minister of Defense; Fi was Chief of Staff; Denise was Minister of Finance (now Economic Development); and David and Gloria were Field Marshals.

Denise had joined the Party in October of 1969, when she was twenty-three. Before, she had attended the State University at Old Westbury, the last of several universities she had attended, all filled with empty promises. Denise had been raised in a "Black Bourgeois" (really middle-class) family, but she knew that reality was in the ghetto, with the people of the streets, and the workers who came home late for little pay. This is where Denise made her home.

Once, Denise worked in an *El Barrio* anti-poverty program. In the Lords, she rose to her natural level, and went through the ranks to become a minister. Besides contributing to the struggle against male chauvinism and female passivity, she has helped in eliminating the racism that exists both with the Party and among our people.

(In March of 1971, Denise Oliver left the Young Lords Party to join the Eldridge Cleaver faction of the Black Panther Party. This was not part of a collective decision by the Central Committee, but rather was an individual decision on Denise's part. We in the Lords still relate to Denise as a sister, in the same manner as we would relate to any Panther. As a result, the position of Minister of Economic Development is now vacant.)

Gloria became a Lord in February of 1970. Born in Puerto Rico, she was a strong supporter of the Nationalist Party. To make a living in New York, she became a health worker in Gouverneur Hospital. There she saw conditions which led her to join community struggles for better health care. For this, the sister was fired, but not until she had helped found HRUM and its newspaper, *For the People's Health*, two people's tools that still fight on. That ain't bad for a junior high school drop-out.

Through HRUM, she came in contact with the Party; Gloria went through the People's Church Offensive, and joined the Party afterward. She rose through the ranks, aided by her organizing of our Health Offensive that reached a peak in Lincoln Hospital in July. In August she and Juan celebrated a revolutionary wedding. She joined the Central Committee in September, at age twenty-six.

On September 22 and 23, the Young Lords Party and the

Puerto Rican Students Union sponsored a conference for Puerto Rican students at Columbia University. The theme was the liberation of Puerto Rico. Over 1,000 high school and college students attended. September 23, El Grito de Lares, the conference marched for a celebration to plaza Borinqueña in the South Bronx.

In August, our branch in Philadelphia was recognized. This has been one of our most effective branches, having dealt with the drug problem (pushers) in the colony, taking over a church to support the demands of rebelling prisoners, and now organizing a conference for church people on the problems of brothers and sisters in the prisons. For this, they have undergone practically the heaviest attacks of any branch; there have been numerous beatings, false arrests, and several firebombs which have wrecked their offices.

We first got involved in the prisons struggle when the prisons in New York City first got taken by the inmates. Many of the sisters and brothers in jail had come from the streets we had worked in, and had read *Palante*, or were reading smuggled copies. In October of 1970, an organization that arose from the prison rebellions came from the concentration camps to become a section of the Young Lords Party. This was the Inmates Liberation Front (ILF).

Our attention had turned from the prisons toward organizing a national demonstration when we were brought sharply back to the brutal oppression of the inmates. For years, there had been reports, many published in the press, of Puerto Ricans and Blacks committing suicide by hanging in precincts and jails. Such a large number of these deaths were reported that the circumstances were highly suspicious. On October 15, 1970, a Young Lord joined the statistics. Julio Roldan, arrested on the whim of a pig in *El Barrio*, was said to be found hung in his cell in the Tombs, the Manhattan Men's Prison. We were told it was a "suicide."

We knew we were being taken for a ride. Julio was a Young Lord, and we are not about useless, wasteful suicide. There had to be some action taken to provide an example for our people; a demonstration just wasn't going to make it.

On October 18, at the end of a funeral procession of 2,000 people for Julio Roldan through the streets of El Barrio, we took the People's Church once again. Only this time we took it armed, with guns. Our message was clear: When attacked, defend yourselves. This was the Party's Fourth Offensive.

Where does the Young Lords Party go from here? At this point, we are going ahead with plans to step up the forward progress of the Puerto Rican national liberation struggle. On October 30, 1970, the anniversary of the day in 1950 that the Nationalist Party started a rebellion in Puerto Rico, we organized a march to the U.N. of 10,000 people. On March 21, 1971, we held a demonstration in Ponce, Puerto Rico, in remembrance of the massacre of innocent people in 1937 by Amerikkkan orders. We announced that day that a YLP branch had opened in Ponce. This has been done to unite our people on the island and the mainland with a common goal: liberation. Wherever a Puerto Rican is, the duty of a Puerto Rican is to make the revolution.

Our new branch in Bridgeport is carrying the Party line to Connecticut. This line carries our belief that national liberation will be won by uniting the most exploited parts of our society, the street people and the workers, in a common effort. We also believe that our fight here on the mainland is fought at the side of many peoples, particularly the people of the Third World, people of color. We are eliminating the racism that divides us.

Our past examples, our present work, and our future successes make victory certain, because we are backed by our people. The enemy, the United States Government, respects us because of our people; we are always humble before our people, and will always be vicious before the enemy.

LIBERATE PUERTO RICO NOW!
VENCEREMOS!
CENTRAL COMMITTEE

People always look for the beginnings of the Party. We started the Young Lords because we just knew something had to be done. If we didn't find or create an organization that was gonna do something then everybody was gonna get shot, see, because it would have gotten to the point that people got so frustrated, they would just jump on the first cop they saw, or just snap, do something crazy.

At first the only model we had to go on in this country was the Black Panther Party. Besides that, we were all a bunch of readers, when we first came in we read Che, Fidel, Fanon, Marx, Lenin, Jefferson, The Bill of Rights, Declaration, Constitution—we read everything. Now there ain't too much time for reading.

We also felt that the potential for revolution had always been there for Puerto Rican people. If we had gone into the thing from a negative point of view, we wouldn't have made it, right. 'Cause a lot of times when things were really rough, it's been that blind faith in the people that keeps us going. The problem has been to tap that potential and to organize it into a disciplined force that's gonna really move on this government. Puerto Ricans had been psyched into believing this myth about being docile. A lot of Puerto Ricans were afraid to move, a lot of Puerto Ricans really thought that the man in blue was the baddest thing going.

Things were different in the gang days. Gang days, we owned the block, and nobody could tell us what to do with the street. Then dope came in and messed everything up, messed our minds up and just broke our backs—dope and anti-poverty. Anti-poverty wiped out a whole generation of what could have been Puerto Rican leaders in New York City.

For example, in '65, the time of the East Harlem riots, we held East Harlem for two days. We had the roof-tops, the streets and the community—no pigs could go through. It was like back in the old days. A lot of people really tripped off that, a lot of the junkies who had been in gangs remembered that shit. To end it they shipped in anti-poverty. They brought it in full-force, and they bought out a lot of the young cats who were leading the rebellions. A lot of dudes who were throwing bricks one day found themselves directors of anti-poverty programs the next, or workers on Mayor Lindsay's Urban Action Core.

So we had no leadership, and we had no people—our people were dying from dope. But we knew that it was *there*, man, 'cause we knew that the fire was there. Those of us who got together to start the thing, we knew we weren't freaks— we didn't feel that we were all that much different from the people. There's a tendency to say "the people" and put the people at arm's length. When we say "people," man, we're talking about ourselves. We're from these blocks, and we're from these schools, products of this whole thing. Some of us came back from college—it was like rediscovering where your parents had come from, rediscovering your childhood.

Our original viewpoint in founding the Party was a New York point of view—that's where the world started and ended. As we later found out, New York is different from most other cities that Puerto Ricans live in. But even in New York, we found that on a grass-roots level a high degree of racism existed between Puerto Ricans and Blacks, and between light-skinned and dark-skinned Puerto Ricans. We had to deal with this racism because it blocked any kind of growth for our people, any understanding of the things Black people had gone through. So rather than watching Rap Brown on TV, rather than learning from that and saying, "Well, that should affect me too," Puerto Ricans said, "Well, yeah, those Blacks got a hard time, you know, but we ain't going through the same thing." This was especially true for the light-skinned Puerto Ricans. Puerto Ricans like myself, who are darker-skinned, who look like Afro-Americans, couldn't do that, 'cause to do that would be to escape into a kind of fantasy. Because before people called me a spic, they called me a nigger. So that was, like, one reason as to why we felt the Young Lords Party should exist.

At first many of us felt why have a Young Lords Party when there existed a Black Panther Party, and wouldn't it be to our advantage to try to consolidate our efforts into getting Third World people into something that already existed? It became apparent to us that that would be impractical, because we wouldn't be recognizing the national question. We felt we each had to organize where we were at—so that Chicanos were gonna have to organize Chicanos, Blacks were gonna have to organize Blacks, Puerto Ricans Puerto Ricans, etc., until we came to that level where we could deal with one umbrella organization that could speak for everybody. But until we eliminate the racism that separates everybody, that will not be possible.

What happened was, in 1969 in the June 7 issue of the Black Panther newspaper there was an article about the Young Lords Organization in Chicago with Cha Cha Jimenez as their chairman. Cha Cha was talking about revolution and socialism and the liberation of Puerto Rico and the right to self-determination and all this stuff that I ain't *never* heard a spic say. I mean, I hadn't never heard no Puerto Rican talk like this—just Black people were talking this way, you know. And I said, "Damn! Check this out." That's what really got us started. That's all it was, man.

We started by trying to pick something that would introduce us to the community. It had to be an action. See—it was summer, it was hot, the people were just, like, sweltering in the heat, nobody was doing nothing. For four years there had been no action. Puerto Ricans hadn't had a good riot since 1965, not even a good fight, a good brawl. Something had to happen that would stun the community. It had to be something with a sense of drama, and a flair, right—but it also had to be something that was real, so the people would know that this wasn't just a bunch of young punks messin' around.

The best thing to hook into was garbage, 'cause garbage is visible and everybody sees it. It's there, you know. So we started out with this thing, "Well, we're gonna clean up the street." This brought the college people and the street people together, 'cause when street people saw college people pushing brooms and getting dirty, that blew their minds. It also got us out of our shyness. When we began, people said, "Well, what are you doing with those berets?" and "What are you doing with those buttons?" and "What does 'All Power to the People' mean?" and things like that. The bolder ones in our group would get out there and yell to people, and everybody else would jump with shock. It was frightening, man, to go on the street and to walk up to some strangers and just start rapping, and give 'em a leaflet—that's frightening shit. And we just forced ourselves to do it, and it got to a thing where nobody wanted to be the one who didn't talk that day, because everybody else would criticize you.

At first some people thought we were part of Lindsay's Urban Action Task Force, and some thought we were just a gang that was trying to be a social club. People couldn't figure us out, man. If we said, "All Power to the People," some of them who read the *Daily News* right away said, "Well, those are the Panthers, and they're Communists." A lot of people thought we were the Panthers, and to that we got a bad reaction, 'cause they were afraid of us. But some people just came out and looked.

This is all we did for the first two Sundays—clean up the street, make it look nice, and put the stuff in garbage cans. We picked Sunday 'cause that was one of the few days when everybody could get together. Some of the members of the Party got pissed. We'd have general meetings and they'd say, "I didn't do this for this *shit*, to clean up no garbage. I came here to off the pigs"; they were comin' from that, right. So, it was hard, man, 'cause we had a bunch of crazy people who just loved fighting, loved getting into shit. And cleaning garbage was not where it was at, so it was a kind of discipline for us, to go through that and learn patience. We didn't realize that what we were doing at that time was building the proper conditions for struggle. I mean, we could have gone underground and started blowing shit up—the thing is, nobody would have understood where it was coming from. Those people who didn't think it was the pig, would think it was some lunatics, and they'd probably be right. So we were just getting ourselves known.

By the second time around, everybody said, "Hey, here they come again! Here come these nuts!" They were calling their friends out—"Look at these fools cleaning off the street!" It was a big thing. They were coming from blocks around. We cleaned 110th Street from Second to Third to Lexington.

By the third Sunday we did something we had learned from what we had read about the Chicago group, and that was to get the people involved through "observation and participation." This time we got the people to clean the shit up with us. We knew somehow we would take them through some kind of a struggle, we didn't know where the hell we were going, but we had to get them involved.

And then came the Sunday of July 27, when we had a lot of people and not enough brooms, and we went to the Sanitation Department. . . . Now understand this—for the Young Lords Party, this July 27 is probably a historical date. It was a Sunday, right? When four of us went to pick up some brooms, they told us, "Well, you can't have any brooms." And we said, "Why?" and they said, "Because it's Sunday." Now the sanitation cats are just second cousins to the cats in blue, 'cept that they wear green. This fool at 106th Street which was the nearest branch of the department asks us, "What area are you cleaning up?" So we tell him 110th between Second and Third. He says, "That area is serviced by 73rd Street and York." So we had to go about a mile and a half outside where we were, when there was this place four blocks down. And the dude at 73rd and York says, "Well, you can't have any brooms." So, we were pissed, you know. We had gone through all the legal machinations, and now we were pissed. We were looking for a rationale for what was going to come next.

In the car on the way up, the four of us said, "Look, we're

going to take the garbage and throw it in the street and that's all there is to it—we're just going to dump it." And that's what we did. We blocked Third Avenue to traffic, right. The people, they went and blocked 111th Street and Third Avenue, blocked 112th, and what was developing was a riot situation. When we saw that happening, we set up a line of garbage cans at the end of 112th Street and we set up a line of Lords and said, "We ain't lettin' nobody through." There was this one cat who said, "Let's go! Let's take it all the way up to the Bronx!" This cat was freaking out, and we were saying, "No, you ain't going noplace—we're stoppin' right here because if we keep going, this is what the pigs want, they just going to pick us off. You ain't got no guns, you know." And this guy kept saying, "No, no, let's go! We got all these people here!" 'Cause people had come out, they come from all over East Harlem for this, they moved a truck into the street, they turned cars over, they were ready to go crazy. The pigs showed up and didn't do nothing, 'cause the pigs believe that Puerto Ricans are docile, you know. We didn't know what kind of reaction we'd get. I mean, all we were doing was throwing some garbage in the street, but we saw that it turned the people loose, it was what they needed, it just set them going. So, we had a quick rally and signed up some recruits, and we said, "Well, we're gonna do this again next Sunday."

When we went back the next Sunday, more people came —but it was a different thing. This time it wasn't "Here come those nuts . . ." but "Here come those people who started the shit last Sunday—let's get together." And people were just, like, waiting, waiting like this on the corner, waiting for us to throw the garbage so they could get involved in the shit.

The next day, Lindsay's office called a meeting. Gottehrer and all those dudes came down to East Harlem to this poverty place. That's when we found out what poverty pimps were really about—they're like outposts in Indian territory, like Fort Apache and Fort Savage, they are the eyes and ears of the mayor of any city. And they're supposed to keep the savages down, right. In this case, we weren't working with the poverty pimps. This was coming from the people, and the poverty pimps are far removed from the people. When they couldn't explain to their masters what was going down in East Harlem, they said, "Well, we have this under control . . . there are these leaflets that are going around. . . ."

We found that a lot of people thought we were there just to throw garbage in the street. They couldn't understand that we were really there for a Socialist revolution, we were really there to off the government of the United States. They just couldn't deal with that, you know. So we tried setting up political education classes.

I remember a lot of those being really funny. Juan had become Deputy Minister of Education, because he knew the most, he had the clearest mind. Juan was dealing with books, right, but, like, ain't nobody could read the books, and then those who could read, let's say something like Che on *Man and Socialism*, threw the book away and said, "This is boring." Juan could not understand how Che Guevara could be boring. But these cats said the dude was boring. You know, it blew his mind. We had to try to find some way of reaching brothers and sisters who did not dig school, the concept of school or the classroom. And how the hell were we gonna do this? This is a problem we're still dealing with. We tried everything, man, from jokes to getting high together, everything to try to bring the point across.

Then there were other problems like people's commitment. Like, "Well, how come you wasn't here last Sunday?" "Ah, man, you know, my mother told me not to come," or like, "I was out late Saturday night, and I just wanted to sleep. . . ." I mean, how do you build up discipline? If you were going to divide fifteen people into three groups that could block an avenue at a given time you needed discipline. How could you cool out cats who knew nothing but fighting and say to them, "Listen, this is not when you hit this pig—you do not hit this pig now."

It was very difficult, it was very hard to do. . . .

Well, after the First Offensive, the Garbage Offensive, all Puerto Ricans in New York knew about us. Then it was the People's Church Offensive that put us on a national level in terms of the United States and Puerto Rico. This was through the correct use of the media. We said, "Look, you know, the media is gonna have to be used. Until we can put out the *Daily News* regularly, until we have a TV station and a radio station, chalk it up. Everybody on welfare got a TV set, everybody got a radio, everybody buys the *Daily News* and *El Diario*, so as long as the people already got access to these things, we might as well use them to the best of our advantage."

It was December 28 that we took the church and during the eleven days we were in there we learned a lot of things about the media. The first day there was this quick press conference on the steps of the church. That night I saw myself on TV, and I didn't like myself, you know. I came across as this stereotyped image of what a militant was supposed to be —the Afro and the shades and all this. I was up there talkin' all kinds of shit about this, that, and the other. And it was so routine and blasé, I said, "Damn," you know. I didn't dig myself. So the next day we had the press conference indoors behind a table. It was a relaxed atmosphere, I had my clear glasses on, so people could see my eyes, and as the press was settling down, I said, "How you doing?" introduced myself and got into raps. All the time we were in that church we had something to give the media people every day, that's how we had 'em going, 'cause they had no other news going on at the time. I got to know 'em, I know everybody in New York City in the media, you know, and we developed a kind of rapport, 'cause they understood they could talk to me, and that meant they could talk to the Party. I learned a lot of things out of that. I learned that a reporter could be your best friend, you shouldn't classify a reporter immediately as being a pig, especially now that they are letting a lot of Black and Puerto Rican reporters in. The real enemy is up on top—management levels. I had some good people, man, who wrote some good things for us—the editors came and hacked the shit up, and it was nothing like what they put in, and they proved it to me, 'cause, like, at first I distrusted them also. There's that whole Movement orientation toward distrusting and watching out for the media—a lot of times, man, the Movement people come up there and treat the media people like shit, you know. Then they say, "Well, they put me on the air bad." *Of course* they put you on the air bad, you came across like an idiot.

And TV gets into somebody's house, man. You know, when you're on the screen in somebody's crib, you better not be saying things that come out with a lot of blips on the screen, 'cause you're gonna turn off whole families like that. You should understand what you're doing. The whole thing is to forget the person behind the mike that's asking the questions and imagine that you are talking to 300 of the most assorted kind of Puerto Ricans in the world in one room, in one little room—just do it like that, and as long as you keep the people in your eyes, you've got it.

Too many people tend to get into arguments with reporters. There are some reporters that come in there red-baiting—what you gotta do is use that, and that's where a little humor doesn't hurt. You can turn things around to make them look like jackasses and expose their game to the people right there on TV or radio. The people dig an underdog, that was the great appeal of the Mets at one time, and you have to understand that that's exactly what we are, underdogs. Once the people can start digging us for that, we can tell them, "Dig yourself for that."

When we're standing up there tellin' the pigs off—they dig that, man, whether or not they're of the same political persuasion. When the chips are falling down for us, a lot of times there have been Puerto Rican reactionaries that have defended us—sometimes *before* the Puerto Rican liberals, because at least they realized that one thing they can never say about us is that we are against the nation. We know for a fact that because of the way we've used the media, people dig our audacity, they love us, they feel like we're their grandchildren.

There was a period in our Party from July of '69, when we first started, to about August of 1970 or July of 1970 when we ran really on the personal magnetism of the leadership. But as we started to grow we said, "Look man, there ain't no way you can get a party going on that—you can't build a national liberation movement on the charisma of five or six people." 'Cause that would mean they would always have to be traveling everyplace to keep the whole machinery together. And if you want to keep a thing together, you've got to lay down certain principles that people can pick up on and go to town with—like the Thirteen Point Program and Platform. We have also developed our own political analysis. Right now we are going through a whole big thing of teaching ourselves to think in scientific terms, to study the theories of other revolutionary philosophers—people like Marx, Lenin and Mao.

Actually, we have made *two* analyses because we have to think of two struggles which are interrelated and at the same time not related—like the law of opposites. In other words, we have to make one analysis for the Puerto Rican nation that includes Puerto Rico, the island and the mainland; then another one for the Puerto Ricans who are struggling in the United States.

Within the Puerto Rican nation, there have been many groups who have been struggling for a long time, and our analysis has shown that the correct method of bringing about revolution is to isolate the enemy to as small a number as possible and unite the greatest number of people. Our major goal at this point is defeating the U.S. enemy. Right now we work with anybody who has the same goal. We're trying to work with the greatest number of people. In doing this, one of our most important concepts is that we are humble before our people, and vicious before the enemy. If you read *History Will Absolve Me*, you will see Fidel was *very* good at isolating the enemy into this little clique. See, when people think the enemy is this big mass, it wears away at the will to fight, but when people see that the enemy is just this bunch, right— this *Tame* Bunch—people begin to move.

The first segment of our people that will join, work with, and support the revolution is the *lumpen*, the street people: prostitutes, junkies, two-bit pushers, hustlers, welfare mothers. That's the group that got the Party through its first two years. Marx and Lenin said the working class would be first, right. But we have to examine the Puerto Rican reality. The street people come into the revolution because they've got nothing to lose. And it's a law of revolution that the most oppressed group takes the leadership position.

After the *lumpen* come the lowest classes of workers. For a long time in America, for a lot of reasons, the importance of the worker has been underrated, and when people have said "Power to the people," they have talked about only one segment, and have sort of isolated everybody else. In the phase we are entering now, we are pushing very strongly for a *lumpen*-worker alliance as being the basis for the revolution within the Puerto Rican nation—an alliance of working people and street people, which will build and see this revolution through to the end.

We're going very heavily into worker organizing while we continue the organizing of street people, and we will continue to create situations where the two can come together because this system has created an antagonism between the working people and the street people of the same nation. In the ghettos of the city you have poor working-class people living in projects, and poor street people living in the tenements. And the people in the projects always think that they're better than the people in the tenements, and the people in the tenements can't stand the people in the projects. I mean, there are junkies ripping off the working people when they come home from the subways with their paychecks, and then the workers want to get together to form vigilante groups. . . . So we have gone out into the community to end this antagonism. This is one of the things that came out of the Second People's Church, this alliance. We know this will bring on a lot of repression from the enemy, because that's been one of their greatest games—like racism, like sexism—to keep the lower classes fighting each other, because they have the greatest revolutionary potential.

The group that comes in between the *lumpen* and the worker is the student. A student is this weird thing—a student actually could be classified as *petit bourgeois,* because the student, see, doesn't have much to do, the student is not working, has nothing to support except himself or herself. The student just has to worry about term papers and grades and scholarships. Once the student gets over that hangup, the student then begins to join the struggle. But the student doesn't have the same kind of gut commitment that the *lumpen* has, or the same kind of overall response coming from prolonged pressure that the worker has.

Many of us in the Party were students. But after checking it out, we saw that we were the children of workers or *lumpen,* so this prevented us from tripping out into a real *petit-bourgeois* vacuum.

Among *petit-bourgeois* people—lower-*petit-bourgeois* people like teachers, certain poverty pimps that ain't gettin' too much bread, middle-class professionals—there's almost a fifty-fifty split in the time of revolutionary struggle. Some will join, and some go against, there's a left-wing *petite bourgeoisie* and a right-wing *petite bourgeoisie.*

When you get to the ruling class, you'll find very few of our people there. And very few of the people who are actually a part of the elite in Puerto Rican society are going to join and support our struggle. Anybody who comes along is considered a bonus.

When we talk about our role in terms of creating the American Revolution, we are not saying we are going to take

Puerto Rican people and ship them back to Puerto Rico. We are saying that we have been here in this country for two generations—in some cases, maybe three generations—we've been here for so long, right, that it would be too convenient for us to move back now, and just create a revolution there. We're saying that we want pay back for the years that we have suffered, the years that we have put up with cockroaches and rats. We had to put up with snow, we had to put up with English, we had to put up with racism, with the general abuse of America. And we are gonna hook up with everybody else in this country who's fighting for their liberation—and that's a whole lot of people. We know that the number-one group that's leading that struggle are Black people, 'cause Black people—if we remember the rule that says the most oppressed will take the vanguard role in the struggle —Black people, man, have gone through the most shit. Black people, along with Chicanos and native Americans, are the greatest ally we can have. So we must build the Puerto Rican-Black alliance. That is the basis of the American Revolution for us. Actually, the first group in America that we had a formal coalition with was the Black Panther Party. Also we must further the Latino ties, especially as we move west, and here in New York City, we must work with Dominicans—to further eliminate the racism that has deeply divided Black people and Spanish people.

We are also coming very close together with the struggle of Asians in this country, Asians who have been disinherited from the land that was theirs. Hawaii, for example, was made a state. One of our immediate struggles is to prevent that from happening in Puerto Rico. The Asian struggle is, like, twice as hard, because now they have to free a state, which is different from freeing a colony, right. That's actually going in and busting up part of a union.

Now the time has come for the Young Lords Party to begin organizing on the island. I mean, that's inevitable— we're not fighting just for Puerto Ricans in the States, we are fighting for all Puerto Ricans, you know, and in turn, we're fighting for all oppressed people. In the fourth point of our Thirteen Point Program and Platform, we say we are revolutionary nationalists, not racists. That also means that we recognize the struggle of white people.

One thing we always say in the Young Lords, "Don't ever

let any particular hatred you have prevent you from working. Always take it into you and let it move you forward. And if it's strong, change it, because it stops your work." We tell all Puerto Rican youth to listen to this. High-school-age Puerto Ricans are into a *big* thing about whitey, and we tell them, "Man, it's not white *folk*. What we are trying to destroy is not white people, but a system created by white people, a capitalistic system that has run away from them to the point that it is now killing white people, too." And in fact, in that struggle, we're gonna hook up and we're gonna be allies with white people, like the Weatherpeople. The fact that the Weatherpeople rose is important to us because for a long time it was very theoretical talking about white allies. Every time we talked about it with somebody, the brother or sister would say, "Well, where are they?" And it was a good point. You know, where was everybody when Fred Hampton was killed? So that the emergence of the Weatherpeople—their beginning was very shaky, but it's a good, solid, steady group now—has given us a lot more trust and has helped us a lot in relating to other white people.

You know, when we meet somebody from the Third World, we immediately call them brother or sister, right. And then they have to prove to us through their practice that they are not our brothers or sisters—like Gene Roberts, who infiltrated the Panther Party. We view white people, when we first see them, with mistrust and suspicion, and then they have to show us by their practice that they are really our brothers and sisters—and that is the difference in the two.

It would be totally naive for us to openly embrace white people, even if they are in the Movement, simply because they're supposed to be revolutionary. We've gone through too many frustrations with white people in the Movement to have that happen. 'Cause you really want to hope that once you get into the Movement there ain't no more racism. But that's a joke. In many cases racism becomes sicker than what you see in the so-called "straight" world, because it's kind of like a psychopathic hero-worship. You know, everything the Panthers do is right simply because they're Black, the Young Lords are fantastic because they're Puerto Rican. That's ridiculous. The Young Lords make mistakes, and if we make mistakes we want our white *compañeros* and *compañeras* to criticize us. If they really love us, that's what they'll do. That's one of the weaknesses of the Movement, you know, that people do not want to criticize the Panthers because the Panthers are Black. But in doing that they do more harm to the Panthers than they do good.

We try to encourage honesty in our relationships with white people. I think that we've gone a long way toward eliminating a lot of the shit in the Movement. And I think a lot of people get good vibes when they're around us. I think a lot of people in the Movement dig us because of that.

The Young Lords Party today is the fastest-moving group of people inside the Puerto Rican nation. We're moving faster than anybody else, and this means that all the contradictions that exist among our people are much more highlighted among us, that things come out much more quickly. That's why you have the Young Lords arguing about male chauvinism, female passivity, racism, Viet Nam. People on the street ain't talkin' about all those things yet, you know. We try to take that word "vanguard" and give it a new definition, because the definition that it has now is that the vanguard is some elitist group, that they're better than everybody else, and they tell all the other groups, "Go fuck yourself." Like, to us, the vanguard means that we have a great responsibility. It means that we are in front of the people and show the people the way, but at the same time we are among the people, because we are the people. We are also in back of the people, you know, because sometimes you got to lay back to check the people out. And that's where we get our strength from.

We're here because we are trying as best we can to take the power of the State and put that back in the hands of the people who for so long have been denied everything. It's a very deep, emotional thing, you know, for people who've been told for so long that they're fucked up, that they're niggers, spics, that they ain't worth shit, to be doing this.

We are showing people an alternative to living under a capitalistic society—an alternative to the tenement, to the street, to the workplace, to the *fanguito*. Each generation that comes up is taught that this is the only way things can be done, this is life, right. It's a fact of life that you're poor, that there are some people on top, and that most people are on the bottom. It's a fact of life that this is a dog-eat-dog world, and if you want to make it you got to make it by yourself. But we're gonna take them facts of life and turn them around. We're saying that it is gonna be a new fact of life that what counts first is not so much the individual but the group, and in order for the individual to survive, the group, the nation, has to survive.

There's a whole new way to live, you know, if the people together are planning where their nation's gonna go, how their government is running, how much they're going to produce, who's going to produce what, and what they're gonna do with it once they get it. In cold, scientific terms this means that production and distribution get put in the hands of the people. That's a phrase that everybody can sing by rote, but if we think about it and if we understand it, it's a whole mind-blowing concept to oppressed people, because we've never been shown that we can succeed in anything.

You know, there was a way that the people used to walk in the street before 1969, before the Young Lords Party began —people used to walk with their heads down like this, and the pigs would walk through the colonies, man, like they owned the block. They'd come in here with no kind of respect in their eyes. They'd *walk* through, they wouldn't ride through. See, when a pig *walks* through the street that means they got less respect than if they gotta ride. But after the Garbage Offensive and the Peoples' Church it was a whole new game.

As these things started to happen, as each one came, it was like boom, boom, boom. You and the enemy are standing there like this, right, and the enemy's been kicking your ass. But suddenly you throw up a couple of blocks, right, and you land a couple of solid ones, and people start digging this, and they see you're landing more solid ones. You're fighting toe to toe and, like, you're takin' some shit, but you know, you can take his best. For 400 years, you've taken the best that this mother-fucker could throw at you, and now you're gonna deal. So now, what's he gonna do- He wants to land his haymaker, he wants to round everybody up—you know that's coming. But we are a tempered people, we have been tempered like the blade of a knife by years, man, of living under this shit. When fascism comes, people gonna be ready for it. It's gonna blow the pigs' minds, right, but we ain't gonna give up. Because the people have seen that there's a way.

At the Second People's Church, we brought guns out into the open, and these guns were definitely illegal, they were unregistered, right. But because we had our people with us, Mayor Lindsay had to say the guns were legal. He had to hold his police back, because the white racists in the department wanted to kill us, you know, and they couldn't. And when people saw this, people said, "Wow!" We took the guns out of the church and we showed them—like we say in the street "we showed our shit" and got away clean. We still ain't been popped for that one.

Now, when they catch us, when they start rounding up the first bunch of Lords, they're gonna throw everything on us. But the point is the people now have hope. They can round me up, they can round up the Central Committee, but they're gonna have a hard time. First of all, the explosion that's gonna come if they touch anybody on the Central Committee will be tremendous. We already know what happened when they tried to take our Chief of Staff, Fi, and that was months ago. The main thing is that they can take any Young Lord now, because now they've got to kill an idea. Like, we have a second-, third-, fourth-level leadership. This is one of the greatest things we've done. Ain't nobody done this in the Puerto Rican nation—build something that's gonna live on. The Nationalists tried and failed because they were centered around this one cat—Albizu Campos.

Our people have been taught to believe that when they rounded up Albizu Campos and two thousand members of the Nationalist Party they broke the back of the Nationalist Party. But now the people can think about Albizu and all of a sudden it seems like the Nationalist Party has just been going through different kinds of changes for twenty years. "Well, man, we thought you all lost—it looks like we're gonna start winning." And, like, the concept of winning, right, that is the number one contribution of the Young Lords Party—that is what we are, man, the concept of winning.

One thing about us I really dig is that we don't get so hung up in theory that we don't move. We can still jump out into the street, we still do battle with the pigs, we still haven't lost our heart. That may sound like a whole big *macho* thing, but it's not, see, because it's important that we understand that the thing that kept the Puerto Rican nation intact, the thing that made us was the soul and strength of our men and women. That's what did it. When people would get put up against the wall, it wasn't because they had read Marx or Mao, it was because deep down inside there was this basic nationalist feeling that said, "Get off my back, you don't belong here—you ain't got no business bugging me. Get the hell out! And if you don't, I'm gonna punch you in the mouth!" This is the thing that is in our core, this is our nationalism.

Now, there are some people who would say that there's a contradiction in being a revolutionary nationalist—in fact, they say you can't be a Nationalist and a Socialist at the same time. Well, that's wrong. See, for these people I would quote Mao, where he says that loving your people and your country and fighting to liberate your people is the best way to aid the struggle of all peoples around the world. It's ridiculous to say you're an internationalist and you're going to struggle for all oppressed people, without picking a particular segment of people you're gonna work in. Because the people, you know, are divided along nation and class lines, and we have to recognize both. In this country, for example, racism is like a stick that the pigs are clubbing you on the head with. Now you got to grab the other end and hit them back with it— and the other end of the stick is nationalism. And if you do it righteously, if you do it with the interest of the people and with the backing of the people, then it becomes revolutionary. Now that's revolutionary nationalism—that is the kind of nationalism that says, "Yes, we are proud to be Puerto Rican, we are proud to be number one—but we want everybody else to be number one too, and we're gonna help everyone else be number one." See, 'cause the other kind of nationalism is reactionary nationalism—where you say, "Well, I'm number one. Fuck everybody else."

We've seen how the Black colony in America has been divided in terms of culture versus politics. We don't want to see the Puerto Rican colony divided that way. We don't want to create divisions where there need not be any. So that we do promote interest in the culture of the nation, right—but we only want to take from the culture what has been good. We're not gonna go into a trip glorifying the *pava,* which is a straw hat, or the *guayabera,* which is a kind of shirt, 'cause there ain't no hat or no shirt gonna free anybody. But the fact that our people, when put up against the wall, have managed to kick ass for centuries—that is good, that is part of our culture, right. That's why we say that the most cultural thing we do is pick up the gun to defend ourselves.

Culture, see, is the gun—as long as we understand that it is not the gun that should control us, but the Party that should control the gun. That is a rule that our Minister of Defense has made very clear. And that was the whole lesson of the People's Church. It can be said that the Second People's Church, when we took the church with guns, when we armed ourselves in our own defense, was probably one of the most cultural events in the history of the Puerto Rican nation—on the same level with the uprising at Jayuya in 1950, and *El Grito de Lares* in 1868. The only cultural form that's gonna go beyond that is armed struggle.

We are not nihilists, you know, we're not just destroy, destroy, destroy. We're saying to our people, yes we've got to destroy, but we have a new system that we're already starting to build, right. Taking the whole Puerto Rican nation into account, we're a small group, but inside that small group we're dealing socialistically with one another in a very human manner, and as we move, that influence is gonna spread out in many ways.

YOUNG LORDS PARTY

13 Point Program and Platform

**The Young Lords Party is a Revolutionary Political Party
Fighting for the Liberation of All Oppressed People**

1. We want self determination for Puerto Ricans, liberation on the island and inside the United States.

For 500 years, first Spain and then the United States have colonized our country. Billions of dollars in profits leave our country for the United States every year. In every way we are slaves of the gringo. We want liberation and the Power in the hands of the People, not Puerto Rican exploiters. *Que Viva Puerto Rico Libre!*

2. *We want self determination for all Latinos.*

Our Latin Brothers and Sisters, inside and outside the United States, are oppressed by American business. The Chicano people built the Southwest, and we support their right to control their lives and their land. The people of Santo Domingo continue to fight against gringo domination and its puppet generals. The armed liberation struggles in Latin America are part of the war of Latinos against imperialism. *Que Viva La Raza!*

3. We want liberation of all third world people.

Just as Latins first slaved under Spain and the yanquis, Black people, Indians, and Asians slaved to build the wealth of this country. For 400 years they have fought for freedom and dignity against racist Babylon. Third World people have led the fight for freedom. All the colored and oppressed peoples of the world are one nation under oppression. *No Puerto Rican is free until all people are free!*

4. We are revolutionary nationalists and oppose racism.

The Latin, Black, Indian and Asian people inside the u.s. are colonies fighting for liberation. We know that Washington, wall street, and city hall will try to make our nationalism into racism; but Puerto Ricans are of all colors and we resist racism. Millions of poor white people are rising up to demand freedom and we support them. These are the ones in the u.s. that are stepped on by the rulers and the government. We each organize our people, but our fights are the same against oppression and we will defeat it together. *Power to all oppressed people!*

5. We want equality for women. Down with machismo and male chauvanism.

Under capitalism, women have been oppressed by both society and our men. The doctrine of machismo has been used by men to take out their frustrations on wives, sisters, mothers, and children. Men must fight along with sisters in the struggle for economic and social equality and must recognize that sisters make up over half of the revolutionary army: sisters and brothers are equals fighting for our people. *Forward sisters in the struggle!*

6. We want community control of our institutions and land.

We want control of our communities by our people and programs to guarantee that all institutions serve the needs of our people. People's control of police, health services, churches, schools, housing, transportation and welfare are needed. We want an end to attacks on our land by urban renewal, highway destruction, and university corporations. *Land belongs to all the People!*

7. We want a true education of our Afro-Indio culture and Spanish language.

We must learn our long history of fighting against cultural, as well as economic genocide by the Spaniards and now the yanquis. Revolutionary culture, culture of our people is the only true teaching. *Jíbaro Si, Yanqui No!*

8. *We oppose capitalists and alliances with traitors.*

Puerto Rican rulers, or puppets of the oppressor, do not help our people. They are paid by the system to lead our people down blind alleys, just like the thousands of poverty pimps who keep our communities peaceful for business, or the street workers who keep gangs divided and blowing each other away. We want a society where the people socialistically control their labor. *Venceremos!*

9. *We oppose the Amerikkkan military.*

We demand immediate withdrawal of all u.s. military forces and bases from Puerto Rico, VietNam, and all oppressed communities inside and outside the u.s. No Puerto Rican should serve in the u.s. army against his Brothers and Sisters, for the only true army of oppressed people is the People's Liberation Army to fight all rulers. *U.S. out of Vietnam, free Puerto Rico now!*

10. *We want freedom for all political prisoners and prisoners of war.*

No Puerto Rican should be in jail or prison, first because we are a nation, and Amerikkka has no claims on us; second, because we have not been tried by our own people (peers). We also want all freedom fighters out of jail, since they are prisoners of the war for liberation. *Free all political prisoners and prisoners of war!*

11. *We are internationalists.*

Our people are brainwashed by television, radio, newspapers, schools and books to oppose people in other countries fighting for their freedom. No longer will we believe these lies, because we have learned who the real enemy is and who our real friends are. We will defend our sisters and brothers around the world who fight for justice and are against the rulers of this country. *Que Viva Che Guevára!*

12. *We believe armed self-defense and armed struggle are the only means to liberation.*

We are opposed to violence, the violence of hungry children, illiterate adults, diseased old people, and the violence of poverty and profit. We have asked, petitioned, gone to courts, demonstrated peacefully, and voted for politicians full of empty promises. But we still ain't free. The time has come to defend the lives of our people against repression and for revolutionary war against the businessmen, politicans, and police. When a government oppresses the people, we have the right to abolish it and create a new one. *Arm ourselves to defend ourselves!*

13. We want a socialist society.

We want liberation, clothing, free food, education, health care, transportation, full employment and peace. We want a society where the needs of the people come first, and where we give solidarity and aid to the people of the world, not oppression and racism. *Hasta La Victoria Siempre!*

PART IV:

EDUCATION ON THE MAINLAND

Eugene Bucchioni

A SOCIOLOGICAL ANALYSIS OF THE FUNCTIONING OF ELEMENTARY EDUCATION FOR PUERTO RICAN CHILDREN*

The curriculum is but one of the many factors affecting life within the classroom. Daily, in the classroom, the teacher, in discharging her professional duties and responsibilities, attempts to implement the curriculum and its numerous provisions by making available the suggested experiences and activities, by utilizing the recommended materials and methods of instruction, and by observing the required time allotments. Children arrive early in the morning, their attendance is taken, and the acting out of the curriculum then begins.

Concurrently with the acting out of the curriculum, however, other things occur as well. Along with the mandated experiences and activities of the curriculum, children talk, become noisy, and are reprimanded accordingly. There are many requests for permission to get drinks or to use the toilets. The pencil sharpener and the waste paper basket become the crowded sites of frequent small meetings as children approach these locations, ostensibly to sharpen their pencils and discard paper but instead remain to chat or to laugh and play. Questions and answers, the playing of games, singing songs, recess periods for milk, class room monitors performing their roles, the giving of homework assignments, fire drills, getting on line, standing up and sitting down are all significant components of classroom life.

The combination of the interaction of various curriculum

* Eugene Bucchioni. A *Sociological Analysis of the Functioning of Elementary Education for Puerto Rican Children in the New York City Public Schools*. Unpublished doctoral dissertation, New School for Social Research 1965, pp. 73–111.

requirements and these patterns of child behavior in the classroom result in an intricate round of life that is repeated daily, weekly and monthly in each elementary school. But this round of life, as varied and highly complicated as it is, becomes still more complex as Puerto Rican children interact with it and act out their several roles as children in elementary school, and as young members of lower classes and participants in Puerto Rican culture.

Miss Dwight, the Curriculum, and los Niños Puertorriqueños[1]

Miss Dwight was seated at her classroom desk handscoring her fourth grade class's achievement tests when the 8:45 bell rang. She clipped the papers and arranged them in a neat pile on the metal file cabinet to her right, put out the room lights, and locked the door after her.

The third grade and other fourth grade teachers had begun to gather inside the side entrance to the building and took the opportunity to talk among themselves for a few minutes before admitting their lines of classes into the building.

Miss Dwight joined the group and said, "I've just been marking the achievement tests and I wish they hadn't been given."

"I know what you mean," said Mrs. Maran.

"How can almost everyone of the children miss a simple question like the one about musical instruments?"

"The Puerto Ricans seem to learn absolutely nothing—either here or at home."

[1] The data presented in this chapter, including incidents within the classroom, teacher attitudes, etc., were derived from an extensive series of observations made in various classrooms. Observations revealed the occurrence of similar events and incidents in each of the classes observed. Since curriculum content, teaching methods, and reactions to these were essentially similar in each of the classes, one such classroom was then selected for detailed discussion. Miss Dwight, her pupils, and the other teachers to whom reference was made are real persons; the names of both tachers and pupils were changed to conceal their identities. Several details concerning other incidents occurring within the classroom on the same day were eliminated in order to prevent a repetitive discussion; the details eliminated include classroom routines such as distribution and collection of materials, collection and correction of homework, several interruptions by children with messages from other teachers, much informal conversation among children during the transition from one subject to another and when lining up, and a fire drill.

"Yes," said Miss Dwight, "all they seem to care about is sleeping, eating, playing, and having parties."

"But you know . . . the ones in my third grade class are very well behaved. Authority means something to them."

"Too bad they have to grow up!" said Miss Dwight. "Things sure take a turn for the worse then."

"Something's wrong somewhere," said Mrs. Maran.

"Well, we'd better get the children."

Miss Dwight moved to the door, beckoned her class to enter the building, and led the double line to their classroom. She held the keys out to Juan, who opened the door and switched the lights on quickly before another classmate, running to the switch, could beat him to it.

The children talked quietly among themselves as they went past the bookcase to hang their coats on the hooks in the closets. The two coatroom monitors took their stations in the closet at either end and saw that no one remained there longer than necessary. They also made certain that the children entered the closet at the left side and went out at the right.

María was watering the plants which sat on the long shelves built in front of the windows. She took particular care of the cactus plants and consulted with Miss Dwight as to the proper amount of water to be given them. Antonio adjusted the shades so that the bright morning sunlight did not streak across the desks and into eyes.

The bulletin board on the wall opposite the windows was filled with samples of children's written work, arranged in columns, some papers boasting glittering colored stars while others were devoid of similar commendation. To one end of the bulletin board were charts with colorful pictures illustrating words that begin with different consonants. The remainder of the bulletin board was devoted to a crudely drawn map, water colored by the children, with street names indicated, of a twenty block radius around the school. Cracked, yellowed plaster hung from almost all of the room's wall space. The lighting for the room came from two rows of three huge globes that were suspended from the ceiling by long chains.

Miss Dwight finished looking over the plans she had written for the day's work. She took the classroom in with a glance and noticed that about half the class was already seated and ready for the day's work with a notebook and pencil on most desks.

"Children," she said, "please get to your seats now."

As the children moved to obey, some a little slowly, some more rapidly, Miss Dwight called the name of each child in the first seat across the room for the attendance of each row. The names of the boys and girls absent were called out and Miss Dwight made the appropriate notations in her attendance register.

As she closed the book, about to put it in its place in the metal file cabinet, Dolores and Jesús entered the room, late. Miss Dwight glanced at them, made the necessary corrections in her register, and asked, "Do you have a note for being late?"

Dolores replied breathlessly, "*Maestra, el reloj despertador se rompió y. . . .*"

"Dolores, speak in English please. You know that I don't understand Spanish."

"*Sí, mastera. ¡Cómo no!* Deh alarrme clock. Eet broken bery bad. My mama say. . . ."

"Please, Dolores. We've taken enough of the class's time for this. Furthermore, if it's not your alarm clock, it's having to go to the store, or helping dress your brother or some other excuse. You will have to learn to come to school on time. You too, Jesús! You have been coming to school long enough to realize that one of the important rules is to be early in the morning. And another thing, you are to bring a note each time you are late or absent. I expect a note from each of you tomorrow morning. And I'm tired of changing my attendance report every time you both come in late."

Miss Dwight turned to the class and asked for two volunteers to be Mr. and Mrs. America for the opening exercises. She looked at the many hands that were raised in her class of thirty-three children, and selected Alan and Carmen. Carmen smiled as she walked quickly to the front of the room. She joined Alan in asking the class to rise for the pledge of allegiance to the flag. Miss Dwight also rose, faced the flag, and helped to lead the class over such words as allegiance, republic, indivisible, and justice.

During the first few months of school the class sang *America,* but Miss Dwight had recently advanced them, after much drilling, to *The Star Spangled Banner.* Miss

Dwight winced when she heard such phrases as "was so proudly we held" and "brought estripes and bri destars." Other words were also unintelligible: perilous, proof, ramparts.

Some of the children moved to seat themselves after the song. Miss Dwight stared in the direction of several of them, folded her hands, bowed her head, and followed Alan and Carmen as they led the class in prayer.

"Almighty God, we acknowledge our dependence on Thee. We beg Thy blessings on us, our parents, our teachers, and our country."

The children seated themselves and Miss Dwight looked at her planbook briefly. Some of the children talked with each other, a few looked through their desks for various papers and books, and others slumped down in their seats.

"Class, please open your number books to page 46. Henry, would you start reading the instructions at the top of the page."

Henry read the title, " 'Learning more about subtraction.' These are problems that ask how many are left. To find the answer you must subtract."

"Helena, please read the first problem aloud."

"Dere were seex duckes esweemin een a pon. Two a dem eswam away. How many were lef?"

Miss Dwight said, "Helena, that's not quite right. You're not pronouncing the words correctly. Say, there were six ducks swimming in a pond. Two of them swam away. How many were left?"

Helena repeated the question incorrectly. Miss Dwight said, "That's better. Now, how many do you have left?"

Miss Dwight called on Juan. He tilted his head to the side and stared ahead, as Miss Dwight waited for an answer. Several children raised their hands to be called on, and others buried their heads in their books or rummaged through their desks.

"Juan, do you or don't you understand this problem?"

He did not answer. His grip tightened on the book as he continued to peer into it.

"Juan, I asked you a question and I expect an answer."

"*Mastra,* dees word I donno. *¿Qué quiere decir?*"

"Spell the word for us."

"S-w-i-m-m-i-n-g."

"That's swimming. To move in the water."

"*Nadando,*" called out Manuel in explanation.

Juan looked into his book again and Miss Dwight waited in silence, keeping the class quiet by glancing around and resting her gaze on those who talked or fidgeted in their seats.

Manuel raised his hand and asked to go to the boys' room. "No, Manuel, you will have to wait until I take the entire class at ten o'clock."

Manuel turned to his neighbor, Pedro, and spoke rapidly and not too softly. "*Pero Tengo que ir al baño ahora mismo,*" Miss Dweight heard him say.

"No talking, Manuel! Juan please read the problem aloud to the class."

"Dere were seex duckes esweeming to. . . ."

"To-geth-er," said Miss Dwight.

". . . to-ged-der een a pon. Two a dem eswam away. How many were lef?"

"What is it, Juan?"

"Lef? *No comprendo* lef. What mean lef, teacha?"

"It means how many stayed together after the two ducks went swimming away."

"*Ah, sí, ahora comprendo,*" he said rapidly, sitting taller in his seat.

He looked into his book and his lips began to move as he reread the problem silently. Miss Dwight said, "Juan, we have taken a long time on this problem. Do you know how to solve it?"

"Seex . . . takeaway two."

Manuel shouted, "*Seis menos dos.*"

"Quiet, Manuel," said Miss Dwight. Juan turned his head to the window. "Juan, please try to pay attention. Take out your squared material and work it out. And," she addressed the class, "if you do not have the answer, I want you to do the same."

The children, some quickly, and others more slowly, searched in their desks for the arithmetic materials. Books from overstuffed desks fell onto the floor and some children took this opportunity to walk to the basket with crumpled scrap paper they found in their desks. Others went to the pencil sharpener that was attached to the side of the book-case where they conversed in soft tones.

"Get to your desks," called out Miss Dwight. "This moving

about has got to stop!" When order was restored, she continued, "Class, how many ones' squares do you need to solve this problem?"

The same few hands that were raised previously went up again. Miss Dwight ignored these offers of assistance. The remainder of the class looked back into their books at the problem. More hands were raised.

"Juan, how many do you need?"

"Seex."

"Fine. Now take them out of your holder and place them separately on your desk. Now, how many should you take away?"

Again, heads turned to page 46.

"Two," Juan answered, as he picked up two squares of paper.

"How many are left?"

"*Uno, dos, tres, cuatro*," he answered as he tapped each square that remained.

"No, Juan, One, two, three, four."

Miss Dwight took a deep breath and adjusted her posture. She then read the second problem to the class. She called on Marvin for the solution and received an immediate correct answer.

"Children, these problems go on to the next page. When you have free time today, you are to do these two pages. Otherwise, they are part of your homework. Make an example of each one. And now, put all your arithmetic materials away. It's ten o'clock and we must go the the lavatories and then to the basement for physical education. Row one, line up. No talking."

The children began to talk loudly. Miss Dwight said, "Sit down, children. We will have to stay here if you do not line up quickly and quietly. And Manuel and Pedro, school is no place for you to be leaping out of your seats and racing others to the front of the room. Behave yourselves."

"Now, let us try again. And keep quiet on line. Row one, stand. Walk to the front of the room. Row two."

Miss Dwight gave each row time to move slowly and then called the rest of the class in the same manner. She gave the keys to Juan, watched him lock the door and turn off the light switch, tried the door handle to make certain it was locked, and reminded him to pull the door closed after the class was out of the room. He nodded and gave her a grin as he said, "Sí, *maestra*."

Miss Dwight led the class to the end of the hallway and lined the boys in front of the boys' toilet and the girls at theirs. "Hurry, boys, three at a time. Girls, four at a time. Please don't waste time as it's ten past ten and we have the basement only until it's ten thirty."

As a boy or girl came out of the lavatories, another child went in. Miss Dwight opened the door to the boys' room frequently and could see, through the mirror to the left, the boys standing at the urinals. "Wash your hands, boys, and if you are ready, come out so that the others might come in."

Antonio was out as fast as he had gone in. Miss Dwight felt his dry hands and sent him back to wash them. The girls were finished and standing on line. Miss Dwight said, "Girls, I'm sure you remembered to wash your hands. If anyone has forgotten, please go back and do it now."

Four girls returned to the girls' room and came out complaining that there was no soap in the dispensers. "Well, girls, we have soap in our room. You can wash your hands later. Now, class, let's be on our way."

Miss Dwight walked to the left of her class line and kept at about the middle. In this way, she was able to control the stragglers at the end of the line and watch for talking in the hallway. The line leaders stopped at the end of the next hall, waiting for instructions to make a turn to the left. There was some talking, but Miss Dwight restored silence and then instructed the line leaders to continue. She moved to the front of the line when they reached the staircase, and led them slowly down to the basement.

"Children, this morning we are going to continue with the square dance. You remember that I explained that this is an early American dance that the first settlers in this country used to do. Today, many people still enjoy doing this kind of dancing. I need eight children; four boys and four girls for the first set."

Most of the children showed eagerness to participate by waving their hands and calling out, "Me!" or by shouting, "Pleez, teacha!" Some children hopped up and down and a few took their partners' hands and skipped about. Miss Dwight asked the class to calm down, selected one of the more eager children, and told the rest of the class to sit on the benches along the wall.

She arranged the four boys opposite the girls and gave brief instructions as to how to begin the dance. She put the *Virginia Reel* on the record player and started the record. The children danced in time to the rapid music. Miss Dwight took the arm of different children at times to help them with directions and to lead them to the new partners during the successive phases of the dance.

"Miss Dwight," complained Arthur, "Carmen doesn't know how to do this dance. She is always going the wrong way and getting me all mixed up."

"Arthur, be patient. You did this dance last year. And besides, Carmen is just learning our language. It is not easy to be new to everything all at once and maybe she doesn't understand directions."

Miss Dwight's attention was suddenly diverted to the children seated on the benches. They were talking, some were pushing and teasing others, some were laughing, and some were just moving about. She asked the children who had danced to sit down, then asked for quiet, and proceeded to select the next group of eight. She chose the children who had been making the most noise and disturbance, gave them the necessary instructions, and played the record once more. When the group had gotten halfway through the dance, another class entered the basement. Exclamations of annoyance came from those who had not yet danced. Miss Dwight lined up her class and spoke with Mrs. Frazier who had led her class to the benches.

"Hi, Mary. Boy! What a waste this morning has been. Two arithmetic problems and only half the class danced."

"Same here. All I do is give directions and explain, explain, explain! You'd think that by the time they get to the sixth grade they'd be able to read ten science pages by themselves."

"But we haven't even got enough texts, even if they could read them. It's a joke. I'm supposed to find time today for social studies, reading, language arts, writing, and health. Not to mention art and music."

"The third month of school and nothing across yet," said Mrs. Frazier.

"Yes, and I don't dare question most of the children about their work. I'm sure that most of what I say has gone out of the window. Most of them listen quietly and never ask a question, except now and then. Well, see you at lunch, Mary."

Miss Dwight reorganized her class and led them back to

the classroom. Felipe came up to her at her desk and asked to go to the boys' room. "No, Felipe, you were there only twenty minutes ago."

"But, teacha, I deen have to make den.'

"All right, but this will be the last time you leave the room this morning. And don't call me teacher. I have a name. Learn it!" Felipe left the room quickly. When he returned, the class was ready to begin a social studies discussion of the neighborhood.

"Yesterday, class," said Miss Dwight, "we talked of the block you live on. Many of you told us about your own block: what the houses look like, where you play, where you go to buy your groceries, drugs, and candy, and where your library, church, and police station are located. Today, let us talk about different neighborhoods right here in New York City and decide whether the differences make people live in different ways than you do. Who can tell me what the five boroughs of New York City are?"

Ronald, Frieda, and Stephen raised their hands. Some children opened their notebooks to find their listing of the boroughs, but other children went to the pencil sharpener or waste paper basket.

"Boys and girls, sit down and keep still." "Now what is the answer?"

Miss Dwight called on Frieda who answered, "Manhattan, Brooklyn, Queens, Bronx, and. . . ." She could not think of the fifth borough, and Stuart completed the answer with, "Staten Island."

"Children, please sit up tall," said Miss Dwight. Your feet belong on the floor, and not on the rungs of your desks. And everyone should be listening. Some of you do not look as if you are paying attention. To continue, let us talk about the borough of Queens where I live. I'll write a list on the blackboard of points of comparison that we can make between your neighborhood and an average neighborhood or suburb of Queens. Now, what things can we compare?"

Many hands were raised, and a list was developed:

> kinds of houses
> places to shop for food and clothing
> churches
> schools
> libraries
> playgrounds

Miss Dwight explained, "Many of the houses in my neighborhood are two family houses. One family lives on the first floor and another family lives upstairs."

Jesús asked, "Each family—they have their own baño?"

Miss Dwight asked, "Baño?"

Jesús replied, "Sí, where you go to wash yourself."

"You mean bathroom," said Miss Dwight. "Yes, they do."

"Dees I like," said Jesús. "The same baño the odder people use, we use too. And sometimes I cannot get een dere neber. For dat, I am een the morning late."

María added, "I too. And mama rrush me when I trry to take a bat. Me she tell not to make people in the beeldeen wait. *Dice que no tengo derecho a hacer, que espere tanto a la gente.*"

"English, children," requested Miss Dwight. "You will find, children, that many families have houses all to themselves, with sometimes two bathrooms upstairs—one for each bedroom and one on the first floor too."

"Only bery rreech peepool leebe een doz places," said Juan.

"Not exactly rich, Juan. But they do work hard, and every day."

"My papa, he say he work hard, ebery day—eben on Sunday. Sometime he don habe to work on Sunday. He get a day to estay home." Juan added, "And heem I hear say, and my mama say too, neber weel we be able to move to a more better place to leebe."

"It is difficult, sometimes, to earn enough money to do everything we want. It's important for you to remember that your work in school will some day help you to get a better job, earn more money, and live in a good home. This is why I am here: to help you live better. But let us remember that while we work toward something better, we must accept what we have now and try to appreciate the good things we have. For instance, what do you have that is good in your way of living?"

Faces took on various expressions and mixed comments were made.

"A lot—we gotta lot een weech to play."

"I habe a bedroom weed my brodder."

"And neber I am hungry like do oder keeds in my beeldeen who are bery hungry all dee days."

"Yes, when we have these basic comforts, we do have something to be thankful for. And that reminds me that it is time for our milk. Will the people we chose to give it out this week please do that now? And if you brought cookies, you may get them."

Miss Dwight sat at her desk and worked on the achievement tests while the children drank their milk and chatted. She overheard a few children make complaints about their living conditions. There was some talking in Spanish. When the milk containers had been discarded, she resumed their social studies lesson. Marvin began to tell of his cousin who lives on Long Island.

"My uncle drives my cousin, Raymond, to school every day. And I saw his school. It's not big like this one. And it's new. They have a gym with everything in it. They even have one of those things that they use in the circus to jump on. There's a big cafeteria and they have flowers and trees in front of the school. And the walls in the room are pretty colors."

"Long Island, children, is not in New York City. It is an island, almost 800 miles long, right outside of New York City. Many people have moved there because it is like the country, and they have built new modern schools and they have shopping centers where you have all the stores you need all together. There are very few apartment houses. Almost every family has its own house. The people who live near each other often get together for parties and dinner."

"Dat we'll do neber. My papa say eet ees too hard to change. Peepool won let you."

"No, Juan. That is not always true. If you study and work hard, and show people that you want to do what is right, they will let you improve yourself. It takes time and patience. We've seen today, children, that people in different places live in different ways, and I hope to continue this discussion tomorrow. For homework, I would like you to bring in pictures of houses, schools, churches, and playgrounds. And tomorrow, we will try to decide what kind of community these pictures fit into and compare them with your own. We have a half hour before lunch. Please open your notebooks to the English section and write a heading for today's work. I would like you to write a paragraph about our discussion today in social studies. Elsa, why is it taking you so long to find a page to write on?"

"An emty page, I cannot fin, teacha."

"How many times have I told you to keep at least five blank pages in each subject section of your notebook?"

"I don have no more paper."

"Well, why don't you ask your mother to buy you some?"

"I deed. Friday she say."

"But tomorrow is Tuesday. That means that you will have to borrow paper from a classmate for the entire week."

Several children were quick to offer Elsa paper. She accepted a few sheets and inserted the pages into her book. Miss Dwight walked around the room and stopped at many of the desks to help pupils in their work and to prod others to begin. Several children asked for the spelling of certain words. Miss Dwight stopped at Pedro's desk.

"Pedro, not 'Today we learn about new york.' It's 'learned' with an 'ed' ending to mean past time. Also New York is capitalized because it is the name of a place."

"I teenk New Yor ees only where I am."

"No, Pedro, you live in Manhattan which is only a small part of our state, which is also called New York."

Pedro shrugged his shoulders and Miss Dwight moved a few desks away and read, silently, the paragraph that Juan had written:

> I libe in nu yor city and so do oder many pipul who hab ril jauses i wil not oways lib were I lib because i wil studi in escool.

Miss Dwight smiled and pointed out the spelling, punctuation, and capitalization errors. "Juan, this is a very good beginning. I hope you will add a few details to show in what ways other people live differently than you do."

"Sí, maestra, cómo no." He took his pencil and proceeded to the next sentence.

"Tomás, please stop holding your head up and get your elbow off the desk. What time did you go to bed last night?"

"Carajo," whispered Tomás. "Twelve o'clock, teacha."

"Why so late?"

"My moder and fader had a party. Eet was een de room where I esleep."

"Well, couldn't you have slept in your parents' room until the party was over?"

"No, on de bed were too many coat. We don habe no room in de closet for de coat of de peepool."

"Well, Tomás, I hope you will go to bed early tonight so that you are rested tomorrow."

"Sí, maestra, I am bery tied."

"Children, it is time to get ready for lunch. Will those children who are going home for lunch get their clothing?"

The children made much noise as they got their clothing and moved back to their seats. Most of the class remained in school for lunch, and Miss Dwight called them, row by row, to get their clothing. At the sound of the bell, she dismissed those who were leaving the building, and after having reminded them to go directly home and to be back before the late bell, then called the remainder of the class on line.

"Children, the principal made a definite point of telling the teachers that the behavior and noise in the lunchroom is terrible. I hope I can be proud of you and that you will behave as you should, get your food quietly, eat quickly, and clean your places before you leave."

Juan took care of the lights and door and Miss Dwight led the class through the crowded hallways to the lunchroom. She stopped at the entrance and observed the actions of many of the children as they pushed each other, called out to friends, approached their tables at a half run, and slammed the metal trays down. She saw many children who had already finished eating return their trays with salads and vegetables untouched. She turned to enter the teachers' room.

She poured herself a cup of coffee, chose a seat next to Mary Frazier, and began to unwrap her sandwich. The teachers' room was not large and was undecorated, except for a small bulletin board with leaflets tacked to it and notes and letters from teachers who had either left or were on leave. There was a brown leather couch along a small wall space and three matching easy chairs along another side. Teachers from all grades filled the three tables. Conversation ranged from fashions to housework to theater to curriculum.

"How was the rest of your morning, Frances?" Mary Frazier asked Miss Dwight.

"Not too bad. I did some social studies and a little English. But I must tell you about Juan."

"Before you do," interrupted Mary, "why not get your coffee and relax a little?"

Frances Dwight went to the small kitchen in the teachers' room and poured herself a cup of coffee. Edith, who sat opposite Mary said, "What's the use of worrying about these kids? Between their lousy way of living and their Spanish, we're lost before we begin."

Frances returned to the table in time to hear Edith's remark and said, "That's just what I mean about Juan. This morning we had a class discussion in social studies and he told how his father works so hard. His parents are sure they'll never get anywhere. It's sad."

"Well," said Mary, "how can they when they don't know anything, go anywhere, or read anything?"

"That reminds me," said Edith, "of a story I heard of a kid who had an assignment to collect pictures of colorful gardens from magazines. He came in the next day without any pictures. When his teacher asked why he replied, 'All we got home is love 'n murder.' Really, I can't wait to get away from these dirty kids. Sometimes, I could faint when I get close to them."

"Edith," said Mary, "let's face it. We are in a slum neighborhood, and as far as the Puerto Ricans go, only the lower class has migrated here."

"True," said Frances. "They're told about the wonderful opportunities for them in America. If they knew any better, they wouldn't live the way they do."

"They act like animals, too. But they're worse in high school. I wouldn't teach there if you doubled my salary."

"You'll have tenure this year, won't you?" Mary asked Edith.

"Yes, and then the hell with all this. No more of this for me."

"But," said Mary, "what if all the teachers felt the way you do. I get discouraged too, but they are in this country and we have a job to do. They are American citizens you know, and we have to teach them how to live here."

"So far, they've been useless," said Edith. "All you see in the newspapers are gang wars, dope addicts, and rapes. You know it is so dangerous here that we have to walk to the subway together."

"Oh, Edith, it's not really as bad as all that," said Frances.

"No, it's worse. It was bad enough when we had the

Negroes. Now the goddamn spics too. Why even the Negroes despise these damn Puerto Ricans."

"Look," said Mary, "we've got them, so let's do the best we can."

"Another thing. What can you do with all this experience learning?" asked Edith. "If you fit in all these experiences, there's no time left to teach. These kids need good old fashioned drill and lots of it. And what child can count from five to ten without fingers or one's strips?"

"What really bothers me," said Frances, "is all the talking in Spanish. And I'll flip if just one more child calls me 'teacha' today."

"When they speak Spanish, they really prattle like monkeys. I'm sure they're not even trying to learn English," said Edith.

"Wait," said Mary. "Remember that Spanish is natural to them. How would you like the pressure of learning a new language and new subjects all at the same time?"

"Mary," said Edith, "you're entirely too sympathetic. You live in a dream world. Do you really think for one minute that these kids will ever amount to anything? In ten years you'll be unable to recognize New York because there will be so many Puerto Ricans here."

"Well," said Mary, "I can't help feeling sorry for these people. They are so persecuted from all sides and they need help, and lots of it."

The bell rang and the teachers cleared their places at the table and filed out to the yard to get their classes. Miss Dwight called her class into the building, led them to the room, and Juan opened the door. The children seated themselves and Miss Dwight called them, row by row, to put their clothing away. She attempted to keep the children quiet by alternately saying, "Quiet, boys and girls," or "keep still, children."

"I noticed, children, that the lunch didn't go over too well today. I saw many salads and vegetables untouched. Would someone care to explain why?"

María raised her hand. "*Si, maestra*, the corn eet habe no taste, and the sald was just *lechuga*."

"Lettuce," called out one of the children.

María continued, "My mama she make a sald dat taste so good."

"Well, we all do have different ways of preparing food so that it tastes good to us, but isn't it necessary to have a variety of foods each day?"

The class showed no response to this query. Miss Dwight continued, "Let us discuss a proper breakfast."

"Who has a suggestion?"

Roger and Antonio began to talk and Miss Dwight asked them to pay attention. They glanced at each other and smiled. Roger looked at the clock and then stared ahead, while Antonio picked up a pencil and started to scratch a groove deeper in his desk.

"Antonio, that is not your property that you are ruining. Many children will use that desk after you. I think you should leave it as you found it. Now put the pencil down and stop this nonsense. Do you hear?"

"*¡Coño de tu madre!*" Antonio did not lower his voice when making this remark. Most of the children looked at one another, showing shock, and some giggled.

"Antonio, what did you say? In English!"

"*¡Coño!*"

"Antonio, stand up and tell me in English what you said."

Antonio did not answer. He looked away from her.

"I'm waiting for your answer, Antonio. What does that mean?"

He stared at Miss Dwight.

"Would anyone in the class care to translate for me?"

"*Maestra*, it ees a bad teeng he say. We cannot say."

"Thank you, Juan." Miss Dwight turned to Antonio and suggested, "Perhaps you would like to repeat it to your mother at a conference."

"No, teacha, I am bery sorry. I do not mean eet. No more will I say eet."

"All right, Antonio. I will believe you. And I hope you will control your feelings better in the future. People just don't burst out and call each other names whenever they feel like it. You must learn how to cooperate more with others. We have to live with many people in this world, and it's time you've learned that everything does not always go the way you want it to. Now sit down and behave yourself."

She turned to the class. "Now, what is a food that we should eat at breakfast time?"

Marvin said, "Cereal."

"Fine. What else should you have for breakfast?"

"*Café*," answered another child.

"Coffee? No, coffee does not nourish you. It doesn't help you to grow strong. What can you drink that is good for your bones and teeth?"

Several children called out, "Milk!"

"Yes, milk. Milk has calcium in it. There is one more thing you should have at breakfast time."

David interrupted, "Miss Dwight, what is calcium?"

"I'm glad you asked, David. Children, I wish more of you would ask me to explain words that you don't understand. Calcium is a mineral. Our bodies need minerals and vitamins, just as a car needs gas and oil. Without the different minerals and vitamins, our bodies would break down and become sick. Each vitamin has a special job to do. Calcium makes our bones and teeth strong. Now what else besides milk and cereal should we have at breakfast time?"

She paused for a suggestion. None came, so she added "orange juice. Orange juice is for vitamin C."

María raised her hand. "What ees beetameen C?"

"Each vitamin has a letter and that is a vitamin we get from citrus fruits. I'll make a list of these items on the blackboard while you are making a heading for today in the health section of your notebooks and copy the list. Perhaps you can show the list to mother so that she, too, will understand what the best foods are for you and the family. Now, what are other foods that we should eat each day?"

"Bread?"

"Yes, and whole wheat or rye bread is better than white because the flour has not been whitened. That means that there is more food value in these other breads."

"Meat?"

"Good. Each day you should have some meat or eggs or cheese. These are called protein foods and they help to build your bodies. What goes with meat?"

"Tomatoes?"

"Well, yes. Also, vegetables that are green. Can you name some?"

"Espeenach?"

"Peas."

"Fine. We have others, too, cabbage, stringbeans, broccoli, asparagus, and many more. Every day you should have a salad, too. If you have these foods each day, you are sure to be getting all the vitamins and minerals that your body needs and you will be healthier and stronger."

Manuel raised his hand. "Teacha, my mama she cook so deeferent. Our beshtabools are oways jellow and white, like corn and rrice. We habe beans, too. But mama don make doz oder teengs. Neber I heard of some of dem."

"This is why we are making a list, Manuel. Perhaps your mother will be interested in trying some of these foods. I think your family might find it fun to eat different foods. Children, why not ask mother to give you, each day, one of these foods on the list? And if you like it, she can serve it again. Little by little, you will have a balanced diet."

"It's almost one-thirty and we had better get into our reading groups. I'll work first with the bluebirds. While I do that, I want the Little Red Group to finish the reading exercises you started yesterday, and the Thunderbirds can work on the paragraphs you started this morning in social studies. Bluebirds, bring your chairs and reading books up to the front of the room."

Some children pushed their chairs and Miss Dwight told them to carry them. Others who were talking were told to stop or they would be given additional homework assignments. Miss Dwight wrote a list of words on the board and said to the children, "Today we are going to read a story about a little boy and girl just your age who go with their uncle to a wharf. As I say the words on the board, you look at them and try to remember them. 'Wharf, trawler, pier, cabin, galley, stern, aft, salmon.' Now I want you to look these words up in the dictionary that is in the back section of your reading books and be prepared to tell me the meaning of each word."

She then addressed the children of the Little Red Group. Some were still working on the exercises in the reading workbooks. Three children who had finished this work were standing at the bulletin board before a world map and appeared to be discussing anything but geography.

"Will the children in the Little Red Group take your workbooks and chairs to the back of the room now?" The ten children followed directions and Miss Dwight started the review of the first exercise. "Vera, read the first sentence with your answer."

" 'Fran has a . . . .' I don't know that word."

" 'Ewe.' You pronounce it like the word 'y-o-u.' "

" '. . . ewe lamb.' "

"Yes, that is right. José, do the next."

"I couldn't do eet, teacha."

"Why not?"

"I deen read destory. I was home."

"Don't you know that you are supposed to catch up on your reading when you come back after being absent?"

"Sí, but I deen habe not enough time."

"Well, take the book and go to your seat and read it now."

Miss Dwight looked over the Bluebird group. "Bluebirds, if you continue to talk, I will have you write the meanings of those words and write them in sentences of your own. Continue your work quietly."

She turned back to the Little Red Group. "Susan, do the second one."

"The name of the ewe lamb is Fluffy."

"Correct. Antonio, the next."

"I don know what eet mean."

"Linda, read it please. Read it without the answer so that Antonio can answer it."

" 'Jerry works in a . . . .' "

"Antonio, finish the sentence."

He looked into his notebook. Miss Dwight asked, "Antonio, do you know where he worked?"

"No."

"Get the book and look for the answer."

Antonio went to his desk for the book, came back to his chair, and turned the pages slowly, trying to find the story.

"Antonio, why don't you use the table of contents?" You can find the story very quickly this way."

He turned back to the table of contents, found the page number, and after several moments, found the story.

"Now, look quickly," Miss Dwight said, "for the part that tells where Jerry works."

He used his finger to underline the sentences as he began to look methodically down the first page.

"Antonio, we read the story only yesterday. Can't you remember that the first few pages are about the lambs? You will find your answer further on in the story. There is no time to wait for you to find it now. Continue to look for the answer when you return to your seat. Children, we will finish this exercise tomorrow. Make sure that you have completed all the questions, so that we will be able to review this rapidly."

She spoke to the third reading group. "Thunderbirds, we have no time for reading today. I will start with your group in the morning. Bluebirds, go back to your seats now. We will start to read our new story tomorrow."

The children moved noisily. Miss Dwight ignored the momentary confusion while she continued to consult the planbook at her desk.

"We just have time before the bell rings to talk about our Christmas party. First, we need to divide the class into committees for entertainment, decorations, and refreshments. I'll write the committee titles on the blackboard and you decide which ones you want to be on."

Many children raised their hands. When Miss Dwight had finished writing on the board, she turned to see almost every hand waving energetically and voices grew louder as children began to call out. When Miss Dwight called for silence and asked each child for his and her preference, many more hands went up. The lists of names were noted on the blackboard.

"Each committee will have a special assignment and special things to do. Today, let's decide what the decoration committee will do."

Suggestions were shouted out from different parts of the room. The voices resounded. Miss Dwight raised her voice. "Children, if you continue to call out like this, we will have no party. We studied in our language arts lesson yesterday about how to hold a discussion. Please try to remember this discussion and all the rules we talked about, and be courteous so that you will all have a chance to be heard."

The class quieted down and Miss Dwight nodded to different children for their suggestions.

"Let's make baskets for our candy."

"I can make a Santa Claus for the door."

"Esnow for de weendo."

"Paper Christmas trees for the bulletin board."

"Fine. Those are enough ideas for now. Tomorrow, the decoration committee can meet and plan the work to be done. Let us give the entertainment committee something to work on."

Again, there was much rapid talk while the children offered suggestions and decided upon a program. The class soon developed a long list of dancers and singers.

"I can see that we will need several more hours for our party than we have planned in order to fit in all of this entertainment. The bell is about to ring! I will write your homework on the blackboard after I explain the assignment. Copy it and be sure to take home all the books you need. Do spelling unit number ten, part B. Look at the new words carefully and write the answers to all the questions. If you did not finish your social studies paragraphs today, finish them for homework. And last, I want each of you to find at least three pictures from magazines and newspapers of different kinds of homes, schools, churches, and communities."

Miss Dwight called the class row by row to get their coats. When they were ready to leave, she asked the first person in each row to go down the row and point out papers and pencils left on the floor so that they might be picked up. She then walked around the room for a final check and called the class to line up. She led the children to the outside door where many wishes for a pleasant afternoon were exchanged between her and the children. The children burst through the door to the street where they shouted, talked, laughed, and ran.

HEMOS TRABAJADO BIEN[*]

The recommendations which came out of the workshops have been combined and listed according to major categories. Participants in the Conference agreed that the true test of the value of these recommendations will be the extent to which they generate positive action. To this end, specific targets for action requests are suggested:

a. NYC Board of Education
b. NY State Education Department
c. US Office of Education
d. Private Agencies
e. Foundations
f. Mayor's Office
g. War on Poverty Agencies
h. NYC Board of Higher Education

New York City and State agencies are named with the understanding that groups in other locales and states will need to identify their own appropriate targets.

I. *To Increase and Upgrade Puerto Rican and Bilingual Educational Personnel and Administrators:*

a. Examine and change teacher certification standards to reflect real needs and competencies. (b)

b. Re-examine job descriptions and tables of organization to make it possible for more minority people to enter teaching at a full professional level and advance to administrative levels. (a, b)

c. Involve teacher training institutions, especially pub-

* *Hemos Trabajado Bien.* A Report on the First National Conference of Puerto Ricans, Mexican Americans and Educators on the Special Needs of Puerto Rican Youth. New York: Aspira, 1968, pp. 64–66.

lic universities, with retraining and recruiting programs for bilingual personnel. (b, h)

d. Examine potential for increasing recruitment of teachers in Puerto Rico. (a, b, h)

e. Examine possibilities for supplementing present guidance system with outside, non-profit agencies focused on problems of Spanish-speaking students. (a, d)

f. Establish effective liaison with organizations such as United Federation of Teachers and National Education Association to encourage development of policies sympathetic to these goals. (d)

II. *To Improve School-Community Relations:*

a. Work out concrete programs for communication on an equal footing between Spanish-speaking parents and schools. (a, b, d, e)

b. Utilize parents and community leaders in as many school capacities (such as guidance, vocational instruction, etc.) as possible in order to share educational tasks and deepen mutual understanding. (a)

c. In workshops and through other means, have parents actively participate in in-service training for teachers in the urban Puerto Rican culture. (a, b)

d. Begin now to educate the Puerto Rican community to the meaning and machinery of decentralization so that they may effectively participate in its implementation:

  1. Utilize the mass media in a planned program of education towards decentralization. (a, b, d, e)

  2. Provide bilingual materials related to all phases of decentralization. (a, b, e)

III. *To Make Curriculum Relevant:*

a. State and City education agencies should allocate funds for the translation and distribution of materials from Puerto Rico. These materials to be relevant to the need for giving the child a sense of pride in his bilingualism and heritage. (a, b)

b. Produce new materials as needed. (a, b, c, e)

c. Produce bilingual textbooks for primary schools and wherever needed. (a, b, c)

d. Develop and fund a Puerto Rican "writers' workshop" to prepare special materials. (d, e)

e. Set up a Spanish-speaking advisory board to evaluate all present textbooks, curricula and materials. (c, d)

f. In the teaching of the Spanish language to all students, give greater emphasis to Latin-American rather than Iberian culture. (Adopt standard Latin-American pronunciation rather than the Castillian which is irrelevant and tends to stigmatize the Spanish spoken by many Americans.) (a, b, c, h)

IV. *To Increase Puerto Rican Political Power and Community Action:*

a. Develop leadership training programs through community-run organizations. (d, e)

b. Increase voter registration. (f, g)

c. Organize on both city-wide and local levels for participation in school decentralization. (d)

d. Create Puerto Rican community committees to continuously evaluate and report on public education agencies which affect them. (d, e)

V. *To Strengthen Adult Education:*

a. Provide meaningful adult education at all school levels. (a, b, c, h)

b. Use educational television facilities, VHF and UHF, to bring interesting and informative programming into the lives of Puerto Ricans just as such programming is brought into the lives of English-speaking Americans. (a, b, c, e, h)

c. Prod cultural facilities such as museums and libraries to augment their services to Puerto Ricans. (d, e)

d. Develop ways of teaching English which are relevant to the culture and lives of adult Puerto Ricans. (a, b, c, e)

VI. *To Prepare Youth for Post-Secondary Education:*

a. Conduct a drive, on a national scale, to sharply increase the number of Puerto Rican youngsters attaining post-secondary education through the expansion of Aspira and any similar agencies. (d, e)

b. Use all available Puerto Rican professionals to stimulate the demand among youth for post-secondary education and to act as role models. (d, e)

c. Coordinate through a private agency efforts of post-secondary institutions to recruit and provide scholarships for students to assure sensitivity to student's special needs and optimum matching of students and institutions. (d, e)

d. Review, through a panel of college officials, administrators in public education, and representatives of private agencies such as Aspira, standards for college admission and allocation proportions and recommend appropriate remedial steps to "open wider the doors" to capable but underachieving youth. (a, b, e, h)

VII. *To Act on the National Level:*

a. Develop among all 7.5 million Spanish-speaking Americans a single voice which can advocate the case for special assistance in Washington. (d, e)

b. Create a central, nationwide clearing house for all educational information and materials related to bilingualism and Hispanic culture with the stress on Puerto Rico and the Western Hemisphere. (c, d, e)

Vera P. John and Vivian M. Horner

EARLY CHILDHOOD
BILINGUAL EDUCATION[*]

"A bilingual school is a school which uses, concurrently, two languages as a medium of instruction in any portion of the curriculum, except the languages themselves. The teaching of a vernacular solely as a bridge to another, the official language, is not bilingual education in the sense of this paper, nor is ordinary foreign language teaching."[1] Our working definition of bilingual education, restated in this quote from Gaarder, is more often the long-range goal rather than an actual description of current bilingual programs. The demand for a realistic and effective educational approach for non-English-speaking children has produced many new programs, but at present most schools are improvising with meager resources based on limited objectives. Those educators still committed to the English-only policies of the past are reluctant to engage in the major staff and structural changes necessary for the implementation of a truly bilingual system of education. Some members of the non-English-speaking communities themselves express ambivalence towards the idea of bilingual instruction. Speaking of one such commuinty, Gil Murello observes:

> Frankly stated, bilingual education threatens the identification with the dominant group that some socially mobile Mexican-Americans maintain. . . . These same professionals dimly, if not explicitly, realize that to accept the concept of bilingual education for their Mexican-

[*] Vera P. John and Vivian M. Horner, *Early Childhood Bilingual Education.* New York: Modern Language Association, 1971, pp. 178–187. Reprinted with permission.
[1] A. Bruce Gaarder, "Organization of the Bilingual School," *Journal of Social Issues*, 23 (1967), 110.

American students is to admit grave failure on their part over many years through the use of traditional materials and methods and an implicit "melting pot" philosophy.[2]

Even the administrators who agree that there is a need for bilingual education programs find themselves confronted by many problems: a shortage of bilingual teachers, a scarcity of appropriate curriculum materials, limited opportunities for teacher training, and lack of special funds. While the passage of Title VII of the Elementary and Secondary Education Act, and the subsequent funding of experimental bilingual programs, has contributed to the moral and financial support of bilingual education, the resources available for such programs continue to be limited. In addition to these problems, educators face the major decision of choosing a suitable model of bilingual instruction.

A systematic exploration of the considerations that enter into the selection of bilingual models has been developed by Mackey, based on information gathered in the files of the International Center for Research in Bilingualism.[3] Mackey proposes four levels of dimensions of varying bilingual educational settings: the learner in the home, the curriculum of the school, the community (or area) in the nation, and national language patterns. He notes that language is the basic component in each of these dimensions; that language "is itself a variable," and that "each language appears in each pattern at a certain degree of intensity" (p. 20).

A useful illustration of this concept of intensity appears in Valencia's study of three Mexican-American communities of the Southwest.[4] Valencia compares the intensity and usage of the native language with English among children in Laredo, Texas; Pecos, New Mexico; and Albuquerque, New Mexico. He observes, for example, that the child living in the border town of Laredo is exposed to and uses a great deal

[2] E. M. Bernal, Jr., ed., *Billingual-Bicultural Education: Where Do We Go from Here?* San Antonio, Texas; sponsored by the Bureau of Educational Personnel Development, U.S. Office of Education, and St. Mary's Univ., 28, 29 March 1969.

[3] William F. Mackey, "A Typology of Bilingual Education" (Quebec: International Center for Research of Bilingualism, 1969), mimeo.

[4] A.A. Valencia, "Bilingual/Bicultural Education: A Perspective Model in Multicultural America," Southwestern Cooperative Educational Laboratory, April 1969.

more Spanish than the child living in Albuquerque. Valencia recommends, with Mackey, that the language competence of the child be examined in the context of community patterns in language use, and that the interaction of these and other variables be considered in the planning of bilingual schools.

Most present programs of bilingual education, however, are not organized with these socio-linguistic and demographic variables in mind. While the importance of such research is recognized as an aid to evaluation, it does not play a significant role in the current planning aspects of the education of non-English-speaking children.

Although we recognize the value of a deductive scheme for classifying bilingual schools, we will limit ourselves, in this chapter, to a simple and descriptive framework. Our approach is dictated by the relatively meager information available on the use and functions of language in the home of non-English-speakers in the United States.

A. THE INFORMAL MODEL

In a surprising number of classrooms throughout the country, two languages are spoken. The native languages of American Indian and Spanish-American children, and those of many other communities, co-exist in the school with English as a means of communication, and, occasionally, as a medium of instruction. This development is less a reflection of recent community and educational interest in bilingual education than an indication of certain organizational and ideological trends in anti-poverty programs. Office of Economic Opportunity-supported programs, whether of the Head Start or Follow-Through variety, have included from the very beginning the employment of members of the low-income communities which they serve. While in many classrooms, the activities of parents and community aides have been restricted to menial jobs (e.g., clean-up, cooking, and transportation), in some instances paraprofessionals have participated in the actual planning and execution of educational activities.

Parents and aides, by their very presence, have altered traditional preschool education. This change is particularly significant in non-English-speaking communities, where these paraprofessionals have brought about an informal use of the child's native language in the classroom, a language usage often unplanned or accidental. Thus the Puerto Rican classroom aide in New York City, in helping to ease the Spanish-speaking child's difficult adjustment from home to school, explains school routines to the child and his parents in Spanish. Occasionally, she may be encouraged to present a lesson or an activity to the class in Spanish because the teacher is usually fluent in English only.

Communities in which such informal classroom experiences in two languages take place are large in number and different in character. Mackey's typology for assessing bilingual education offers one means of systematically identifying these community differences. Mackey refers to patterns of language usage in the home and identifies five types of "learners in the home." An illustration of one type of "learner" is the child from the monolingual home, where the language spoken is not that of the school, for example, a Navajo child living on the vast, isolated Navajo reservation. This child's pattern of language usage in the home would contrast sharply with that of a child raised in a Spanish-speaking home in a city with a bilingual tradition, such as Santa Fe. In spite of the differences in these two environments, the Head Start and Follow-Through programs conducted throughout much of the reservation are similar in their informal use of the native language and English to those in Santa Fe. These preschool programs often lack a clearly articulated policy toward the native language of the learner. A much-debated question here is whether the native language should be encouraged or should only be tolerated until the child acquires English.

A typical example of this ambivalence in classroom policy (and also of the mistaken belief that bilingual instruction consists of teaching the native language as a subject) is illustrated by the comments of a teacher participating in the Bureau of Indian Affairs kindergarten programs. "At first I did not consider this as a bilingual program, because we did not use materials published in the Navajo language, and were not attempting to teach it as a separate subject. . . . I now believe our efforts can be called bilingual and bicultural, and we are seriously considering extending bilingual instruction to other grades."[5]

A similar confusion is voiced by a very able Spanish-

[5] See "Bureau of Indian Affairs Kindergarten Programs," pp. 98–100.

American aide in one of the leading Follow-Through programs in the Southwest, who reports he is neither encouraged nor discouraged from speaking Spanish to the chlidren in the classroom; the Anglo teacher he works with is trying to learn Spanish and the children laugh good-naturedly at her pronunciation. However, the idea that learning to read in Spanish may be helpful to these children upsets him. In his own life and in that of his relatives, he has accepted the idea that Spanish is the language of oral communication, intimacy, and friendship, and that English is the language of literacy.

Much of the confusion in these informal programs derives from a lack of systematic planning in the instructional use of the two languages. While these programs cannot be considered bilingual education, as defined at the beginning of this chapter, they have increased the interest in bilingual instruction and have led to requests for more bilingual experiments.

B. THE SUPPLEMENTARY MODEL

In a number of school systems throughout the country, limited attempts at using two languages as instructional media are in effect. These programs are supplementary in nature: some are organized in communities with scant resources for bilingual education (e.g., Pecos, New Mexico); others are aimed at small numbers of non-English-speaking children in a primarily "mainstream" community (e.g., Englewood, New Jersey).

A well-established supplementary program is found in Pecos, a community in northern New Mexico with limited resources for a bilingual program. All the children in the Pecos school, including the small number of native speakers of English, receive half an hour of Spanish instruction daily. In spite of limitations in staffing and time devoted to instruction in the native language, the Pecos program has been a pioneer in bilingual education in New Mexico. Since its establishment in 1965 with Ford Foundation funds, the program has served as a demonstration center. Recent and more ambitious programs in New Mexico are based upon the success of Pecos.

As Puerto Ricans continue to move into small communities on the Eastern seaboard, school systems count an increasing number of Spanish-speaking children among their pupils. In Englewood, New Jersey, the introduction of a non-graded multi-educational system offered an opportunity for educational innovation. Teachers work with children in small groups; bilingual tutors work with groups as small as two or three children. Their aim is to achieve a third grade proficiency in Spanish among the Puerto Rican children before moving them into reading in English.

In both the Pecos and the Englewood programs, instruction in the native language is limited to a small portion of the school day. The approach is similar to the "Spanish S" programs, familiar to many high school teachers. The inclusion of these efforts in our bilingual program descriptions is justified by their importance as starting points. Once a shift is made away from the English-only policy of public schools, no matter how minor the change may be, parents, educators, and community leaders become interested in exploring an alternative model of education for children in the non-English-speaking communities.

C. TRANSITION MODEL

Mackey states that the long-range goals of bilingual schools are two-fold: the curriculum can be directed toward the language of the wider culture, thus promoting *acculturation;* or the curriculum can be directed toward the regional, national, or neo-national culture, thus promoting *irredentism.*

In most programs in this country there is no clear direction in language policy. The following recommendations of the Texas Educational Agency, while ascribing an important role to the Spanish language as a transitional medium leading toward acculturation, illustrate the general lack of a defined, long-range language policy:

> Non-English-speaking children needing special instruction to adjust successfully in school and to use the English language may be placed in a modified program which makes full use of the pupils' ability in the language they understand and speak when · enrolled in public schools. . . .

The modified program should have the following characteristics: The first language of the child is used as a means of instruction in developing the basic skills of reading, spelling, writing, and arithmetic.

English is introduced as a second language; as the child becomes more proficient in understanding and speaking the second language, the use of the first language as a means of instruction should be decreased, while the use of English for this purpose is increased.

The use of both languages as a medium of instruction is continued for a minimum of three years and thereafter until such a time as the child is able to comprehend and communicate effectively in English.

To assure the development of a literate bilingual, the child is given the opportunity for continued study of the four basic skills of his first language (understanding, speaking, reading, and writing).[6]

Note that the last recommendation adds, almost as an afterthought, the phrase, "to assure the development of a literate bilingual." The student is offered the option of continuing his studies *of* (though not *in*) Spanish.

For many bilingual programs, the use of the native language serves mainly as a bridge to the national language. Mackey describes such a curriculum as the Transfer (T) type: He notes that "The transfer pattern has been used to convert from one medium to another. . . . In schools of this type, the transfer may be gradual or abrupt, regular or irregular, the degree of regularity and gradualness being available as to distinguish one school from another."[7]

The Follow-Through Project at Corpus Christi, Texas, is an example of a transfer program. Concepts are taught first in Spanish, then in English; at all levels the intensive language approach is aimed at developing proficiency both in English and in Spanish. The bilingual program ends after the third grade.

[6] Principles and Standards for Accrediting Elementary and Secondary Schools" (Austin: Texas Educational Agency, Spring 1967).

[7] "A Typology of Bilingual Education," p. 8.

Bilingual educators, ideally, would like to develop in their students the skills of coordinate bilinguals; educators at Corpus Christi share these objectives. But frequently the funding available for pioneer programs (particularly before the passage of Title vii legislation) has imposed limitations on comprehensive planning. Follow-Through funds, for example, span only the K-grade 3 years of elementary instruction. Parent enthusiasm and community support have aided in expansion or reformulation of these early programs, but this process is just starting.

It is difficult to predict at this early stage of programmatic development of bilingual education in the United States how much interest students will display in the acquisition of literacy in Spanish. Educational programs affect as well as reflect language policy. During the three years that we have been engaged in the study of bilingual education, we have witnessed great variations, reversals of position, and significant new developments in the way in which the meaning of education in two languages has been interpreted by members of interested groups.

Some educators who doubted the wisdom of teaching children in their native languages modified their attitude after the publication of the Coleman report. The Coleman finding that a positive self-concept is a crucial attribute of the successful student has contributed to a re-evaluation of the role of the minority child's language and culture.[8] Bilingual education is now envisaged by an increasing number of administrators as one aspect of programmatic endeavors to increase the self-respect of children who are not part of the "mainstream."

The feelings and hopes of members of non-English-speaking communities toward the future of their language is difficult to assess. Some recent events may be of significance in this regard. Spanish-speaking students in high schools and universities are asking for Chicano studies, Puerto Rican studies, and a larger role for Spanish in these settings. In Spanish-speaking communities, the more militant members rely upon their native language increasingly in their publications, meetings, and press conferences. At the same time, others in these communities continue to emphasize assimila-

[8] James S. Coleman, *Equality of Educational Opportunity* (Washington, D.C.: U. S. Office of Education, 1966), No. OE-38001.

tionist trends. Additional socio-linguistic studies, such as Fishman's *Bilingualism in the Barrio,* are needed to develop a fuller picture of the language aspirations existing in the diverse communities of America's minorities.

D. THE TWO-WAY MODEL

Mackey, in his typology of bilingual schools, identified two major variants that we would categorize as two-way schools: the *Dual Medium Differential Maintenance* (*DDM*) and the *Dual Medium Equal Maintenance* (*DEM*). Mackey describes the *DDM* model as follows: "In maintaining two languages for different purposes, the difference may be established by subject matter, according to the likely contribution of each culture. Often the culture based subjects like art, history, literature and geography are in the dominant home language."[9]

In our concern with early childhood bilingual education, this model is not quite as relevant as some of the others already described. However, the debates concerning this model are of interest. When the Rough Rock Demonstration School was first established on the Navajo reservation, it conformed to this description of the *DDM* model. Culture-based subjects (e.g., social science, tribal organization) were taught in Navajo, while more traditional academic subject matter was taught in English. Visitors from other Indian tribes, among them Robert Thomas, the Cherokee anthropologist, criticized the restricted role given to the Navajo language in the curriculum. Subsequently, Rough Rock's Board of Education, made up of Navajo elders, outlined a new policy with regard to the language, and many traditional academic subjects are now taught in Navajo.

Some sociologists, including Fishman, have argued in favor of the *DDM* model as the most accurate expression of the actual uses of the native and national languages in bilingual communities. On the other hand, others interested in the development of balanced bilinguals have argued in favor of a dual system characterized by equal treatment of the two languages. Mackey describes this system, the *Dual Medium*

[9] "A Typology of Bilingual Education," p. 14.

Equal Maintenance (*DEM*), in the following way: "In some schools . . . it has been necessary . . . not to distinguish between languages and to give equal chance to both languages in all domains. This is done by alternating on the time scale—day, week, month, or year from one language to the others."[10]

In the United States, the best-known example of a two-way bilingual school is the Coral Way Elementary School in Miami, Florida. Two important, long-range conditions of bilingual education are exemplified in this program: (a) equal time and treatment are given to two languages (Spanish and English), and (b) monolingual English-speaking children are integrated with Cuban immigrants into this bilingual system. The Miami experiment has been highly successful locally and nationally and is a much-admired exemplar of what bilingual education can become.

A few other school systems have tried to adopt the equal time and treatment approach. The comprehensive program developed in Las Cruces, New Mexico, with the aid of New Mexico State University, is one such attempt: "In the early stages of the program the day was divided in half, instruction in Spanish in the morning, and English in the afternoon. However, as the program developed, the teachers developed their own class schedules. While about half of the day continued to be spent in each language, individual instruction varied; in some classes both languages may be mixed in one lesson, or a lesson in English may directly follow a lesson in Spanish."[11]

E. CONCLUSIONS

Although theoretical concerns enter into the choice of a model for bilingual education, most bilingual schools develop their curriculum as a function of practical considerations. Basic research, the preparation of materials, and the training of teachers lag severely behind the needs of existing and projected bilingual programs. Consequently, administrators and

[10] "A Typology of Bilingual Education," p. 14.
[11] See "Sustained Primary Program for Bilingual Students," Las Cruces, N.M., pp. 39–42.

parent advisory committees are often forced to choose programmatic models that fall short of the long-range goal of developing balanced bilinguals.

We have speculated earlier in this book that, once the prohibition against instruction in a language other than English is overcome, a series of new possibilities may be considered by individuals who have previously played a passive role in the education of their children. When bilingual programs are first started, they usually serve as demonstration programs only. The reactions of parents, of teachers in other schools, and of administrators often add the impetus necessary to implement comprehensive programs that include more than the beginning grades of school.

The participation of parents is a critical aspect of bilingual education. Although many bilingual educators support this view, they fail to implement it. When programs are planned in isolation from the community, parents' contributions become merely incidental. Parental participation and community control do not guarantee relief from the shortage of qualified teachers, the lack of curriculum materials, limited funds, or from any other of the problems specific to bilingual education. Such participation and control do, however, provide support for and continuity to the school's efforts.

Educational innovations will remain of passing interest and little significance without the recognition that education is a social process. If the school remains alien to the values and needs of the community, if it is bureaucratically run, then the children will not receive the education they are entitled to, no matter what language they are taught in.

David Perez

THE CHAINS THAT HAVE BEEN TAKEN OFF SLAVES' BODIES ARE PUT BACK ON THEIR MINDS*

Cultural genocide is the destruction of a people's awareness of themselves—as a nation, as a people. It also means the destruction of those physical things that represent a people's culture, such as their food, their language, their music, their poetry, their history. It's very necessary for an oppressor to destroy a people's ability to communicate among themselves. In this country, for instance, one of the first things that was done with African slaves was to separate people from the same tribe so that they couldn't get together and build a resistance movement to the slave traders. Language is one of the ways that people are able to communicate and to build a way of fighting back against the enemy—to maintain those ties of identity and therefore strengthen themselves to fight. Destroying the language, as the Americans did with the African slaves and with our people in Puerto Rico, is the initial step to breaking down the people's connection with one another.

To support its economic exploitation of Puerto Rico, the United States instituted a new educational system whose purpose was to Americanize us. Specifically, that means that the school's principal job is to exalt the cultural values of the United States. As soon as we begin using books that are printed in English, that are printed in the United States, that means that the American way of life is being pushed—the American way of life with all its bad points, with its commercialism, its dehumanization of human beings.

* David Perez, "The Chains that have been taken off Slaves' Bodies are put back on Their Minds," *Palante* (McGraw-Hill, 1971), pp. 65–68. Reprinted with permission.

At the same time that the cultural values of America are exalted, the cultural values of Puerto Rico are downgraded. People begin to feel ashamed of speaking Spanish. Language becomes a reward and punishment system. If you speak English and adapt to the cultural values of America, you're rewarded; if you speak Spanish and stick to the old traditional ways, you're punished. In the school system here, if you don't quickly begin to speak English and shed your Puerto Rican values, you're put back a grade—so you may be in the sixth grade in Puerto Rico but when you come here, you go back to the fourth or fifth. You're treated as if you're retarded, as if you're backward—and your own cultural values therefore are shown to be of less value than the cultural values of this country and the language of this country.

What all this does is to create severe problems for our people. First, it creates a colonized mentality—that means that the people have a strong feeling of inferiority, they have a strong feeling of not being as worthy as the Americans because the structure tells them that to become American is always a goal they have to attain. Now it's not easy to shed years of one culture for another—so we have people struggling with themselves to throw off the old way, instead of questioning whether it's correct to throw off the old way or not. Because it's a matter of their survival in this country. The people get a sense of frustration with themselves, because they can't change themselves as fast as is necessary.

In the Young Lords Party, we talk a lot about the colonized mentality when we're frightened of taking on responsibilities. We've been conditioned to feel that we can't lead other people. The school system doesn't develop an individual's initiative and creativity. It develops your ability to follow, it develops a worker-employer mentality, which is suited to this country—the teacher is the employer and the students are the workers.

Puerto Ricans here and in Puerto Rico are taught three things: Puerto Rico is small and the United States is big; Puerto Rico is poor and the United States is rich; Puerto Rico is weak and the United States is strong. Sort of a national inferiority complex. These things are constantly put in our heads and in this way people are conditioned to believe that independence is impossible because our country could never survive without the help of big brother United States.

In this country education is used as an extension of the American economic system. We understand as we go through school that we are being prepared for one of the various positions there are for people in America. Now, the ruling class of this country doesn't go to public school—so we can eliminate that consideration. Then there are the lackeys of the ruling class who run the businesses for them, the managers and corporation heads. The next class is a more functional class of people who are doing the actual work of running the corporations of America: they may be typists, file clerks and secretaries, or assistant managers who are just the lackeys of the managers. And last of all, on the level below that, we have people who are what used to be called blue-collar workers—who work with their hands and they don't wear a suit and tie if they're a brother, or they don't wear a dress if they're a sister, and they wash dishes, and they push pushcarts with clothing, and they do more or less the slop jobs, the un-skilled jobs in society. In the schools, right from the begin-ning, Third World people are programmed for the lowest-level jobs. Because right from the beginning, IQ tests are given to determine where a kid is going. And the IQ tests are based on a white Anglo-Saxon norm that's established in this country, which doesn't apply to the cultural background of Third World people—so you're not gonna do good on the IQ test. Those tests have to some extent been discarded, but they've also been disguished in other ways. Now you get a reading test. Kids read shit about houses with trees and fam-ilies with two cars and dogs and everybody going to the swim-ming pool—and that's bullshit, man. It doesn't relate to them and therefore they don't get into it, and they don't do well on the tests. So if you don't do well on those tests, right from the beginning it shows on your record that you're a slow student.

As you move up in the school system, the guidance coun-selor looks at your record and says, "Well, you did so poorly in reading last year—why don't you go into a general program in high school. You won't have to do too much reading there." When you go into high school, you can either go into an academic program, a commercial program, or a general pro-gram—this is called the tracking system. Actually you have very little choice because you're simply put into a specific program, and unless you bring a lot of parental and outside pressure on the school system, you stay in that one, whether you like it or not. And our people end up in the last level, the general program—people who are being prepared to do shitwork for America. That means they're not being prepared to do anything, basically. The highest level of preparation in the general program is to be a cashier; or if you're a brother, they train you in mechanics, but you find out very soon that everything you've been trained on is outdated already, so you can't get a job. Also, if you're a brother, to get out of school with a general diploma means that you're going to Viet Nam. Students with academic diplomas get college deferments.

When we talk about cultural genocide, we have to see what it does to an individual that goes through this school system. When you raise your hand in class and the teacher, instead of listening to what you have to say, begins to correct your accent and insists that you're gonna talk perfect English, whatever thoughts are coming out are just gonna be ignored until this superficial thing is corrected according to what the system has set as a standard. We're faced with an education that isn't relevant to us. We're faced with reading books that have nothing to do with what we know to be our people's experience and what we know to be our personal experience. We're faced with out-and-out racism, not only the racism of textbooks, which ignore the contributions of the Third World to the development of civilization—but also the out-and-out racism of the teachers who instruct us, who have already been told that they have a class of slow learners and so therefore they feel that they don't have to work too hard, because we can't learn too much anyway. We have the racism that this society generates in white people that tells them that people of color are inferior, and therefore you can treat them like inferiors. We still have the vestiges of slavery, the slave trade, left over. The chains that have been taken off the slaves' bodies are put back on their minds.

Besides boredom, besides racism, we have the fact that the educational system is a mediocre system. It doesn't educate people, it doesn't provide a forum for opposing points of view, it doesn't develop the creativity of the individual. It tends to smother people, it tends to value conformity instead of orig- inality. It tells you, "Don't be different—be like everyone else," it tells you to sit still, raise your hand if you want to go to the bathroom, you have no rights as an individual once you're in the system. Instead of developing the potential of human beings, we're putting young people into a jail—locking up their heads, locking everyone into a dead-end street.

We don't want our children to go through this school system—this is the school system that creates My Lai massacres, the school system that dehumanizes us to the point where we can watch someone killed in the street and not feel pain and not feel the need to intervene, that teaches us it's dog-eat-dog in America—that's how the pioneers lived so that's how we should live. We see a need to create our own school system, a school system based on developing each person to the fullest potential that they have, and bringing out the beauty that we know is inside our people, that's being buried in the American school system.

We have to understand that cultural genocide is being used to destroy the strength of people so that they can be used to perform certain low-level tasks in industrial society. At the point when that society no longer needs these people to do those tasks, the logical progression from cultural genocide will be physical genocide—the systematic elimination of Third World people who are no longer needed by a highly technological society. Many of our people see that our culture has been destroyed by this country, and they react in an extreme way, and become cultural nationalists—whose sole purpose in life is to revive the culture of the Puerto Rican nation and to keep it alive, to speak only Spanish, to relate only to our music, to dress the way we dressed when we lived on the island. Now, our feeling is that nationalism is important—that we have to be proud of our nation, our history and our culture—but that pride alone is not gonna free us, the ability to play congas is not gonna free us, the ability to speak Spanish fluently is not gonna stop landlords, the ability to run down Puerto Rican history like it was right from the beginning is not gonna stop the exploitation of our people on their jobs and everyplace else. We know that just going back to our culture is not gonna make it in and of itself. We have to use our culture as a revolutionary weapon to make ourselves stronger, to understand who we are, to understand where we came from, and therefore to be able to analyze correctly what we have to do in order to survive in this country.

G. Ramsey Liem

NON-ENGLISH SPEAKING STUDENTS*

The New York City public schools have been especially slow in recognizing the need for system-wide bilingual education for it's large number of non-English speaking students. The federal government, too, has not supported bilingual education until as recently as 1968 when federal laws prohibiting education in foreign languages was repealed. Title VII of the Elementary and Secondary Education Act appropriating money for bilingual education was not created until 1967.

In 1968, approximately 175 full and part-time teachers of English as a second language were employed by the New York City Board of Education. These instructors are specially licensed English teachers who are certified to teach English to non-English speaking students. Generally, these instructors do not have a foreign background and are not necessarily fluent in a second language. Rather, they are specialized English teachers. During the school year 1967–1968, fewer than 25 special classes for non-English speaking students were operated in the total public school system.

Currently, the available services for children who do not speak English are not considerably improved. The total number of teachers of English as a second language has only been increased to approximately 200. Two new categories of instructors have been created to meet the needs of Spanish-speaking youngsters. One is bilingual Spanish-speaking teachers who function in school-community relations and the other is bilingual common branch teachers. The Office of Personnel, Division of Recruitment and Training of Spanish-Speaking Teachers estimates the current number of these instructors to be less than 200 and 100 respectively. The only other potential source of manpower for bilingual programs in the public

* G. Ramsay Liem, . . . and others: A Report Card for the New York City Public Schools. New York: Aspira, 1971, pp. 65–72.

schools is the small number of regularly licensed Hispanic teachers, fewer than 500 as of March, 1969. Together, these teachers number fewer than 1,000, the majority of whom have no special training in bilingual education. The Board of Education has assessed the number of Hispanic students who do not speak English to be over 100,000. When to this number are added those non-English speaking pupils of other backgrounds, the result is a large group of students with special needs for whom little is being done.

Only two schools in New York City are operating major bilingual programs. During 1969–1970 they were the only programs funded through Title VII, ESEA. The largest of the two is P.S. 25 in the Bronx. Among the school's objectives are:

1. to develop proficiency in Spanish and English,
2. to improve academic achievement,
3. to improve the pupil's self-image.

This school conducts classes in all areas of the curriculum in both languages for the entire elementary school enrollment (approximately 900). The program includes an in-service training component that provides teachers with techniques relevant to bilingual education. A bilingual school library is being organized and special curriculum materials developed.

The second school with bilingual education is P.S. 1 in Manhattan. Pupils in pre-kindergarten through second grade are included in the program. Unlike P.S. 25, this school has large numbers of both Puerto Rican and Chinese students, and each group receives bilingual instruction. In addition, English speaking students participate in the non-English instruction of the other children. Greater emphasis is placed in this school than in P.S. 25 on intensive instruction in oral English and reading readiness, and bilingual instruction at grades one and two is limited to mathematics. Teacher-training and self-evaluation are both central aspects of the program. During 1969–1970, approximately 180 students participated.

In contrast to these programs is a project conducted by the Central Board of Education, *Improving the Teaching of English as a Second Language, K-12.* With a 1969–1970 budget over twice the size of the combined support for P.S. 25 and P.S. 1, this program represents the Board of Education's major educational effort for non-English speaking students. Its goals are to:

1. improve pupils' ability to understand, speak, read, and write English,

2. improve pupils' self-image,

3. improve social interactions.

The program consists of a core of expert teachers of English as a second language (42) who provide supervision and guidance for teachers and principals in schools with non-English speaking students. Through this consultative service, the program claims to have served all 900 schools and 120,061 students.

What is disturbing about this program as compared with the two bilingual schools, are the apparent assumptions that service to non-English speaking students means teaching them English, and that improving a pupil's self-image means enabling him to be "on a par with native speakers of the English language." These assumptions reflect the general attitude of the public schools that there is one educational method suitable for all students and that special education means "raising the child's skill and abilities" so that he can compete successfully in the present system. The emphasis placed solely on improving skills in English also implies that the schools have no room for the language and culture of students of different backgrounds. The Teaching of English as a Second Language program does conduct a limited number of bilingual science classes in a "selected group of poverty-area junior high schools" which, however, are referred to as "subsidiary projects." The bilingual programs at P.S. 1 and 25, on the other hand, are concerned with a child's competency in both his native language and in English. They also view positive self-image as equally dependent on developing the students' awareness of his native language and background as on teaching him English. Their programs, thus, redesign the entire learning environment instead of only providing remedial service. They address the school as the object of change, not the student.

A handful of additional programs (approximately 25) are also being conducted in both elementary and junior high schools. For the most part, these projects are either limited to one or two classes in a school or involve consultative services to teachers by a bilingual teacher or a teacher of English as a second language. In those instances where bilingual teachers are employed, programs tend to respect the importance of both languages and an attempt is made to develop appreciation of cultural background as well as language proficiency. Programs for the teaching of English as a second language, however, focus primarily on improving English language skills. Support for these services comes largely from Title I and VII, ESEA, and the State Urban Education Act.

In order to increase its effort in the area of bilinqual education, the Board of Education is currently proposing a Bureau of Bilingual Educational Services to serve the centralized high schools and special schools to provide resources and support to community school districts, and generally to coordinate and evaluate bilingual programs. The proposed bureau would include the following services: Teaching of English as a Second Language, Bilingual Instruction, Recruitment and Training, and the Bilingual Program in School and Community Relations. It would also create a Research and Evaluation component.

The primary existing mechanism for increasing the number of bilingual Spanish-speaking teachers is a special Title I financed program within the Board of Education, Office of Personnel. It seeks to recruit and train graduate and undergraduate candidates to meet the licensing requirements of the Board of Examiners, and to provide in-service training for bilingual Spanish-speaking teachers to enable them to serve in supervisory and administrative capacities. Goals set for the 1969–1970 school year were to recruit and train 100 graduate and 100 undergraduate candidates for the teaching license, and 10 graduate candidates for the license of guidance counselor. This office was originated in 1967 through the efforts of the New York City Council Against Poverty and the Puerto Rican Committee on Educational Policies.

While the current program response for non-English speaking students is minimal, both an administrative mechanism and a variety of excellent program models exist. Whether or not these assets are used to benefit children depends on the degree to which the Board of Education can be persuaded to support large scale, bilingual education. Stronger advocates for these programs are needed.

Hernan LaFontaine

BILINGUAL EDUCATION*

INTRODUCTION

It is quite clear that modern technological advances have virtually transformed our world into what Marshall McLuhan describes as a "global village." With intercontinental communications accelerated beyond jet speeds, events occuring this morning on opposite sides of the planet become this afternoon's news broadcast. Unfortunately, in spite of the almost instantaneous delivery of information there has not been an equivalent development of probably the most basic medium employed in communication: language. It is a shame indeed that this is particularly true of the United States. We must now abandon the parochial monolingual attitude that dominated the early history of our country. The evolution of international relations has placed us in a position of leadership which makes it mandatory that we develop a corps of well trained linguists capable of working harmoniously with people of other lands by demonstrating a knowledge and respect of their culture and their language.

Domestically, we must strive to reduce the conflict which plague us throughout the nation by making any and every effort which could conceivably· enhance inter-cultural and interracial relations, including the learning of other groups' languages. There is a wealth of resources to undertake these tasks but it is tragically being wasted.

Particularly in New York City, have we ignored the richness of language talent offered by the diverse ethnic groups living here. Even a cursory glance at any tourist map immediately reveals the wide diversity of ethnic and racial groups which have concentrated in particular sections of the city.

* Hernan LaFontaine, *Bilingual Education* (1969). Reprinted with permission.

Chinatown, Germantown, Spanish Harlem, Harlem, Little Italy are just some of the more famous areas. Other sections can be easily identified as one walks through neighborhoods which are in reality microcosms of the "old country" of the local residents. On any given day a trip on any public transportation will likely afford several opportunities to hear one or more foreign languages spoken. (It is interesting to note the apparent lack of reaction on the part of other riders in the vehicle. I use the word "apparent" because in many cases although the novelty and curiosity of hearing a foreign language has long disappeared, the individual listener may still be inwardly annoyed at not being able to understand what is being said.)

One of the languages most commonly heard throughout the city is Spanish. The large numbers of Spanish-speaking people living in the city include Cubans, Spaniards, Dominicans, Mexicans and many other national groups, but the greatest majority are Puerto Rican. Puerto Ricans have been coming to New York for decades with especially large migrations in the years after World War II. In fact the numbers increased so rapidly and to such a large extent that we now account for almost one quarter of the entire student population in the schools of New York City. In actual figures this amounts to almost 250,000 Puerto Rican students, a number approximately equal to the total population of Albany, Schenectady and Oswego together. Certainly, when we talk about tapping the extensive resources of our city we cannot possibly overlook this student population with its rich cultural background and linguistic potential waiting to be developed. And just what have we done with this potential?

THE IMMEDIATE PROBLEM

Let us look briefly at the status and progress of the Puerto Rican population in New York City. According to the U.S. Bureau of the Census only 13 percent of the Puerto Ricans 25 years and older in 1960 had completed either high school or more advanced education.[1] In other words, 87 percent had dropped out without graduation from high school.

[1] *United States Book of Facts.* United States Bureau of the Census, 1967.

Among New Yorks non-white (predominantly Negro) population, nearly a third had at least completed high school. There is also evidence that Puerto Rican youth, more than any other group, is severely handicapped in achieving an education in the New York City public schools. In 1961, a study of a Manhattan neighborhood showed that fewer than 10 percent of Puerto Ricans in the third grade were reading at their grade level or above. In comparison, 19 percent of the Negroes in the same schools and 55 percent of the others, mostly whites, were reading at grade level. By the eighth grade the degree of reading retardation was even more severe. Almost two thirds of the Puerto Rican youngsters were retarded more than three years.[2]

Although figures are almost impossible to secure in the area of school completion and dropouts, a special study conducted by the Board of Education of the June 1963 graduating class indicates the almost complete failure of the public school system of New York to successfully prepare Puerto Rican youth to pursue post-secondary education. Of the nearly 21,000 academic diplomas granted, only 331 were received by Puerto Ricans; 1.6 percent of the total academic diplomas. Of the 1,626 Puerto Ricans who succeeded in graduating from high school, only 20 percent qualified for academic diplomas, while for the "other" category, 59 percent of the graduates were awarded academic diplomas.[3] There is no data available indicating just how many of those receiving academic diplomas actually were admitted to college.

In the critical area of English language proficiency, Board of Education data indicate that in 1964 there were almost 89,000 or 8.4 percent of the total student population in the C through F categories on the Scale for Rating Pupils Ability to Speak English.[4] The vast majority of these students are Puerto Ricans. The scale rates students in categories from those who speak English as well as a native to those who speak no English. Evidently, thousands of students are being

[2] *Special Study of Reading Grades in Selected Manhattan Neighborhoods.* Columbia University School of Social Work, Research Center, 1961.

[3] *Unreleased Report on Analysis of High School Graduating Class of June 1963.* Board of Education, New York City.

[4] *New York City Public Schools—Facts and Figures, 1965–1966.* Board of Education, New York City.

considerably handicapped in their academic progress by their inability to communicate in English. Needless to say, this is one of the most significant factors to be considered in attempting to improve the educational status of Puerto Rican children.

APPROACHES TO THE PROBLEM

Many attempts have been made to develop methods, materials and programs to meet the needs of the non-English speaking students. Probably the most extensive attempt was a study conducted during a period from 1953 to 1957 by Dr. J. Cayce Morrison, which became known as the Puerto Rican Study.[5] The study focused on the consideration of three main problems: 1. What are the most effective ways and materials for teaching English as a second language to newly arrived Puerto Rican pupils? 2. What are the most effective techniques with which the school can promote a more rapid and more effective adjustment of Puerto Rican parents and children to the community and of the community to them? 3. Who are the Puerto Rican pupils in New York City's public schools? There is no doubt that Dr. Morrison's study was responsible for developing a wealth of excellent materials which were specifically designed to meet the educational needs of Puerto Rican children. Unfortunately, it appears that not enough effort was expended in following up the actual implementation of these materials in the schools. I personally recall being the only teacher in my junior high school using some of these materials and even then it was merely on an optional basis. Teachers today often ask, "What ever happened to the Puerto Rican Study?"

Another approach was already being attempted by the Board of Education by establishing the position of Substitute Auxiliary Teacher in 1949. The auxiliary teacher's primary duties were vaguely defined as assisting the principal and teachers in working with Puerto Rican pupils and parents. In some cases the auxiliary teacher spent the majority of his time translating or interpreting for the staff. In other cases, he played a more significant role by undertaking a variety of

[5] Morrison, J. Cayce. *The Puerto Rican Study, 1953–1957.* Board of Education, New York City, 1958.

activities involving teachers, supervisors, students and parents. The newness of the program was reflected in the lack of clearly delineated operational roles for the personnel. Gradually, as the program expanded, the function of the auxiliary teacher came more and more into focus making it possible in 1967 for a special committee to develop a comprehensive outline of the duties an auxiliary teacher should fulfill.[6] Basically, the committee described three major functional areas for the auxiliary teacher:

1. As a community relations agent
2. As part of the guidance process and
3. As a resource person.

A more recent change indicating a trend toward giving the auxiliary teacher more status in the profession was the official change in their title to "Bilingual Teacher in School-Community Relations." Apparently, the term "auxiliary" seemed to connote a level less than that of full professional status.

In general, the bilingual teacher program has made an appreciable contribution to the effort in alleviating the many problems of adjustment for the newly arrived Spanish-speaking children and their families. Whether it has had any influence on the actual achievement of these children is not clear. The one area which the bilingual teachers did not undertake was actual classroom teaching. It does seem a shame indeed, that with a manpower source of over 150 bilingual teachers, not one of them was directly involved in the classroom instruction of Puerto Rican children.

Curiously enough, another program which was introduced in the elementary schools and which focused directly on teaching English to Puerto Rican pupils, had virtually no bilingual personnel. Although the knowledge of Spanish may not be essential to successful teaching of English to Spanish speaking children, most educators would agree that it would at least be a useful tool in communicating abstract concepts. On the junior high school level a different position was established with the title of Puerto Rican Coordinator. Again the primary function of these individuals was to teach English. Out of these early attempts grew a more comprehensive and structured program which today is headed by an Assistant

[6] *"Suggested Duties of Auxiliary Teacher."* Report of Select Committee on Functions of Auxiliary Teachers. Board of Education, New York, 1967.

Director of English as a Second Language. This E.S.L. program as newly structured is still in the pilot stage in many respects. New materials and modified class organizations are being tried out. All of these practices will have to be evaluated periodically and it is too early to make any fair determination of their value and impact. Suffice it to say that a broad approach to the problems of non-English speakers is being designed and implemented and we shall eagerly await the appraisal of the results of this comprehensive program.

THE SOCIAL CLIMATE

Although I recognize the contribution of the many efforts made to date towards improving the education of Puerto Rican students, there remains an impression that professional educators have been wrestling with this task for many years with little visible effect. To the Puerto Rican community however, this failure is more than just an impression. The reality of seeing their children become disinterested in school, fail in their courses and finally drop out, is too vivid to be pacified by saying to them "We're doing the best we can." Their reaction is that our best is still not good enough. It is difficult to argue with a parent whose child has experienced twelve years of public education only to receive a general diploma and not have the necessary skills to compete in today's complex, technological world of work. The long range result is that parents have lost confidence in our educational system and have begun to view the schools and everyone associated with them as "the enemy." The traditional concept of teachers being "in loco parentis" has gradually dwindled to teachers being just plain "loco."

Events during the past three years are witness to the fact that our system is in a state of turmoil. Beginning with the tragic situation of Intermediate School 201 to the recent occurrences in the high schools there has been a constant attack, verbally and psysically against representatives of the schools at all levels. Parents and community persons in general have exhausted their patience in waiting for things to happen. They are now initiating their own actions, bypassing normal but inadequate channels of appeal, demanding full participation in the decision-making processes which so intimately affect their children's lives. And these same feelings and attitudes are mirrored in the behavior of the children in school. Vandalism in many schools is a common place occurrence. Physical attacks on teachers take place even more often than is publicized. A general disregard for school regulations and a total lack of interest in school work are evident in many schools throughout the city. All of these are manifestations of the tense and vitriolic conditions which have been simmering in our city for so long a time. They reflect too, the general demoralization of our entire country over issues such as Vietnam, racial prejudice and poverty.

With an environment of such deep social unrest it is sometimes difficult to pay attention to the demands of the community, while simultaneously trying to put out fires. And yet we cannot run the risk of adding more fuel to the fires by ignoring these demands.

Among the many demands being presented by the Puerto Rican community to the educational establishment there is a recurrent theme that Puerto Rican youngsters be aided in retaining and developing their knowledge of the Spanish language. In 1966, the Puerto Rican Committee on Educational Policies included as one of their ten broad concerns that there should be an "immediate implementation of a program to teach Spanish to our youngsters in the elementary schools."[7] A year later, at the Puerto Rican Community Conference sponsored by Mayor Lindsay, the more than 200 people attending the panel on education developed a series of 32 recommendations clarifying their concerns regarding the educational needs of Puerto Rican children. Among those recommendations were requests that "1. the Board of Education continue to expand the present pilot projects so that more subject areas be taught in Spanish; 2. the teaching of Spanish to Puerto Rican students in the elementary level be provided in order to develop and maintain bilingualism."[8]

The community's call for improved quality education and the specific demands for bilingual education certainly seemed to stimulate the thinking of many educators. In November,

[7] *Memorandum to Members of the Board of Education.* Puerto Rican Committee on Educational Policies, May 17, 1966.

[8] *Puerto Ricans Confront Problems of the Complex Urban Society: A design for Change.* Proceedings of Puerto Rican Community Conference. New York: April, 1967.

1967, the Board of Education adopted a comprehensive statement of policy to guide the staff in building a program of quality education for pupils of Puerto Rican background. This statement included a call for the use of Spanish as much as possible in their school careers. Fortunately, the statement came at a time when one of the significant curriculum trends in education was the exploration of new methods. The professional community appeared to be more amenable to experimenting with ideas that would rapidly have been labeled foolish and radical not many years before. Bilingual instruction as a new method therefore, did not seem to shock many teachers and administrators. However, there were many questions posed as to how this new approach could be implemented and what were the possibilities for any degree of success.

A NEW APPROACH: BILINGUAL EDUCATION

Certainly, bilingual education is not really new when we go beyond our own New York City school system. A significant experimental approach toward the development of a philosophy of bilingual instruction was initiated in Dade County, Florida in January 1962.[9] Responding to the sudden and large increase of Cuban students in the county schools, the office of education established the Coral Way School, a bilingual project. English was the medium of instruction for all pupils for approximately half of each day and Spanish the medium of instruction for all pupils during the other half. The experiment appears to be having considerable success. At the fifth grade level the children have been found to be able to learn equally well through either of the two languages. Also, since half of the children are Cubans and half begin as monolingual speakers of English, it has become apparent that a truly comprehensive bilingual education program can serve not only the non-English mother tongue children who must necessarily become bilingual, but also the monolingual American child who speaks nothing but English and whose parents want him to become bilingual. The project has led

[9] Rojas, Pauline. "The Miami Experience in Bilingual Education" in Kriedler, J.C. (Ed.) *On Teaching English to Speakers of Other Languages.* San Diego: National Council of Teachers of English, TESOL Conference Paper, 1966.

to the development of the Miami Linguistics Program which is being used in other areas. One of these areas is in Santa Fe, New Mexico. I recently had the fortunate experience of attending the National Conference on Educational Opportunities for Mexican Americans in Austin, Texas and of meeting with Dr. Henry Pascual, Director of Bilingual Education, Santa Fe, New Mexico. He described their program at the West Las Vegas Schools as a modified Miami Linguistics approach and was very pleased with the results they were obtaining. In a report describing the program, the students were evaluated in their overall progress in acquiring nineteen different reading skills.[10] They were rated "excellent" in 11 items, "good" in 7 items and "satisfactory" in 1 item. Together with other results in oral expression, written expression and actual test scores, the administrators have seen sufficient progress to warrant the expansion of the project to many more schools.

In San Antonio, the bilingual program is based on materials developed under the direction of Dr. Elizabeth Ott of the Southwest Educational Development Laboratory.[11] The approach is very much similar to the audio-lingual method used in the teaching of foreign languages. The teacher presents certain patterns of speech as models for the class to hear and the class then repeats the patterns both as a group and individually. A demonstration of this program which was given at the conference, presented a class of first graders learning mathematical concepts related to shapes and dimensions. The children were enthusiastic and eager to participate in the lesson and all those who responded did very well. What impressed me most however, was to see these very young children change from one language to another with relatively little difficulty. Although their English was spoken with a slight accent in some cases, I felt that these children, if continued in this program, will quite definitely be truly bilingual long before they finish their school careers.

The number of programs in bilingual education currently being undertaken is much too great to attempt a comprehensive survey in this paper. However, just to give an idea of the

[10] Leger, Mela and Griego, Gavinia. *Report of Miami Linguistics Program.* West Las Vegas School, Las Vegas, New Mexico, April, 1968.

[11] For Information Contact: Dr. Elizabeth Ott, Program Director Language-Bilingual Education, Southwest Educational Development Laboratory, Austin, Texas.

scope of this effort I would like to include a partial list of areas involved in bilingual instruction.

Arizona: Douglas, Phoenix, Sahuarita

California: Brawley, Calexico, El Centro, Fresno, Imperial, Los Angeles, Merced, San Diego

Colorado: Denver, Pueblo

New Mexico: Albuquerque, Pecos

Texas: Brownsville, Edinburg, El Paso, Laredo, Pharr, San Antonio

Additional programs are being or have been established in Florida, New York, and Maine.

RELATED RESEARCH

Underlying all of these programs is an extensive body of research on bilingualism, which has been added to by workers in many disciplines. For example, the literature in psychology indicates that researchers have traced the development of native language from the incomprehensible odd sounds of an infant to the full mastery of self-expression.[12] However, the most relevant information lies in the studies done in psycholinguistics.

Haugen[13] pointed out in 1956 that little had been done to study the effects of bilingualism beyond studying the individual's intelligence test performance. He feels that the "locus of the bilingualism is in the individual mind" and therefore the psychological study of the bilingual is of central importance in the analysis of bilingualism. He argues that the motivation for the effective learning of a second language must have its roots in the needed social adjustment. Similarly the extinguishing of a background language depends to some extent upon the individual's attitude toward the language. Ervin[14] refers to the psycho-social influences upon the child's

[12] Ervin, S. M. and Miller, W. R. "Language Development." Stevenson, H. W. (Ed.) *Child Psychology*. 62nd Yearbook of the N.S.S.E., Part I, Chicago: University of Chicago Press, 1963.

[13] Haugen, E. *Bilingualism In America: A Bibliography and Research Guide*. Publication #26 of the American Dialect Society, University of Alabama; University of Alabama Press, 1956.

[14] Ervin, S. and Osgood, D. E. "Second Language Learning and Bilingualism" in C. E. Osgood and T. Z. Sebcok (Eds.) *Psycholinguistics: A Survey of Theory and Research Problems*. New York: Holt, Rinehart, Winston, 1961.

receptivity to a new language. He indicates that a child adopts models which relate to his own self-image. In other words, for most of our Puerto Rican students, the retention of their native language while learning a new one, depends on the displacement of their discouraging view of Spanish, with a more positive socially advantaged association. They must overcome the effect of the admonitions of many teachers not to speak Spanish in school because "it isn't nice" or because "in this country we speak English." In fact this psychological conflict may cause bilingual children to be handicapped in their intellectual development according to Jensen.[15] He feels that the burden of two or three languages causes a child of normal intelligence to become mentally uncertain and confused. In addition, he cites evidence of research which finds that the bilingual may become schizophrenic as a result of the frustration and insecurity of not being able to communicate effectively. Jensen's position goes along with that of some educators who feel that bilingualism is a handicap. On the other hand, there is a group who oppose this position on the basis that the research has not shown that bilingualism, per se, is the cause of low performance on intelligence tests. Gaarder[16] claims that the research simply points out the consequences when the child's mother tongue is ignored or deplored or otherwise downgraded. He stresses the fact that other investigation has shown that it is how and to what extent and under what conditions the two languages are taught that make the difference. Supportive of this opinion is Lambert's work in Montreal. He found that if there had been equal, normal literacy developed in both languages, the bilingual subjects were markedly superior to monolinguals on verbal and non-verbal tests of intelligence and had greater flexibility, a superiority in concept formation and a more diversified set of mental abilities. Modiano[17] found similar results while investigating language learning in Mexico. The study involved students in Federal and State schools in which all reading instruction is offered in Spanish, and National

[15] Jensen, V. J. "Effects of Childhood Bilingualism." *Elementary English*. February, 1962.

[16] Gaarder, Bruce. *Statement at Congressional Hearings on Senate Bill #428*. U.S. Congress, 90th Congress, First Session, May 18, 1967.

[17] Modiano, Nancy. "*Reading Comprehension in the National Language: A Comparative Study of Bilingual and All Spanish Instruction in the Schools of Chiapas, Mexico.*" Doctoral Dissertation, New York University, 1966.

Indian Institute schools in which literacy was developed in the native Indian tongue prior to being attempted in Spanish. In each of the three "municipios" she investigated she found significantly better reading ability among children who were first taught to read in their original language. Further, a higher proportion of literate adults had had native-language-first instruction instead of all Spanish.

One of the most recent pieces of research was done in our own New York City schools. Raisner, Bolger and Sanguinetti[18] sought to determine the educational effects of bilingual instruction on junior high school students of Spanish-speaking background. The approach consisted of bilingual science instruction and an accelerated course in the Spanish language. Very briefly summarized some of the results were as follows:

1. student achievement was positively affected in science and in Spanish, but not affected in social studies or mathematics
2. bilingually taught students excelled in learning Spanish
3. in the area of classroom English achievement, the experimentals did as well as the controls, and in the area of English reading ability they did much better than the controls
4. in the area of bilingual dominance the bilingually taught students tended to use Spanish more frequently than the controls.
5. experimental students were superior to the controls in effort and reliability but no better or worse in conduct and self-control
6. there were definite decreases in anxiety among experimental children
7. bilingually taught children tended to retain the parental culture more than the controls.

The report's statement of results actually presents the findings on nineteen different factors. In general, however, the findings seem to support the investigators' recommendation that simi-

[18] Raisner, A., Bolger, P. and Sanguinetti, C. *Science Instruction in Spanish for Pupils of Spanish Speaking Background.* Cooperative Research Project #2370, U.S. Office of Education and Bureau of Educational Research, Board of Education, New York, June 1967.

lar projects be initiated at the elementary and high school levels.

It does seem strange that the New York City schools system has this recent Science-Spanish experiment as its only source of raw data on bilingual instruction. We are generally in the forefront with a myriad of experiments in all aspects of education. Evidently, this is one area where other cities and states have taken the lead in searching out innovations designed to meet the very pressing needs of their student population, even in spite of state education laws. Fortunately, the federal government has finally recognized the need for a concentrated, national attack on the educational problems of the bilingual child. On January 17, 1967, Senate Bill #428 was introduced to Congress by Senators Yarborough, Javits, Kennedy, Kuchal, Montoya, Williams and Tower, members of a special sub-committee on bilingual education, as an amendment to the Elementary and Secondary Education Act of 1965.[19] Its declaration of policy reads:

> "In recognition of the special educational needs of the large numbers of students in the United States whose mother tongue is Spanish and to whom English is a foreign language, Congress hereby declares it to be the policy of the United States to provide financial assistance to local educational agencies to develop and carry out new and imaginative elementary and secondary school programs designed to meet these special educational needs."

Having had the privilege of testifying before the committee, I must admit that I was favorably impressed by the sincerity of the sponsors of the bill in attempting to assure that significant programs be designed and implemented as soon as possible.

THE NEW YORK CITY BILINGUAL SCHOOL

The passage of the Bilingual Education Act in November, 1967 opened the way for the establishment of the first com-

[19] "Bilingual American Eduaction Act." *Senate Bill #428*, January, 1967.

pletely bilingual school in the history of New York City. In the spring, under the direction of the district superintendent of District #7, approval for the initiation of such a program was obtained from the local school board and then from central board headquarters. The actual work of organizing the school was begun in June after the principal of the school was selected and was available to enter the project. The school P.S. 25, was scheduled to open in September, 1968.

Of course, the usual problems of establishing a new school organization had to be resolved (i.e., personnel, supplies, curriculum materials, etc.). However, additional problems arose unique to the project because of its bilingual nature. For example, it is difficult enough to recruit and select a staff of 40 teachers for any school but when we stipulate that each of these persons must also be bilingual, the selection procedure becomes a major challenge. Indeed, it developed into an extensive search for staff with candidates responding from across the country and from abroad. Among those selected were teachers who were either natives of or who had experience in New York City, Puerto Rico, Colombia, Mexico, Spain, Peru, Dominican Republic, Cuba, Venezuela, and even Cambodia.

While teachers were being interviewed and selected other tasks had to be undertaken simultaneously. Efforts made in the selection of appropriate instructional materials immediately revealed a paucity of textbooks and workbooks in Spanish. Consequently, normal channels of procurement had to be by-passed in order to begin to contact those sources which already had some materials available and could deliver in time for September. This aspect of organization eventually led to contact and correspondence with individuals, agencies and companies from a variety of places such as Puerto Rico, Mexico, Southwestern United States, Florida, South America and Spain. However, in spite of the utilization of a wide variety of sources of materials, it was foreseen that a great deal would depend on the teachers' ability to create and develop those materials which were most appropriate and relevant for the children.

Another concern requiring immediate attention was that of providing the staff with some orientation and training regarding bilingual education. Although everyone selected had indicated a high level of interest in this particular educational philosophy, few had explored it in depth. Thus it was necessary to review with the staff the rationale for this program, related programs being undertaken, evidence and conclusions available through research and a possible approach for the implementation of the program in P.S. 25. All of this was carried out within a two week period prior to the opening of the school with financial support secured by the principal from Title I funds. Obviously, a comprehensive training program could not be complete in a two week period so that additional in-service training had to be provided during the school year. This was accomplished primarily through a weekly after-school workshop conducted by one of the assistant principals.

The instructional program itself was based on a model developed by the administrators of the school which provided specific guidelines as to how the elementary school curriculum could be implemented through the use of two languages.[20] Although the model clearly delineates specific time allotments for each subject area and for each language, teachers were encouraged to report their experiences in the classroom to their supervisors and to indicate whatever modifications might be deemed necessary. This feedback would then become the basis for the development of an even more relevant and workable model for the following year.

It would be premature to consider an analytical evaluation of the school program after seven months, however, there are certain subjective signs which indicate that the program is enjoying some degree of success. In general, there is an excellent rapport between teachers and pupils so that disciplinary problems are reduced to a minimum. The majority of the children, including those newly arrived from Spanish speaking countries, are actively participating in their classroom work. (Although this may not seem especially unusual, it seems to be somewhat significant in view of the chaotic conditions of many schools throughout the city.) Parents and other community persons are very supportive of the school and do not hesitate to visit and express their opinions on many school matters to the teachers and to the supervisors. Teachers are intimately involved in the process of educational experimentation and are able to contribute their find-

[20] LaFontaine, H. *"A Model for the Implementation of the Elementary School Curriculum Through Bilingual Education."* New York 1968.

ings to the total school program. Pupil attendance is steadily increasing and the turnover in registers is generally limited to students moving away to distant places.

Other incidents occur frequently which, because of their intangible nature, are impossible to measure with any kind of objective instrument but which sometimes reveal significant glimpses of the possible effects of the program. A mother, bringing her son to be admitted to a New York City public school for the first time, entered the principal's office. While she spoke to the principal the boy stared constantly at the wall until finally he could contain himself no longer. Spontaneously, he cried out "Mami, mira, un retrato de Vieques!" His chest fairly stuck out as he proudly announced that Vieques was his hometown. There was no mistaking the effect on this youngster of that picture on the principal's wall.

Undoubtedly, there is a need for a comprehensive evaluative study to determine the success of the program and provisions are presently being made to initiate such a study in the second year. Notwithstanding the lack of hard data to substantiate the subjective judgements indicated above, there is a strong feeling that bilingual education may be the single most significant pedagogical innovation in our many attempts to improve and enrich the lives of our Spanish speaking youngsters in the city and in the nation. There can be no guarantee of success nor should there be any expectations of instant miracles, but there should be an air of optimism which will encourage and stimulate the efforts of those involved.

Francesco Cordasco and Eugene Bucchioni

THE REALITIES OF
PROGRAM IMPLEMENTATION*

In the last analysis, it is the program which addresses itself to the educational needs of the Puerto Rican child which must be evaluated with recommendations made for its continuing improvement. The evaluation of a particular program for Puerto Rican children in a large urban school district and the recommendations which were made for its improvement and expansion are, in themselves, instructive: they delineate the contemporary educational experience for the Puerto Rican child, and they point the way to meeting the needs.

The recommendations which are subjoined derive from a study and evaluation of the educational programs for Puerto Rican students underway in the Jersey City (N.J.) school district in 1971–1972. Over 5,000 Puerto Rican pupils (out of a total school register of some 38,000) were in the city's schools. The recommendations provide a profile of contemporary Puerto Rican educational experience (practice that lends itself to improvement), generally encountered on the mainland.

PROGRAM RECOMMENDATIONS

Elementary Level

1. The basic recommendation to be made for the elementary schools involves the establishment of functional bilingual programs wherever there are Puerto Rican students in attend-

* F. Cordasco and Eugene Bucchioni, *Education Programs for Puerto Rican Students: Evaluation and Recommendations* (Jersey City: Board of Education, 1971), pp. 27–37.

ance. The basic premise of bilingual education involves the use of Spanish to provide instruction in most curriculum areas when English is not the mother tongue of the children and when there is insufficient fluency in English to profit from school instruction in that language. Thus, for example, instruction in basic curriculum areas such as mathematics, social studies, *etc.* would be in Spanish. At the same time that instruction is given in the basic content areas in Spanish, an intensive program in the teaching of English as a second language must be conducted. As children develop greater fluency in English, additional instruction in the basic curriculum areas should be given in English. This approach would assist children in becoming equally fluent in both Spanish and English, and at the same time it would also assist children to develop the appropriate knowledges and skills in curriculum areas other than Spanish and English. Bilingual education should also provide for the teaching of Spanish as a second language for those children who are dominant in English. Such programs should begin in September 1972.

At the present time in the bilingual classes in the Jersey City schools, this approach is not in widespread use. Teachers who speak Spanish are used for the most part to interpret what the English speaking teacher has said, and (as noted above) often at the same time, a practice resulting in considerable confusion. In addition, the practice of assigning two teachers to a room, one of whom functions as an interpreter, represents poor utilization of personnel, both educationally and financially.

2. The bilingual program recommended by the evaluators would also necessitate the regrouping of participating children more carefully. In addition to using the traditional criteria for grouping, in a bilingual education program it is necessary to develop parallel classes or sections of children who are dominant in either English or Spanish. In developing bilingual programs, however, it is essential that priority be given in class assignment to children who are dominant in Spanish, rather than to those dominant in English, because the greatest immediate need exists for children who are dominant in Spanish and who cannot derive as much educational value as possible from school programs conducted solely in English.

3. It is recommended that two schools [perhaps, Public

School No. 2 and Public School No. 16 in view of the very large number of Puerto Rican students in attendance] develop complete bilingual programs beginning with the kindergarten and including each grade in the school. In other schools, bilingual classes should be established as needed.

4. A committee on bilingual education at the elementary school level should be established immediately in order to plan for the development of bilingual programs in Public Schools Nos. 2 and 16, and in other schools of Jersey City where there are large Puerto Rican enrollments. The bilingual education committee will also give attention to the development of a bilingual curriculum encompassing the usual curriculum areas as well as the teaching of English as a second language, the teaching of Spanish as a second language, and the history and culture of Puerto Rico as an integral part of the elementary school curriculum. The present Hispanic Culture Committee is a beginning; but it must deal with a Puerto Rican studies curriculum and only ancillarily with Hispanic cultures in general. Membership on the committee should include parents, teachers, principals and should also make provision for student input.

5. A city wide Puerto Rican advisory council composed of parents, high school and college students and community leaders should be established. The advisory council can advise school officials on the needs, aspirations, sentiments and responses of the Puerto Rican community insofar as educational matters are concerned. The existence of a community advisory council will assist in making public schools with large numbers of Puerto Rican students "community schools," furnishing educational and other much needed services to the Puerto Rican community. Such an advisory council on a city wide basis [and articulated with local advisory councils for specific schools] will provide much needed community participation in education in Jersey City for the Puerto Rican community.

6. Parochial schools with large numbers of Puerto Rican students should also participate in special programs funded with federal monies.

7. All communications from school officials to parents should be available in both English and Spanish.

8. Additional Puerto Rican personnel should be recruited for positions at all levels in the public schools including

teachers, principals, school secretaries, a curriculum specialist, teacher aides, *etc.* Special attention should be turned immediately to the employment of a curriculum specialist in bilingual education.

9. At the present time, no city wide coordinating effort involving existing bilingual programs is available in Jersey City. It is recommended, therefore, that a city wide office at the level of coordinator for bilingual education be established. This office will have jurisdiction over planning, developing, implementing, supervising and evaluating all bilingual education programs, programs in the teaching of English as a second language, and other special service programs for Puerto Rican elementary school children and high school students. The office would also provide liaison with the Puerto Rican community.

10. Bilingual classes as envisaged in recommendation #1 should also be made available in the Summer of 1972. [The period January 1972 to June 1972 should be used as a planning period for the bilingual programs to be established in the Summer and Fall of 1972].

11. It is recommended that provision be made for the establishment of a continuing consultancy in the implementation of the recommendations contained in this report. Consultants would work with school officials and members of the Puerto Rican community in the implementation of the recommendations and would assist in the development of other programs and special services that may be needed by the children of the Puerto Rican community.

12. Parent education programs conducted in both Spanish and English should be developed for the Puerto Rican community.

13. An in-service program for teachers and other school personnel should be developed as soon as possible. Current and past efforts in Jersey City in the areas of in-service courses include the offering of a course in "Teaching English as a Second Language" that was to be given in the 1970–71 school year, beginning in November, 1970 and a request to develop and finance an "In-Service Course Involving Philosophy, Approaches and Methodology of Bilingual Education," to be given during the 1971–72 school year. In-service efforts should be expanded, and should include both professionals participating directly in bilingual programs or English as a second language programs as well as other professionals in

the Jersey City Public Schools who may not be participating in special programs for Puerto Rican children but who do work with Puerto Rican children in regular classes. Such an extensive in-service program might be developed and offered during the regular school year, or might be given as a special summer institute for participating personnel.

14. Greater numbers of Puerto Rican student teachers should be recruited from Jersey City State College. An expanded student-teaching practicum drawn from the cadres of Puerto Rican students at Jersey City State College represents an important source for recruiting larger numbers of Puerto Rican personnel for employment in the Jersey City Public Schools.

15. A continuing and expanding liaison between the Jersey City Public Schools and Jersey City State College is recommended. Here, an important beginning and model [Title VII, at School No. 16] has been provided by Professor Bloom and Jersey City State College personnel.

Secondary Level

1. The city wide Community Advisory Council described in recommendations for elementary schools would also turn its attention to secondary education and make recommendations relevant to the educational needs of Puerto Rican high school students in Jersey City.

2. A testing and identification program should be developed at the secondary level. Such a program would attempt to identify Puerto Rican students in need of intensive instruction in English as a second language or in other important school subjects such as reading.

3. A special committee to deal with secondary education for Puerto Rican students should be established, with the membership drawn from teachers, principals, guidance personnel and other school professionals; and including parents and students from the Puerto Rican community. The committee should give special attention to the current basic offerings: industrial arts, college preparatory, business and general studies. It should consider ways of increasing the holding power of the secondary schools so that greater numbers of Puerto Rican students remain in high school and graduate.

4. Special work study programs for Puerto Rican students

might be developed in connection with the basic offerings now available. Such work study programs could become a very significant phase of the industrial arts and business education programs, and should, consequently, carry high school credit.

5. An immediate attempt should be made to increase the number of Puerto Rican students in the college preparatory program. This can be done by teachers, guidance personnel and administrators. More information about current high school programs should be made available, and students should become familiar with the implications of selecting specific programs and the out-of-school consequences of enrollment in any given program. In addition, talent-search programs might be initiated to increase the number of Puerto Rican students entering college.

6. Secondary school teachers should participate in in-service programs dealing with the education of Puerto Rican students.

7. It is recommended that high school students having little fluency in English be given basic instruction in Spanish in the various classes required in the four curricula. Instruction in Spanish would be in addition to intensive instruction in reading, writing and speaking English as a second language. When high school students have achieved a sufficient degree of fluency in English, they may then receive all or most of their instruction in English. Bilingual education at the high school level at the present time is essential, and it is especially important when large numbers of students are dominant in Spanish rather than in English. It should be remembered that it was not possible to secure from school officials data concerning the number of Puerto Rican high school students dominant primarily in Spanish.

8. At present, a secondary school curriculum committee is working on a course of study in Puerto Rican history. The work of this committee should be accelerated and a course of study in Puerto Rican history and culture should be developed as rapidly as possible. The committee might then turn its attention to the development of a course of study dealing with the Puerto Rican experience on the mainland. At present, there are no student members of this committee. Students should be a significant and contributing part of this committee. Indeed, greater participation by high school stu-

dents in the decisions affecting their school careers is vital, and it becomes especially crucial when there are large numbers of students dropping out of high school programs as is true for many Puerto Rican students.

9. The high schools should make available to all high school students without cost all special examinations such as the National Education Development Tests or the College Boards. Such examinations now require the payment of fees by candidates taking them. There may be many Puerto Rican and other students unable to take the examinations which require the payment of fees because of inability to afford the funds required.

10. The continuing consultancy referred to in recommendations for elementary schools should encompass secondary education as well as elementary education.

11. It is recommended that an experimental program involving independent study be instituted for those students who are considering leaving high school before graduation. This program would provide the opportunity for independent study under supervision, for which credit leading to a high school diploma would be given. Such a program would also provide for attendance in organized classes in the high schools, especially where remedial or advanced programs are required. Students would participate in developing their programs. Such supervised independent study programs could be related to jobs which students leaving high school before graduation may have secured.

12. It is recommended that additional Puerto Rican personnel be recruited for employment in Jersey City secondary schools. The two Puerto Rican guidance counselors at Ferris High School are an important beginning.

These recommendations are, essentially, reaffirmations of the cogency of those made years earlier in *The Puerto Rican Study*. One cannot help but wonder how differently meaningful educational opportunity for Puerto Rican children may have been had *The Puerto Rican Study* been implemented. In its cautions and admonitions, *The Puerto Rican Study* was prophetic: "A study, however good, never solves problems. At best it finds solutions that will work. To translate proposed measures into practice is the greater task. At the very best it will take three to five years to translate the proposals of *The Puerto Rican Study* into an effective program. . . . The real question is, how rapidly can the school system move? . . . there are thousands of Puerto Rican children in New York City schools who have been here two, three, four or more years and are still rated as language learners. The task is twofold—to salvage as many as possible of those currently retarded, and to reduce the numbers that thus far have been added annually to the list. The time to begin is now—A year gone from a child's life is gone forever." (p. 237)

Francesco Cordasco

EDUCATIONAL ENLIGHTENMENT OUT OF TEXAS: TOWARDS BILINGUALISM*

It has long been an ethnocentric illusion in the United States that, for a child born in this country, English is not a foreign language and virtually all instruction in the schools must be through the medium of English. Some of our states (New York included) have mandated this ethnocentrism in a plethora of statutes which expressly forbid instruction in any language but English. Of course this is not difficult to understand. Despite the ideals of a democratic society in which the schools were to serve as a basic vehicle of cohesion, the schools instead became the agencies of social disaffection, cultural assault, and enforced assimilation. How could it have been otherwise, since the schools had to minister to children who brought with them myriad cultures and a multiplicity of tongues? More often than not (almost always in the urban immigrant citadels) the American schools found their children in poverty and neglect. If there is a common denominator which must be sought in the millions of American children who presented themselves to a society's schools, it is poverty. And its ingredients (within the parameters of this poverty) were cultural differences, language handicaps, social alienation, and disaffection. In this sense, the Negro huddled in the urban ghettos, the Puerto Rican poor in search of economic opportunity on the mainland, and the Mexican-American poor, largely an urban minority, are not newcomers to the American schools, nor do they present American educators with new problems. The American poor,

* Francesco Cordasco, "Educational Enlightenment out of Texas: Towards Bilingualism," *Teachers College Record* (May 1970), pp. 608–612. Reprinted with permission.

traditionally, are the ingredients out of which our social institutions have fashioned the sinews of greatness.

In its efforts to "assimilate" all of its charges, the American school assimilated (and in consequence very often destroyed) the cultural identity of the child; it forced him to leave his ancestral language at the schoolhouse door; it developed in the child a haunting ambivalence of language, of culture, of ethnicity, and of self-affirmation. It held up to its children mirrors in which they saw not themselves, but the stereotyped middle-class, white, English-speaking child who embodied the essences of what the American child was (or ought) to be. For the minority child, the images which the school fashioned were cruel deceptions. In the enforced acculturation there were bitterness and confusion; but tragically, too, there was the rejection of the well-springs of identity, and more often than not, the failure of achievement. The ghettoization of the European immigrant is, in substance, exactly analogous to the ghettoization of the Negro, Puerto Rican, and Mexican-American poor. Louis Wirth, a long time ago, called attention to the vitality of the ghetto in its maintenance of the life-styles, languages, and cultures of a minority people assaulted by the main institutions of a dominant society.

When the Congress discovered poverty in the enactment of the Economic Opportunity Act of 1964, and fashioned the cornucopia out of which the schools have plucked endless "goodies," the schools largely fashioned programs born out of this new federal largesse which reflected their continuing pursuit of the stereotyped middle-class, white, English-speaking child in whose image all of our children were to be cast. And so Head Start taught its children middle-class table manners; the Neighborhood Youth Corps took its social adventurers to museums and opera houses whenever they could be found; Upward Bound, too, became preoccupied with the cultural refurbishing of its charges and took for granted miraculous cognitive blossoming; and Title I Programs of the Elementary and Secondary Education Act did a whole host of things which were designed to elevate "culturally deprived" children to levels of middle-class conformism, *de rigueur.*

THE NON-ENGLISH SPEAKING CHILD

Those of us who have been concerned with Puerto Rican children in our major cities have for some time struggled with what was actually a very old problem. If all children presented themselves to the American schools with many differences, how graphic was the immediate difference epitomized in the non-English speaking child. The history of the American school has not been the evangelical triumph which the New England sage and historian Ellwood Cubberley sketched in such bold relief; rather, the non-English speaking child (almost inevitably in a context of poverty) was the easy victim of cultural assault, and his ancestral language was at once a target against which the school mounted relentless resources.

Against this tragic background and quixotic effort, largely unnoticed, has been a "sleeper" amendment to the Elementary and Secondary Education Act which in essence would propose that we wash away the haunting ghosts of ethnocentrism and cultural affectation, and turn to the meaningful cultivation of individual differences which better reflect the pluralistic base out of which the children of an open society truly come.

THE SLEEPER AMENDMENT

The history of this "sleeper" amendment is a good illustration of what Kenneth Clark has characterized as "the dilemmas of power." Where would one have sought the power in the Congress to recognize the particular needs of Puerto Rican children, if previous Congresses had chosen largely to ignore those millions of children who were non-English speaking who had passed through the portals of the school? The tactic here was obviously to relate the Puerto Rican child to the needs of another group long indigenous in our society but equally long disenfranchised, and for whom English was not the native language. In the five state area of the Southwest (Texas, New Mexico, Colorado, Arizona and California) there are at least 1.75 million school children with Spanish surnames, whose linguistic, cultural and psychological handicaps cause them to experience, in general, academic failure in our schools, or at best limit them to only mediocre success. The Mexican-American child classically demonstrated that an almost inevitable concomitant of poverty was low educational achievement. Thus, it was out of unlikely Texas that an extraordinary amendment to the ESEA was proposed: an unlikely provenance, since one would have expected that the provisions of this liberal and enlightened amendment would have been born in the great egalitarian citadels of the North.

On January 17, 1967 Ralph Yarborough (D.-Texas) introduced in the Senate of the United States S.428, which proposed "To amend the Elementary and Secondary Education Act of 1965 in order to provide assistance to local educational agencies in establishing bilingual American education programs and to provide certain other assistance to promote such programs." At long last the Congress had before it legislation which would legitimatize the cultivation of individual differences in our schools. Understandably, Senator Yarborough was concerned with the problems of his Mexican-American constituents, but his bill explicitly noted that: "For the purpose of this Title, Spanish-speaking elementary and secondary students means elementary and secondary school students born in, or one or both of whose parents were born in, Mexico or Puerto Rico, and, in states for which such information is available, other students with Spanish surnames." The very proposal of the bill was tantamount to the recognition that Mexican-American children had been neglected by American schools. But Senator Yarborough's legislation went far beyond this elemental recognition. It proposed (1) bilingual educational programs; (2) the teaching of Spanish as the native language; (3) the teaching of English as a second language; (4) programs designed to impart to Spanish-speaking students a knowledge of and pride in their ancestral culture and language; (5) efforts to attract and retain as teachers promising individuals of Mexican or Puerto Rican descent; and (6) efforts to establish closer cooperation between the school and the home. What extraordinary proposals! Those millions of children who had been denied what a mature society was now proposing might well have served as a Greek chorus intoning social amens.

As was to be expected, Senator Yarborough's bill (which

had as co-sponsors both Mr. Javits and Mr. Kennedy of New York) created a flurry of activity in the House (though largely unnoticed outside the Congress) and a veritable spate of companion House bills were proposed, chief amongst which was H.R. 9840 mounted by James H. Scheuer (D.-New York). Congressman Scheuer would have everything that Senator Yarborough had proposed, but he chose not to accept the Yarborough bill's limitation of its provisions to Spanish-speaking students. For Congressman Scheuer the school would respond in much the fashion that Yarborough proposed, no matter what the student's native language might be, and Congressman Scheuer simply chose to increase five-fold the allocations which Senator Yarborough had proposed ($25,-000,000 as against $5,000,000 for fiscal 1967–68), and further to allow participation by full-time nonpublic school students (children in parish schools).

TOWARDS BILINGUALISM

There are of course some objections which have been raised against the legislation. Some linguists have objected to the pegging of the bill to the poverty context, and have been adamant in proposing that the bill be unrestricted in its provisions and allow the cultivation of a vast bilingual resource. But this is truly another problem. What the legislation has really proposed (no matter how awkwardly, and with full cognizance of all the programming intricacies which will have to be worked out) is that the social institution which is the school and which serves the children of an open society must build on the cultural strengths which the child brings to the classroom: to cultivate in this child ancestral pride; to reinforce (not destroy) the language he natively speaks; to cultivate his inherent strengths; and to give this child the sense of personal identification so essential to his social maturation. We can only lament the lost opportunities of other eras. The legislation proposes that there is no excuse for failure at this juncture in our society. Senator Yarborough's "sleeper" legislation will have thrust greatness upon him, and Texas will have become in educational history as illustrious as Massachusetts. In August, 1967 his Senate Bill 428 was unanimously reported out of the Senate Sub-Committee on Education, and in the closing sessions of the 90th Congress became law. In the long interim which followed, a reluctant Congress finally authorized $7.5 million for fiscal 1969.

Secretary of Health, Education, and Welfare Robert H. Finch said on February 12, 1969, that he considered prompt, massive upgrading of bilingual education one of the major imperatives confronting HEW. He announced at the same time that he was establishing a new post, Special Assistant to the Commissioner of Education for Bilingual Education, as a first step in meeting this challenge. Proposals requesting some $47 million were received prior to the December 20, 1968, deadline from local agencies in 40 states, the District of Columbia, and Puerto Rico. Following review of the proposals by a panel of outside experts, selected applicants were asked by the Office of Education to submit formal proposals by May 5, 1969, for final evaluation. From a $7.5 million budget for the program for fiscal 1969, direct grants are to be made to those agencies that propose programs and activities which present innovative solutions to bilingual education problems. Projects must focus on schools that have a high concentration of children of limited English-speaking ability and who come from families earning less than $3,000 per year. Emphasis may be on planning and developing research projects; conducting pilot projects to test the effectiveness of plans; developing special instructional materials; and providing training for teachers, teacher aides, and counselors. Bilingual educational activities may be designed to impart to students a knowledge of the history and culture related to their languages; establish closer cooperation between the school and the home; and provide preschool and adult educational programs related to bilingual education.

Seventy-seven public school agencies in 27 states have been invited by the U.S. Office of Education to prepare formal proposals for grants under the authority of the $7.5 million Bilingual Education Program, Title VI of the Elementary and Secondary Education Act, as amended. These education agencies were selected from 312 which submitted preliminary proposals to the U.S. Office of Education by the December 20, 1968 deadline. Approved projects will be operating during the 1969–70 school year.

BIBLIOGRAPHY OF SELECTED
REFERENCES

I GENERAL BIBLIOGRAPHIES

Cordasco, Francesco with Eugene Bucchioni and Diego Castellanos. *Puerto Ricans on the United States Mainland: A Bibliography of Reports, Texts, Critical Studies and Related Materials* (Totowa, New Jersey: Rowman & Littlefield, 1972). An annotated bibliography of 754 main entries dealing with bibliographical resources; the migration to the mainland; the island experience; conflict and acculturation on the mainland; education on the mainland; and social needs encompassing health, housing, employment, and other human needs.

Cordasco, Francesco and Leonard Covello. *Studies of Puerto Rican Children in American Schools: A Preliminary Bibliography.* New York: Department of Labor, Migration Division, Commonwealth of Puerto Rico, 1967. [some 450 entries] Also published in *Education Libraries Bulletin*, Institute of Education, University of London, #31 (Spring 1968), pp. 7-33; and in *Journal of Human Relations*, vol. 16 (1968), pp. 264-285.

[Cordasco, Francesco]. *The People of Puerto Rico: A Bibliography.* New York: Department of Labor, Migration Division, Commonwealth of Puerto Rico [1968]. Some 500 entries.

Dossick, Jesse. *Doctoral Research on Puerto Rico and Puerto Ricans.* New York: New York University, School of Education, 1967. A classified list of 320 doctoral dissertations completed at American mainland universities.

II GENERAL STUDIES

Burma, John H. *Spanish-Speaking Groups in the United States.* Duke University Press, 1954. Includes a sketch of "the Puerto

Ricans in New York" (pp. 156-187). Burma assumes that there is a fundamental "unity of culture" among diverse groups put together because they speak the same language. In light of the widely differing historical backgrounds which have given rise to different cultures among Spanish-speaking groups the assumption does not seem valid.

Chenault, Lawrence. *The Puerto Rican Migrant in New York City.* Columbia University Press, 1938. Reissued with a New Foreword by F. Cordasco. New York: Russell & Russell, 1970. The one book that puts together data available on the early movements to New York City of Puerto Rican migrants. Includes a discussion of the various ways these movements affect the established community and the migrants.

Cordasco, F. and David Alloway, "Spanish Speaking People in the Unted States: Some Research Constructs and Postulates," *International Migration Review*, vol. 4 (Spring 1970), pp. 76-79.

Fitzpatrick, Joseph P. *Puerto Rican Americans: The Meaning of Migration to the Mainland.* Englewood Cliffs, N.J.: Prentice Hall, 1971. An overview and trenchant study with materials on the dynamics of migration: the problem of identity; the family, problem of color; religion; education; welfare. See *New York Times*, September 12, 1971, p. 96.

Glazer, Nathan and Daniel P. Moynihan. "The Puerto Ricans." In: *Beyond the Melting Pot: The Negroes, Puerto Ricans, Jews, Italians, and Irish of New York City,* by Nathan Glazer and Daniel Moynihan. Cambridge: M. I. T. and Harvard University Press, 2nd ed., 1970. Puerto Ricans in New York City are discussed in terms of who migrates to the United States, their relationship to the island of Puerto Rico; business, professional, labor opportunities, and average earnings in New York; and the effect of migration on the culture of the migrants. The Puerto Ricans are compared and contrasted with immigrant groups. [1st ed., 1963]. The 2nd edition updates some of the material, and includes a new introductory essay and analysis.

Lewis, Oscar. *La Vida: A Puerto Rican Family in the Culture of Poverty—San Juan and New York.* New York: Random House, 1966. 669 pp. Begins with a long introduction which describes Lewis' methods, the setting, and the family involved in the study. A discussion of the theory of the "culture of poverty" is included. The rest of the book is the story of a Puerto Rican family, as told by the members of the nuclear family and some of their relatives and friends. See also Oscar Lewis; *A Study of Slum Culture: Backgrounds for La Vida.* New York: Random House, 1968. Provides the general background, data, and statistical frame of reference for *La Vida*.

Mills, C. Wright; Clarence Senior; and Rose Goldsen. *The Puerto*

Rican Journey: New York's Newest Migrant. Harper, 1950. Reissued, New York: Russell & Russell, 1969. A carefully researched field study of the Puerto Rican population in two core areas of New York City. The study was done in 1948 by a research team of the bureau of applied social research of Columbia University. Although many of its statistics are now out of date, the book deals with basic concepts, such as the factors in "adaptation," cultural and language differences, and their influence on the progress and problems of the migrants. Includes much data on the characteristics of the Puerto Ricans in the two core areas —family, age, sex, education, occupation, income, etc.

Puerto Rican Community Development Project. Puerto Rican Forum [New York], 1964. This report was developed as the basis for an antipoverty, economic opportunity project, and is subtitled "A Proposal for a Self-Help Project to Develop the Community by Strengthening the Family, Opening Opportunities for Youth and Making Full Use of Education." The forum is a private agency, with a professional and secretarial staff of New Yorkers of Puerto Rican background. It has received some financial support from foundations to develop self-help projects as well as some public money to develop its proposal. Thus the concern in this report is to highlight the problems—income, housing, education, family, *etc.*—that confront the Puerto Rican community in New York City, though not all of its population. Data are presented to support the thesis that Puerto Ricans generally are not well off and need to make much more rapid gains in a contemporary technical, urban society such as New York. As a Forum summary indicates, the report is advanced as a rationale for a project "which takes into consideration both the problems of poverty in New York City and the complex realities of the cultural community pattern of the Puerto Rican New Yorker." The report is not intended to be a rounded picture of the total Puerto Rican population in New York City. Read from the point of view of its purpose, it is an illuminating study.

"[The] Puerto Rican Experience on the United States Mainland," *International Migration Review*, vol. II (Spring 1968). Entire issue devoted to a comprehensive account of the experience.

Sexton, Patricia. *Spanish Harlem: Anatomy of Poverty.* Harper & Row, 1965. Report by a sociologist who spent part of two years "getting acquainted" with East Harlem. Shows awareness that she is dealing with the pathologies of a minority of the area's population ("still, the majority of the people are self-supporting"). However, she does not gloss over the problems that confront many of the self-supporting, low-income urban dwellers. The book is informed by the important insight of the need for "the poor" to be involved in working out their destiny. See F. Cordasco, "Nights in the Gardens of East Harlem: Patricia Sexton's East Harlem," *Journal of Negro Education*, vol. 34 (Fall 1965), pp. 450-451; and F. Cordasco, "Spanish Harlem: The Anatomy of Poverty," *Phylon: The Atlanta Review of Race & Culture*, vol. 26 (Summer 1965), pp. 195-196.

III EDUCATION

Anderson, Virginia. "Teaching English to Puerto Rican Pupils," *High Points* (March 1964), pp. 51-54.

Bilingual Education: Hearings, U.S. Senate, Committee on Labor and Public Welfare. Special Sub-Committee on Bilingual Education, 90th Congress, 1st Session. Washington: U.S. Government Printing Office, Part I, May 1967; Part II, June 1967. On Title VII (Elementary and Secondary Education Act) which was enacted in 1968.

"Bilingualism," *The Center Forum*, vol. 4 (September 1969). Entire issue is given to analysis of Title VII (Elementary and Secondary Education Act), programs and related matters. Includes an important annotated bibliography.

Bucchioni, Eugene. *A Sociological Analysis of the Functioning of Elementary Education for Puerto Rican Children in the New York City Public Schools*. Unpublished doctoral dissertation, New School for Social Research, 1965.

Cordasco, Francesco. "The Puerto Rican Child in the American School." American Sociological Association *Abstract of Papers*, 61st Annual Meeting (1966), pp. 23-24.

Cordasco, Francesco. "Puerto Rican Pupils and American Education." *School & Society*, vol. 95 (February 18, 1967), pp. 116-119. Also, with some change, in *Journal of Negro Education* (Spring 1967); and *Kansas Journal of Sociology*, vol. 2 (Spring 1966), pp. 59-65.

Cordasco, Francesco. "The Challenge of the Non-English Speaking Child in the American School" *School & Society*, vol. 96 (March 30, 1968), pp. 198-201. On the proposal for the enactment of the Bilingual Education Act. (Title VII, Elementary and Secondary Education Act), with historical background.

Cordasco, Francesco. "Educational Pelagianism: The Schools and the Poor," *Teachers College Record*, vol. 69 (April 1968), pp. 705-709.

Cordasco, Francesco and Eugene Bucchioni. *The Puerto Rican Community of Newark, N.J.: An Educational Program for its Children*. Newark: Board of Education, Summer 1970. A detailed report on the implementation of a program for Puerto Rican students.

Cordasco, Francesco and E. Bucchioni. *Education Programs for Puerto Rican Students*. [Jersey City Public Schools]. Evaluation and Recomendations. Jersey City: Board of Education, 1971.

Cordasco, F. and Eugene Bucchioni. *Newark Bilingual Education Program, 1970-1971*. Newark: Board of Education, 1971. Evaluation report of a massive program for Puerto Rican students.

Cordasco, Francesco and Eugene Bucchioni. *The Puerto Rican Community and its Children on the Mainland: A Sourcebook for Teachers, Social Workers and other Professionals*. Metuchen, N.J.: Scarecrow Press, 2nd ed., 1972. "The original structuring of the text has been retained, and it is within this framework that new materials have been interpolated. New materials have been added to Part I (Aspects of Puerto Rican Culture) whose basic design is to afford a politico-cultural kaleidoscope of island life; to Part II (The Puerto Rican Family), bringing into clear focus the family's transition to mainland life; to Part III (The Puerto Rican Experience on the Mainland: Conflict and Acculturation), in bringing into sharp view the new politicization of the mainland experience; and in Part IV (The Puerto Rican Experience on the Mainland: Puerto Rican Children in North American Schools) in affording additional materials on bilingual education and in providing outlines for course content and staff-training. Appended to the bibliography are selected additional references." [Preface to the 2nd ed.]

Cordasco, Francesco and Eugene Bucchioni, "A Staff Institute for Teachers of Puerto Rican Students," *School & Society*, vol. 100 (Summer 1972).

Diaz, Manuel and Roland Cintrón. *School Integration and Quality Education*. New York: Puerto Rican Forum, 1964.

Hemos Trabajado Bien. A Report on the First National Conference of Puerto Ricans, Mexican-Americans and Educators on the Special Educational Needs of Puerto Rican Youth (New York: Aspira, 1968). Includes a series of recommendations.

John, Vera P. and Vivian M. Horner. *Early Childhood Bilingual Education*. (New York: Modern Language Association 1971). Invaluable. Includes a "Typology of Bilingual Education Models;" excellent documentation and bibliography.

Margolis, Richard J. *The Losers: A Report on Puerto Ricans and the Public Schools* (New York: Aspira, 1968). An important report on visits to a number of schools with description and evaluation of programs for Puerto Rican children.

[Puerto Rican Children] "Education of Puerto Rican Children in New York City," *The Journal of Educational Sociology*, vol. 28

(December 1954), pp. 145-192. An important collection of articles.

Morrison, J. Cayce, Director. *The Puerto Rican Study: 1953-57.* New York City Board of Education, 1958. Final report of the most complete study of the impact of Puerto Rican migration on the public schools of New York City, and how schools were affecting Puerto Rican children and their parents. Though sponsored by the New York City Board of Education, matching grant-in-aid of half a million dollars from the Fund for the Advancement of Education made the study possible. Specialized studies were done within the framework of the large-scale study. These smaller studies focused on the "socio-cultural adjustment" of the children and their parents, and digests are presented in final report. About a third of the book deals with the special non-English-speaking program developed by the city school system. Description of some of the methods and materials developed is included. Study discovered some unresolved problems in the areas of learning, effective grouping of pupils, staffing those schools with Puerto Rican children, and teacher education. Study led to many research and curriculum publications, and 123 major recommendations, all designed to achieve three purposes: "° ° ° [developing] better understanding of the children being taught, [relating] the teaching of English to the child's cultural-social adjustment, [improving] the integration of ethnic groups through the school's program" (p. 247). With respect to the children, the major conclusion is contained in the following statement: "The children of Puerto Rican background are exceedingly heterogeneous. This is true of their native intelligence, their prior schooling, their aptitude for learning English, and their scholastic ability ° ° °" (p. 239). Reissued with an introductory essay by F. Cordasco (New York: Oriole Editions, 1972).

A BRIEF CHRONOLOGY OF PUERTO RICAN HISTORY*

1493—On November 19, Christopher Columbus discovers the island of Borikén on his second trip to the New World and calls it San Juan Bautista.

1508—Juan Ponce de León is made Governor of the island and founds the first settlement, called Caparra.

1509—The seat of government is moved and called Ciudad de Puerto Rico.

1521—The capital city is renamed San Juan, and the island takes the name of the capital: Puerto Rico.

1530—With the limited gold supply exhausted, many colonizers are attracted to Peru; others devote themselves to agriculture.

1595—Sir Francis Drake's fleet attacks San Juan but is rebuffed.

1598—George Clifford, the Count of Cumberland, captures San Juan with 4,000 men and holds it from June through November.

1625—Dutch fleet attacks San Juan on September 24, but is rebuffed after its troops sack the city.

1631—Construction begins on the massive El Morro Fortress to protect the city.

1660—Governor Pérez de Guzmán writes to the King that "eleven years have passed since the last ship came to this island."

1680—The city of Ponce is founded on the south coast.

1760—Mayagüez is founded on the west coast.

1775—Population is 70,250, including 6,467 black slaves.

1797—San Juan is attacked by the British, who retire after a one-month siege.

1812—Ramón Power represents the island in the Spanish Cortes.

1868—On September 23, patriots in Lares declared a republic, but the revolt is quickly squashed.

1873—Slavery is abolished.

* Adapted from Kal Wagenheim, *Puerto Rico: A Profile.* New York: Prager, 1970.

1897—On November 25, Spain grants autonomy to Puerto Rico. Population is 894,302.

1898—On February 15, the battleship Maine blows up in Havana Harbor; on April 21, the Spanish-American War begins; on July 25, American troops land at Guánica, on Puerto Rico's south coast.

1899—The Treaty of Paris is ratified on April 11, and Spain cedes Puerto Rico to the United States.

1900—The Foraker Act makes the island a U.S. territory. The U.S. military government is replaced by a civil administration, headed by an American governor.

1917—The Jones Act is passed in Washington on March 2, granting U.S. citizenship to Puerto Ricans.

1930—Pedro Albizu Campos is elected President of the militant Nationalist Party.

1934—President Roosevelt visits the island and affirms support to rehabilitate the island's economy.

1935—Five people die in a clash between Nationalists and police at the university.

1936—Two young Nationalists kill insular police chief Riggs and are later killed by the police who arrested them. Albizu Campos and eight followers are jailed for sedition.

1937—On March 21, nineteen are killed and 100 injured in "the Ponce Massacre," as police open fire on a Nationalist parade.

1938—In July, Nationalists fire at U.S. Governor Winship during a ceremony to mark the fortieth year under American rule. Two Puerto Rican bodyguards are hit; nine Nationalists are indicted for murder.

1940—The new Popular Democratic Party wins the elections. Luis Muñoz Marín becomes Senate President.

1941—Rexford Guy Tugwell is named the last U.S. Governor of the island and joins with Muñoz in an ambitious economic development program.

1944—Popular Party wins the election with 383,000 votes, compared to 208,000 of the combined opposition.

1946—On July 21, President Truman names Jesús T. Piñero as first native Governor of Puerto Rico.

1947—On August 4, President Truman signs Crawford-Butler Act, permitting Puerto Rico to elect its own governor.

1948—Populars win the election, with 392,000 votes against 346,000 of the combined opposition. Luis Muñoz Marín becomes the first popularly elected Governor.

1950—On July 4, President Truman signs Public Law 600, permitting Puerto Rico to draft its own constitution. On October 30, five armed Nationalists attack the Governor's mansion; uprisings erupt in other island towns, causing twenty-seven dead and ninety wounded. On November 1, two New York Puerto Ricans try to kill President Truman; a White House policeman and one assailant die. Albizu Campos and other Nationalists are given long prison sentences for complicity.

1951—On June 4, 387,000 Puerto Ricans favor Public Law 600, 119,000 vote against; over 200,000 registered voters abstain.

1952—On March 3, the new constitution is approved in a referendum, 374,000 to 82,000. On July 25, the Commonwealth Constitution goes into effect, after some changes insisted upon by Congress are approved in a second Puerto Rico referendum. Populars again win the election, with 429,000 votes against a combined opposition of 232,000. The Independence Party is second, with 125,000 votes.

1953—The United Nations authorizes the United States to cease transmitting information on Puerto Rico as a nonself-governing territory.

1954—On March 1, four Nationalists open fire in the U.S. House of Representatives, wounding five Congressmen.

1956—Populars win the election with 62 per cent of the total vote. The Statehood Republican Party doubles its 1952 total with 172,000 votes; the Independence Party drops to 85,000.

1959—Congress rejects the Fernos-Murray Bill, which aimed to amplify Puerto Rico's autonomy.

1960—Populars win the election with 58 per cent of the 800,000 votes. The Statehooders are second, and the Independence Party drops to only 3 per cent.

1964—The Status Commission begins to study the island's political status. Muñoz Marín retires from the governorship; his handpicked successor, Roberto Sánchez Vilella, becomes the Popular candidate and easily wins the election.

1967—On July 23, in status referendum, commonwealth wins 60.5 per cent of the votes, compared with 38.9 per cent for statehood and .6 per cent for independence. *Ad hoc* committees are to be formed to work out the perfection of the commonwealth status.

1968—A rift in the Popular Party causes Sánchez Vilella to leave, and he forms his own People's Party. Luis Negrón Lopez is the Popular candidate. Luis A. Ferré and the pro-statehood New Progressive Party win by a narrow margin, interrupting twenty-eight years of Popular Party rule.

1970—Governor Ferré and President Nixon form an *ad hoc* committee to discuss the U.S. presidential vote for Puerto Rico. Muñoz Marín retires from the Senate.

INDEX